RUDOLF STEINER

HANDBOOK

A comprehensive illustrated guide
to the ideas of Rudolf Steiner

ADRIAN ANDERSON Ph. D.

Threshold Publishing
Australia

Copyright © 2013 Adrian Anderson
ISBN: 978-0-9581341-2-5 (pbk)
ISBN: 978-0-9581341-5-6 (hbk)

on-demand

Also by this author

The Way to the Sacred.
The Foundation Stone Meditation: a new commentary
Hellenistic Mysteries and Christianity
Living a Spiritual year: seasonal festivals

Books under the name Damien Pryor

Lalibela
Stonehenge
Externsteine: the world's greatest Celtic site
The Great Pyramid and the Sphinx
The origin and nature of the tropical zodiac

E-booklets available from the author's website:
www.rudolfsteinerstudies.com

Also available the author's Ph.D. thesis:
"Dramatic Anthroposophy" from Otago
University, German Dept. (monograph 19)

DEDICATION

The interaction with my students in the Steiner Studies program over many years – their questions, thoughtful observations, 'in-tranquillities' and insights have been very helpful in bringing this book into the world. The help of the nine friends who proof-read the manuscript – George, Ian, John, Leah, Margot, Peter, Philip, Ramana, Ruby – offering important feed-back, has been very helpful. Above all, without the insightful suggestions and constant support of Marguerite this book could not have been written.

CONTENTS

Introduction

Chapters

    Architecture of the Goetheanum,
    Art: its spiritual value, Colours: their influence on us,
    Eurythmy: a new kind of dance,
    Goetheanum Cupolas: their paintings,
    The four Mystery Plays, The Group sculpture,
    Paintings valued in anthroposophical circles,
    The Planetary Seals,
    The Windows of the Goetheanum,
    Voice (acting, recitation).

    Akashic Record, Ancient Egypt, Chakras, Emptiness
    of soul: the battle for meaning, The First Class,
    The Foundation Stone meditation,
    Festivals of the Seasons: spiritual ecology in action,
    Freemasonry, Hierarchies and the human soul, Holy Grail,
    Meditation, Religion and anthroposophy, Sacred Sites and
    Mystery Streams of earlier times,
    Vidar: inspirer of anthroposophy

    Education: the Steiner schools, Philosophy,
    Plagiarism, Psychology,
    Seven Planets, their influences,
    The Three-folding of society,
    Twelve senses and the zodiac,
    The 7-year Phases of life

List of Illustrations

INTRODUCTION

In recent years I have had the privilege of teaching Steiner's ideas to many people who are seeking to understand life more deeply, and who find the compassionate and ethical foundations of these ideas, as well as their exceptional depth, really inspiring.

If this book has clarity and a relevance to today's world, it is greatly due to the many conversations I have experienced with my sincere, idealistic students; students who have become my friends. Their constant request for a book that would provide a reliable and clearly written guide to the main elements of Rudolf Steiner teachings, led to the project of writing such a volume. Over the years, hundreds of graphic illustrations were presented during our lecture and discussion sessions, and effort has been made to include some of these.

We explored many inspiring and uplifting thoughts, finding references that clarified or supported Steiner's ideas from the wisdom of earlier ages, or from contemporary research. Extracts from original texts of Homer, of the Hebrew and Greek scriptures, of the Edda, of the Hellenistic thinkers, of medieval German mystics, were translated from time to time. The artworks of pre-literate and mysterious pre-Flood cultures, of the ancient Egyptians and Sumerians, the Greeks, the Carolingian era, the Renaissance and of later eras, discussed in the light of Rudolf Steiner views, became a fascinating guide to the way the human spirit manifested humanity's journey in ways beyond words.

I hope that this Handbook will provide a reliable and insightful guide to the ideas of Rudolf Steiner. It seeks to place Steiner's teachings in a non-sectarian way in today's world, and to assess how his ideas relate to current knowledge and values.

As such, it is an introduction to his worldview, called 'anthroposophy'. It may be of help to all who are studying Steiner's ideas in Courses at tertiary level. But I also hope that it will offer an opportunity for those who are already familiar with Rudolf Steiner's works to deepen and clarify their understanding.

To achieve these goals this handbook attempts to dialogue, even if only briefly, with evidence supportive of, or opposed to, Steiner's ideas and to assess whether his students have at times misinterpreted him.

I am aware that hostility towards Steiner can be found in articles on the Internet. This is partly due to the fact that there are some statements in Steiner's Complete Works which are not compatible with today's cultural values. This has led to various criticisms of his work, including that of racism or ethnic insensitivity. These accusations are upsetting to those who have experienced a profound spirituality throughout Steiner's works. But the most obvious factor here, pointed out by supporters of Rudolf Steiner, is that there are many people involved in anthroposophy from different ethnicities who do not consider him to be a racist.

But it is nevertheless true that many of Steiner's statements on ethnicities, on historical and cultural issues are seen as inappropriate in today's world. This theme is quite complex and is not explored in this book. I have endeavoured to avoid presenting teachings which, in the social context of today, may be regarded as inappropriate. An e-booklet which explores the negative reactions to Steiner, *Opponents and Critics of Steiner*, is available on the website, www.rudolfsteinerstudies.com.

In attempting to present the core themes in anthroposophy in one book, it is inevitable that some topics could not be covered in depth, especially those that involve complex issues. These became brief foot-notes, or the subject of e-booklets. Some simplifying of the complex dynamics and data involved in Rudolf Steiner's worldview is unavoidable here, as this is not an advanced study in Rudolf Steiner's work.

A user-friendly text
The exclamation mark is set one space away from the end of a word, not right next to it, as modern style dictates. A number of compound words have a hyphen, for example, semi-conscious, not semiconscious. And also some other compound words have a hyphen, such as Life-spirit, to give a more accurate rendering of the German meaning, where such 'double nouns' are commonly found; at times Rudolf Steiner uses even triple nouns. These features result in a clearer and more user-friendly text for the reader.

1: RUDOLF STEINER: A SKETCH OF HIS LIFE

In June of 1922, amidst the distress surging through central Europe after the war, the grand city of Vienna hosted an influx of visitors. They were there to attend a ten-day Congress of lectures and artistic performances which offered new ideas and new perspectives to a war-weary world. Every day some two thousand people crammed into the rooms of the Music Association of Vienna. Every evening as the keynote speaker entered the great hall, a thunderous round of applause greeted him. When he finished his lecture, given without the aid of a microphone, there would be a standing ovation, lasting several minutes.

Rudolf Steiner spoke to the eager audience of how a new, more spiritual attitude to life, to various academic fields of knowledge, and to social and political questions, could offer hope to a devastated Europe. Every day hundreds of people gathered at the Hotel Imperial, each hoping to have an audience with Rudolf Steiner. It was the pinnacle of Steiner's interface with the public.

So what kind of person was Steiner? What do people find so valuable in his teachings? How and why did he set out to communicate his spiritual ideas, to eventually become an internationally renowned thinker and spiritual teacher?

Rudolf Steiner was born on the 27th February 1861 into a poor Austrian family, living in a village near what was then the Austrian-Hungarian border (now Croatia).[1] His father was a stationmaster in the Austrian railways. The family also had a daughter, and another son, who had severe speech and hearing difficulties. His father was transferred to a number of railway stations in villages in the vicinity of Vienna during Rudolf Steiner's childhood.

The young Rudolf Steiner at fourteen years of age took up the study of Kant's Critique of Pure Reason, a very difficult philosophical text. Kant's book examines cognitional processes; that is, how we perceive and know anything, often called 'epistemology'. This study is evidence of a brilliant intellectual capacity; however, already at ten years of age Steiner had shown artistic gifts as well. A portrait he made at that age of an Hungarian hero was found in the Steiner archives in the 1970's. It is very impressive for its technical skill and artistic sensitivity.

In 1879 Steiner entered university, where his intellectual brilliance allowed him to study more than a full curriculum of scientific subjects, and he also coached fellow students to finance his own studies. His academic achievements led to him being appointed to the editorial team producing the first edition of the scientific writings of Johann Wolfgang von Goethe, Germany's greatest literary figure. For a young man of

---

[1] For years it was thought that he was actually born on Feb. 25th, not the 27th as was usually stated. This earlier date derives from an error in reading an abbreviated version of his birth certificate. Three years ago the original full birth certificate was examined, and the correct date, the 27th, fully established. The number 25 on the short version only refers to the consecutive number of births for that month, in that diocese of the church.

21 years, this was an exceptional honour. From the 1880's to 1900 he undertook a vast and arduous project of studying all major philosophical streams as well as most of the crucial scientific research of his times.

In 1891 he attained the degree of Doctor of Philosophy from Rostock University. This was for a thesis which examined the process of cognition, and argued against aspects of mainstream philosophy, strongly influenced by Immanuel Kant. As a young person Steiner had been experiencing and researching spiritual realities as well as undertaking his academic studies. But he did not teach or write about spiritual themes until 1900, when he entered his fortieth year. Until then he was active as editor of a literary journal, tutor and as a writer of philosophical, cultural articles and scientific material.

In 1890 he moved to the German city of Weimar, where he remained until 1897; here he worked as co-editor of Goethe's complete works. In 1892 he married a widow, Anna Eunicke. Weimar is where Johann Wolfgang von Goethe's archives are to be found; he is commonly regarded as the greatest literary genius of Germany. Steiner found many observations in the works of Goethe which stimulated him towards his own spiritual attitudes to life. Steiner found in Goethe a great help in formulating his philosophical and his spiritual worldview with respect to cognition, that is the process whereby we perceive a sense object or have an 'inner perception' of an idea.

In 1897, with his work at the Goethe archives completed, he moved from Weimar to Berlin, a thriving hub of European culture, where he lectured in Adult Education and briefly worked as a school teacher. He was also extensively involved in the literary and artistic culture of the times, and contributed to a literary magazine, writing some 270 articles on theatre, and many others on cultural issues.

During the 19th century, a particularly nihilistic attitude had developed in philosophy with regard to the process of knowing in its most direct manifestation. That is, our capacity for sensory perception and also for flashes of insight (rather than laboriously elaborated ideas). Philosophers had come to regard sense perceptions as illusions, concluding that we may not be really seeing, hearing, smelling, touching, what we think we are.

And therefore they concluded, since sense perceptions are an illusion, no one can defend spiritual perceptions, since the way we may experience those are even subtler, even less understood. In his time at the Goethe archives Steiner had argued against these philosophical theories. To him, they cast a destructive shadow over the attitude towards our capacity as human beings to have any real knowledge of anything, especially things of a spiritual nature.

In 1894 Steiner's book, "The Philosophy of Freedom" was published. Through an insightful reflection on how our consciousness functions, (not by any appeal to a belief system) this book showed that our sensory perception is indeed inherently reliable: it does convey to us valid information about the world around us. Beyond this the book demonstrates that our mind has an equally valid capacity to perceive deeper truths, and to act from a deeply moral volition.

It was precisely because of his vital interest and extensive research into cognition, that Steiner would later be in a position to assess the validity of his own spiritual perceptions. This also enabled him to pioneer a way to maintain a rigour and reliability in spiritual insights. Hence as from 1902 he would refer to his research as 'spiritual science' which he saw as deriving from 'anthroposophy'. The word 'anthroposophy' is derived from the Greek language, and means the wisdom in the human soul.

He was acutely aware that materialistic science viewed spiritual experiences as merely illusory or subjective, but his intense engagement with philosophical studies had given him an expertise. He was also urgently pressed by the owners of the estate of Friedrich Nietzsche to become the editor of his complete works. He declined this position discerning that the politics of the Nietzsche Archives scene would hamper his editorial freedom.

But to actually teach his spiritual wisdom later on, after 1900, he would need to confront modern materialistic philosophy, which uses acute analytical skills. For he would be speaking not only from intellectual analysis but from wisdom united to an exact clairvoyance which enabled him to research spiritual realities. His approach was designed to achieve results with the clarity and internal consistency of scientifically disciplined research.

He saw it as his task to bring the fuller, spiritual aspect to life into areas of knowledge which were becoming viewed in a one-sided materialistic way, due to the prevailing scientific attitude. In order for him to bring the other side of the equation, the spiritual perspective, he needed a thorough knowledge of the scientific conclusions about every subject, such as the mind or the ecology, or education or medicine. But he also needed a capacity to perceive the activity or influence of subtle energies and spiritual realities within these areas of life.

At first it is a puzzling fact that the younger Steiner would devote so much of his life to mastering scientific works and non-spiritual philosophical texts. One might think that a person who would later bequeath a vast heritage of spiritual teachings, obtained by first-hand spiritual experience, would find such studies of little interest. In effect Steiner was mastering the intellectual currents of the times, when the prominent thinkers of the dawn of modern science were deeply materialistic, and often atheistic, rejecting any non-physical ideas.

But bringing the spiritual aspect of many areas of knowledge to modern times, required a very capable and reliable capacity for higher perception. It was this exact, precise higher perceiving that he set out to achieve during his earlier years, so that his research would not land him into the unreliable psychic fantasies. Although Steiner did not refer publicly to spiritual matters in his twenties and thirties, his work on his own faculty of higher perception was already endowing him with knowledge of lofty spiritual realities.

A private document about Steiner's worldview as a young man discovered some decades after his death, written when he was 27, reveals his profound spirituality. It reads in part,

The origin and sustaining principle of all existence is the realm of archetypal Thoughts. In it is never-ending harmony and joyous tranquillity. If any part of Creation were not illuminated by this realm, it would be something dead and without being, and would have no part of the life of the universe....

Devout, truly spiritual Love ennobles the innermost fibre of our being; it refines and uplifts everything that lives in us. This pure, devout love transforms the entire soul-life into something that is akin to the Universal-Spirit...[2]

Steiner made a comprehensive study of modern thinkers because he was aware that the modern materialistic attitude had no feeling for the living environment and for the inner nature of the human being and its connection to the cosmos. He concluded that this modern spirit-estranged attitude would gradually join up with an increasingly powerful technological capacity.

He perceived that this dangerous liaison would potentially have the power to seriously damage the eco-system, and also to bring about changes in the nature of humanity, leading to an increasingly unnatural consciousness state. At the dawn of this new era, the beginning of the twentieth century, Rudolf Steiner functioned as a kind of solitary prophetic conscience of modern humanity. He could see future trends and knew that it would be vitally important that humanity did not continue to exclude the spiritual side of life. He saw that scientific research, although accurate, and important for the welfare of civilisation, saw only one side of any situation. He realized the need for a more inclusive perspective to be developed and then integrated into modern scientific modes of thinking.

Whilst he had been acquiring a competent knowledge of the newly emerging scientific view of the world, he had also been mastering the process of meditation. Through this a person can enhance their spirituality and alertness of mind and gradually achieve higher consciousness. In 1900-1903, he worked as a lecturer in adult education, in a private girls' school, in the independent Literary Association, and gave adult education classes to employees in the Berlin Workers' Tertiary Education College. People in the audience of the latter institution soon noticed that someone exceptional was speaking. Steiner would begin his lecture precisely on time and, speaking without any notes at all, finish precisely on time, without reference to any clock or watch. Whilst Steiner was lecturing in adult education, his wife Anna and her daughter often accompanied him to the talks. People noted the deep respect these two ladies showed to him.[3]

During this first phase of his life, he received an invitation to lecture about medieval mystics from a group of people in Berlin who had an interest in medieval spirituality, the Giordano Bruno Society. But in the audience were some Theosophists, and they were deeply impressed. This led to him being appointed General Secretary of the newly formed German branch of the Theosophical Society. He agreed to do this on the

---

[2] "Credo" in GA 40, p. 271. (GA 40 is German for Complete Works volume 40).
[3] Alwin A. Rudolph, in *Erinnerungen an Rudolf Steiner und seine Wirksamkeit an der Arbeiter-Bildungschule in Berlin*, Blätter für Anthroposophie, 3. Jhrg. 1951, Nr. 12, December.

basis that he would only teach what his own spiritual research had revealed, and not what was accepted generally in that society.

A Russian woman, Marie von Sivers, who had been a Theosophist already in 1900, became Rudolf Steiner's foremost student and closest associate. She became deeply involved in the work of supporting his mission and established a publishing company to ensure that his books were available. But as interest in his spiritual wisdom increased, he took on the task of lecturing throughout Europe, travelling extensively for years, speaking to Theosophical groups, and also to the wider community. Anna was not interested in this aspect of his work, and they separated (she died in 1911). Later on, her daughter joined the Anthroposophical Society which was formed in 1912, see below.[4]

He spoke of higher spiritual realms from his own experience, and explained the difference between the soul worlds, and the divine spiritual worlds. He taught that the soul realms are intermediate realms, where souls exist shortly before birth and briefly after death. The spiritual realms, (referred to in his Credo), are the famous Idea realms of Plato, where the archetypal Ideas, emerging from high spiritual beings, (as an expression of God), are moulded and metamorphosed by great, but lesser divine beings.

Steiner also taught a spiritual aspect to cosmology and the creation of the universe. He described how the universe condensed out of subtle ethereal energies, after being first conceived in the mind of high spiritual beings, their concept being taken up and realized over aeons by ranks of divine-spiritual beings. This activity is a 'workshop' of divinity, where the archetypal ideas underlying creation are developed.

Local newspaper reports show that this unusual enterprise, of speaking publicly to whomsoever was interested, on previously veiled spiritual teachings, brought excellent responses from the community. A reporter for the Local News in Weimar, Germany reported in 1903,

> "Lecture held by Dr. Rudolf Steiner: "*Theosophy and the evolution of world religions*". Yesterday evening, Dr. Steiner from Berlin held the first of three lectures. In a fascinating manner the speaker considered to begin with, the origin of 'theosophy' or divine wisdom. The talk was followed with the greatest attentiveness; it was an extremely interesting lecture, the entire content of which we are unfortunately not able to detail here. 16.April. 1903." [5]

The newspaper reported on the next two lectures, saying that, "…unanimous applause greeted the speaker at the end, from the otherwise intensely silent audience in the auditorium." He spoke extensively about subtle ethereal energies which maintain the eco-system of the planet, and the role of cosmic influences from planets and the zodiac in the life on our planet, and in human psychology. He later gave visual architectural expression to this interaction between cosmic forces and humanity in his great

---

[4] Wilhelmine Eunicke, born 1876 - died 1969.
[5] Reported in Beiträge zur Rudolf Steiner Gesamtausgabe, Nr. 99-100, Easter, 1988.

building, called the Goetheanum, in honour of Johann Wolfgang von Goethe (see below). Steiner also gave sessions about the way to develop spiritually through meditation, explaining what occurs as the meditant's consciousness becomes spiritualized, and the student encounters the soul-spiritual realms. He referred to this as 'crossing the threshold' between this world and the higher realms. He spoke of the living Earth and how specific spiritual forces are active in the different seasons, and how our consciousness and our life-processes are significantly interwoven with these.

He also lectured on various religious themes, especially on Christianity, presenting it as a limited cultural expression of a sacred reality of cosmic dimensions. He describes the Gospel narratives as indicating a union of a cosmic being of great significance, the 'Logos' of St. John, to the soul of the Earth. He also lectured extensively on psychology – in a more spiritual sense – and also on history, showing the gradual evolution of humanity's inner life and bodily form through the ages. Steiner also spoke on destiny (or karma) and repeated earth-lives, and how this was compatible with the underlying truths of Christianity.

From 1910-1913 he wrote four dramas about the dynamics that occur in the spiritual quest within a group of people. One of these was performed in Munich each of those years. As the momentum gathered around his work, plans were made to establish a centre in Munich, but the town authorities declined permission as the proposed large building was seen as incompatible with the surrounding architecture. But within ten years the Great War would commence, and then Rudolf Steiner's attempts to bring what he regarded as a more complete, spiritually balanced view of life and of one's own human nature, would be severely limited. During these years of travelling and lecturing, and on to the end of his life, it was Marie von Sivers who took on the responsibility for supervising the details of his strenuous existence. In 1912 his association with the leadership of the Theosophical Society ended; he had been General Secretary of the German Branch for ten years. This Society, based in India, and led by Annie Besant, announced in 1910 that they had found the Indian teenager who was the vessel for the returned Christ, and who was the same as the anticipated world-teacher, known in some Oriental circles, as the Maitreya Bodhisattva.

The young Indian man, Krishnamurti, was to become famous later on. Leadbeater reported that, "In Esoteric School meetings I have said, that the boy's body will be used by Lord Maitreya... Lord Christ and Lord Maitreya are the same."[6] (The name Maitreya refers to the great saintly spiritual teacher who is understood in Buddhism to become the next Buddha.) A number of theosophists world-wide became convinced of the deceit. Steiner in his lectures on Christianity pointed out that his research had clearly shown that Jesus would never reincarnate. He also pointed out that a so-called Second Coming would occur, but it would occur in a non-physical way (see Chapter Eight).

Steiner continued on his increasingly successful path, but difficulties were now obviously brewing between Berlin and Adyar, where the headquarters of the Theosophical Society was located. On Dec. 30th 1910, a new branch of the

---

[6] Reorted in the Indian newspaper, "The Hindu" on 4. April 1913, and elsewhere.

8

Theosophical Society was dedicated in the town of Esslingen, followed by a lecture in the museum in Stuttgart. Steiner's social profile was such that the Mayor had the street between the railway station and the Museum cleaned, and he joined the audience. Three hundred members of the Theosophical Society arrived by train.[7] Membership of the German branch of the Theosophical Society was increasing substantially.

Soon Steiner's growing success led to the head of the Theosophical Society, Annie Besant, waging a campaign against him. She declared that Rudolf Steiner was an agent of the Jesuits (!) and consequently informed the Members of the Theosophical Society that, " The T.S. is face to face with the most dangerous enemy that liberty or speech ever had…"[8] Her subsequent actions of cancelling a conference in Genoa in September 1911 with Rudolf Steiner as the keynote speaker, just a few days before it was to begin, made a split inevitable.[9]

Steiner refrained from any polemic against her, no doubt hoping that she would find her conscience. When after a lecture in 1911 someone in the audience asked him for his view of the reincarnation of Jesus as Krishnamurti, he simply replied,

> "It is not necessary for the spiritual research {he was conducting} to speak about everything that happens in the world. Such spiritual research speaks about that which arises from its own worthy, earnest research; and such research only wants to offer this to those who are interested. In regard to your question, I only have this to say; the spiritual research which is presented from this place (Berlin) does not have anything at all to do with this matter, and does not want to have anything to do with it."[10]   (translated, the author)

So various Theosophists began to see the need for a society that would be open to Rudolf Steiner's research. They put the idea to Steiner, who affirmed that he would lecture to such a society. In December 1912 the Anthroposophical Society was founded by a number of members (ex-members) of the German branch of the Theosophical Society. Steiner explained that anthroposophy is "A knowledge which becomes born in the heart as wisdom, when the heart is raised to selfless love". On another occasion, Steiner defined anthroposophy as "A path of knowledge which seeks to guide the spiritual in the human being to the spiritual in the cosmos."

In 1929, four years after Steiner's death, the young Krishnamurti, who had been holding conferences around the world as the returned Christ, declared right in the midst of a world conference, that as he was not a world teacher, he was dissolving the Order of the Star of the East, which then ignominiously collapsed.

---

[7] Reported by one of the 13 members, Mina Gerst, in *Mitteilungen aus der Anthroposophischen Arbeit in Deutschland,* 33. Jhrg. Nr. 128, Johanni 1979, p.151.
[8] Published in *Mittelungen für die Mitglieder der Anthroposophischen Gesellschaft,* No. 1, Cologne, Mar. 1913, p.11. (T.S. is the accepted way to refer to the Theosophical Society.)
[9] The Italian General Secretary of the Theosophical Society, Prof. O. Penzig, wrote to Steiner informing him of Besant's actions and declared it to be in contravention of the statutes of the T.S. in *Mitteilungen der Deutschen Sektion der Theosophischen Gesellschaft,* No. XV, Cologne, Jan. 1913, p. 5.
[10] Archive document: a question & answer session from 1911.

During Steiner's tenure as General Secretary of the German branch of the Theosophical Society, he had introduced the world of Art to his fellow members, many of whom had not previously incorporated art into their spiritual interests. Steiner insisted that the wholesome spiritual life, and indeed the effective spiritualization of the soul, and thereby society in general, is assisted by the exposure of the soul to the beauty offered in artistic activity. As he told his listeners, in a 1907 conference,

> "… indeed I am convinced that when the artistic element draws ever more into our ranks, then it shall also become more possible for our friends to overcome the difficulties in attaining to actual spiritual consciousness".

That this element of art was a major factor in the motivation for his decision to take up such a challenging activity can be seen in a statement made to Theosophists in 1907,
> "…in so far as we carry out spiritual science, we are not following some woolly theories, and not something that is life-alienating and rejecting of the world. But rather, we do this in order to seek out in the spiritual that which can very directly uplift and ennoble the soul and the life-forces behind our physical body…"[11]

The point that he is making here is that we have a life-force organism that maintains our body and makes sense perception possible, and this needs to be refined and ennobled; not only the soul. If people are exposed to works of beauty and art that present higher ideals, then gradually these images have a beneficial effect on humanity. But he also wanted people to try to develop their spirituality and to thereby let spiritual reality shine through their art,

> "Spiritual Science has to begin to incorporate itself into human endeavour, in the evolution of humanity, or else we will become inwardly empty, unfruitful. Today one encounters in the area of the Arts that humanity is spiritually deserted, has an inner emptiness as they seem able to portray in their artwork only what is to be seen outside in nature. The inner fertilization from the spirit is already lacking."[12]

(See Chapter Twelve, entry, *Emptiness of soul; the battle for meaning*, for more about this.) This attitude was embodied in his work as a spiritual adviser. On the occasion of the dedication of a new branch of the Theosophical Society in the town of Esslingen, Rudolf Steiner suggested to the thirteen members of the new group that they could consider themselves to be "a Raphael Sanzio circle". They consequently began each weekly branch meeting with a half hour of painting practise or a study of art.[3]

In 1910, lecturing on the account of creation in the book of Genesis, Steiner brought in an artistic element to deepen the audience's understanding. It was the last, unfinished painting by the Greek artist, Nikolaus Gysis (1842-1901), called "Vision from the Gospel", also known as, "The Heavenly Bridegroom". Steiner commissioned an art firm to make a copy of this painting for him. In his work, Gysis presents a great

---

[11] GA 96, lecture, 4th March 1907 p. 255.
[12] From an archive lecture, 20th March 1916.

number of spiritual beings gazing towards a majestic Christ figure, in the centre – and all of this in a vibrant red colour, framed by a rich indigo blue. He took it along to the lecture and for about fifteen minutes he spoke to his audience about this painting. He commented that one could feel something of the mood of the opening lines of Genesis,

> "The spirit of the Elohim brooded over the gathered up elemental substances".... this carrying in the gold into the closely linked red, and then into a blue which attunes one to reverence, brings to expression deep, deep secrets of the heart."[13]

From 1910 through to 1913-14 Steiner lectured extensively on an esoteric approach to Christianity and also to cosmology, writing in this time his major anthroposophical work, "An Outline of Esoteric Science". In these years, he was also working on a new form of organic architecture, designing a building to serve as the cultural centre for his life's work. Land had been donated in the village of Dornach, near Basel in Switzerland. As the First World War began, the earlier plans for a centre in Munich, declined in June 1913, were transferred to the site in Dornach. Immediately a number of anthroposophists, including an architect, Schmidt-Curtius, moved to Dornach and began to purchase further large amounts of the land on the hill there, where only two houses stood.

By December the building project commenced; the first spade was placed ceremonially in the soil and the foundations of the large building were laid. In early 1914, a small canteen was established and funds started to pour in.[14] The construction of the First Goetheanum quickened in its pace; this was an extraordinary double-domed wooden building named in honour of Johann Wolfgang von Goethe. A leading anthroposophist, Carl Unger, undertook to financially support the initial stage and to also supervise the project.[15] The donations eventually totalled some 8 million Swiss Francs, worth about US $46 million in today's market. Soon the first signs of religious opposition emerged to the large anthroposophical initiative within the tiny village of Dornach. In early 1914, the local protestant pastor announced a lecture "What do the anthroposophists intend?"[11]

Steiner had been teaching for a little more than a decade when the first World War began, severely restricting his lecture activity. He hoped to bring about a deepening of the cultural life of Europe (and beyond), as well as to renew various areas of vocational endeavour, such as education. He felt a deep concern about the tragedy unfolding around about him. In addition to the enormous personal suffering war brings, Steiner was also aware of the destruction it would bring to the spiritual and cultural life of central Europe, which he viewed as immensely valuable. As the war dragged on, he made a public appeal concerning ways to bring it to an end. In private he made contact

---

[13] From an address by Rudolf Steiner in Munich on 25th August 1910, published in *Blätter für Anthroposophie*, 3.Jhrg. Nr.12, 1951, p. 424-5.
[14] Reported by Helene Kober, "Erinnerungen an die ersten Dornacher Jahren" in *Mitteilungen für die Mitglieder der Allgemeinen Anthroposophischen Gesellschaft*, 2. Jhrg. Nr.10, Oct. 1950.
[15] In 1928, Unger was shot in the midst of giving a lecture becoming the first anthroposophist to lose his life on behalf of the movement.

with powerful figures in authority, hoping to reduce the length and severity of the conflict. At this time, Marie von Sivers was given the task of returning to the war zone, in order to reach Berlin and to arrange for the Society's publications and documents to be freighted to Switzerland. To enable her to enter German territory, she and Rudolf Steiner underwent a formal civil-wedding ceremony, to give her Austrian citizenship.[16]

The Goetheanum building, embodying an organic architectural style, was constructed during the war years by people from many different nations. Some of these nations were at war with each other. This building can be regarded as one of the greatest achievements in European architectural history. Built from wood, its form was based on two large intersecting cupolas, one smaller than the other. These represented the emergence of the higher spiritual humanity from the lower self; and it also represents the emergence of humanity from the cosmos. Its hand-carved interior, extensively painted in plant-based watercolours, was intended to embody the organic architectural feature of surfaces that metamorphose naturally into associated forms.

Teams of people from various countries worked at this task in relative harmony, shaping the interior to remove angular surfaces, to bring out flowing, organically metamorphosing forms. They also began painting scenes from the spiritual history of humanity on the ceilings of both domes. In 1915, architects from around the world came to see the scaffolding removed, fully expecting it to collapse as the feat of joining two large domes, without the normal quota of support-columns in place, was regarded as impossible to achieve. (For more about this building see entries in Chapter 11.)

Steiner was also busy developing a new approach to the use of colour in art, emphasizing water colours in painting, to allow more subtle spiritual nuances to emerge. He developed a new art of movement called eurythmy, creating hundreds of choreographic settings, and also gave instruction as to how it could be applied for therapeutic purposes. In eurythmy, the dancer strives to make moving, metamorphosing forms, with her or his arms, which in effect makes visible the extraordinary forms which musical sounds, and vowels and consonants form in the air and ether as we speak. He also created many paintings or pastel drawings, and designed 13 other buildings in an organic architectural style.

From 1918, in war-devastated Europe, extremely serious questions about the nature of society, of economics and government were discussed. Rudolf Steiner was approached by people who wished to find ways to approach their work that would create a better society. People found that Steiner's far-reaching knowledge of the interrelatedness of the earthly reality and the spiritual could be put to practical humanitarian use. His knowledge of the subtle ethereal forces at work in living organisms enabled him to lay the foundation for valuable organic farming known as bio-dynamics.

Bio-dynamics is an enhanced form of organic farming, a fully commercially viable system of agriculture which does not put poisons and synthetic fertilisers into the soil,

---

[16] This was a pragmatic arrangement; otherwise Steiner's life was that of a spiritual seer, teacher and scholar. Steiner made the situation clear to a student, Alfred Meebold, (noted in Meebold's unpublished memoirs, p.41b).

but which also actually enhances the life of the soil, both the micro-organism and the subtle 'ethereal' energies which we need to take into our bodies through our food.

In the area of animal husbandry, he warned against feeding meat pellets to animals, saying that it would bring epidemics of insane cows; if this advice had been taken seriously in mainstream circles, the horrific effects of the mad-cow disease of the 1990's would have been prevented.[17] Likewise he predicted the mass dying of bees, by the early 21st century if the stress placed on them by new trends in apiary practice of using the larvae of worker bees for breeding queen bees was not stopped.[18]

Rudolf Steiner 'spiritual science' is rigorous in its logic and clarity, enabling his insights to be applied to vocations, such as medicine, education and agriculture. The practical application of Steiner's works in the medical field alone is astonishing; it would eventually include medical and pharmaceutical data which has resulted in many hundreds of medicinal products and medical therapies, used by general practitioners around the world (see the entry under medicine in Chapter 15).

He founded the Weleda Company, which now produces some 2,000 medicaments for use by doctors and other practitioners. Steiner's lectures to doctors and medical students, laid the foundation for a broader model of health and illness in the allopathic medical world. Steiner gave detailed guidelines for the understanding of the origin of illness. He taught that the origin arose in disturbances to the interface between the physical body, the subtle life-force organism which maintains our body, and lastly, our consciousness (or soul).

Although anthroposophical doctors and therapists do use allopathic medications and procedures when necessary, they have a large body of non-toxic medicaments and therapies, and above all a new view of the nature of the human body and its interdependence upon the human soul inhabiting it. From this, new therapies for the treatment of illness and the maintenance of wellness, is at their disposal. Another aspect to Steiner's pioneering work in developing a new perspective towards illness and health is the application of his ideas to counselling, to the care of people with disabilities, to drug addiction and to personal development issues.

But he is best known for his contribution to new approaches to education. Steiner's educational principles are based on his direct knowledge of the changing consciousness of the growing child, and are published in some 24 volumes.[19] A basic perspective in his approach is that the child gradually 'grows down' into earthly consciousness, leaving behind its innocent and highly imaginative 'pre-birth' condition. The gentler is this interface with the world in early childhood, the stronger will be the psychological foundations of the young adult. The young adult is consequently more empowered in his or her search to find themselves, that is to sense their own deeper potential and to exert their will to develop this.

---

[17] GA 353, lecture, 13th Jan. 1923.

[18] GA 351, lecture 10th Nov. 1923.

[19] Not to be confused with the Montessori system which has entirely different educational principles, influenced by her Theosophical worldview.

The young person is then empowered as to his or her own inner compass, and becomes more resilient to the negative influences. Steiner educational principles are applied in some 800 schools worldwide. These 'Steiner schools' are also referred to as 'Waldorf schools', after the name of the company which financed the first Steiner school, in Stuttgart). The Steiner schools became more widely known after an international Steiner School exhibition travelled the world in the 1990's, under the auspices of UNESCO.

The first, pioneering Waldorf school in Stuttgart – and also the Anthroposophical Society itself – were forced to close in the mid 1930's when the Nazi party came to power in Germany. Rudolf Steiner's work was high on their list of hated movements; in 1935 the Anthroposophical Society and the Waldorf Schools were banned. The Nazis could see the degree of interest in Steiner's ideas and the potential that this had to become an opponent of their own social-political goals. (But they did at times allow bio-dynamic agriculture, as they misread this as a kind of pagan nature-deity movement.)

This opposition began when in the 1920's Steiner had to deal with political thugs attacking the people gathering to hear his lectures. Bolshevik socialists and nationalist socialist extremists were already active by then. The infamous Nazi publicist Karl Rohm published an article in the anti-Semitic journal Leuchtturm, in 1920, in which he threatened the burning down of the Goetheanum, ("...it will sure need some cleverness of Steiner... to prevent a real shower of fire... one day bringing an ignominious end to the Dornach splendour.")[20]

In the years after the First World War Central Europe was in crisis. Both Nazi and Communist violence was spreading, assisted by the prevailing financial and industrial devastation. Rudolf Steiner spoke on urgent social issues, on the governance of society, including the role of money. He set out to explain how 'the body social' is threefold, that is, it consists of three independent but interrelated spheres, just as our consciousness has three faculties, namely thinking, feeling and will.

During the war he took the unusual step of issuing an Appeal to the people of Europe for a quicker end to the hostilities. It was in the form of a pamphlet, which was also printed in various newspapers. His Appeal made suggestions for a new political and financial way of governance for Germany and other lands.[21] Steiner enlisted the help of gifted anthroposophists, asking them to undertake extensive lecture campaigns, to spread the word about a better way to resolve the conflict and to re-think the way that society functioned.

He also sent documents to heads of State or their senior cabinet ministers, in particular Austria and Germany, (Prince Maximilian, briefly the German Reich chancellor, and Emperor Charles of Austria, and Ernst Siedler, Minister-President of Austria). This action was undertaken in an attempt to offer them advice on how to steer their country through these dangerous times. Prince Maximilian consequently went to see Steiner in

---

[20] C. Lindenberg, *Rudolf Steiner eine Biographie*, vol. 2, p. 733.
[21] This document is referred to in English as a "Memorandum".

Berlin, before he became Chancellor, in October 1918. Steiner was aware that if the war dragged on, it could end with a peace treaty that would make a second world war inevitable. But his attempts to bring about the end of the war in 1917 failed to change the course of the disastrous political-military juggernaut.

By now and on into 1921 Steiner's lectures were in such demand that a professional agency had to be used to arrange his lecture tours, and he filled the largest venues in the great cities of Europe. Steiner did not give a utopian prescription for solving society's ills, rather he urged people to recognize the nature of, and then encourage, the various aspects of society to function healthily together. He called this approach to social renewal, 'the threefolding' of society, by which he indicated what would naturally happen if people could recognize the inherent triune nature of society, and let it come to expression in a system of governance.

He then began negotiations with a media proprietor, about acquiring his own newspaper, so he could write articles about ways to help society out of the disastrous situation. The proprietor, an anthroposophist, was happy to oblige, but the crisis situation, intensified by the financially ruinous state of central Europe made it impossible to go ahead.[22] See Chapter 13 for a brief summary of this threefolding concept.

Violent Communist agitators prevented him speaking to the workers in large factories. It was not only their hatred, but also the germinal form of the Nazi party exerted its hatred against Rudolf Steiner. This led to violence against his efforts, and eventually the German police were unable to guarantee the safety of Steiner's audience (or of himself) and his lectures had to be cancelled. Prominent in the Anthroposophical Society, (including in its executive) amongst Christians and Theosophists, were some Jewish people with a vital interest in spirituality, who found Steiner's esoteric inclusive Christianity quite acceptable. It seemed that this also fuelled the nationalist-socialists hatred of Steiner's initiative.

In 1921 Steiner had responded to requests from Christian clergymen and theological students to advise them on how they could bring a renewal to the role of the church. His lectures and texts presenting a new style of religious rites, led them to found a church, eventually called the 'Christian Community'. It offers religious services with qualities similar to both Protestantism and the more liturgical churches. A highly regarded German priest, the Reverend Friedrich Rittelmeyer, left his Lutheran church to become the first head of the newly formed church called the Movement for Religious Renewal.

In response to this, the German Protestant churches placed a discrete embargo on any reference to, or critiquing of, this startling event. This embargo lasted for some 65 years, until in 1998 an article was published in a theological journal discussing this

---

[22] Karl Künstler owned the newspaper. Reported in, *Mitteilungen aus der anthroposophischen Arbeit in Deutschland,* 26. Jhrg. Nr. 99, Ostern 1972, p.59.

situation.[23] Similarly when the world-famous missionary, theologian, musician and Nobel Peace prize recipient, Albert Schweitzer, praised Rudolf Steiner his remarks were censored from his books, published in 1960.[24]

From 1920 opposition to Rudolf Steiner from religious groups grew stronger. As the construction of the Goetheanum neared completion, the building became a noticeable landmark, and increasing numbers of people from beyond Switzerland began to attend conferences there. In April 1920, a local Catholic priest in his weekly pastoral letter wrote of how, "the huge new temple of Dornach, with its immense cupolas, is devastating the beautiful area."[25] And a campaign was launched by the local priests against Rudolf Steiner's work, using their weekly church newsletter to spread disquiet. This led to resolutions being passed in meetings of the Catholic People's Party of the Basel area, declaring their support for the church's actions.[26] Then in July 1920 a meeting of Swiss Catholics was arranged in Dornach.

A notice of the meeting in the newspapers called for direct action against the Goetheanum saying, "Catholics – rise up, to Dornach !"[27] No public protests actually came as a result of the meeting, but further events were held, and their tone became more strident. In late December 1922, opponents of Rudolf Steiner' work, presumably spearheaded by religious zealots, burnt down the Goetheanum. Tragically one man perished in the flames. With the mysterious disappearance from the local court room of the files about this arson attack, assembled by the police and the insurer, the conclusion as to who were the actual culprits remains unknown.[28] The famous theologian Karl Barth, whose writings have obscured much of the deeper spiritual truths in the New Testament, wrote about this,

> "We have heard with satisfaction about the burning down of the Goetheanum. {Our colleague} Emanuel Hirsch, thinks that the arm of the Lord is still outstretched {against evil-doers}".[29]

The year 1923 consequently began as a time of anguish for many, and concern as to how to continue with the work, with the building no longer available. In particular Rudolf Steiner was concerned with the dilemma of giving his work a stronger foothold in an antagonistic and changing world. In an effort to give his listeners a deeper grasp of spiritual realities, Steiner spoke more than ever before on the spiritual forces which maintain the planet's life-processes in each hemisphere. He hoped that festivals about the spiritual significance of a hemisphere's seasonal cycle would be created. These public festivals would also incorporate spiritual elements derived from a cosmic view

---

[23] Ute Gause, *Friedrich Rittelmeyer (1872-1938)* in *Zeitschrift für Religions-und Geistesgeschichte,* 48. Jhrg.1996, E. J. Brill pp.153 -171.

[24] A. Schweitzer, Meine Begegnung mit Rudolf Steiner, 37th letter to the Schweitzer Friends Circle. Written on 5th Nov. 1960.

[25] Reported by R. Boos in, Die Hetze gegen das Goethanum, Nov. 1920, Dornach, p. 55.

[26] Boos, Die Hetze gegen das Goethanum, p. 91.

[27] Nordwestschweizerische Katholikentag, 25. Julz, 1920, quoted in, Die Hetze gegen das Goethanum, p. 93.

[28] The building was insured with the local government body, the Canton of Solothurn.

[29] C. Lindenberg, *Rudolf Steiner eine Biographie*, vol. 2, p. 985

of Christianity, and help imbue people's everyday life with something higher, something of the spirit. (For more about this theme, see Chapter 12).

In Germany in November 1923, political extremists including Adolf Hitler, launched the abortive Putsch, seeking to gain power in Germany. News of this ominous event reached the villages of Switzerland. Anna Samweber, a student of Rudolf Steiner, reports that when he read the news of this attempted coup in a broadsheet, he announced, "If these men are to become the government, then my feet can no longer tread upon German soil."[30] And soon thereafter the Berlin apartments used by the Society for its work, were relinquished, such was the threat that Hitler posed. This was referred to in the second issue of the 'Journal For Anthroposophy in Deutschland' to be published after World War II had ended.[31]

> "...when the Hitler Putsch was mentioned amongst other anthroposophists in Steiner's presence, he said, 'If these people are to take hold of the rudder in Germany then I have nothing more to say there'." [32]

Steiner transferred his entire activity to Dornach, and rarely set foot in Germany again. A few months later, on New Year's Day of 1924, someone very close to Steiner, caused him to be poisoned during a social gathering.[33] He had just completed a special conference, held in the carpenter's shed, next to the ruins of the Goetheanum. This event was intended to link the members of the Anthroposophical Society to the wellsprings of spiritual inspiration.

Steiner recovered from the poison, but from then on he was weakened; almost immediately he appointed two people to serve as food-testers, who sampled for poison all liquid or solid nourishment.[34] After September 1924, when Rudolf Steiner was confined to his sick-bed, these two people lived day and night in an ante-room.[35] The effect of this poisoning and the destruction of the Goetheanum building started to take its toll on his health.

By now Steiner was internationally renowned as a spiritual thinker and as a spiritual teacher of impeccable moral integrity. So large numbers of people began to flock to Dornach from all over the world for their own personal reasons. Steiner's energies were now declining, he was unable to walk the 100 metres from his residence to his office near the ruins of the great building. Young members of the Anthroposophical

---

[30] Anna Samweber, Aus meinem Leben, p. 44, Vlg. Die Pforte, Basel.

[31] This was in October 1947.

[32] An article by Friedrich Husemann, in *Mitteilungen aus der anthroposophischen Arbeit in Deutschland,* Nr. 2, Oct. 1947, p. 21.

[33] There are denials of the poisoning in some anthroposophical texts, usually from circles associated with the main suspect. But several eye-witnesses provided a clear account of this event.

[34] They were Maria Kleiner (1888 -1966) and Sofie Bauer (1882-1958).

[35] Rudolf Steiner left arrangements that at his funeral ceremony, the Executive members of the Anthroposophical Society should travel in the first car behind the coffin, and these two ladies in the second car.

Society worked as chauffeurs, taking him there and watched him struggle to get up the fifteen steps into his room.[36] After lecturing, his energies often recovered, at least for some hours.

Steiner was now at the peak of his spiritual capacity, and perhaps sensing the end of his life may not be so far away, he worked at an extraordinary pace, delivering six lectures a day often in several different towns, despite the exhaustion. Each of these lectures in 1924 was in itself a work of genius, giving the foundations of his research into medical, educational and agricultural areas, as well as regarding the arts and art therapy, and advanced spiritual development themes. In the decades after his death this material would be used and explored by hundreds of thousands of people, seeking to help society by creating a broader, more spiritually aware approach to life. This includes a new approach to social and economic problems, to education, medicine and psychology, to agriculture and to the Earth's ecological needs, and to both the performing and visual Arts.

The demands for personal advice from him began to take their toll, and as word spread that he was very unwell, many more people, fearing they might not get a chance to put their personal question to him, flocked to Dornach. He issued a statement to the effect that personal consultations were especially tiring on him. But still people came. On some days up to 400 hundred insistent people would be lining the pathway leading to the venue where he was to speak, forcing his exhausted body to 'run the gauntlet' of their questions before even getting inside to deliver a lecture.

Finally in late September 1924, he was too ill to finish a lecture, and was forced to the sick bed, to undergo a period of convalescence. His personal physician was unable to nurse him back to health. His condition deteriorated, and on March 30th 1925 he died, after a few hours of suffering a sudden and acute deterioration of his general condition. The underlying medical cause of his death is unknown. The entries on his death certificate specify general medical conditions that are not usually considered life-threatening.

Steiner's labours on behalf of humanity were to intended to offer ways to alleviate potential harm caused by a one-sided application of modern technological-scientific attitudes. One of the great outcomes of his life's work was in effect to provide an understanding of the spiritual nature of the cosmos and of human beings. This reduces the impetus towards ideas and processes that de-humanize human nature.

During his last years of lecturing, he was not only poisoned and subject to assassination attempts, and his audience subject to violent assaults, he was also the victim of smear campaigns. Even today this happens from people ill-disposed towards him or unaware of his selfless humanitarian will, his personal integrity and inherent goodness. His lifework has led to a detailed and profound new perspective on the spiritual nature of the human being, and our potential for spirituality.

---

[36] Reported in *Mitteilungen aus der Anthroposphischen Arbeit in Deutschland*, 24. Jhrg. Nr. 93, Michaelmas, 1970 p. 201.

He provided invaluable perspectives on medicine and ill-health, which is today used by many anthroposophical doctors. He also gave very valuable indications into ecological questions, both the practical and spiritual aspects. His research here shows how deeply we are connected to subtle life-forces that are influenced by the planets and the stars.

In summary, during his life he gave 6,000 lectures, designed 14 buildings in an organic style of architecture and drew or painted 100 graphic works showing a new way of working with the inner language of colours. He created about 800 choreographic forms for the new art of eurythmy, and wrote about 700 meditative poems and four dramas. His teachings on cognition and psychology provide a view of the soul that has led to innovative counselling models, residential communities for people with intellectual disabilities, and also to drug rehabilitation therapies. Recognition of the value of his work in education and agriculture is growing continually, around the world.

His last poetic text, found by his death-bed, expresses the drama of his life, and his yearning to see every human being find his or her inner truth, and to allow the spirit to enliven and ennoble the soul, despite the power of forces which oppose this,

I wish to enkindle every person, from the
spirit of the cosmos,
so that they may become a flame,
and fierily unfold the essence of their being.
The Others, they wish to take water
from the cosmos,
which quenches these flames,
and by its dampness,
lames the inner nature of all being.
O joy, when the human-flame
is glowing, even there where it rests,
O bitterness, when the human-creature
becomes bound there where it wants to be consciously active.

Postscript to a remarkable life.

In 1925-26, the leaders of the Anthroposophical Society endeavoured to carry on after his death harmoniously the impetus developed by Steiner in the many areas that he contributed to. But personal frictions and disappointing behaviour eventually led to divisions, which lasted some decades.[37] Fifteen years after Steiner's death, Europe was once again engulfed war, the inevitable and predictable outcome of the peace treaties drawn up at the end of the First World War. Many of Steiner's initiatives were linked to the cultural heritage of central Europe. But many people and much of this cultural

---

[37] And in the 1970's several falsified letters were circulated in Steiner's name, about a romantic attraction between him and a member of the society. But linguistic analysis reveals their origin with a person to whom German was an acquired language.

greatness were lost in the shadow of Nazism and the destruction wrought by World War II.

Steiner's impulse is today carried on by many groups, by interested individuals, and by the world-wide General Anthroposophical Society. Branches of this Society are to be found throughout many countries around the world. There are also a few independent anthroposophical societies. The international centre of the main organisation, The General Anthroposophical Society is housed in the second Goetheanum, at Dornach, built of concrete in the 1920's, and constructed in a very different style to the first one.

The interest in Steiner's work increased substantially in the 1980's, for much of what he taught and forecast and suggested as solutions to global issues has become more relevant with the passage of time. With the increasingly serious challenges that we now face globally, his work is a source of unique help in the quest to enhance the meaning and preserve the wholesomeness of life on Earth.

Most of Steiner's teachings are preserved in the 360 volumes in German; these are mainly transcripts of his lectures. To read Steiner's lectures requires you need to know his basic terms. The question of where to start with reading Steiner, is dealt with in the last chapter, "How to read Rudolf Steiner".

2: THE SOUL AND THE SELF

To Rudolf Steiner the mind or soul is seen as something derived from spiritual realms, which gradually enters into the embryo during pregnancy. It is not seen as the by-product of chemical and nerve processes occurring in the brain. The body however is constructed with such wisdom that our soul can manifest itself through the body. So, in the spiritual psychology of anthroposophy, the common term 'the mind' is actually the soul, or more precisely, the intellectual aspect of the soul.

The term 'soul' means various strands of consciousness integrated together and which derive from spiritual realms. The soul descends down from divine *spiritual* realms into the less sublime *soul* realms, and hovers above the mother. At conception it has united the underlying energy field, responsible for its future body, with the fertilized ovum.

The seven aspects of human nature
Rudolf Steiner identifies seven distinct aspects to the human being, including the soul and the spirit. He refers to this as 'the sevenfold human being'. We will start with the so-called 'three bodies'. Firstly, we have our physical body. Secondly, we have an ethereal energy form which animates every cell of the body, and thirdly we have our soul. In so far as these three each has a definable appearance and role in our human nature, they are referred to as 'bodies'. Rudolf Steiner refers to the soul as the 'soul body' and the ethereal energies as the 'ether body'.

The use of the term 'body' for two subtle elements of human nature need not be confusing. The term 'body' when used in this way, has a more philosophical meaning, it has the same meaning as 'the body of Shakespeare's plays', or 'the body of medical knowledge'. So, one can call the 'soul body' *the soul,* and the 'ether body', *the life-force organism.* But Steiner has good reasons to refer to the 'soul body' and the 'ether body'.

Our soul has an identifiable set of qualities and dynamics, and appears to the clairvoyant as a glowing aura extending out about a metre around the physical body. This is called by Steiner the 'soul body' since it has its own definite appearance and boundary. The term 'soul' here means our consciousness, which Rudolf Steiner defines as having three primary strands; namely our usual thinking, emotion and will. The higher aspects of these three qualities, such as wisdom, noble emotions and social good-will are part of our spirit.

Exploring these various parts of our being further brings greater clarity to the subject of what is a human being. The ethereal energy form called by Steiner the 'ether body' is becoming increasingly accepted as a reality. Wherever Western knowledge is enriched by ancient Oriental wisdom, it is quite accepted. This is because the Ch'i energy of Chinese acupuncture, or the prana of Indian literature is the same thing as the ethereal energy form which Rudolf Steiner clairvoyantly researched.

The **ether body** is a definable, gently glowing organism made of energies more subtle than those of the electro-magnetic spectrum. It has approximately the shape of our physical body, but it extends beyond the body, only a half inch or so, except at some points such as the finger-tips, from where it rays out a short distance.

Whereas the **soul** appears to clairvoyant vision as the well-known 'aura', which is a definite oval of living colour forms surrounding our physical body. The aura is like an egg-shaped glow surrounding us. It extends about a metre below our feet and above our head, and on all sides around us. So within the soul, or identical with the soul, is our mind; that is our feelings, intelligence and volitional powers. So far, we have considered three aspects to human nature, the physical body, ether body and soul body.

As a fourth element there is a **'self'** or **'ego'**. By these terms Steiner means 'self-awareness', or the awareness that we are a separate entity. The term ego in anthroposophical literature means the sense of our own being-ness; it is not a pejorative term. To make this quite clear to his students, he often uses the term "I" (in German the word, "Ich") rather than 'ego'.

But for now let's note that in Steiner's psychology, the "I" is a sense of self which gradually arises in the little child, usually appearing a short while after the second birthday; which is when we enter our third year of life. This is happening when the child stops saying for example, "Johnny wants a biscuit" and says, "I want a biscuit". The 5th, 6th and 7th aspects belong to the spiritual part of us, and he calls these the **Spirit-self,** the **Life-spirit** and the **Spirit-human**. We shall consider these three aspects later on. Thus, working upwards from the physical body, we have,

> Spirit-human (or Spirit-man)
>
> Life-spirit
>
> Spiritual-self (or Spirit-self)
>
> the "I" (or ego or self)
>
> Soul body (or soul)
>
> Etheric body
>
> Physical body

The soul or soul body is also referred to as the 'astral body'. This term 'astral' is a Latin word which means 'of the stars' and it is also used by astronomers. The reason that in 15th century Europe seers and esoteric thinkers, such as Paracelus, used this word for the soul is that they were aware that the soul is permeated by energies from the planets and the zodiac. From the zodiac and the planets our soul derives its qualities on the journey down to birth.

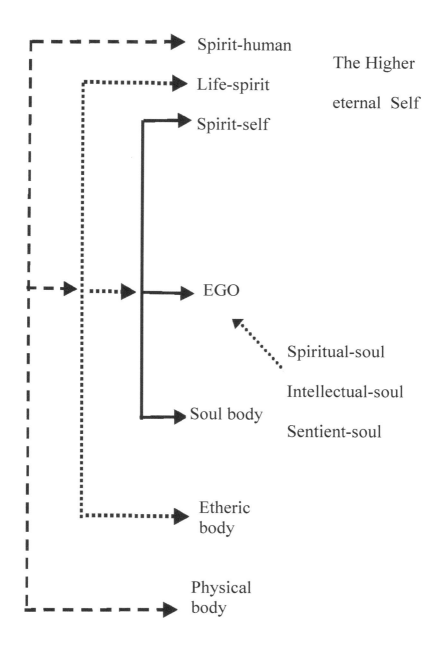

Diagram of the human being: body, life-force, soul & spirit

The threefold structure of the soul

This perspective on the human being resolves itself into a triune structure. We have three 'bodies': the physical, etheric and astral bodies. We have three souls: the sentient, intellectual and spiritual souls. Finally, we have three aspects to our spirit: the Spiritual-self, the Life-spirit and the Spirit-human. Before we discuss the threefold spiritual aspects, we need to consider again this central factor about the soul. That in Steiner's view, the soul has three components or dynamics, namely, thinking, feeling and will. This was also the case with ancient systems of spiritual knowledge. So in various ancient languages there are often three terms for 'soul'.

In Hebrew, there are the terms Nephesch, Ruach and Neschamah, each referring to a different soul dynamic. Likewise in ancient Greece, there is Orektikon, Kinektikon and Dionetikon. In ancient Egypt, amongst a variety of terms, there are the words Kha(ba), Akhu and Putah for these three components. These three terms in these different cultures, are seen by Steiner as referring to the emotional soul, the intellectual soul and the intuitive soul respectively, in the order as given for each language. Let's see what Steiner means by these terms.[38]

Firstly, we have the capacity to have **emotions**, and these manifest from the lowly to ever higher kinds. There are primitive emotions; such as the survival instincts, and aggression, fear, lust, vengeance, envy, etc. There are transitional emotions, such as humour, basic dislike and liking, anxiety, jealousy, etc. We note that in a simple way, there are a few more intelligent animal species which have some of these.

Then there are the more sophisticated emotions, which are only in human beings; intellectual humour, duty, romantic love, artistic responses, altruistic compassion, etc. So as we human beings leave the other kingdoms of nature behind, we discern their footprints. The capacity to experience these emotions is called the 'sentient-soul'. But the sentient soul is also the faculty in us that registers sense impressions, such as coldness or warmth.

Secondly we have our **intelligence**; that is, the capacity for logical, analytical thought. This Steiner calls the 'intellectual-soul'. This term refers to our reason, our capacity for logic, for analytical thinking, and for mental picturing. We note that the animal realm is represented here only in a small way, and not at all with respect to higher kinds of personal intelligence.

With the writing of the play, "Hamlet" or the designing of sophisticated medical equipment, for example, we enter the uniquely human sphere. But here we need to note that one can indeed discern intelligence in the animal kingdom; they do possess some quasi-personal intelligence.

---

[38] Hebrew examples are Nephesch: psalm 43,5 'Why art thou cast, O my soul'. Ruach: Deuteronomy 2,30 'The Pharoah's soul (mind) was hardened'. Neschamah (very rare) Proverbs 20, 27, 'The soul (intuitive mind), of the human is the lamp of the Lord, shining into his innermost being'.

A sensitive observer discovers that the intelligence in some animal species is startlingly powerful, but it is also instinctive; in other words it is not personally present in, or personally 'owned' by the creature. So when a wasp makes a hardy form of paper to construct its nest, or the spider makes its geometrically sophisticated web, or a newly hatched turtle moves off down to the sea, these creatures are manifesting an instinctive intelligence. Steiner explains this instinctive knowing as deriving from the group-spirit of the particular species.

Thirdly, we have our **will**, the aspect of our mind which has the capacity to make a resolution to do something, to carry out an action. This 'will soul' is called by Steiner 'the spiritual-soul'; one could also call it the 'intuitive soul'; and it is often called the 'consciousness soul'. Most of our will is subconscious, only a small part is consciously functioning in us. Do we really know why we are doing our jobs, or even in many cases, married to whom we are married, or living in this country? And ultimately, do we know why we were born in these times? It is often our intuition that has made these decisions! Our will or volition, being in essence intuitive, functions primarily behind our conscious mind, and thus is not accessible to our ego or self.

Now, it is helpful to look at the threefold soul structure of the human soul again from different points of view, to get clearer about it. The three elements to our soul – our emotional capacity, logical thought, and will – despite being an integrated unity in us here on the Earth, **have their own spiritual origins**, and so after death, or in the person undergoing real spiritual development, they become more independent of each other. Steiner therefore refers to the human being as possessing 'three souls', rather than being 'a threefold soul'. Let's consider these three soul qualities again.

Sentient-soul
What Rudolf Steiner calls the sentient-soul is our emotional capacity, but it also is the part of us which registers the sensations of cold, heat, darkness, light etc. Sentiency is the capacity to experience desires, yearnings, fears, joys, happiness, pleasure and pain and so on. It is also the capacity to experience what our senses tell us of the physical world, such as coldness, heat, movement, sounds, odours and so on. If we can experience our 'inner life' (all our emotions) then we can also experience, so long as we are in a physical body, what our senses report to us.

Intellectual-soul
Secondly we have our logical, intellectual, rational capacity; the capacity to think clearly and analyse situations. We normally call this our intelligence; Steiner refers to this as our '**intellectual-soul**'. Steiner points out that the intellectual-soul is often at the mercy of the sentient soul, in other words, our emotions can damage the clarity and truthfulness of our thinking. If we desire that a certain attitude of ours be seen as correct (by ourselves or others), then the power of our wishes can overwhelm the objectivity of the intellect. However the reverse is also true, that so often in the heavily intellectualized and technological cultures of today, rational thinking can be oblivious to our emotional needs. The logical capacity is a vital tool of our life, as medical-therapeutic knowledge, as literary skills and engineering achievements, etc; these are all derived from the intellectual capacity.

Spiritual-Soul

Rudolf Steiner's vast body of teachings, called '**anthroposophy**' (a Greek term which means the wisdom in the human soul) derives from his insights. But from what part of our consciousness do these insights derive? They derive from our third soul, the '**spiritual-soul**'. This is the third member of our soul, and it is the least known and the hardest to understand, in terms of psychological dynamics. The fact that the soul is seen to have three aspects means that the list of seven members of human nature has to be expanded, to add these additional three elements. The psychological force operative in the will, especially in deeper decision-making is **intuition**, it is not emotion and not logic. This capacity of intuition is in effect, the spiritual-soul.

Summing up

Our soul has three aspects, **emotion**, **logic** and **will**. We have seen that our emotions could be termed our 'sentient soul' and our intelligence, which uses logic, could be termed our 'intellectual soul'. Our will is a mysterious and complex part of our soul or mind, and it is the forces operating in our will that create a third aspect to our consciousness, or the third soul. This third soul is called the spiritual soul or consciousness soul.

When we make a deeper decision, indeed when we act in a split second in a dangerous or very challenging circumstance, then we are of course, using our will – but often we cannot really claim to be fully in charge of such powerful volition, because often it surprises us through its power and complexity. See Illustration One for a view of the three soul aspects that together constitute our aura.

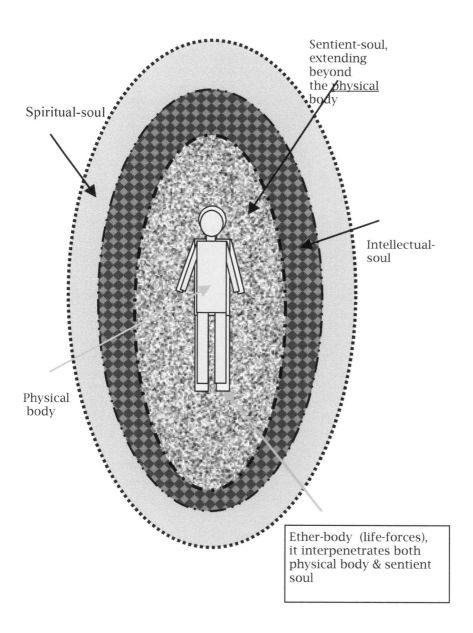

Sentient-soul,
extending
beyond
the physical
body

Spiritual-soul

Intellectual-
soul

Physical
body

Ether-body (life-forces),
it interpenetrates both
physical body & sentient
soul

1: The spatial relationships of body, life-forces and our 3 souls
(A simplified diagram. not to scale)

The Spiritual soul: pathway to the human spirit
This faculty of intuition is a soul-power which gives us insight into a situation – and it is this same capacity which **is** our third soul, the **spiritual soul**. It is this same soul that gives to us – in rare moments – spiritual insights. Such insights into deeper spiritual truths need not be rare and unpredictable, they can become ever more present. This is what the meditative life is all about – giving us a stronger, more vivified spiritual-soul.

But as one strives towards higher wisdom and compassion, then one is invoking the presence of one's 'spirit'. This brings us to the three aspects of the human spirit which we listed above, but did not explain. The '**Spirit-self**' is Steiner's term for that part of our spirit which is brought into a faint but real relationship to the human being when we begin to feel ourselves to be an individual entity. This emerging of a sense of "I" when we are about three years old is basically the everyday "I", the normal personality.

Here you could wonder why Steiner would connect the eternal human spirit to this everyday personal I. You could conclude that Steiner was unaware of the entire discussion in eastern religions and in modern psychology, of the tenuous nature of the "I", of how it is considered to be an illusion.

But Steiner was very aware of the debate and ideas on this subject. We can note that what he taught in his many lecture cycles is that the "I" or ego is a dual thing. Firstly, our "I" is our personality, the outcome of the unique combination of our three souls, which indeed has many illusory aspects to it. But secondly, this "I", he taught, has an immortal and spiritual aspect to it. This aspect is **our threefold higher spirit, which exists in a germinal form, and which is held and nurtured for us by our guiding Angel**. This higher aspect of the "I" is seen by Steiner as always being faintly in connection with the personal self or the earthly "I".

In Chapter Six these three parts of our spirit, and the Self or Ego, are explored in more detail. But we can note here that the Spirit-self arises when the soul – the emotions, the thinking and will – start to become spiritually attuned and selfless, no longer earth-bound. And this Spirit-self is part of our spirit. Whereas the Life-spirit arises when in turn, the spiritualizing soul allows the life-energies (or etheric body) to be conserved and refined.

The third part of our spiritual ego or eternal self is the Spirit-human, and it is only a distant potential in us, and difficult to conceptualize. It arises when the refined soul and life-forces enable a further subtle spiritualizing of the human being, which releases a hidden spiritual energy that maintains the over-all form and functioning of the physical body. We shall consider this triune spirit further in a later chapter.

Lastly, we can note that the number of the components of the human being can be defined differently. Steiner also shows how the sevenfold human being, once these three souls are added to the list, creates a *ninefold* being. One would expect a listing of ten elements, because there should be, as the tenth one, the ego or "I". However in *Theosophy*, this is dropped as the three souls are added to the list, making a total of nine.

Spirit-human
Life-spirit
Spirit-self

Spiritual soul
Intellectual soul
Sentient soul

Soul body
Ether body
Physical-body

The list is to be understood in this way; the three souls together comprise the everyday personality or normal 'ego', the three spiritual aspects together comprise the higher self or eternal "I". See Diagram "The Sevenfold Human Being" which clarifies the above descriptions.

The Evolution of the individual ego-sense over millennia

A particularly important theme in Rudolf Steiner's anthroposophy, forming a basis to much of his teachings about human nature, concerns the changing, evolving nature of the "I", our ego, or our sense of what we are as human beings. In past ages we experienced ourselves and our environment very differently from the way we do today.

How did people in earlier millennia actually experience their own self? Can we ever know the answer to this, since in times prior to Aristotle (about 350 BC) few people attempted to form philosophical thoughts about questions which explore the nature of consciousness? An avenue to explore in the search of an answer here, is how did mothers name their babies, long ago.

According to Rudolf Steiner, in millennia prior to the Greek civilisation, people lived with both a natural psychic tendency and, without being specifically aware of it, a kind of group ego-sense, or group-soul. A group ego-sense, instead of what we all take for granted, namely an "I", an individuated ego-sense. These two characteristics made earlier humans, up to about 700 BC, quite different from ourselves. Illustration Two shows a carved gemstone for ritual-cultic purposes from the Mycenaean civilisation in the area of the Aegean Sea, from about 1,250 BC.

If you asked a modern scientist to draw a scene from the life of the bees, thinking of the flowers that they fertilise, you would perhaps get a drawing showing the structure of the hexagonal cells inside the hive, or perhaps a close up of the inside of the flower and its pollen. But 3,250 years ago, it was natural to depict some nature spirits, clad in bee skins, worn in the manner of two priests at an officiating ritual, passing on some nourishment to the plant. In other words, the plant owes its life to the activity of nature spirits, who work in a sacramental way in service of bees, the spirit of the bee colony. This is a totally different attitude to that of modern people.

29

2 The old psychic consciousness: a Mycenaean gemstone ca. 1,250 BC

Two nature spirits, empowered by the bee-spirit, nurture a plant.

(Colours enhanced for clarity)

Ancient naming customs

And how did mothers name their babies in much earlier days? If we go back to the ancient Sumerian-Babylonian and Egyptian cultures of about 3,000-2,000 BC we find an astonishing fact. The world's earliest writings are from these cultures, and on the clay tablets that have survived, experts were astonished to find sentences such as,

> *The Queen of heaven is my mother* writes to *the words which the god spoke, shakes the heavens*, to assure him of her loyalty.

Or

> *My king, whose decrees in the sanctuary ceases not* has contracted to buy from *May I go forth in the light of Marduk*, ten head of cattle.

Eventually it became clear to the linguists that parts of these sentences (put into italics here) were in fact substitutes for personal names or rather, what we would today think of as personal names. They show that to people of those ancient times, divine beings were considered to be deeply important. Now in fact when a mother gave the baby such a name, there was no interest or striving to find out what this baby should be called – in our meaning of that idea.

That is, no need was felt to determine what name resonated with the qualities of that soul as a (future) self-aware adult. And in other parts of the world the custom of naming a baby could include names which were actually numbers, such as 55 or 71. Or a name could be "bring on a younger brother" if the child was female, and males were more valued. Or the name could be, "house-fire", or "flood". Why was this done? Because in the case of a number such as 55, that was the age of the matriarch of the extended family when the birth occurred. If the name was "house-fire", then this meant that the birth occurred in the same year as when a fire occurred in the village.

In these customs the main focus was not to find a name that resonated with the personality of the new baby. According to Rudolf Steiner a sense of individual personality was quite faint in those times. The birth of the individual ego-sense had not yet occurred. And therefore also the spiritual-soul, which is such an individuated part of our soul-life, was also not very developed.

Amongst the Mesopotamian people, unusual lists of ancient kings and the dates of their rulership have survived. For example, a King Gelumin ruled for 900 years; king Zugagib ruled for 840 years and, coming towards the end of this culture, king Aripi ruled 720 years. In the Bible the patriarchs are likewise listed as living for centuries. Adam lived for 930 years; and Seth for 912 years, and Methuselah lived 969 years.

Rudolf Steiner pointed out that of course these figures are not to be taken literally, but they are spiritually true. He explained that as people had no real ego-sense, the founding patriarch – his deeds and decrees – was in effect the core of the tribe's sense of identity. His being resonated inside the people as their own core element. They had no individual ego, but rather a group-ego. These centuries-old life spans indicated for how long the memory of the patriarch reverberated in the souls of his descendants in the tribal-group. And since these people were naturally somewhat psychic, the patriarch after death still exerted a huge influence; and from this came the cultural customs that we refer to as ancestor worship.

But as time moves towards the Hellenistic Age, amongst only the Hebrews and Greeks, a personal name arose, but this would be placed <u>after</u> the tribal or family name. So you could be called the equivalent of "Smith, John". No truly individual name arose until the Christians in Europe unconsciously brought about this momentous change. Consider the case of the person whom we call "Julius Caesar". If you were to go back in time to ancient Rome and ask to meet Julius Caesar, people would be confused; no Latin document exists which bears this name. For this would be like asking, in 19th century America, to meet "Lincoln tribal-group President", instead of President Abraham Lincoln. Julius Caesar was actually <u>Caius</u> Julius (i.e., <u>John</u> Smith) and 'Caesar' was his epithet or special title, that is, Emperor.

Although he was part of the Greco-Latin world that developed a personal name, these were still not felt as something to use really freely, as happened later on in early European cultures. So he, like the other emperors, was known amongst his contemporaries as "Caesar". There is no recorded usage of the name Julius Caesar by the ancient Latin people.[39] The Roman historian Suetonius called him "divus Julius" which actually means: a 'deified member of the Julius family'!

A personal name
Referring to someone by his or her first name only became culturally universal in early European Christendom. But unawareness of the development of the personal ego, and hence the significance of the development of the personal name, and how the family name predominated over it at first, led to the Renaissance custom of calling him "Julius Caesar". Perhaps these Europeans meant 'the Julius-family Caesar' which is in accordance with the general attitudes of the ancient Romans, but amongst the less educated it quickly became falsely viewed as a personal name.

Starting to some extent amongst the Hebrews and the ancient Greeks and Romans, it was in early Europe for the first time in history that people walked the Earth who felt themselves to be first and foremost individual beings, without any known tribal-family name of any kind. Each mother made an effort to find a name for her baby that seemed to be expressive of the individual. Each person had only a first name which they called their 'Christian' name; they had no other name, no family name, at all. Their names were often taken from Bible and church history, such as John, Miriam, Joseph, Dorothea, etc. Or their names came from Latin or Greek terms, such as Leonides, Albanus, Basil, or from Celtic terms, such as Lorna or Roger.

So when Lorna married John what was her name then? Simply, Lorna, as there were no family names. And if John lived near the forest, he could be called "John attwood" (that is near the woods), but if he moved into the village and lived near the church, he was called – not <u>named</u>, just referred to – as "John church". So if Lorna married "John

---

[39] The definitive biographical reports of Ancient Latin writers and poets about this Caesar never use the name Julius Caesar: namely, Suetonius in *De Vita Caesarum* and Plutarch in *Marcus Brutus.* Nor does Virgil in his Aeneid, despite Dryden 'helpfully' adding it in centuries later; nor Lucan in his Pharsalia, and Catallus refers to him as Caius Julius Caesar.

attwood" she still remained Lorna. In the communal monastic life of the 12th century, scholars have discovered an enhanced tendency towards a greater focus on the self.[40]

But these people were the same ones who were losing the age-old psychic state and thus gradually, by the 15th century, in Europe a humanistic or agnostic state of mind arose, followed soon by an Earth-bound attitude. The mineral physical world envelops European humanity, as people found themselves stripped of belief in, or perception of, the spiritual.

Gone were intimations of the unborn babe, of the recently deceased elders, of the nature spirits and of the gods. But this bare physical world, bereft of any tangible sense of a living milieu, served as the womb of the personal ego. The individual ego-sense had been born, amongst the people whose religion was essentially an appeal to the individual self, to one's own conscience. Christianity is the religion of the individualized person, and therefore the spiritual dimension, in terms of many deities, nature spirits, heavenly realms, was kept to a minimum in this religion.

No Bible in the western world could tell people about 'the Kingdom of the Heavens', it had to be falsely translated as the Kingdom of Heaven. No multiple heavenly realms, no multitudes of gods or nature spirits were proclaimed, all serving a great Uncaused God. (In eastern Christendom – Greece, Serbia, etc – the Greek text with its plural is naturally there.)

An indicator of how the older, more psychic or spiritual feelings lingered on in Asia is a tapestry made by order of the atheistic Chinese government in 1956. This shows a Soviet rocket flying in the heavens amongst happy, celestial goddesses; see Illustration Three. This first ever intrusion of a mechanical device into the firmament was possibly going to lead to civil unrest in China. The tapestry was made to pre-empt feelings of outrage and anxiety, which could have caused social unrest, because the old feeling for gods and goddesses in the heavens was still present.

Artworks reflecting the evolving of the ego-sense
But we also can trace this process of the loss of awareness and consequent development of an ego-sense in the way that works of art were made over the millennia. Most art from pre-literate societies around 5,000 - 9,000 years ago, or even much earlier, is that of a crude depiction of the natural world and of gods and spirit beings.

The **Egyptian-Mesopotamian** cultures appear to be the earliest civilisations with cultural achievement such as writing and substantial artworks, apart from pre-diluvial civilisations. Among these artworks some very substantial and impressive architecture remains, of course. We find still the focus on spirit beings and gods, but in paintings this was often very awkwardly done. There is a kind of naïve unreal realism in which the head of a person is seen in profile, but the eyes are seen from in front of the person.

---

[40] Caroline Bynum, "*Did the 12th century discover the individual*", Journal of Ecclesiastical History, vol. 31, No.1 Jan, 1980.

And there was no ability to put an object into any perspective in terms of its position in space.

When a king was depicted, the depiction of personality was not striven for, but rather his divine empowerment. Art works were designed to impress enemies and vassal states of the ruler's might, and also to support the priesthood in their task of encouraging veneration of divine beings. But in this age where the ego-sense had not yet developed, and a strong group-soul awareness prevailed, no artist or artisan ever signed their artwork. And with a weaker sense of the physical world around them than that of later peoples, paintings had distorted perspective on spatial reality.

See Illustration Four, a papyrus drawing from ancient Thebes, revealing how the artist was unable to portray the actual way that we perceive things in space. In this picture of a lake in a garden setting we have four different points of view. The trees appear as if growing flat along the ground. The ducks on the pond are seen as if we are standing on the edge of the lake; the fish are seen as if we are down inside the water. The aquatic plants are seen as if the viewer were down under the water.

In this ancient era with such vagueness about the physical environment, the night-time journeying of the soul was very vivid. Upon awakening, the body was still felt to be taking the person into darkness; so the radiant realms above were deeply attractive. Hence the so-called Egyptian Book of the Dead was actually called The Book of Coming Forth by Day. Compared to the later Greco-Latin Age, the Egyptian-Mesopotamian peoples still had a feeling for the link to the cosmos.

In their destiny, unfolding here upon the Earth, people felt themselves as dependent upon the movement of the stars and planets, and from events occurring in the great universe. From this arose the beginnings of what developed into astrology. Although individual horoscopes have not so far been found from the early phase of this Age, the wisdom gained created the basis for this immensely important branch of knowledge. But as only a small percentage of the ancient Mesopotamian tablets have been translated so far, individual horoscopes may be found when further research is done.

Then came the **Greco-Latin Age**. Personal names started to emerge, even if placed after the tribal name. Artists had discovered perspective and foreshortening, and so their artwork was now accurately reflecting the way we see the physical world. Rudolf Steiner points out the Greeks felt much more at home in this world and in the body, and hence they could reflect the interplay of gravity versus levity, of the three dimensions of space in their creative works.

Art ceased to be at the service of religious and esoteric themes only; art now portrayed human personality and struggles, it could 'interpret reality'. And in this age where individuals were having more or less individualized names, the individual ego was more present. And this meant that when a person such as Pericles spoke in Athens, people felt it was right that he did this, because they could sense that the impulse to do this was living in his **will.** Whereas in earlier ages, a god had to be the authority behind a speaker or leader, especially a high priest/priestess.[41] And as the individual ego arose, so did individuated thinking; so there arose the world's first 'intellectuals', a phase pioneered by the great Greek thinker, Aristotle.

And towards the late classical period of Greece artists began to sign their artworks. But a much stronger focus on the physical world would develop in the next epoch; for the Greeks could still sense, if semi-consciously, the presence of the etheric energies behind living physical forms. Rudolf Steiner put the question, how is it that the ancient Greek statues are felt by us as so living?

He answered, because in this epoch human souls felt themselves to be one with etheric energies which formed the arm...they could feel the etheric energies behind the creation of matter.[42] But later on, in pre-medieval times there was a Dark Age, and the superb mastery of physical perspective developed by the ancient Greeks was gradually lost and less skilled art forms predominated. During the Greco-Latin Age body identification developed for the first time in history, and gradually the soul-life began to be identified with the bodily life-vitality. And hence gradually they were left with only a vague feeling about existence after the death of the body.

In the 15th century as the Renaissance began in Italy, this started what Rudolf Steiner calls the **Central-European & Anglo-American Age**; which still has 1,500 years to run. It is fascinating to follow this process in the development of Art from the medieval times into the Renaissance. In the medieval period, and into early Renaissances times, painting of sacred themes would almost always have a golden background, the physical environment being ignored.

Rudolf Steiner comments that there was a feeling in the artists of the medieval times that a holy person was spiritually located in, or resonated with, divine realms where gold is a predominating colour.[43] Illustration Five shows paintings of this kind. But in later Renaissance artworks this feeling for the transcendent faded out and personal emotions came into expression. But above all the focus of the artist became the portrayal of the physical world as a reality, almost as precisely as if photographed.

See Illustration Six, a painting by an early Renaissance painter, Baldovinetti, who created an extraordinary scene of considerable historical importance. For he, like a few other painters of this time, has placed the natural world with its sky and trees as intruding into the divine realms. The golden area indicating the divine realms is still there, but this has now shrunken to become a smaller area directly around The Virgin Mary and Child. Coming across this painting in the Uffizi gallery is quite an experience ! And then see Illustration Seven, where, in the new medium of oil

---

[41] GA 62, p. 466.
[42] GA 62, p. 373.
[43] This is mentioned in GA 264, p. 197 & GA 291a, p. 219.

**3
Chinese
govt.
tapestry
1956:**

A Soviet
rocket happily
received by
the celestial
deities.

36

4 Egyptian tomb painting from Thebes, ca. 1400 BC

Note the inability to portray spatial reality. There are 4 different viewpoints mixed up in this.

Colours enhanced for clarity

37

painting, which enables fine details to be achieved, van Eyck ostensibly portrays The Virgin Mary and Child being revered by a church dignitary. But in fact the artist is really demonstrating how he can portray the physical world with extreme precision, and the two holy people are reduced to almost an ornamental feature.

In the 20th and 21st centuries this general trend has developed further, but we don't have room to explore the various shorter-term phases of art works here. There is now generally speaking, no longer a sensing of the souls awaiting birth, or of the ancestors who have departed from this life, of the four ether energies underlying the Earth's life processes.

The personal ego

The personal ego awoke alone in this world, being no longer immersed in the umbrella 'ego' of the tribe, nor in a living milieu of spirit beings with whom one felt oneself to be livingly connected. The bare physical world became the womb of the earthly ego, so to speak. For the first time in history, painters began to repeatedly paint their own faces. This is an action which is motivated by the specific wish to experience, or dialogue with, one's own ego. The ego is more clearly expressed in
the countenance than anywhere else in the body.

Albrecht Dürer, van Eyck and Jean Fouquet are noted for this in particular. An ancient Greek artist, Phidia, had made one small self-portrait on the back of a shield dedicated to the goddess Athena, but was jailed for doing so. The intrusion of self into the divine was still experienced as immoral. But this was, in any case, prompted by a much lesser ego-centric motivation.[44] By the fifteenth century as the physical world became the only convincing reality, people set out to explore it; the Age of Exploration of the physical world had begun.

The European and later the American peoples pioneered this push into the individual ego, and hence straight into the double-edged sword. For the personal ego, devoid of any sense of a spiritual matrix around it, has two future possibilities. One is the spiritualization of this ego-sense into a real conscience with regard to the community in general and also a capacity for personal development. The other is to harden it into a destructive, self-serving, self-centredness, which all too easily leads to ways of living and using the resources of the world that damage its ecology. In Chapter Six we shall consider the nature of the higher ego and the human spirit in more detail. There is a higher spirit reality which encompasses and guides the earthly ego-sense. But it's now time to consider a little more about the twofold ego, and how it differs from the Buddhist idea of the ego.

The twofold ego

What appears in us as the normal every-day ego, is what Rudolf Steiner terms the 'concentrating deed' and 'purposeful action' of our karma. That is, our ego is an integral part of the focus, the purpose, the stream of further developmental possibility, within our karma. This is not the same as the Buddhist teaching which states that the

---

[44] And a self-sculpture by an ancient Egyptian artist, Bak, of himself and his wife ca. 1350 BC is a still weaker example of a self-sense, as the image has to do with the after-life beliefs.

so-called 'ego' is only the incidental result of the skhandas or astral energies from the past life, that re-emerge in this life, following karmic laws, without any deeper basis to them.

In contrast to this, Rudolf Steiner teaches that following karmic laws, the personality or ego has come into being, and this as a consequence of the stream of evolution, guided by divine-spiritual beings. This karmic effect flows from the past into the future, guided by the gods, and is an organic metamorphosis of the previous personality or earthly ego. And within this activity is the other part of our 'ego', namely the higher, eternal self. In anthroposophy, in contrast to Buddhism, the ego (the earthly partially illusory personality) does not bring into being the karma. So in anthroposophy, the word 'karma' refers to an immensely valid, complex activity from high spiritual beings who are assisting the soul to move to ever higher states of development in life after life, by assisting the earthly ego to become ever more a vessel of the eternal self. As Rudolf Steiner explained in a lecture,

> "Thus the Buddhist extinguishes the ego and only allows karma to have a validity, which works over from one life into the next, and creates there an illusory ego. Whereas the follower of anthroposophy or spiritual science, for whom karma and ego are not the same, says my ego departs from my present earthly stage endowed with an inner intensification and shall reappear in a new state in my next life, and it will then unite itself with the deeds {and personal qualities} of this next life. Thus if I as an ego have done something, then *my ego* remains connected with the core of that deed, and moves on with that deed from incarnation to incarnation. And whilst all other deeds are temporal and are extinguished in time, that deed of karma which has led to the ego-consciousness of the human being, is not within time…it constantly intensifies its own inner reality."[45]

Now when contemplating these teachings, it is very important to note a remarkably profound element in the spiritual psychology developed by Steiner. Careful study of Steiner's psychological texts reveals that he often speaks of "the ego" in a way that includes both the personal and the eternal in the one entity. The term in italics above – *my ego* – is actually an example of this. Logically, here it has to refer to both egos at once, intertwined into a single higher over-seeing entity, so to speak. If this were not the case, then Steiner would be saying something quite inconsistent, because the personal ego can not remain with the deed, at least, not unless it is deeply interconnected to the higher eternal ego, because this is the only 'ego' that is able to "move with that deed from incarnation to incarnation."

In other words, in anthroposophy, the self or ego here in our earthly world is basically our astral body, our soul, our personality. But in spiritual realms exists our germinal spirit ego which incorporates the deeds of our previous life into the new

---

[45] GA 61, lecture, 21st March 1912, p. 474.

5 The gold of heaven: typical examples of inherent other-worldly (Devachanic) mood that permeated Art prior to the focus on the physical plane.   Left: Refettio de Santa Croce by Nardo di Cione 1366   Right: St. Lucy by Jacopo del Casentino 1340 ?

6 Renaissance art with medieval nuance: the physical intrudes into the sacred: The "Madonna and Child with Saints" ca. 1454 by Alesso Baldovinetti, 1427 - 1499 in the Uffizi Gallery. An extraordinary transitional painting: the natural world's sky & trees are now intuding into the divine realm, which other wise for centuries, as a golden colouring, formed the entire background of holy persons.

(Faded and darkened colours enhanced by computer)

7 A van Eyck painting, Adoration of the Virgin by Cardinal Rolin, 1435.
In this Renaissance painting, the two sacred persons are ornamental, the real
focus is the extremely detailed portrayal of distant physical features, beyond
what the eye can actually see.

personality. And if we enquire how can a germinal entity produce such a wise and extraordinary achievement as the complex tapestry of karma, the answer is that each human being has a guiding Angel, who nurtures this germinal spirit ego.

This Angelic being is one evolutionary step beyond the human life-wave, and it assists higher spiritual beings to weave the tapestry of our karma. There are eight other ranks of such spiritual beings. (See Chapter Nine for more about the 'divine hierarchies' or gods.) Because the concept of the 'I' is so important, in Chapter Six we shall again consider the contrast of the anthroposophical view to the Buddhist view of the ego (the Anatta doctrine).

Further reading
Rudolf Steiner: Theosophy
               At The Gates of Spiritual Science (also published as,
               Founding a Science of the Spirit)
               The Theosophy of the Rosicrucians

3: DESTINY: OUR ABILITIES AND LIFE EXPERIENCES

Our experience of life differs from person to person. Someone's life can be subject to terribly tragic incidents and hardships, whilst another person has abundance and many happy events. Our individual talents can be so varied. There are many profoundly moving features of the human landscape: the musical genius of Mozart, the artistic skills of the Renaissance painters, the determined courage of people in crisis and the inherent selflessness of humanitarians. But also the absence of such talents, or the absence of any socially positive tendencies in other people' is likewise very striking. Sone people experience many harsh experiences, and others have wonderful, life-transforming opportunities.

In the modern western world, there have been historically two explanations for these facts, neither of which is particularly satisfactory. A common explanation in the western world is that it is due to chance, or to the will of God. But in earlier times, in the Hellenistic age, as indeed in Asia today, there are other explanations. And sometimes, awareness of these other solutions appears unrecognized, in the language of the western world.

For example, a Russian music critic a century ago wrote a review of a concert and especially praised the gifts of a singer, a lady who at that time was not prominent. His good review greatly helped her career. When the war broke the Bolsheviks listed the music teacher as an enemy of the state and within a few days was taken out to a lonely harbour, to be shot. The troops readied themselves, taking aim, when a mounted soldier galloped in, with orders to halt the execution. Bewildered and relieved, the music teacher went back to his apartment, where a lady was waiting to see him. She was the singer whose performance he had praised several years earlier. She was now a close friend of the commanding officer of the regiment, and hearing of the music teacher's plight, she had pleaded for his life.

We all probably know of similar examples, and hearing about this sort of event, we might say it's a bit strange, or even a bit 'weird'. But in saying this, we are saying something more significant than our conscious western minds realize. For the word 'weird' is a modern form of the old Celtic 'weordhen', which means 'Fate'. But fate, or destiny, or weordhen, did not mean to people long ago, our vague, fuzzy idea of 'fate'. But rather it meant a pre-destined event which the gods had specially arranged for us, before we were born. Now this idea which underlies fate or destiny or weordhen, is in effect the oriental idea of karma, because these three words do imply a past life on the Earth. The idea of karma appeals to a lot of people, although it is not acceptable to most Christians.

So, how did Rudolf Steiner explain the differing life experiences and abilities in humanity? He taught that there is indeed a deep truth in the idea of karma, with its related idea of repeated earth lives, provided it is understood in a certain way. So he affirmed that this is a truth, and furthermore, that it is compatible with Christianity. He didn't speak in a sensational way about anyone's past life; instead, he sought to show people that it was possible to accept the idea that one's life experiences and talents are the outcome of a past life, without being irrational or superstitious.

We can note that many other great minds in the western world also accepted this solution to this challenging riddle of human existence. In Friedrich Schiller and Johann W. von Goethe's works are various indications that these great German poets were convinced of reincarnation. The composer Richard Wagner in his opera 'Parsifal' actually merges the concept of reincarnation with that of Christianity.[46]

So how does Rudolf Steiner approach this theme? Two aspects stand out here. Firstly, he asserted that he was 'a scientist of the spiritual', rather than a person who received at random psychic images, for he researched very carefully such realities with his extended consciousness. Secondly in his teaching activity he strives to show how it is possible with an enlivened thinking or intuitive insights, to arrive at this idea by acutely observing the phenomena of life. He does not make any sensational claims about his own past, nor provide some strange psychic impressions as a basis for proof. He takes a different approach to this question.

Intuitive thinking points to karma

By sheer clarity of thought, a kind of intuitive thinking, he demonstrates that the idea of karma is thoroughly correct, and indeed logical. It is in his book *Theosophy* that he writes some of the greatest passages of western literature on deeper life-questions. You may need to read it a few times before it is really clear, but it is well worth the effort. The way Rudolf Steiner teaches these things means that there is no need to betray the integrity of one's logical, rational mind, to grasp these spiritual truths. Let's now see what he writes about this, from his book ***Theosophy***, my comments are in brackets,

> "... the soul mediates between the present and duration (eternity). It preserves the present for remembrance.... it thereby rescues the present from impermanence, from fading away, and takes the present up into the duration of its own spiritual being. But the soul also gives an ongoing, enduring quality to the impermanent, temporary world in another way. That is, apart from yielding itself up to the transient, temporary sense impressions of the world, and making these ongoing, it also determines things by its own initiative, i.e., by embodying its own nature in the things which it does, in the actions which it carries out. By remembrance the soul preserves yesterday, by its actions it prepares tomorrow."

So far, Steiner is saying that we have the power of memory, and this power in effect preserves some short-term fleeting moment forever, by keeping it in the memory. Furthermore, we can carry out a deed, and this short-term action keeps living on, in so far as it triggers off changes in the world, Steiner continues on by repeating what he just said, but at the same time unveiling the deeper significance of these apparently simple truths;

---

[46] The evil seducer Kundry, is told by the evil magician Klingsor that she is the rebirth of a person who lived in ancient Gaul, called Grundrygia, and earlier she was also Herodias, who demanded the execution of John the Baptist.

"My soul would always have to perceive again the redness of the rose, in order to have it in consciousness, if it could not retain it through remembrance, the power of the memory. So, what the soul can retain after an external sense impression has faded, can again become an image – a memory picture of the object, independent of the original external impression.

Now, one can say, that through this power of forming mental images, the soul makes the outer world into its own inner world, so that it can retain the outer world in the memory, and independent of these acquired images, lead a life of its own.

So, the soul-life becomes the ongoing result of a cause, namely, experiencing the temporary sense impression from the external world. But, action also receives permanence, once it is stamped into the outer world. If I cut a branch from a tree, something has taken place through my being, my soul, which completely changes the course of events in the outer world. Something quite different would have happened to that branch, if I had not interfered by my action.

I have called into life a series of effects, which without my existence, would not have been present. What I have done today endures for tomorrow. The decision of yesterday becomes lasting through the deed, just as the impressions which I received yesterday have become permanent for my soul, through memory."

In other words, imagine that we all live in a large pond, and as we row our boats across this pond of life, at some point we throw a stone into the water. What then happens? Well, you can see what happens by getting a bucket of water and gently dropping a little pebble into it. From the point where the pebble enters the water, ripples move out like circular waves. They move out until they reach the edge of the bucket. Now if the dropping of the pebble represents us hurting or really helping someone, in the actual vast pond of life, then these waves will last a long time. Steiner continues,

"We have a definite concept, and therefore a definite name, for the process whereby a sense impression becomes eternal, or ongoing in the soul – namely Memory. But we do not have a definite concept of, or awareness of, the other process, wherein **we become permanent**, where the decision becomes an ongoing, enduring reality in the outer world.
But, will not the self, the ego, of a human being be just as much linked to the alteration which occurs in the world as a result of its deed – as it is to a memory, which results from seeing something?

The soul assesses new impressions differently, according as it has or does not have this or that recollection....But, the self (ego) has entered into a different relationship to the world, according as to whether it has performed this or that deed."

46

In other words here Rudolf Steiner is saying, if I am a different person according as to what sense impressions I have experienced, am I not a different person as far as the world is concerned, depending as to what deeds I have done to it?

And here we return to our pebble in the bucket example. For, if you watch carefully after dropping a pebble in the bucket, after a brief moment another series of waves arises, starting from the circumference of the bucket. They proceed to move inwards, contracting into a tiny point – at the very place where the pebble was dropped, see diagram ! Steiner continues,

> "If one really thinks out what is being presented here, the question must arise as to whether the results of a deed on which the ego has stamped its own nature might not **retain a tendency to return to the ego**...just as a sense impression, preserved in the memory, returns in response to the appropriate inducement.
>
> Could not that which retained the imprint of the ego, in the external world also wait, **so as to approach the human being from without**, just as a memory approaches from within?"

So here he is saying, this process whereby some particular cause creates a result (known as an 'effect'), has the name in the East of, 'karma'. But the modern western world has never had a feeling for this, and hence never coined a word for this process. What Steiner has done here is to show that intuitive, living thinking can lead one to conclude that karma is a reality. The ancestors of the western peoples, the Celts and Romans and Greeks, did have the term 'rebirth' in their vocabulary in the early centuries of Christianity as there were still some people who believed in this. But this died out before the Middle Ages. However, it was only in 1828 that the word reincarnation and only in 1858 that the associated word, karma, entered the English language. They were taken from the Sanskrit texts of Buddhism and Hinduism.

Repeated Earth-lives
However Rudolf Steiner's research into how a person experiences their life-times on the Earth led him to reject some of the beliefs now current in the East about the way in which repeated earth-lives occur. So what did he teach specifically about this? He found that a person's gender tends to alternate in the successive lives. Thus one can live as a woman in a particular life, then as a man, then a woman and then as a man, etc. He also found that there are usually two life-times in approximately every 2,000 years, and that this process, which encompasses millennia, is due to a kind of cosmic rhythm affecting humanity's existence.

This rhythm also harmonizes with the need for life on Earth to have changed enough to make available new life experiences. But Steiner also pointed out that it is true that this pattern can be broken, by the special karmic requirements of a person or of a group of people. Another point he emphasizes in regard to this theme, in contrast to the Oriental teachings, is that a human being never reincarnates as an animal. Since we belong to the human life-wave, there are parts of our higher nature, our higher self, which no animal possesses. As we saw earlier, these include the Spiritual-Self and the Life-Spirit, although this latter part is only slightly developed so far. The divine-spiritual beings who have created us in response to the will of the great uncreated God, do not allow such a retrograde step in the cosmos to occur, as a human being returning to a new life without their ego-sense.

We have the human capacity of ego-hood or self-awareness, and yes, this is to quite some extent based on illusory values and a vague awareness of separated being-ness, but it is, as we saw earlier, always linked to an eternal higher self. As we shall see when we consider Steiner's teachings on religion, it was a specific outcome of the actions of the cosmic Christ (or Osiris or Apollo or Ahura Mazdao) in Palestine long ago, which ensured that this core part of our being is protected from such debasement. This dual ego entity is never exterminated between one life and the other; this is an impossible action which would force a human being to live next time as a monkey or fish, etc, and thus without any sense of the individual self.

The next point that Rudolf Steiner makes here is that we are not caught in a circle of rebirth, but rather live in a spiral of development. In other words, we are not in a perpetual cycle of lives, just repeating the same level of being, but rather humanity does very slowly progress over the millennia from life to life, evolving the soul to a higher level. Over the ages, different aspects of our own being, and of the greater world, are experienced. Indeed, this theme of specific attributes to our human nature being slowly experienced in the different lifetimes, and thereby evolving further, is a central theme in anthroposophy, which we shall examine later in this book. It is also directly relevant to the question of interest to Christians, as to why it was not taught by Christ, if it is true? Before we consider this theme, let's look at some core aspects of Rudolf Steiner's teachings on karma.

How does Karma work?
There are two aspects to it; there is outer karma and inner karma. Outer karma occurs when what we have done in a past life comes back to us. That is, the actions we have carried out of a good kind or an unethical nature have sent their waves out through the pond of life and these come back to us, suitably metamorphosed.[47] They can be experienced as blows that inflict suffering upon us, bringing ill-health or accidents, etc; or they can return as opportunities that bless us, such as kindness from others, avoidance of illness and violence, etc. Inner karma occurs by bestowing upon us our new personality (sometimes termed the 'inner life'). In other words, the kind of thinking, feeling and the general intentionality which we harboured in the last life, metamorphoses into our new personality.

In the current life if we have a gift in mathematics, this derives from substantial involvement with music in the past life. And if in the current life we have a gift for music, this derives from a quality in the past life, which Rudolf Steiner described as "an open, sensitive predisposition, easily finding the inner transition from sadness to happiness, and happiness to sadness through Nature, in response to Nature".

In the current life if we have a tendency to premature ageing, then it is possible, amongst other possible causes, that this derives from a lack of caring and warmth in the

---

[47] For those who want to push ahead a little in their knowledge, we can mention here that the outer edge of this pond is the sphere of the planet Saturn.

past incarnation. Whereas by contrast, if in the current life we manifest an outpouring of loving kindness, then in the next life we shall inherit, from ourselves (!), the gift of remaining young in the next life. Rudolf Steiner also taught that if in the current life we have a tendency to easily becoming infected, then it may derive from greed for possessions in the past life. However, it is very important to note that other factors may have been operative in a person's life, to cause this weakened state of the immune system. Such as being exposed to deadly chemicals or it may be due to stress that weakens the stomach's ability to digest food, creating systemic toxicity as undigested foods poison our body.

This leads us to the next aspect of karma; namely to never negatively judge a person who is undergoing terrible times, or who suffers from inherent soul disturbances. Because they may well be more ethical than ourselves, or be suffering these things for a higher spiritual purpose. For example, they may have invoked a variety of awful situations, because prior to re-birth they felt the high moral impulse to 'cleanse the stables'. That is, we may have the same negative soul-quality, but failed to find the courage to invoke the circumstances in our life where we will have to directly confront it, and thereby overcome it. So, it lingers on hidden within.

The essence of this striving by the soul through karma, to improve itself from life to life, is beautifully expressed by a noted American, Benjamin Franklin. He wrote a humorous epitaph for his own gravestone, in which he uses terms borrowed from the book-binders trade;

> "The body of Benjamin Franklin, like the cover of an old book lies here, its contents torn out, and stripped of its gilded lettering, lies here. Food for worms. But the Work shall not be lost, for it shall – as he believed – appear once again, in a new and elegant edition, revised and corrected by the author."

So here Franklin, an esotericist, is hinting at his new incarnation as a more evolved soul.

Remembering past lives
The question is often asked, "Why do we not remember our past lives?" The answer firstly is that some people do, namely those people with whom the veil between the incarnate physical consciousness and awareness of the spiritual realms is very thin. This includes little children and very sick people and those who were born with a natural psychic ability. Although statements from such sources may be viewed as lacking a scientific standard of proof, and self-made illusions or fraud often occur in this area, many of the anecdotes from such people will be genuine recollections of the past.

A common mistake occurs when a person in the above categories gets a glimpse back to that century in which they once lived, and in this haphazard experience, they notice the personality of the Pharaoh or of a great saint, and think that they were that person. What happens, in fact, is that they do get a glimpse of the right century, wherein the most potent ego of that time, usually a famous person in history, has left the most noticeable footprint. They gain a glimpse of this after-echo of some potent person, and conclude that they were this person. The situation is similar to a person gazing back across an abyss to a far distant mountain ridge. The person will see the largest trees on the ridge; they just won't notice the small bushes or shrubs. Rudolf Steiner points out that when people have such a recall, this is why they often claim to have been a famous and powerful person, such as Rameses IV, or Joan of Arc.

Back to our question of why most of us have no recall of a past life. Our current personality needs to have something eternal incorporated into it, something that goes as part of us, from life to life, to make recall of a past life possible. We need to have this higher mind inside us, which gives us spiritual thinking and absence of sensual desires, in order to inwardly make a link back to our previous life in an earlier time.

If we don't have this, then we take on a new personality each time, and then there is no part of our consciousness, as earthly or incarnate people, which goes back to that past century. It is possible to have a visionary glimpse from previous centuries about that past personality of whom we are the outcome. This can happen in times of severe illness or if one has a psychic capacity which is simply there from childhood. It is, however, a special requirement of the anthroposophical path of spiritual development that the meditant is able to spiritualize their consciousness through strenuous meditative exercises, so that this recall occurs without any strange or harmful intervention in our psychology or bodily health. Additionally, the current ego-sense should so deepen and widen its nature by the meditative exercises that these visions or insights merge into the sense of self, rather than act as a kind of add-on.

The cosmic clock regulating our lifetimes
We mentioned earlier Rudolf Steiner found in his research that there is a template according to which people return to the Earth; because we do not live in a simple linear time frame that goes on in a simple straight line from the past to the future ! Instead, a kind of cosmic clock determines much of our evolution on Earth. So looking at Illustration 8A, we see how there is the pattern of having lifetimes which alternate between the genders, and which occur about twice every 2,000 years. Now Rudolf Steiner goes on to point out that the evolution of humanity is governed by a cosmic clock, namely the movement of the sun backwards through the zodiac. It takes 2,160 years to pass through a zodiac sign, and it is this movement which creates the sequence of zodiac ages, such as the Age of Taurus, during which the ancient Egyptian and Mesopotamia cultures reached their peak. Now looking at Illustration 8B, these ages are indicated by the symbol of the various zodiac influences.

If we ask the question, why are so many people not inclined to accept the idea of repeated earth-lives, then this same diagram gives an answer. It was back in the time of the Age of Taurus that the spiritual realms and the gods (and to some extent awareness of repeated earth-lives) were a regarded as sacred truths. This more spiritual attitude is shown by the golden colouring in the arrows; over the millennia this awareness fades out and gives way to an earth-focussed attitude (hence in the diagram the golden colour fades and is replaced by a dark grey).

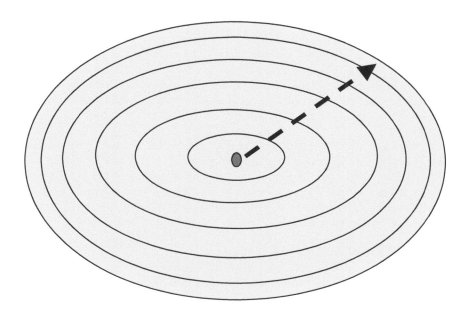

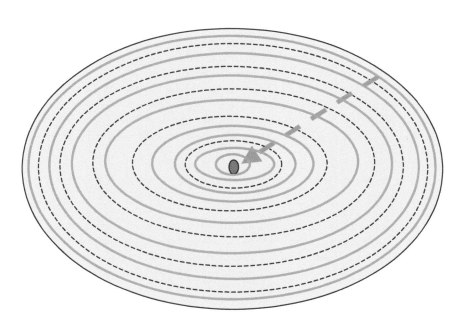

The pond of life: the results of our deeds ripple out, and after a pause, they return to meet us.

So the last major culture which placed the after-life and the gods and initiation in the centre of its life was the Egyptian, and the Mesopotamian. In our age this sensitivity to the spiritual dimension to life is re-developing. In any event, by the Hellenistic Age of the Greeks and Romans the old more sensitive attitude was fading, and modern western cultures have inherited at least 1,500 years of a much more limited and non-mystical viewpoint.

This important discovery of Rudolf Steiner's, namely of the changing nature of consciousness over the millennia, has huge implications for how Christianity would historically develop. For those readers who are Christian or feel there is something sacred about Jesus, we shall have a separate chapter to show how Rudolf Steiner approached this theme, which he also held as a sacred, although he saw it in a more esoteric light than is normally done.

Karma and reincarnation in the New Testament

But for now we can briefly explore why Jesus did not emphasise or indeed even teach the idea of karma and repeated earth-lives. Jesus Christ was aware that humanity in the Hellenistic world, which is where the gospels would be first presented, was undergoing this fading of awareness of the spiritual dimension; this is connected to a developing sense of a personal ego or self-hood. These two phenomena are closely connected. Hence he specifically refrained from emphasizing this truth, but he also refrained from in any way condemning or denying this ! He remained somewhat neutral in this regard, in order to assist the dynamics unfolding in the consciousness of the people.

There are two episodes which relate to the idea of karma and hence reincarnation. It concerns the great Hebrew saint, called Elijah and John the Baptist. People were expecting Elijah to re-appear, in effect to be re-born (as the idea of reincarnation was still alive amongst some of the Hebrews).[48] It was inevitable that when the Baptist began to become prominent as a preacher in the Holy Lands, many began to wonder if the Baptist was perhaps Elijah reborn. Matthew tells us that when Jesus had to comment on this idea to a large group, he gave a curiously complicated answer (Matthew 11:13-15),

> For all the Prophets and the Law prophesied until John. **And if you are willing to accept it, he is the Elijah who was to come**. He who has ears, let him hear.

In verse 14, we encounter a truly unusual answer, which is interpreted differently by different scholars, because it is so strange. The solution commonly chosen today is to make the word 'it' into 'him', thus; "…**and if you are willing to accept him**…" So now this sentence can mean that people might not want to regard the Baptist as so great a figure since he was now under arrest. This translation is saying that the people were placed before an important choice: whether to receive this strange person as the one who ushers in the age of the Messiah.

---

[48] In old Judaism the concept was known as 'gilgul ha'ne'shamot' which means the transmigration of souls. Josephus the great historian refers to it, as does the Zohar (I: 186b).

But to translate the sentence this way requires the grammar to be stretched unacceptably. The solution Rudolf Steiner gives is much truer to the grammar, and means the following: 'If you have the capacity to hear a deeper truth, namely, if you are willing to allow _it_ (the idea of reincarnation) into your view of life, then yes, the Baptist is the reborn Elijah'. But later in this gospel, in chapter 17:11-12, St. Matthew tells of another incident where Jesus is discussing this same subject, but now only to his inner circle of disciples. To them he is much more direct,

> Jesus replied, "To be sure, Elijah comes and will restore all things. **But I tell you, Elijah has already come**, and they did not recognize him, but have done to him everything they wished. In the same way the Son of Man is going to suffer at their hands."

Then the disciples understood that **he was talking to them about John the Baptist.** In effect, the Baptist is declared to be actually the reincarnated Elijah.

Other examples of how karmic laws work
Karma is very much a matter of balancing up our account book with the cosmos; there are as it were, debit and credit pages, as in an accountancy ledger book. Our life is an opportunity to make up for previous errors, and thereby work effectively towards balancing the entries in the 'book of life'. A personal example of this is known from a student of Steiner's. It was a man who was approached by Rudolf Steiner to work in the first Waldorf School. But the man, knowing already just how hard the work was in this new initiative, declined to be of assistance.

A few years later, he came to see Steiner, looking haggard and in a bad state of nerves. He complained of a really difficult, unpleasant event that had plunged him into severe crisis; he was reminded by Rudolf Steiner that some years ago, he had the opportunity to join in the hard work at the new school. If he had done so then, day in day out, year after year, "he would have worked off his bad karma". But he declined, and consequently "encountered his negative karma in one potent blow". An example Rudolf Steiner gives of the subtleties of karma, and how there is a balancing to be achieved, concerns a tragic incident from his lifetime when a large group of people perished in a fire that burnt down a theatre.

He points out that the fact that it was those persons specifically who died may be just entirely a tragic chance event. Or it may be a kind of 'group karma', wherein for a variety of serious reasons, their deaths were to occur together, which would have some really positive outcome in a future life. Or it may go back to a common guilt incurred by all those persons in a past life; and finally it may be that all of the victims had a karmic requirement to die at that time in that way, but in fact they were not linked together by any past karma. So, the above statements also mean that it is true that accidents, as such, do happen.

He also taught that the family and childhood friends of our early years in the previous life are usually met again in the prime, in the middle phase of the next life. Whereas the friends and associates which we had in the previous life in our prime, our middle phase, become our family and childhood friends in the next life. But again one has to avoid being simplistic in looking at our links to other people. Some of our close friends or people with whom we have a serious karmic involvement, may not be able to return at the same time as we do. So our resolving of that karma is put off until a later life.

We can also start an encounter with someone in any phase of this life, with whom we had almost no association from the past at all; so new (or almost new) karma is now starting. But it is also the case that this starting up of new karma more often occurs in the last third of life, especially after the age of 72. Interestingly, this is the time it takes the sun to go one degree further along, as it slowly moves or retrogrades around the zodiacal circle, when viewed on the same day, year after year. As part of this process, Rudolf Steiner reports that 72 years is the age when we enter a phase wherein our past karma normally ceases to demand anything from us. On the other hand, Rudolf Steiner does mention in this regard that, if a person has the inner strength and commitment to seek their own betterment, they can invoke a challenging episode in these latter years, for the purpose of reducing a karmic debt as yet unpaid.

Furthermore, once we have knowledge of the laws of karma, we can start to work towards a bettering of our karma, and thereby be of more help to the world. We can actually have the initiative to formulate a new goal to improve our self, such as developing an artistic appreciation or artistic skill, or learning about a specific spiritual theme to develop inner wisdom. This kind of spiritual development is as helpful to the world as being a humanitarian.

Further Reading
As for Chapter Two

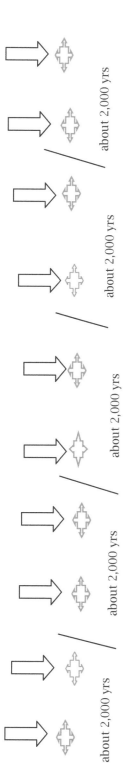

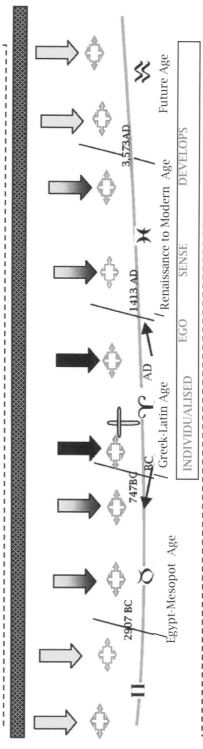

2907 BC

Egypt-Mesopot Age

747BC

BC

Greek-Latin Age

AD

1413 AD

Renaissance to Modern Age

3.573AD

Future Age

| INDIVIDUALISED | EGO | SENSE | DEVELOPS |

55

Appendix

<u>Elijah became John the Baptist</u>?
We need to note that there is an ambiguous statement in a different gospel, that from Luke (1:17) in regard to the Baptist;

> [Lk 1:17] "And he will go on before the Lord, in the spirit and power of Elijah, to turn the hearts of the fathers to their children and the disobedient to the wisdom of the righteous – to make ready a people prepared for the Lord."

This sentence could possibly mean that Elijah was only overshadowing the Baptist, and not actually reincarnated in him. But it is invalid here to mix this report with Matthew's gospel, as Matthew is reporting on how Jesus dealt with the dynamics involving those Jews who were involved in the (centuries old) speculation that a physical re-birth of Elijah was possible, in order for the prophecy about his return to be fulfilled. If the incidents recorded by Matthew were only a matter of speaking with people who believed that Elijah might over-shadow the Baptist with his spirit and power, then there would be no need for Jesus to offer to shield his audience from this much less confronting idea.

We shall explore the implications about the need to focus people's attention on the one life on Earth, and not emphasize reincarnation, later. So the above verses could be seen as confirming reincarnation, even though in a tenuous way. They directly thereby confirm Rudolf Steiner's perspective that karma and reincarnation are true, but not suited to a culture where such subtle awareness was fading out; it was fading out amongst the Mediterranean cultures due to wise, if perplexing, dynamics operative in our historical evolution.

4: THE ENIGMA OF EVIL

In this chapter we are going to consider the contributions that Rudolf Steiner made to our understanding of what causes people to manifest unethical or even criminal ways of being, and in the light of this insight, how to counteract the tendencies, so far as is possible. And this includes the question, why the quest for something apparently sacred sometimes lead into malignant results. It does happen occasionally that someone who is focused on the spiritual quest becomes a sinister, dictatorial figure. In earlier ages the cause of evil was understood to come from the influence of evil beings. In more recent times, the question of why evil exists has been the focus of serious attention by many people in the western world, but usually not from an esoteric or spiritual perspective.

Rudolf Steiner has provided some invaluable insights into this serious issue from his spiritual research, although he does caution that a 'final' resolving of the enigma of evil is scarcely possible. He points out firstly that, as a general underlying dynamic, our capacity for free will is involved. That is, if we had no free will, there would be no evil, as we would simply be ethical, for we would mirror the nature of our creator. This viewpoint is based on his perception that humanity was created by a divine being, and therefore could be expected to reflect the goodness of our creator.

Looking around our modern society, especially where the humanistic or materialistic attitude is prevalent, one cannot really find any answer to the question of evil. For millennia religion taught that it is due to evil spirit beings known in the Judaic-Christian tradition as Satan or the Devil. However, religion in the Western world is no longer a major force, so for many people the enigma has no answer.

The materialistic view
When Rudolf Steiner spoke on this theme, he referred to a statement made by a famous materialistic thinker, a Darwinist, Thomas Huxley (1825-85). Huxley once gave a potent, almost emotive, position statement on ethics. He said,

> "I declare that if some great Power were to agree to always make me think what is truthful and therefore always do what is right, on the condition of me becoming a sort of clock-like person, I would instantly agree to the offer." [49]

This quotation has enormous significance! He is of course saying that evil is connected to the freedom to do good or bad, so Huxley wants to become a robot, and in that way he shall always only do the good. So as his highest ethical attitude, he is offering to surrender his freedom in order to not become a producer of evil. We shall return to this quote later on, for now we just want to note that this is the ethical principle of a non-believer in all things religious or spiritual. Rudolf Steiner has a number of entry points into this deep theme, and one of these is this,

> "In this current epoch {starting in 15th century} a conscious confrontation with evil is taking place... that which people of this epoch will have to experience is

---

[49] From Huxley's essay, On Descartes' 'Discourse Touching the method of using one's reason rightly and of seeking scientific truth'. (1870)

a fully conscious encounter with evil, because this is now becoming an active factor in evolution. People will now have to become conscious of much which in earlier times was permitted to remain in the subconscious. Indeed the purpose of this present epoch is that people shall become inwardly mature to become informed about certain truths of our soul-nature which in earlier ages were kept away from consciousness." [50]

These words were spoken in 1917, and like so much of Steiner's teachings, they are becoming ever more relevant as the decades go by. In effect he is saying that the good spiritual Powers guiding humanity require human beings to encounter the lower self. There is a deep reason for this; namely that we learn how to effectively counter it. But to do this, we first have to be fully awake to its existence. Once we realize that this is the dynamic, then we cannot help but feel the need for some assistance in dealing with this unpleasant demand placed upon us now. What Rudolf Steiner taught about the actual origin of evil impulses inside the human soul, provides valuable guidance to this entire theme.

First, let's note the lack of real insight in our culture on this, but not by considering terrible atrocities. Instead, we shall be examining the more subtle, but equally important, manifestations of unethical actions caused by a wrong attitude, a wrong kind of thinking. In the media, terrible crimes are often described as "senseless". And this is understandable enough for us to say, from our feelings. However, it is a sign of the inner blindness, because all deeds, all acts of will, have a causative factor! There is no such thing as senseless deeds ! Especially deeds that require forward planning, and cunning. So where is the cause, where is the intention? If it is not inside the mind of the criminal as such, then where is it?

Two kinds of evil
To answer this question we have to go deeper than the usual, materialistic views of today. We have to look at the idea once taught by religious teachers, namely that there are influences inside the human soul from malignant spiritual sources. Rudolf Steiner taught that if this ancient idea is approached in a new and clear-sighted way, it could lead to some really valuable answers. To see how Rudolf Steiner approached this, we need to get a little clearer about the two different kinds of unethical tendencies, (which become sources of evil in their stronger modes). There are spontaneous bad deeds, when someone is "carried away" with overwhelming emotion, such as impassioned jealousy. The offender often says he was "out of myself". This is especially the case in crimes of passion, involving 'love triangles'. But there is another type of unethical deed, one that needs to be planned, and in fact, has the polar opposite dynamic to the first, it is the premeditated crime. These involve intelligence and will; here there is no remorse, no sympathy for the victims. But with the first type of wrongdoing the perpetrators very soon feel strong remorse and shame for what they have done. There are these two kinds of evil.

Now the second kind of evil has two parts to it, a much more subtle part which is apparently quite respectable. It is the foremost enemy of human life today. It is what

---

[50] GA 178, 18th Nov. 1917.

Rudolf Steiner calls 'dead thinking', by which he means the utterly non-spiritual attitude to life. This is the major cause of most of today's problems. Damage to the Earth's ecology, to our own soul-life, to society in general from these harmful, negative actions may be described as having their origin in dead thinking. This kind of thinking is often so widespread and subtle that it takes on an air of respectability.

Dead thinking as unethical

The institutionalized use of money in a way that is harmful to society, or the use of genetically altering agricultural technology, or the concept of 'self-regulating industries' and 'self-regulating' policies regarding the censoring of films and the internet, are all harmful realities which derive from what Steiner refers to as 'dead thinking'. The static thoughts behind these policies is harming large parts of our planet's eco-system, and threatens the moral integrity of people.

All of these negative factors derive from this second type of evil, the one which produces dead thinking or conscienceless attitudes. It is a way of thinking, and type of attitude that has no feelings, that is, no conscience. Hence its most prominent trait is that it functions in complete unawareness of, and indifference to, the inter- dependence of both human society and the eco-system. Many of the social structures, or technologies that we use today are based on clever processes, but these are devoid of any sensing of the real nature of life.

Some strange earlier examples include the use of x-ray machines as novelties in shoe shops in the 1930's to allow a customer to see the bones of their feet. This exposed the customers to large doses of dangerous x-ray radiation. Another example was the attempt to teach mathematical data and other information to unborn babies, by mean of trumpets used by the mother and aimed at her abdomen; a technique now applied to the defenceless babe by the more sophisticated technique of a CD, played during the night-time, as the mother sleeps.

As Rudolf Steiner points out, the unborn baby has descended down from spiritual realms, and lives within a wonderful, blissful semi-awareness of the spiritual sphere. The baby is still part of the spiritual realms, but also has a dreamy awareness of its mother and the new, developing body. So, the intrusion of detailed intellectual data into this living transcendent consciousness could have a negative impact, impairing the baby's empathy with the enchanted and comforting world in which it finds itself, and thereby predisposing it to a weakened capacity to feel a real meaning to its adult life.

Another serious example of the dulled empathy and dead thinking which is causing trouble in our times is the use of nuclear power. In this technology the structure of matter is forcibly smashed, violently releasing as an inevitable consequence a deadly energy. Whereas a better solution here would be to focus on the several subtle energies which are the crucial carriers of the life-processes of nature and of our own bodies. These energies are referred to as 'etheric energy' by Rudolf Steiner, and as 'Ch'i' or 'prana' in the East. It is these which make possible the rise of sap in every plant in the springtime, or the healing of damaged cells in a living organism.

Now the question arises, why is it that people are subject to these two kinds of unethical tendencies? And in particular, why is the second tendency, in its more pervasive and subtle mode, this dead thinking, so prominent in our times? Rudolf Steiner begins to answer this question by affirming that the old spiritual or religious viewpoint, as regards this theme at least, was on the right track. He explains the effect of two classes of spiritual beings involved in our soul-life. And he taught that these ranks of beings were once known to seers and spiritual teachers, in earlier times, including the writers of early Jewish and Christian texts. Rudolf Steiner teaches that the negative actions and attitudes of the first kind which lead, in the worst-case scenario to crimes of passion, derive from 'luciferic' influences.

Who is Lucifer?
Lucifer is a name of Latin origin, and it was used in the 4th century AD, by Saint Jerome, when he made a Latin version of the Bible, and was trying to find a way to translate a mysterious statement in the Hebrew original of the Book of Isaiah. The statement is about a self-centred, proud, fallen spirit, not a hate-filled one. This is quite different to the second influence, one which leads to crimes of hate which usually require planning and scheming. These derive from what Rudolf Steiner calls 'ahrimanic' influences. 'Ahriman' is in fact a name for a primary evil being in the Persian texts of the old Zoroastrian religion. Zoroastrianism permeated the Hebrew culture, and its ideas and terms became widely known to Jewish people, in the time of the Babylonian Captivity. The term Ahriman was probably seen by the Hebrews as an equivalent to the Hebrew Satan.

So here already we meet another new perspective from the unique work of Rudolf Steiner, who points out that humanity is not placed ethically only between evil and good, or symbolically speaking between light and darkness. Humanity is placed in the midst of three dynamics. There is darkness on the one side (the ahrimanic influence), true light above this, and on the other side, an alluring, selfish light (luciferic). In the latter, souls can be carried away with a potent desire to have some experience which is personally irresistible. This is a highly attractive and egocentric, but not directly evil, form of inner 'light'; leading to goals which are driven by self-indulgent selfish desires. But human beings can also be subject to the 'darkness', of hate, violence, etc. Both are sources of misconduct that lead to social disharmony. But, between these two factors, there exists a true light, in other words a truly ethical way of being.

Normally one finds in religious references to good and evil, a good being (God) and a bad being, called Satan. (Furthermore, many religious traditions refer to a multitude of lesser divine beings, who carry out the intentions of God.) But Rudolf Steiner teaches that there is a more subtle and complex dynamic than this; namely that there are two types of fallen spirit beings. One type could be associated with the old term, Satan, or Ahriman. The Hebrew term Satan means 'adversary', 'enemy' and also has the slight suggestion of an enemy that lies in wait for his victims.[51] There is very little literary evidence for either class of beings in the Old Testament, but there are many references

---
[51] Satan with long 'a's = Sahtahn = adversary (שָׂטָן) and Satan with one short 'a' Sahtan = a lyer in wait (שָׂטַן).

in the New Testament. There the terms Devil or Satan are used almost interchangeably. One reason for this is presumably that the existence of the Luciferic class of beings was only known to a few initiated sages of antiquity. Most people lived within the somewhat inadequate two-dimensional polarity of good and evil, instead of three types of influences.

The origin of the word Lucifer

Rudolf Steiner calls the leader of this first group of beings, Lucifer. So what is the situation here? Exactly what is the origin of this being called 'Lucifer' in spiritual literature? As it is not possible to find an informed explanation in any reference book for the origin of this word, I have researched this elusive theme and shall briefly present the results here. It is important to have clarity about this, as Rudolf Steiner was the editor of a theosophical magazine called Lucifer-Gnosis. This fact has aroused considerable disquiet in religious circles.

The word Lucifer is Latin, and means 'light-bringer'; so how can that be the name for a fallen spirit being, who is a source of unethical impulses in the human being? The actual origin in literature of the idea that there exists a certain spiritual being, one who is full of pride and hence alien to the harmonious and sacred realms of the divine-spiritual hierarchies, is wrapped in mystery. Its origin is actually with the initiates of earlier cultures, whose spiritual wisdom included the influence of the spiritual beings of the solar system on the soul of human beings. One such initiate, who had knowledge of this was the Hebrew seer and prophet, Isaiah.

The early Hebrew culture had a wonderful system of sacred texts in which initiatory wisdom was discreetly interwoven. Isaiah wrote a passage which, like so much of the Hebrew Scriptures, can be read on two levels. The sages of olden times would conceal inside their Scriptures a spiritual truth that they felt was not suitable for the wider community to access. In chapter Fourteen in the Book of Isaiah is the story of the fall of an un-named bad entity. This passage is normally seen by scholars as referring to a Babylonian king, who is not named, but is understood to be Nebuchadnezzar.

But if one is aware that a hidden layer of meaning is often placed inside these Scriptures, it can also be seen as referring to a spiritual entity. On this level, it is saying that a spirit-being fell out of the divine cosmic order, because of his pride and other un-spiritual qualities, although not because he was fully evil. Isaiah 14:12-16 says,

> "How you have fallen from heaven, O morning star, son of the dawn! You have been cast down to the earth, you who once laid low the nations! You said in your heart, 'I will ascend to heaven; I will raise my throne above the stars of God; I will sit enthroned on the mount of assembly, on the utmost heights of the sacred mountain.
> I will ascend above the tops of the clouds; I will make myself like the Most High.' But you are brought down to the grave, to the depths of the pit. Those who see you stare at you, they ponder your fate saying: 'Is this the man who shook the earth and made kingdoms tremble'……"

We can note here that in the Hebrew original the phrase, 'morning star, son of the dawn' literally says, 'shining {one}, son of the morning {or dawn}'.[52] This phrase is actually the established Hebrew phrase for the shining planet Venus, which is called 'the morning star' in other earlier cultures. And yet this long Hebrew phrase itself suggests a specific living being, because it is not actually a neutral term for a planet, like Venus or Mars.

So, there is a hint here of an entity who is equated with Venus. In mystical language this is a way of referring to the primary spirit of that planet, or at least one of its prominent spirits. And the following verses support this hidden meaning, since they are about an entity who is full of pride; so they refer to a specific being, they obviously cannot refer to an inanimate planet.

So we have here a veiled reference to a specific being who is full of pride, and yet who is also somehow linked to Venus. Of course, the non-esoteric way of viewing this is to say that the Babylonian king, Nebuchadnezzar, was so powerful, that he could be likened to the morning star. But the esoteric interpretation has the natural edge here, as it fits the grammar better than the surface meaning.

It is somewhat strained to think of Nebuchadnezzar harbouring such lofty cosmic intentions, and it is also unlikely that such a militant male would be symbolized by the feminine planet Venus. Isaiah intended that both meanings be conveyed, one for the wider readership, and one for the esoterically aware readers. When this Hebrew text was translated into Greek for the Greek-speaking Jews of the Hellenistic world, about the time of Alexander the Great, it appeared as 'heos-phoros' which means 'dawn-bringer'; an established term in the Greek world for the planet Venus.[53] An evocative phrase, but one which is less individualized than the Hebrew version. When in 404 AD the Hebrew Old Testament was translated into Latin by St. Jerome for the Vulgate Bible, he chose the term Lucifer, which means 'light-bearer'. This phrase restores something of the individuated quality; it also fits very well as a personal name. However, modern translations of the Bible usually just have the expression, the morning star. The King James Version however, has the word Lucifer.

The Luciferic temptation
Through a meditative contemplation of this Scripture passage we have discovered a veiled reference to a radiant spirit being who is independent of the divine order of spiritual beings serving God, and who is associated with Venus. But there is another text to be considered now, it is the story in the Book of Genesis about 'the serpent' coming into Paradise and bringing about the ethical Fall of Humanity. In Genesis, chapter Three, we read of how Adam and Eve were in a blissful condition in Paradise until the serpent came along and persuaded them to break some of the rules; Genesis 3:1-5,

---

[52] In the Hebrew, Isa:14:12, leylel ben-schahar (בֶּן־שָׁחַר) son of the morning and (הֵילֵל) shining one.)
[53] In the Septuagint's Greek version of Isa:14;12 it is " ho heosphoros" (ὁ ἑωσφόρος) the bearer of the dawn (ἑῷος).

"Now the serpent was more crafty than any of the wild animals the LORD God had made. He said to the woman, 'Did God really say, you must not eat from any tree in the garden?' The woman said to the serpent, 'We may eat fruit from the trees in the garden, but God did say, you must not eat fruit from the tree that is in the middle of the garden, and you must not touch it, or you will die.' 'You will not surely die,' the serpent said to the woman.
'For God knows that when you eat of it your eyes will be opened, and you will be like God, knowing good and evil'."

Now in the Hebrew original of this passage, the bad being involved here is simply called, 'the serpent'. So, back to our question, who was it in ancient times that referred to some type of fallen spirit being (or beings) as the slanderer? Research has shown that many centuries after the Book of Genesis was written, an unknown author writing in the first century AD, or perhaps a century earlier, refers to this story and calls the serpent 'a slanderer'. This text is called The Wisdom of Solomon. Its author uses a standard Greek term, diabolos, which means slander; it had no other meaning, it was not a personal name.

Diabolos in English is written as 'Devil'. But in so far as Jerome used it as an epithet (or nickname) it became a kind of personal name, 'the slanderer'. And this is fascinating, because it seems that to some people with mystical knowledge, the process brought about by 'the serpent', was not an act of hate, but one of rebelliousness against the divine order of things. This raises the possibility that the fallen spirit-being involved here was not 'Satan' but someone else. Rudolf Steiner teaches that this story in Genesis is very important, it is in effect saying that a class of beings who were fallen, played a very important role in the creating and development of humanity. This story is telling us that long ago, soon after coming into life on the Earth, early humanity experienced the impulse within itself to be exposed to its **own** desires and urges and attitudes; to the desires and values which accrue once one is cast into the flesh, and this creates the possibility of evil, of unethical acts or emotions.

The Creator, or more accurately a group of divine beings, had created humanity in a way that was naturally reflective of his (or their) divine qualities. But the serpent, in persuading humanity to be open to the serpent's influence, was carrying out slander against these divine beings, by saying in effect that God is lying to Adam and Eve when he said that bad things would result if they broke the divine rules.

Through Luciferic attitudes to morality
So, on this basis, it is indeed reasonable to call this action a form of 'slander'. But now observe the outcome of this process. Humanity developed the capacity to experience its own self, its own ego-ic reality. Consequently, we developed the capacity for both good and evil. Rudolf Steiner teaches that the intention of these beings was not to create evil as such, but it was to stimulate the ego-sense of the human being, in a way which would take humanity into ways of being that were no longer an automatic reflection of the divine. But naturally if its influence is too potent, this could, and often does, lead to specifically evil results. The implication of this esoteric view of these sacred texts is profound.

To the sages or initiates of the past, this entire process meant that these beings had, in effect, lit up the soul of the human being. Their influence had flamed into life an earthly sense of selfhood, within the early primitive human being. These beings were therefore indeed, 'light-bringers'. The fallen being mentioned discretely by Isaiah, is that same being. So, when St. Jerome decided upon the term Lucifer for this being, he was very discerning in his choice.

The hosts of Lucifer lit up the otherwise dulled non-egoic consciousness of early humanity, back in the ancient Lemurian epoch (see chapter 10). The 'light' was not that of a spiritual or saintly self, it was that of the normal flawed earthly self. But the Luciferic influence has several modes of manifesting. One is the flaring up or intensifying of the ego or sense of self in the usual desires, yearnings, and excitement. But another is the enflaming or intensifying of the ego-sense with an irresistible, alluring force.

We shall explore the link to Venus in the next chapter. It is interesting to note that when a person is involved in any alluring emotion, they can often say that they are 'caught up' by it, or they are 'out of themselves'. So one can say that these self-centred desires, whether normal or lower, are not fuelled by a selflessness or noble 'inner light', but by some sort of personally attractive force.

The Devil or Satan?
Now this becomes more meaningful, when contrasted with the phenomena associated with the other type of beings mentioned by these old sages, the opposite type, 'Satan'. We need to note here that Rudolf Steiner taught that the being Lucifer is a separate type of being to the one called Satan. For the locality of Satan also hints at his inner dynamics; it is the exact opposite of a brightly shining light, linked to our yearnings and burning desires. For in the Bible, Satan's home is deep inside the dark, cold, subterranean depths of the Earth. This is suggested in the Book of Job,

> Job 1:6 One day the angels came to present themselves before the LORD, and Satan also came with them.
> Job 1:7 The LORD said to Satan, "Where have you come from?" Satan answered the LORD, "From roaming through the earth and going back and forth in it."

So in this mystical text, Satan is a being who dwells in the immensely hard, dark and forbidding realm of the Earth's interior, and his influence is associated with calculating, planning and scheming. This activity of his, of roaming or walking back and forth, is in effect a kind of pacing around, and gives the impression of someone scheming, devising ideas. Further, in the book known as 2 Samuel (24:1), the account of the first census amongst the Israelites being taken is recorded. But when the census starts, a defiant prophet strides into the court of the king, and denounces him as being inspired by Satan.

The intriguing point here is that the scheming, and mathematical planning behind a census which reduces people to units, and gives more authority to those in power, is associated here with the influence of the entity referred to as 'Satan'. Conducting a census is a technique of governance of great help in the planning of society's needs, but it can also be used in a way that ignores the over-all spiritual needs and karma of the nation.

For example, officials can decide to limit the intake of students to certain subjects in tertiary institutions, and encourage students to join other studies, because of their projections as to what they would like society to become in two decades' time. This could prevent the inherent karma of the students from coming into expression, as they bring with them from the realm of spirit, subconsciously at least, an impetus towards various careers. This forces people into pathways for their life which are alien to their life's intentions, as formulated before descent to conception. And by the time the students are ready to enter the work force, the entire dynamics of the country may have changed, and the quantities of personnel ready for various professions could now be out of balance.

The nature of Ahriman

With regard to the incident mentioned above from the Old Testament, it illustrates how there is an ahrimanic aspect to such processes. This example has merit, we need some right light to be shone upon the secretive, hidden influence of these beings. However the Old Testament itself has very little to say about Satanic beings. But it regards any malignant quality in the soul of a human being as coming from Satan or Ahriman. Such an attitude can be of course subjective, but that is not the point; it indicates that in ancient times the influence of these Ahrimanic beings was seen as something which could enter the human soul.

In 1Samuel 29:4 a king who is hostile to Israel calls King David 'a Satan', without any suggestion of David being an evil spirit entity. More significantly, there are passages in the Bible which imply that the evil influence of Ahrimanic beings, though malignant, is specifically permitted by higher divine beings (referred to as 'the Lord' or 'God'). This is the point that Rudolf Steiner also makes; these beings are part of our evolutionary pathway, their influence creates for humanity lessons in developing a clearer approach to ethics.

Rudolf Steiner points out that there is a fully justified operative mode with these both types of entities, wherein their influence, whilst not delightful, is not evil, and is required by humanity in its long journey of lifetimes within the physical plane. Lucifer and his hosts must produce the self-centred pleasures, and inflamed inner life, in order to create a sense of self within the human being. And the repugnant 'satanic' entities are not evil when they produce the appropriate and necessary capacity of calculating and planning, in effect, of dry intellectualism.

Without this capacity, earthly existence would not be viable. These ahrimanic beings are also responsible for the creation of inert mineral substances, which constitute matter itself. And it is just this hard matter and also a dry rationality which is suggested by the Book of Job, when it places Satan inside the Earth's dark interior, amongst the dark layer of minerals and rocks, pacing around, scheming how to destroy the moral integrity of Job.

Lucifer and Ahriman

So, we see that two quite different types of evil or at least of disharmony are suggested by the Biblical references, and that these two are polar opposites, and they precisely dovetail with the inherent dynamics that are present in unethical states of the soul. The worst manifestation of the Luciferic beings is in crimes of passion. The usual manifestation of Luciferic beings is the capacity to be uplifted, thrilled and enthusiastic, and responsive to joy or pleasure. But the unethical manifestation of these beings creates the self-indulgent quest for pleasure, or a naïve and ego-centric search for spirituality.

This is a quest which carrying a hidden egoism, can lead to malignant outcomes. Their influence goes beyond the wholesome mode of the usual kind of pleasures, and of enthusiastic experiences of beauty, etc. For then it severs our connection with wholesome, balanced reality, so we seek to flee responsibility and duties, and to do whatever appeals to our ego-centric state.

The other group of beings is referred to as 'Ahrimanic' by Rudolf Steiner; here he has chosen a Persian term for them. In the Persian scriptures of Zoroastrianism, there is an evil being who is called Ahriman, who fights against the sun god. One reason no doubt for the decision to avoid the term Satan is to avoid using fundamentalist Bible language. From this spirit-being and his hosts, usual human life gets the analytical intellectual capacity which is inwardly 'dead', in other words is divorced from any appreciation of the living reality of life. The extreme manifestation of these Ahrimanic beings has two aspects: one is premeditated conscienceless crime.

This other type of influence is now part of the soul-life of all, or almost all, human beings especially since the 16th century, as rationalism began to emerge. It creates abstract schemes and attitudes, and materialistic attitudes in various forms. These inflict considerable harm on society in all sorts of ways. Materialism, that is, the denial of the reality of anything beyond matter, is a major manifestation of these beings in the consciousness of humanity.

To become aware of just how inwardly dead are many of modern society's thoughts about the deeper issue of life is a tremendously important achievement. Rudolf Steiner once told a student that wherever there is a loveless attitude, pedantic and full of disdain, then Ahriman is active.[54] A sentence from the young Steiner's Credo, which we considered in Chapter One, is relevant here: "One must first know something of the holiness of Love, before one can speak about spirituality (piety)". A serious threat Ahrimanic beings will pose in the future will be their attempt to persuade humanity about the idea of becoming a form of android. An initial phase of this state arises with the idea of people being injected, shortly after birth, with tiny nano-technology devices, such as computers or sensors, so as to change their inherent consciousness. Our consciousness would then change into one rather like a super clever but lifeless intelligence, equipped with faculties for perceiving energies within the coarse electromagnetic spectrum.

---

[54] Heinz Müller, *Erinnerungen*, in Mitteilungen aus der Anthroposophischen Arbeit in Deutschland, 22. Jhrg. Nr. 84, Johanni, 1968, p. 112.

Such future people could not then experience the beauty, the awe-inspiring side of creation, and above all, they would be prevented from developing their own potential to behold spiritual reality themselves, by active spiritual, artistic and ethical development. That is, they would have a state of mind that would imitate real spiritual perception in a nightmarish way. It would be a mentality that also gives perception to humans of ultra-violet or micro-wave or x-ray waves. A future government could then broadcast ideas and requirements on these frequencies, to which people would respond, as they would resonate in the mind as if they were one's own thoughts.

The more this happens, the less capable humanity becomes in developing a new subtle awareness of the ethers, and especially for spiritual realities, or indeed its own conscience. For we have a consciousness that the divine-spiritual beings have striven to develop for us over aeons, and which can develop into a highly spiritual, and highly clairvoyant state, through the correct method of spiritual development. There are also people who actively seek to further the aims of Ahriman, and hence the need for society to actively develop a spiritual or holistic mind-set.

Perhaps the worst form of this Ahrimanic attack on human consciousness is through the move to create the conditions ripe for the acceptance by masses of people of the soul-less android human. The way this is being done now is manifold, but one technique is to use the innocent term, 'singularity' to describe and encourage this new dehumanizing state. Under this deceptive name efforts are underway to work towards a future situation wherein an electronically altered state is imposed onto the new-born or the young child. By getting people to increasingly embrace electronic devices on their body, this next step will be easier.

The human soul in a few generations, could find itself with the perceptive capacity, built into its nervous system, of an infra-red sensor and a mobile phone, etc, but permanently gone from the person will be the capacity to feel wonder and awe at the greatness, the beauty of creation. In the adult, such alterations to the physical body will damage the influence of the etheric body, and the soul (astral body) preventing perception of, or even interest in, the first delicate intimations of the spiritual worlds and the higher ego. The influence of ahrimanic beings encourages attitudes and thinking that hollow-out people's inner being. The soul-less nature of modern society, and its resulting lack of compassion and decent values are the direct result of this

So how does one protect oneself from the subtly unethical influences of these Ahrimanic beings? Rudolf Steiner described that there are various ways to avoid their wish to instil a clever but life-alienating way of thinking that now increasingly darkens modern consciousness. In essence it is to strive to think spiritually about the world, rather than to limit our thoughts to materialistic intellectuality. And the practise of a wholesome form of meditation and a study of spiritual texts especially removes the influence of these beings.

A potent defence against the Luciferic tendency towards self-indulgent, naive feelings and ideas, or harmful sensuality, is provided by the conscientious development of real moral principles. The cultivation of a selflessness in regard to others (but not a surrendering up of one's valid rights) and a striving towards a chasteness, an inner purity, keeps these beings away.

This striving towards integrity and selflessness also has the power to protect oneself from the tendency of these beings to create harmful forms of spirituality. Luciferic spirituality produces the urge to separate the person from their responsibilities which life on the Earth involves. Trying to live on a few grains of rice, or only on breathing the air, or floating in the air, are some of the signs of this ego-centric striving to soar up and away from a balanced life.

Modern life tempts us ever more to take up high-tech solutions with regard to daily chores, to inter-personal relating and also to entertainment. People are thereby being taken away from experiences of nature, of other peoples' inner journey, of the grandeur and life-forces behind the Earth's ecology. To try to live into the natural seasonal processes with a sensing of the spiritual forces that make the seasons possible is a potent way to defend oneself. See Chapter Eight where the actual nature of these energies are explored, and advice given on this wonderful journey. With regard to serious premeditated crimes, society needs to be aware of the need to nurture the potential for goodness in children during their school years. The Steiner School curriculum is designed to do this by various means. Insightful education and parenting will minimize the tendency in the young school leavers to take up the extreme form of Ahrimanic action, through which serious offences can occur, and this also minimizes the tendency towards clever lifeless intellectuality.

It is precisely our modern Ahrimanic abstract attitude which falsely thinks that by giving young children a beautiful environment, many artistic and nature experiences, and uplifting inspiring moral stories, weakens them for entering real life later on. On the contrary, this protecting of children from ugly and harsh architecture, violent art and cartoons, or similar toys, provides the best possible soul nourishment for them, giving them an enhanced inner moral compass when entering adulthood.

Now let's hear again the Huxley version of ethics,

> "I declare that if some great Power were to agree to always make me think what is truthful and therefore always do what is right, on the condition of me becoming a sort of clock-like person, I would instantly agree to the offer."

It is now clear that this materialistic person, devoid of any higher insight, has no other option than to commit himself to the ultimate unethical act, namely of opting out of the battle, out of the entire purpose of humanity being created. To surrender one's inner freedom, and become an automaton, is to stop evolving in life after life; and is thus to fall behind, to fall out of the evolving human life-wave. The fruits of materialism, where spiritual ideas and sensitivity to the spiritual is excluded, whether in an educational syllabus, or in medicine or agriculture, are usually harmful. Whereas, for those people who can acknowledge these two kinds of influences and their corresponding tendencies inside the soul, the only way forward is to seek enhanced morality, even a high spirituality.

The Archangel Michael

Rudolf Steiner taught that an especially empowered archangel provides help with regard to this dynamic of being exposed to influences from two classes of beings; this is a being known in various religions, under different names. In the Judaic-Christian texts it is known as archangel Michael. This being has been portrayed in spiritual texts from Persia as 'Marduk', as well as in Hebrew and Hellenistic Christian material. This archangel is described in these texts, from about 2,200 years ago, as specifically helping those souls who seek to attain to a high spiritual consciousness. This archangel thus became known in antiquity as the dragon slayer. But Rudolf Steiner describes this being as now 'battling for the integrity of the cosmic intelligence'. What he means by cosmic intelligence is the wisdom of the divine beings, which is reflected in a dim way in us humans, as our thinking capacity. So, in simple words, Michael seeks to help human beings to have a spiritual consciousness.

Finally, many people today who are not convinced of spiritual realities, naturally regard the above idea of two classes of spiritual beings as absurd. Here the words of Germany's immortal poet, dramatist and spiritual researcher, Johann Wolfgang von Goethe, about this subject are relevant. His view on this subject is found in his drama *Faust,* which is about a man seeking a spiritual meaning to life, whilst being allured by decadence. The figure of Mephistopheles in this drama presents a composite figure of evil, combining both of the above classes of beings. Although Goethe was not fully aware of these two separate types, his words on this subject are immortal.

Mephistopheles

He implies how naïve is the attitude of modern materialism which feels quite relieved that people have despatched the Devil into fairy stories for children. For Mephistopheles says sarcastically to Faust, "The Evil One has left them, but evil beings remain".[55] In other words, declaring a disbelief in the influence of fallen spirit beings does not mean that they are gone; in fact it allows them to become more potent. Something similar is indicated in Bram Stoker's novel, *Dracula*, where one of the characters says, "The strength of the vampire lies in the fact that no-one believes he exists". In a magnificently deep thought Goethe shows Mephistopheles as being aware that the final result of his evil actions shall be the good. For he says of himself, "I am a part of that Power which constantly wills evil, and constantly creates the good".[56]

Further Reading
As for Chapter Two

---

[55] From line 2509; „Den Bösen sind sie los, die Bösen sind geblieben."
[56] Lines 1336/7, „Ich bin ein Teil von jener Kraft die stets das Böse will und stets das Gute schafft."

5: CHRISTIANITY: AN ESOTERIC VIEW

In today's world, the quest for 'spirituality' can be highly regarded. The same attitude *can* be shown towards religion, but often this is not the case. Christianity is often regarded with indifference or even hostility. In the minds of many people today, spirituality and religion are two very different things.

A century ago, when Rudolf Steiner was teaching in Europe, the situation was very different. Spirituality was a rare term. Christianity was the predominant religion in Europe; it was widely respected, and had an influential role in society. So it was to be expected that Rudolf Steiner would speak about this religion. But today, most people educated in the western world, and referred to as Christian, often have very little knowledge of this religion. Whereas in Steiner's time, school children were given a basic knowledge of the Bible, and Latin and Greek as well. Consequently the reader today has to bear in mind that many of Steiner's lectures assume a more informed religious background in the listener. Steiner presented an esoteric view of Christianity, that is a view not commonly found in religious circles, as it derives from his own spiritual research in higher realms.

In so far as many Theosophists were interested in eastern religions, Rudolf Steiner could also be expected to speak on these as well, but to a lesser extent. However, quite apart from his social context, Rudolf Steiner had other reasons to lecture on Christianity. He had discovered profoundly sacred cosmic processes were present behind the external narrative of the life and teachings of Jesus. His intention was to communicate his research results, but to leave people free as to their decision.

As we have seen in previous chapters, Rudolf Steiner's primary work involved researching the spiritual aspects of the human being, and the connection of these to spiritual realms, and therefore to the beings who exist in these realms. But these topics are generally the same topics that form the focus of the great world religions. So in this area of his work, Steiner's spiritual research does overlap with themes prominent in the religious life.

In this chapter we shall gain a clear understanding of why Christianity, viewed esoterically, is important in anthroposophy. (In Chapter 12, we will clarify the relation of anthroposophy to religion in general.) So we shall consider not only Rudolf Steiner's viewpoint on Christianity, but also the way that religious ideas are related to anthroposophy. To Rudolf Steiner, Christianity is about cosmic, spiritual events of deep importance. He taught that there exists a deep esoteric layer of meaning in Christianity. It is also important to note Rudolf Steiner taught that there would soon be large groups of people who proclaim themselves as Christians, and yet who would be in fact actually deeply un-spiritual, even sinister. They would have an unpleasant, fundamentalist way of misrepresenting this religion.

Now with regard to the 'esoteric Christianity' of anthroposophy, let's note that the religious texts of Christianity contain statements from Christ that are extremely striking, in that they imply a supreme importance of Christ. Various texts refer to an importance beyond that of other founders of religion. For example, in the Gospel of St. John, in 6:51, it is apparently Jesus who says,

> "I am the living bread that came down from heaven. If anyone eats of this bread, he will live forever. This bread is my flesh, which I will give for the life of the world."

But reflecting on this and similar passages, gives the impression that the speaker is more than a mortal human being. It requires the speaker of these words to have a more-than-human status to substantiate such a huge claim. And such words also imply that the speaker has a very important role in the ongoing development of humanity. It certainly transcends the claims of Buddha and other notable religious teachers, none of whom inferred that they were vital to the future life of the planet.

More than human

A similar statement is made on behalf of Christ by the writer of the Epistle to the Hebrews, where Christ is referred to as the son of God, and who as such, created the world. This is usually translated as,

> "…In these last days He has spoken to us by his Son, whom God appointed heir of all things, and through whom He made the universe."

When more accurately translated, from the Greek, it shows an even higher level of cosmic greatness to Christ, as the word translated as 'universe' means actually not only physical creation but spiritual realms as well.[57]

> "…In these last days He has spoken to us by his Son, whom He appointed heir of all things, and through whom God also made the spiritual realms, and {thus} physical creation, with its epochs of time."   (author's translation)

This statement even more clearly points to a spiritual being who far transcends the human state of existence. And many other enigmatic statements indicating a more than human status to Jesus are to be found in the New Testament. Precisely such passages in the Bible have led to many Christians regarding Jesus as divine, and indeed as being in effect, God. This conclusion that has caused confusion, disdain or hostility from other sectors of society and other religions.

Rudolf Steiner's approach to Christianity indicates that statements such as these actually communicate a deeply mystical or esoteric message. Part of that message is that a divine being, not a human being, is involved. And when this deeper message is seen, the relation of Jesus to the divine can be much more clearly grasped. Attempts to discuss this theme are often unsuccessful, as the actual nature of the spirit realms from which Christ comes is unknown to Christian theologians generally, though various groups of Christians over the past two millennia have ventured to study this area.

---

[57] The core Greek phrase here: δι' οὗ καὶ ἐποίησεν τοὺς αἰῶνας·

A good introduction to Rudolf Steiner's teachings on this subject is found in his book, "Christianity as Mystical Fact". And a good place to start with his teachings on Christianity is his statement which has the quality of a Zen Buddhist 'koan',

> "Christianity began as a religion, but is greater than all religions, including Christianity."

In other words, what we know (or, don't truly know) as Christianity is in fact something else, something which transcends the formal structure of a religion. Rudolf Steiner's perspective here is that the scriptures of this religion present a sacred narrative, but they also veil a profound cosmic event, understanding of which requires initiation wisdom.

Once this deeper message is understood, these texts can become a source of real spiritual inspiration, because a deeply sacred, esoteric reality is discovered. To find these special truths one needs a feeling for the underlying esoteric worldview of the gospel writers. The Greek texts of the New Testament will be briefly referred to, in new translations, where it helps to build a pathway to understanding Steiner's research. There are a number of key ideas which are associated with Christianity, and which today can feel to us as very alien, very odd. These ideas are primarily what theologians refer to as Salvation, Damnation, Redemption and Eternal Life.

The key ideas in their esoteric context
Rudolf Steiner taught that underlying the Christian Scriptures is a veiled cosmic viewpoint which sees humanity evolving on planet Earth in a series of Ages or time-cycles, during which humanity descends down from non-material realms into the physical, material Earth through many lifetimes. Then we gradually arise back into these spiritual realms. When Steiner's perspective on the Gospels is studied, these terms take on new meaning. The essential message of his esoteric Christianity is that the death and resurrection of Christ have a pivotal role in this vast process whereby the human life-wave achieves its wonderful future goal.

This idea poses a problem for thinking people today, because it seems to combine two ideas that really have nothing to do with each other. There are people with little interest in the Bible, who are enthralled by the idea of many spiritual realms and many earth-lives (karma). But there are also those who do find a sacred quality in the Bible, but who feel the idea of repeated earth lives deeply alienating, indeed deeply undermining the core teachings of Christ, about being 'saved'. The latter conclude that once a person has died, who has lived an ethical life and had 'faith' in Christ, they shall then exist forever in 'Heaven'.

Rudolf Steiner's teachings on this subject indicate that both these reactions are the result of an incomplete knowledge of this deep theme. We shall see how this is to be resolved later. Firstly, as regards the idea of many spiritual realms, this is in fact thoroughly Biblical. It is only the flattening-out of the scriptures by a modern humanistic mind-set that has made this idea seem incorrect.

You will probably be familiar with the phrase, "the kingdom of Heaven"; there is in fact no such phrase in the Greek text of the New Testament ! Jesus never used it, he always says, 'the kingdom of **the Heavens**'. However, by common humanistic consent, the translations always censor this truth by making it singular.[58]

This flattening-out is done because humanistic Christianity has assumed that a multiplicity of heavens is 'a Jewish superstitious idea'. An idea which Jesus made use of in a kindly way, in order to 'speak the language of the people'.   But such an explanation of the text is both shallow and prejudiced.

This implies that a great religious teacher would use a false term for a very important spiritual reality, namely the nature of the divine itself, in order to appease some current, but false, popular view ! St. Paul wrote about how he arose up into 'the third heaven',

> I know a man in Christ who fourteen years ago was caught up to the third heaven. 2Co.12: 2.

So multiple heavens are literally Biblical; the vague and incorrect phrase, 'the kingdom of heaven' is very inconsistent with St. Paul's own experience. Unfortunately, much Christian theology has had this humanistic veil placed over it. This became much stronger after Steiner's lifetime, carried by an attitude that the Scriptures should be 'de-mythologized' to prevent superstitious, non-critiqued and naïve and interpretations. And indeed it is true that such naïve interpretations are of no value, and can lead to anti-social fundamentalism. And disappointment with the search for the 'historical Jesus' has also led to this approach.

But unfortunately the 'de-mythologizers' themselves were caught in their own desolate mythology. Theirs was a worldview in which any intuitive sense for higher worlds, or of divine spiritual beings, or a path of spiritual initiation towards spiritual perception, was entirely absent. Hence the veiled indications about the cosmic dimension placed in the Scriptures could not be seen. A prominent theologian behind this was R. K. Bultmann (1884 -1976). This situation contrasts strongly with that of other great religions in which an awareness of different levels of meaning in Scripture is retained; namely an esoteric and an exoteric level.

Jesus or Christ ?
So what is then the core difference in Rudolf Steiner's esoteric Christianity to that of the churches today? It is the difference between 'Jesus' and 'Christ'. Rudolf Steiner taught that there is a cosmic deity overshadowing Jesus. And obviously a deity is a different kind of being to a human, even a most sacred human being. However, as we shall see, it is also understood that the person Jesus, after the Baptism in the River Jordan became eternally united to the cosmic deity; becoming the archetype of what future humanity is to evolve towards. (We shall return to this theme, below). To Rudolf Steiner, Jesus was of immense sanctity; and he taught that for a person to be Christian, she or he needs to consciously make a sincere inner decision to be someone who regards Christ as their Saviour.

---

[58] In Greek, *he basileia ton ouranon* (ἡ βασιλεία τῶν οὐρανῶν).

In Rudolf Steiner's teachings on Christianity, in addition to Jesus himself, who is viewed as a most holy human being, there is a sublime spiritual being; the so-called 'cosmic Christ'. Actually the term 'Christ' derives from the Hebrew language and means to be anointed by a divine reality. This is how the term 'Christ' in understood in anthroposophical literature.

Technically, in the old Hebrew world there were many 'Christs' because the term referred to those who were anointed by God, such as their kings. In the usual Christian theology, theologians refer to Jesus as 'Christ', by extending this idea to its highest level; that is he is the **great** Messiah. They understand from Scripture that the most sacred of such an anointing or blessings of a human being occurred in the case of Jesus. This blessing came from a particularly divine source and sanctified him.

The cosmic Christ
In anthroposophy, the term 'Christ' refers to the cosmic being who came upon (or, 'anointed') Jesus at the Baptism in the Jordan River. So in anthroposophy, the person known as 'Jesus Christ' is a being consisting of the man Jesus, and also of the deity, the Christ being, who became present in him, as from the Baptism. This viewpoint of two distinct but deeply interlinked entities being involved, was held by some earlier Christians in the early church, but later was condemned as a heresy.[59]

Rudolf Steiner taught that behind the Christian narrative about Jesus, there is an understanding of the journey of humanity from life to life through various time-cycles, and of the involvement of divine beings in this journey. Originally humanity existed in a non-material state, a kind of Paradise. But in this state humanity was not endowed with a sense of self-hood.

The Fall of humanity as a predestined event
The 'Fall of Humanity' described in the book of Genesis relates to a process, decreed by our Creator through which we lost a divine innocence, but attained gradually an earthly sense of self. (As we shall see, below, humanity has many Creators, serving the one uncaused, Creator.) As we mentioned in the last chapter, in this process the soul was exposed to influences from Luciferic beings. These influences brought about our yearning for the various (often illusory) pleasures and opportunities of the incarnate flesh state.

This yearning, and the associated development of earth-bound attitudes, had an impact upon the tenuous primordial body of humanity. The body became denser, and gradually developed its corporeal, flesh condition. This was a falling away from the divine realms, but it was a process that gave the possibility to humanity to develop a sense of self. When there is a sense of self, the human being in the course of many life-times can lose its earthiness and become spiritualized. Without a sense of self, no spiritualized human self or individualized human spirit can arise. It was for this reason that we began the process of living on the material Earth. So, when in Genesis 3:21 it is

---

[59] Adoptionism, identified as starting with Theodotus in 190 AD, is one form of this awareness; Monophysitism (associated with Eutyches (378-454) is another, and Apollinarianism (Syria 4th cent.) is another.

stated that, "The LORD God made garments of skin for Adam and his wife and clothed them", this refers to the process, taking millions of years, of developing a protoplasm body, and hence no longer existing in an ethereal state of being.

This takes us again to the theme of Lucifer, that spirit being whom Rudolf Steiner saw as responsible for the 'Fall of Man'. He taught that the being called Lucifer is needed to produce the state of mind in humanity through which a sense of self, initially a selfish one, is created. This then serves as the basis for the future Spiritual-self.

Lucifer and Ahriman

Lucifer is 'the old serpent' who in the story from the Book of Genesis enters Paradise and tempts the sentiency or emotional forces of the soul (symbolized by Eve). But it is this which triggers off the actual sense of self; the earthly self, with all of its flaws and dark corners. It is this process which 'opened peoples' eyes', in that humanity began to live within a flesh body and to perceive the sense world. Without this sense of a personal ego, there would be no purpose to our earthly lives. (The Anatta doctrine of Buddhism is explored later.) This sense of self has to start with a very earthly quality, and then gradually become ennobled. So Lucifer is not seen as deeply evil, but rather as a fallen spirit being, filled with pride and self-centredness, whose influence creates naïve and selfish, indulgent qualities in the human being. Lucifer, as described by Rudolf Steiner, is the fallen spirit being referred to by Isaiah, whom we considered in Chapter Four, where he is called 'the morning star'. Lucifer is filled with self-centred desires and ambitions.

So Lucifer is not the source of callous evil deeds, for as we noted in the last chapter, this derives from Ahriman. It is important to note that as from about the time of Christ people in the Hellenistic world became confused about these two separate entities, Satan (Ahriman) and Lucifer (the Devil), and often merged them together in their minds. Consequently, the name Lucifer became associated with evil or satanic beings, and has at times been made a central deity in dubious occult circles. But this is certainly not at all what Rudolf Steiner means by the term Lucifer.

A core element of Rudolf Steiner's teachings about Christianity is that, as the influence of Lucifer and also Ahriman gained momentum, the earthly ego-sense developed, just as was intended. But as this process continued on, the very real possibility arose from the influence of these beings, that humanity would not be able to have the strength in the conscience, to start developing their higher spiritual self. Hence a deed of profound love and compassion on behalf of humanity was needed, a deed from a cosmic being, as these dynamics are cosmic in nature.

The earthly ego has a focus on material goals and pleasures, and over many millennia it has developed a nature which caused the soul to become 'Earth-bound'. In other words, the self was becoming unable to find interest in spirituality, unable to bring about a fusion of the transient earth ego with a germinal higher self. Rudolf Steiner taught that the awareness of spiritual realities, or in other words, a natural spiritual sensing, began to fade out during the course of the Egyptian-Mesopotamian era (ca. 3000-750BC). This process was due to the influence of these two classes of beings becoming strongest by the time of the Christ event. And if this continued without any counter-measures, it would produce a permanent inner darkening of the soul. It is this idea that is referred to as 'Damnation' in theology. To enable humanity to have the needed spiritual capacity, the cosmic Christ descended to the Earth, to sacrificially carry out a deed designed to bring about the reversal of this cosmic process. This deed of Christ is regarded as a manifestation of the love of the Father-God for humanity.

The events on Golgotha

This deed started at the Baptism in the Jordan, through which the divine, cosmic Christ being united spiritually to the soul of Jesus and to the life-forces or etheric body of Jesus. This cosmic being also permeated the energy template sustaining his physical body. It is this process which is referred to as 'Redemption' in theology. This process was carried out by the sacrificial death on the cross; and then it was fully completed by the mysterious event of the Resurrection. Rudolf Steiner refers to these events as the Mystery of Golgotha. And in addition there were spiritual energies permeating Jesus that maintain the underlying energetic structure of the physical body.

Thus through the events which led to the death and resurrection of Jesus, the human soul, and our life-forces or etheric body were rescued from an inner withering and darkening. But there is also the theological concept of the bodily resurrection of Jesus. Rudolf Steiner gives a profound explanation of this enigmatic theme. It refers to the rescuing of the so-called 'phantom' or tenuous physical energy-field, which underlies the physical body. [60] The archetype of the body will be needed forever, and is actually separate from the protoplasm or flesh which fills it out in varying ways in the different evolutionary epochs. The phantom is embedded in an etheric template, and sustained by a 'Devachanic' archetype (Devachan is the name for the true spirit realms).

The process of Jesus being over-shadowed by the sublime deity allowed this cosmic being to speak to humanity through Jesus. But more important than his teachings are the deeds which he carried out, especially that of permeating the planet with His (or more accurately, Its) own divine spiritual light.

Deeds of Christ, even more than the words of Christ

The nature of this deed of Christ is especially important to the future welfare of humanity, and is therefore also regarded by Rudolf Steiner as especially sacred. It is seen as an expression of the kind of selfless love that Jesus Christ embodied in his actions, and in his unique teaching about love. As with so many other founders of a religion, he taught people to forgive their friends and family for any wrongs they may have done, and to love their neighbours.

But Jesus also taught people to love their enemies, that is to refrain from developing hatred and revengeful desires, and to bring good-will towards them. This state of goodness is known as 'agape' in Christian circles. To Rudolf Steiner, such actions by human beings are an expression of the conscience. He regarded the conscience as a kind of semi-conscious voice in us from divine realms proclaiming a deeply ethical, intuitive morality.

---

[60] This 'phantom' organism appears to be sustained by the "First Elemental realm" (mentioned in *Theosophy*; The Three Worlds, section 5).

So in Rudolf Steiner's anthroposophy the deed of the cosmic Christ occurring on Golgotha hill at Jerusalem is understood to result in a permeation of the aura of the Earth with sacred spiritual energies. As Jesus died on the cross, the great deity illumining him, the cosmic Christ, merged its own divine etheric and astral auras with the aura of our planet, with mother Earth. Rudolf Steiner describes this event as the most sacred and important event in the lifespan of the planet.

This event resulted in a radiant spiritual light permanently imbuing our planet; a light from which our Spirit-Self, and the Life-Spirit, derives. Rudolf Steiner describes how to the modern initiate this event can be seen as if from far out in space. The seer then notices a golden light, in the shape of a star, arising in the Earth's own aura.

This anthroposophical perspective is unique in modern religious teachings, it arises from the attitude that the Earth is a living reality with a soul, and so the term 'Christ' refers to a cosmic being who united to the Earth-soul. And here the enquirer can ask, is there any indication in the Bible (apart from Rudolf Steiner's spiritual research) that the cosmic Christ is has spiritually united to the planet? Is there perhaps a verse in the Bible about this?

Christ as the Spirit of the Earth
A particular verse is used some 16 times by Rudolf Steiner to argue that this same perspective does exist in the Gospels. The verse occurs in St. John's Gospel, 13:18, it is in the account of the Last Supper. The verse here is about Judas Iscariot planning to attack Jesus. In English Bibles this verse reads, "He who shares my bread has lifted up his heel against me." This verse apparently has nothing to do with a cosmic being uniting to the Earth, rather it presents the words of Jesus indicating to the other disciples that Judas is the traitor.

But Rudolf Steiner uses the translation of this sentence made by Martin Luther, and in his lectures in English one finds the Luther version translated as, "Those who eat my bread tread on me with their feet". But the German phrase to tread on someone with the feet actually means to trample on someone. Rudolf Steiner however suggests to his audiences that this sentence should be taken literally. If that unusual thing is done, then Rudolf Steiner is in effect saying that this sentence can serve as a pointer to the anthroposophical view that Christianity is about a cosmic being uniting to the Earth. But this is seen as a very odd situation to Bible scholars and others who wish to assess whether the Bible provides any basis for Steiner's comments. The above sentence in the gospel appears to have nothing to do with the interpretation that Steiner gives it.

Some prominent persons in Steiner circles have concluded that Steiner here is in error, but this author has researched the sentence in the original Greek, and can state that it does have precisely the meaning given to it by Rudolf Steiner. This second meaning is concealed within the Greek text, and when this other meaning is unveiled, it has the following meaning,

> **"All people who are absorbing life-forces from plant foods are absorbing that which belongs to me; and they are walking across me."**

In other words, as people walk across the ground, they are walking over a cosmic deity whose body is the Earth itself. We cannot explore this sentence here in more detail, however the author's book, "The Hellenistic Mysteries and Christianity", presents a step by step unveiling of the inner meaning on this sentence, starting with the Hebrew origin of the sentence used by St. John from a Psalm. When Rudolf Steiner's viewpoint is adopted, namely that there is a cosmic being who has united to the Earth, then those extraordinary statements that we noted earlier become deeply meaningful,

> "I am the living bread that came down from heaven. If anyone eats of this bread, he will live forever. This bread is my flesh, which I will give for the life of the world."

These now become the words of a deity and not a man; a deity from whose spiritual energies the higher self was originally implanted in the human soul, and from which this higher self can now develop. It is important to note here that Rudolf Steiner's Christology derives from his independent initiatory research. So it has a cosmopolitan quality which transcends the structure of humanistic western religious ideas.

For example, he taught that the being called 'Christ' is known to the ancient Egyptians as an aspect of Osiris. And likewise he taught that the man Jesus exerted an influence upon the religious life of humanity long before the events of Palestine. His activity being reflected historically in various sacred figures known in myths or religion. He was active within spiritual processes associated with such religious figures as Krishna, Mithra and Apollo, and also in even earlier activity, which is not found in historical records.

To Rudolf Steiner, the theological idea of 'redemption' is best understood through knowing about this action of Christ, which was made possible through the sacrifice made by Jesus. It was an action that involved bringing a divine spiritual light to the Earth, into its aura. So, 'redemption' offers a person the opportunity, if they wish to take it, to avoid what theological discussion refers to as 'damnation'. Damnation can be understood in Rudolf Steiner's worldview as a bleak future in future time-cycles for human souls who continue along a trajectory which takes one downwards into a debased state of being. See Illustration Nine for a diagram showing the basic evolutionary concepts underlying the Christian message.

The above outline of Rudolf Steiner's view of Christianity is only a brief sketch, which is strongly affirmed by a study of the Greek texts of the New Testament. But a clearer grasp of his view of Christianity can be gained by noting how Rudolf Steiner interprets the old festival of Epiphany.

The original cosmic theme of Epiphany
Today the Epiphany festival in the western world celebrates the visit of the Three Wise Men to the baby Jesus. But the original theme of the Epiphany festival was something much deeper. Its focus was the event known as the baptism of Jesus in the Jordan River by John the Baptist. This took place when Jesus was 29 years old, in AD 30.[61] Rudolf

---

[61] Not when he was 30, as is at times suggested (e.g., *The Time of Christ*, Ormond Edwards).

Steiner taught that this event is of great significance to the spiritual life of the planet, because it prepared the way for the Crucifixion and consequent Resurrection of Jesus. The baptism was the event through which the cosmic Christ descended upon Jesus. And the union of the cosmic Christ to our planet's aura occurred as a result of the death of Jesus; he became the paschal Lamb who was slaughtered to secure the world's future, in the fullest sense. But firstly, Christ had to descend upon Jesus, so to speak.

Epiphany is a Greek word that means 'manifestation', and so this festival once focused on the 'manifestation' of the cosmic Christ to the Earth. The original purpose of the Epiphany festival was to honor the great event of the descent of a cosmic being to the Earth; and in eastern churches which are not associated with Rome it still is a celebration of this descent, (referred to as the Holy Spirit).

But for many people this fact will come as a surprise. This surprise can serve as an indicator of the lack of esoteric insight in western humanistic Christendom. It tells us that many other deeper facts about the Christ event have also been dismissed. But such a cosmic awareness was destined to die out, and by the fourth century the Rome-based western church, with little feeling for the initiatory truths of Christianity, decreed forcibly that Epiphany was to celebrate the much lesser theme of the manifestation of the babe Jesus to the Three Wise Men.

St. Augustine of Hippo
It was the famous church father, Augustine of Hippo, whose influence on the history of the church was immense, who enforced this decree on behalf of Roman Christianity. A brief exploration of his role in church history reveals the strange destiny of the Christian religion; it was destined to become emptied of its esoteric depth. For such deep themes would be incompatible with the increasingly earth-bound nature of European Christianity from the Byzantine Age, through the medieval times and the Renaissance, on into the modern era.

The lack of esoteric insight into Christianity prevailing in the Latin Church fathers was partly due to the fact that these church fathers, such as Augustine, were often unable to read Greek, and hence knew only a Latin translation of the Bible. It is so important to realize that the deeper esoteric meanings of the Gospels are totally lost in the Latin translation (or translations in any other language). The deeper esoteric layer of meaning was placed in the Greek, and cannot be carried over into another language.

Nevertheless, there were still leading theologians in western Christendom who had a mystical or esoteric depth, but they had to be discreet. Rudolf Steiner mentions Thomas Aquinas as such a person, saying that he could give accurate and deep interpretation of the Bible "because he could clairvoyantly see the hierarchies of divine-spiritual beings".[62] Whereas Augustine was a man of genius with a vehement conviction of his own insightfulness, his understanding of the veiled initiation truths of this religion was

---

[62] Archive document; 7th lecture given in Rome, late March 1909.

very limited. However he was historically an extremely important theologian.[63] Augustine's lack of esoteric insight inaugurated a narrower, non-cosmic view of a cosmic event. Rudolf Steiner viewed Augustine as the primary western church father in the Latin world, who developed the form of the church for his times and indeed for another 1,500 years. Steiner described him as the most competent interpreter of the writings of St. Paul (for the non-esoteric mindset ordained for Roman Christianity).[64] His theology became the cornerstone of western Christianity. His view of the church as the City of God adheres closely to the non-esoteric viewpoint embodied in the Council of Nicea. But consequently as Rudolf Steiner taught, through his 'City of God' concept Augustine became the most significant opponent of that form of the church (or religious-spiritual understanding) which will be needed for the future. In the future social life of humanity, imposed authority will no longer be appropriate.[65]

An esoteric view of Christ
Now if we ask modern humanistic theologians, just what kind of being is the Christ, they find themselves in difficulty. The related question, 'From whereabouts in Heaven did this being come?' is simply an unanswerable riddle to western Christendom. This is because the church is not able to associate deity with any specific place in the cosmos.

It is not part of the mind-set of the western Christianity to factor in any specific cosmic qualities, or points of origin, of a divine being. We have already seen that the statements from Christ that He (or It) is the 'bread of life' do show a great significance when the cosmic aspect is included. But yet even this is still a somewhat vague concept. How can one approach the idea that the 'cosmic Christ' could be somehow associated with a specific cosmic place or specific divine abilities? To modern minds, a deity with all its special qualities on the one hand, and the structure of the cosmos on the other hand, are two entirely separate things. But this attitude is not true, for in fact, **they are two entirely *separated* things** !

This is the modern dilemma; in ancient times people did not experience this divide. For we have become what Rudolf Steiner calls, 'hermits in the cosmos'. In other words, we have lost the old awareness of the influence of the etheric and astral energies within the material world, influences deriving from spiritual beings. What are the insights of Rudolf Steiner's initiatory wisdom about this being, and are his teachings in any way substantiated by authoritative Christian church fathers?

The Logos
Rudolf Steiner taught that the term 'Christ' actually refers to **two** sublime beings. One of these is the 'Logos' who is part of a sublime trinity of transcendent beings. Such a trinity is found in a variety of religions, such as ancient Celtic beliefs, and Hinduism. The other Christ, as understood in anthroposophy, is not as sublime as the primal

---

[63] It is a memorable experience to stand at the remnants of the very baptismal font, under the entrance to the magnificent cathedral of Milan, where in AD 387 Augustine was baptised (as a convert from Manichaeism).

[64] Archive document; 7th lecture given in Rome, late March 1909.

[65] GA 93, 11th Nov. 1904, p. 78.

Logos but is nevertheless a sublime spiritual being in our solar system. This means in the sun, which is the great centre of our solar system.

But let's just consider firstly the Logos idea. Rudolf Steiner's understanding here is closely linked with that of the Gospel of St. John, where, in the very first sentence, the reader's attention is abruptly drawn to this mysterious being. For St. John begins his Gospel without any reference to the baby Jesus or the holy family. He goes straight to a meditative picture of a sublime being closely associated with the First Principle, or so-called Father God, and who carries out the act of creating the cosmos as an agent of God. In the standard NIV translation it reads as follows,

> "In the beginning was the Word, and the Word was with God, and the Word was God. He was with God in the beginning. Through him all things were made; without him nothing was made that has been made."

However when the subtle nuances of the Greek are translated precisely, a much more accurate (if wordy) and informative translation of this famous text arises,

> "In the beginning was the Logos, and the Logos was inwardly with God, and a god was the Logos.[66] This {same} one, he was in the beginning inwardly with God. All things through him were created, and without him was created not even one thing that has been created."[67]   (translated the author)

We see that the word Logos occurs here as if the readers are already familiar with this term.[68] The Greek word 'Logos' was used by people in the initiatory schools of the Hellenistic Age to mean a high spiritual being who was in effect the 'Soul of the Cosmos', or in modern terms, the high spiritual Intelligence behind Creation. This indicates that the gospel was designed to be a meditative text for those with a more esoteric approach to Christianity.

But it is true that the term was also used by different people to refer to different beings. Its deepest meaning however, is that of a sublime being who brought forth Creation in response to the uncaused, un-manifest primal God. Its usage in Hellenistic literature is not uniform. Knowledge of how the Logos is understood in Hellenistic times is a specialized study, requiring knowledge of ancient Greek itself. This is especially the case as the approximately 1,200 references to the Logos in the writings of the famous first century AD esotericist, Philo Judaeorus, have been removed from the commonly available English translation. This word was changed into a variety of other terms, such as reason, word, idea, etc.

---

[66] The 'anarthrous' condition of the urtext here can be understood to be presenting the Logos as a separate (but reciprocally interweaving) divine being or deity.
[67] The term 'inwardly with' expresses more accurately the reciprocal interacting with God which is implied by the Greek word, 'pros'.
[68] Usually the text says, "and the Word was God", not "the Logos was a god", but the Greek does allow this alternative translation, through the 'anarthrous' condition of the noun here.

Statements from Philo, and from an ancient Greek initiate, Heraclitus, who was writing about 500 BC onwards, convey a good idea of what the esoteric Greek understanding of the Logos was. Heraclitus writes for example,

> "Although this Logos is eternally valid, yet people are unable to understand it….although all things come to pass in accordance with this Logos, yet people seem to be quite without any experience of it…
> Although intimately connected with the Logos which orders the whole world, men keep setting themselves against it, and the things which they encounter every day seem quite foreign to them." (Saying 1 & 64)[69]

Another text about this sublime being is found in the so-called Gospel of Truth, an esoteric text written about 100 AD, included in the collection of ancient texts found in Egypt (Nag Hammadi). It was written only a few decades after the Gospel of St. John,

> "The Logos, the Word of the Father God, rays forth into the world as the fruit of His heart and as the expression of his will." (V.23)[70]

These two texts, from spiritually enlightened people separated by half a millennium, present quite similar insights about this high being. And they are very similar to statements in the Gospel of St. John. Hence the presence of this esoteric idea in a Christian church text was very strange to many early Christians. In Rudolf Steiner's Christology, Jesus is a man whereas the term 'Christ' properly designates the cosmic deity.

Indeed some people in other sectors of the early Christian movement, devoid of a sense for the more cosmic aspects of this reality, tried to have this gospel condemned as heretical ! The above quotations are very similar to the view of the Gospel writer. But there is a large difference in this Christian gospel, for it goes on to declare that through Jesus, the Logos became incorporated into the world of humanity.

Christ as the Logos and also the sun god

Although the way in which "the Logos became flesh" is not elaborated in detail in the Gospels, we need to note that in most Christian circles it is understood that it was by Jesus being born, that the Logos became a flesh and blood person. In other words, they conclude that Jesus is the Logos or God; and it is here that the lack of esoteric wisdom in theological circles becomes evident. Rudolf Steiner taught that Jesus as a human being was not God as such, nor the Logos (except in the sense that all human beings potentially are, for the Logos can indeed become gradually manifest within humanity).

The Logos is mentioned in both the Gospel of St. John and referred to in the Epistle to the Hebrews, and also briefly in the Gospel of St. Luke. However Rudolf Steiner taught that the Logos or God did manifest within Jesus in an exceptional way. The great cosmic Logos was present within another divine being, of lesser rank, namely the sun god Christ, and this latter being is united to the soul of Jesus.

---

[69] On the internet the Complete Fragments of Heraclitus are available.
[70] The Gospel of Truth, The Nag Hammadi Library in English, Leiden, 1977, Brill.

So in Rudolf Steiner's Christology there is a complex reality underlying this cosmic Christ idea. There is <u>another</u> great spiritual being involved, apart from the Logos, who is <u>also called</u> 'Christ'. This second 'Christ being' is from one of the nine ranks of great spiritual beings existing between humanity and God. This other great being is described by Steiner as the 'sun god Christ'; and is the highest of the divine beings in the sun-sphere. They belong to the rank of 'Powers'. This being has been worshipped since ancient times under different names. The term 'sun' here means the spiritual sun, or in other words, a non-material state of this radiant celestial body, perceptible only to clairvoyance.

The sun god and Origenes (3rd century AD)

This same view of the sun god or Power as well as the Logos being called 'Christ' was held by Origenes of Alexandria, the revered third century church father. However other translations of his works fail to make this clear. In his commentary on the Gospel of St. John, he writes about this, and teaches that Christ is the highest of the Powers or 'Spirit-Hosts of God'. But earlier he has been teaching that the Logos whom he regards as the primal wisdom of God is Christ also. Origenes writes in Paragraph 292,

> "***Just as*** therefore numerous mighty Spirit-Hosts of God exist, each one of whom has individualization, (yet amongst all of these is the Saviour, who is higher than the others), ***so too*** even if the Logos is not individualized anywhere outside us - he the Christ {the Logos} will be understood through the elucidations in previous pages as having real being, in the beginning, in Wisdom."[71]   (translated the author)

So Origenes is writing that there exists a specific individual 'Christ' deity who is the foremost of the Powers, but that additionally there also exists a 'Christ' deity who is the primal Logos. This Logos may not be defined as specifically an individualized being, such as the leader of the sun gods is. But this is only because the Logos is so sublimely high, that all such concepts are meaningless. This is obviously a difficult, mystical theology, and the above passage has to be considered in relation to the preceding paragraph (No. 291), but here we cannot go into a detailed assessment of these texts. (The author's book, The Hellenistic Mysteries & Christianity provides more about the statements by Origenes on this subject.)

Rudolf Steiner taught that the 'Christ' is the closely linked to the god the ancient Egyptians called Osiris, the Greeks called Helios, and the ancient Persians called Ahura Mazdao. The initiated priests experienced this being as the primary Creator in our part of the cosmos, namely the solar system. Illustration Ten presents some artistic evidence for the awareness of this solar aspect of the Christ by the earliest Christians. It

---

[71] Origenes text is: Ὥσπερ οὖν δυνάμεις Θεοῦ πλειονές εἰσιν, ὧν ἑκαστη κατὰ περιγραφήν, ὧν διαφέπει ὁ σωτήρ, οὕτος καὶ λόγος – εἰ καὶ ὁ παρ᾽ ἡμῖν οὐκ ἔστι κατὰ περιγραφήν, ἐκτος ἡμιν νοηθήσεται ὁ Χριστὸς διὰ τὰ προεξητασμένα ἐν ἀρχῇ, τῇ σοφίᾳ τὴν ὑπόστασιν ἔχων. In Origenes: ΩΡΙΓΕΝΟΥΣ ΤΩΝ ΕΙΣ ΤΟ ΚΑΤΑ ΙΩΑΝΝΗΝ ΕΥΑΓΓΕΛΙΟΝ ΕΞΗΓΗΤΙΚΩΝ in Sources Chrétiennes Origène Les Éditions du Cerf, Paris, 1996, Tome 1, #291, p. 208.

is a mosaic from an early Christian grave, found under the ground in Rome. It depicts Christ as the new Helios.[72]

The meaning of Easter

What then is the significance in anthroposophy of the Easter events, of the descent of the sun god? Perhaps the most concise way of explaining Rudolf Steiner's view of the impact of the union of the cosmic Christ to the Earth is to note his words that, "Christ died in order that human beings could find meaning in their lives". In these words Rudolf Steiner is indicating that by his sacrificial death, Jesus, through becoming the vessel of the Christ, brought about the process which enabled our planet to be imbued with the spiritual energies through which the human being can develop a truly spiritual, ethical goodness when she or he follows the urge to strive towards the good. As he explained in a 1909 lecture,

> Through the event that we call the Mystery of Golgotha, or in other words, the walking of Christ upon the Earth, that spiritual being who was previously within the sun, united itself to the Earth. And that humanity divided the flow of time into 'before-Christ' (BC) and 'after-Christ' (AD) has its basis in the situation that, this living being who we call the Earth, actually went through an important development. What was previously only to be found on the sun is since then to be found in the astral aura of the Earth.... In the events of Golgotha the {cosmic} Christ-spirit has united with the Earth.[73]

It is important to note in reading the works of Steiner on this subject, that there are two phrases used by him. In English translations of Steiner's books you may come across the expression, "the Christ problem" or "the Christian problem". [74] These translations could give a deeply incorrect impression. The correct translation of his German expression (*"das Christus Problem /das christliche Problem"*) is "the challenging enigma of Christ / the challenging Christian enigma". Because here Steiner is using this word 'problem' (which is foreign to German) in its more learned meaning.

In that context, it means a challenging philosophical enigma, not an annoying problem. (Steiner does not use it in another perfectly acceptable sense of 'the challenging problem for individuals of finding or relating to Christ'.) [75] This usage of the word is especially common in his own Austrian form of German. So Steiner can also say,

---

[72] This mosaic, and another artwork, are discussed further in my book, The Hellenistic Mysteries and Christianity.
[73] GA 108, p. 86, lecture 17th Jan. 1909.
[74] Another example is, "the challenging cosmic enigma which forms the basis of Christianity" not "the cosmic problem which forms the basis of Christianity" (GA 93 p.39)
[75] GA 325, p. 131.

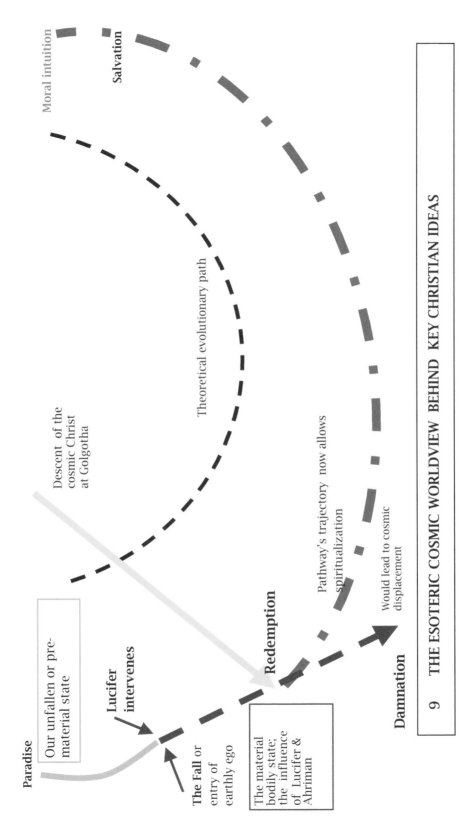

Paradise

Our unfallen or pre-
material state

Descent of the
cosmic Christ
at Golgotha

Moral intuition

Salvation

Theoretical evolutionary path

**Lucifer
intervenes**

**The Fall or
entry of
earthly ego**

The material
bodily state;
the influence
of Lucifer &
Ahriman

Redemption

Pathway's trajectory now allows
spiritualization

Would lead to cosmic
displacement

Damnation

9   THE ESOTERIC COSMIC WORLDVIEW BEHIND KEY CHRISTIAN IDEAS

85

"…this is why over in Asia Minor in earlier centuries the *challenging enigma* (*Problem*) of the union of Jesus to Christ often arose {in theological debates}. The second phrase you will encounter is, "the Christ-impulse". This unusual phrase replaces the normal, simpler expression, "Christ". It is used by Steiner because of his awareness that both the great primal Logos and the sun deity are involved in the Christian reality. He also uses it because there are a number of other divine beings who are actively serving the intentions of these great beings. All this spiritual activity creates various definite streams of spiritual energies which unfold their influence in civilisation across the millennia.

The nature of God
In teaching about the nature of God, Rudolf Steiner points to the existence of three great spiritual realities, namely Wisdom, Power and Love.[76] He explains that God can not be all-wise, as that would prevent humanity attaining to true freedom, because God can only know <u>all</u> things if the decisions that are as yet unborn in the human soul were also known in advance.

Further, he explains that God refrains from being an all-powerful (almighty) ruler, as that would also prevent human freedom. That is, such a condition prevailing in deity would prevent humanity from manifesting its own will. The fact of the existence of Lucifer and Ahriman establishes, he explains, that God does not manifest as an all-powerful ruler. Rudolf Steiner taught that it was only **after** the fourth century AD, that God was considered to be almighty.[77] Many mainstream theologians would find such an assertion very wrong.

Does Steiner's view have any basis in Biblical literature, or is it pure heresy? In the New Testament there are only ten references to an almighty God. It does not occur in the Gospels, so it was never spoken by Jesus. But, and this is the point, none of the ten references ever meant 'almighty'. The Greek word involved, 'pantokrator', is found only in one other early Christian text, and there it is used for Satan![78] The non-Christian Greeks used it for such deities as Hermes and Isis. So in effect it means, 'very powerful, mighty'. The interpretation of such terms to mean almighty probably first occurs in the works of Augustine of Hippo.[79]

The Hebrew word involved is 'shaddai', and it is of unknown origin and hence unknown meaning in any precise sense, but experts suggest from its context that it has to mean something very reverential such as, 'more grand, more powerful' or possibly, 'more bountiful'.[80] And esoterically as it is used of Jehovah (as well as other aspects of Deity in the Hebrew Bible), it cannot refer to the sublime godhead who is beyond such hierarchical beings, and hence is not correctly viewed as meaning almighty.

---

[76] "Love and its meaning in the world" 17th Dec.12 (GA 143).

[77] GA 194, p. 90 (Lect. 29th March 1919).

[78] In the Greek, κοσμοκράτωρ.

[79] His unawareness of the deeper cosmic aspects of this religion is expressed is such words as "…our salvation was brought about when a woman conceived the flesh of the Almighty in her womb…" (Sermon CCLXXXIX, 2., quoted in *An Augustine Synthesis*, E. Przywara)

[80] In the Hebrew, שַׁדִּי.

But over many centuries with Augustine's wrong interpretation of the Hebrew and Greek terms, scholars in recent times, translating ancient Christian writings that pre-dated Augustine imposed this wrong meaning onto the Greek text. Thus not only the few New Testament passages with the Greek word pantocrator have this word wrongly translated, but also for example, Clement of Alexandria (155-220 AD) is represented in English as referring to God Almighty whenever he uses the word pantocrator.[81]

So how then, is God understood in anthroposophy? Rudolf Steiner used the term 'Weltengrund' for God, which means something like, 'the cosmos-foundation' or 'cosmos-fundament' or basis of creation, or substratum of being. This expression is not unique to Rudolf Steiner; it is commonly found in learned theological and philosophical works of 18th and 19th centuries. But he gives a profoundly deeper understanding of this term,

> "The Weltengrund (God) has fully poured out Himself into the cosmos. He has not withdrawn from it in order to guide it from outside. Rather He impels it from within; so He has not withheld Himself from it. The highest mode of His manifestation within the reality of normal existence is (human) thinking (consciousness) and through this factor, the human personality.
> Thus if God has goals, then they are identical with the goals that human beings set for themselves, as He lives within these. But this does not occur through the human being trying to investigate one or other command from this Regent of the cosmos, and acting according to such a perceived goal.
>
> It – the active involvement of God – occurs through the human being, acting from his or her own understanding. For this Regent of the Cosmos is living within these human beings. He does not exist as Will somewhere outside of the human being for he has forgone such a Will of his own, in order to make everything dependent upon the Will of the human being." [82]

In another lecture he presents similar profound insights about Deity,

> "Evolution is to keep on occurring, because God, in infinite Love to all of his separate parts,[83] wants to make these perfect, just as he himself is. This was a free decision not a necessity; it was a sacrifice. Through this decision we have a development of the separate parts of God up to Godliness. Through your inner work, the possibility for perfection which is already within you, comes into manifestation."[84]

-[81] Clement, The Miscellanies, Bk. 6: 5, "...by which the Almighty is glorified among the Greeks...." The Ante-Nicene Greek Library, translations of the Church Fathers, vol. 12, Clement of Alexandria Vol. 2, Edinburgh, 1882, p. 327.
[82] "Outlines of a theory of epistemology of the Goethean world-view" page 125 (German edition), in the chapter, *Human freedom.*
[83] This is in German, „einzelnen Gliedern".
[84] Archive document from 19th Jan. 1905.

It is valuable at this point to see how the initiates of the ancient Mysteries viewed this theme of God, as Rudolf Steiner explained in a different lecture,

> "They understood that God is never a completed Being, it is [in existence] as the ongoing development inside all living beings, in all things….Each one of us is, so to speak, a ray or a reflected image, of God. The relationship of God to humanity is like that of the Sun to its own reflection in a multitude of drops of water…If one asks a Theosophist about God, about what is behind Brahman, he says nothing, for about this being one cannot speak. Everything which people say in this direction is an indicator only." [85]

So, from this we see the very substantial difference between the anthroposophical worldview and the theological views of God and Christ and the spiritual realities in general.

Christ Jesus the empowered saviour

Finally, you need to note that sometimes anthroposophical writers appear unaware of the spiritual greatness of the Saviour of the Christian religion. In many anthroposophical texts Christ Jesus or Jesus Christ is referred to as "the Nathan-Jesus soul". This is a deeply incorrect term for the Christian Saviour. This unusual phrase comes from Rudolf Steiner and means Jesus, as he was 2,000 years ago. It alludes to a priestly ancestor of Jesus of that name, as recorded in the genealogy list presented in St. Luke's gospel. This divine Jesus child became Jesus Christ after the Baptism in the Jordan when he was 29 years old, as the cosmic Christ descended on him. An error found in anthroposophical writings is that this person, whom Rudolf Steiner describes as a "God-man", is presented as a soul without an ego; that is, a person without a self-sense.[86] The reason for such people thinking of Jesus as lacking a sense of self derives from misinterpretation of statements of Rudolf Steiner.

Steiner has explained, as we saw above, that Jesus had never been on the earth before and hence he had little of the earthly ego-hood that normal human beings have. But Jesus Christ is nevertheless presented in Steiner's works as having a personal ego-sense, although not strongly, because during his earthly life in Palestine this naturally developed. Moreover, he had already begun to develop a basis for a sense of ego from activity undertaken to influence humanity from the spiritual worlds about a millennium before the events in Palestine. Certainly the earthly personal-ego does need incarnations on the Earth for it to unfold, but this process is what began in Palestine. However as the momentous event occurred of the cosmic Christ overshadowing Jesus, this same divinity, which is the origin of humanity's higher ego, merged with his delicate ego-sense, with the full power of the higher ego; the eternal self. Jesus then became a person with an immensely real higher ego or sense of self. And he is therefore the most spiritually empowered and ennobled of all human beings. As Steiner

---

[85] From GA 52, p. 44.

[86] Such passages as, "…the Nathan Jesus soul must yet again fashion for the Christ a garment of light {in the 20th century}…" (S. Prokofieff) indicate this misunderstanding.

told one audience, "...although a cosmic principle lives in him, Christ Jesus as an individual personality confronts other human beings quite individually..."[87]

Two Nativity stories

There is another unusual feature to Steiner's teachings on Christianity that needs to be briefly noted here. It concerns the two Nativity stories about Jesus, one in the gospel of St. Luke, the other in the gospel of St. Matthew. Rudolf Steiner taught that the two very dissimilar Nativity stories and two different genealogies given in these gospels indicate that two families were involved in preparing for the coming of the Messiah. He refers to the "Nathan Jesus child" when talking about the Nativity story in St. Luke's gospel, because the priest called Nathan was listed there as an ancestor Jesus. And Steiner also refers to the "Solomon Jesus child" when talking about the Nativity story in St. Matthew's gospel, because this great king was listed as an ancestor Jesus, in that gospel.

There is evidence of knowledge in ancient Hebrew wisdom of a deep mystery concerning two individuals, each of whom are thought of a Messiah. But we need to be totally clear that there is really only one Messiah, of course. Old Hebrew texts refer to The Two Messiahs, but one of them dies in childhood; so there is actually just one Messiah. In an esoteric treatise, assimilated at times into the great core esoteric treatise of the Hebrew mystics, the Zohar, there are references which seem to refer to the birth of two boys, who would spiritually merge their souls, and thus eventually these events would bring forth the expected one Messiah. It is a 13th century text, the Ra'aya Mehemna, which probably went back orally to the time before Christ,

> "There shall be two Messiahs who shall arise from the grace of Moses...One will be the royal messiah, the son of David, a descendant of the royal tribe of Judah. The other messiah, the son Levi, (priestly caste) he holds the pastoral crook. After the unusual death of the royal messiah, the Messiah shall appear; for one of these Messiahs shall die, and yet he shall live on again..." [88]

Further reading
Rudolf Steiner: "Christianity as Mystical Fact"
Rudolf Steiner: The Gospel of St. John (a lecture cycle from1908)
A. Anderson: The Hellenistic Mysteries and esoteric Christianity
Emil Bock: The Three Years

---

[87] GA 139, *The Gospel of St. Mark*, 17th Sept. 1909, lecture 3. Although Steiner reported that as the cosmic Christ descended, the enhancement of his ego-sense which had been especially arranged to help Jesus went away, his own delicate earthly ego (and soul) was nevertheless the vessel into which the true higher, eternal ego came. The departure of the 'ego' actually refers to a powerful, wise ego-sense that was assisting Jesus from his 12th to his 30 year of life.

[88] Parts of the Ra'aya Mehemna are in the Exodus sections of the Mantua Zohar in the 5 vol. English, Sperling edition (Waera par.24 and Bo para. 41). It is available in the Hebrew Zohar, published in Israel, and in French from Jean de Pauly, Sepher ha-zohar: doctrine ésotérique des Israélites; livre de la splendour.

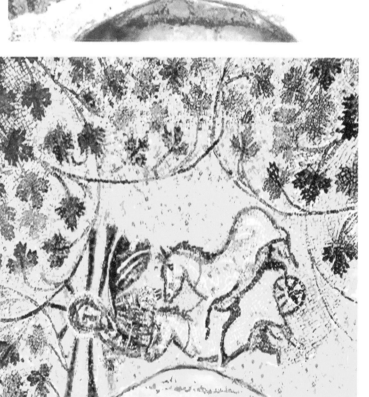

10   Christ as the new sun god, Helios

From a tomb in Rome, from about 250 AD Right: the mosaic in its current damaged and faded state.
Left: The image partly restored (by computer graphics) with its original colours refreshed, by the author.

6: THE SPIRIT, THE SELF AND MEDITATION

A summary of the three strands of the soul

Three elements to our soul – our emotional capacity, logical thought, and will – despite being an integrated unity in us, **have their own separate origins**, and after death, or in the person undergoing real spiritual development, become more independent of each other. Rudolf Steiner therefore refers to the human being as possessing 'three souls', rather than being 'a threefold soul'. The term he uses for the emotional capacity in English would be the rarely used term, 'sentiency'.

Sentiency is the capacity to experience desires, yearnings, fears, joys, happiness, pleasure and pain and so on. It is also the capacity to experience what our senses tell us of the physical world, such as coldness, heat, movement, sounds, odours and so on. If we can experience our 'inner life' (all our emotions) then we can also experience, so long as we are in a physical body, what our senses report to us.

So this part of our soul is called the '**sentient-soul**'. The term, sentient-soul, simply means our capacity to have emotions, but remembering that each of the three souls is potentially a separate entity. Steiner's insistence on this point is very insightful, as mental health problems can be more easily understood and more effective therapies developed when the inherent dynamics of our three-fold soul is understood.

Secondly, we have our logical, intellectual, rational capacity; our capacity to think clearly and analyse situations. We normally call this our intelligence; Steiner refers to this as our '**intellectual-soul**'. Steiner points out that the intellectual-soul is often at the mercy of the sentient-soul. In other words, our emotions can damage the clarity and truthfulness of our thinking. If we desire that a certain attitude of ours be seen as correct (by ourselves or others), then the power of our wishes can overwhelm the objectivity of the intellect. However the reverse is also true, namely so often in the heavily intellectualized and technological cultures of today, rational thinking can be oblivious to our emotional needs. The logical capacity is a vital tool of our life, it is the basis of the scientific, engineering and literary achievements of civilisation.

But the intellect can also become a willing vessel for higher spiritual insights. If spiritual wisdom is gained in a healthy balanced way, the intellect can learn to grasp higher truths to some extent, and express them in a clear, conceptual manner. If this is done, one moves away from spontaneous visions, wherein the spiritual is experienced but cannot really be presented to others, to what Steiner calls 'spiritual science', wherein such truths can be explained to others, and thus used to help society.

However, it is also true – and a common complaint against the intellect – that our rational thinking can refuse to allow a higher spiritual insight to be acknowledged. But as Steiner strongly pointed out, and embodied in his life's work, the intellect can also become a willing vessel for higher spiritual insights. And the fruits of such insights can be used to help renew many fields of work. It was Steiner's special task to do just that. Whereas in psychic moments the spiritual is experienced, but often cannot be explained to others, or be monitored by the self of the person who is undergoing the visions. Such a person is a disempowered spectator, so to speak.

The spiritual-soul

But from what part of our consciousness do these insights derive? They derive from our third soul, called by Steiner, the '**spiritual-soul**' (this term is also translated by the less satisfactory term, 'consciousness soul'). The 'spiritual-soul' is the third member of our soul, and it is the least known, and the hardest to understand in terms of psychological dynamics. An excellent meditative way to understand this soul is to contemplate a sentence from the Hebrew Bible (or Old Testament) which we noted in Chapter Two. The Hebrew word for the spiritual-soul is Neschamah, which is used very rarely,

> Proverbs 20, 27: The soul of the human being is the lamp of the Lord, shining into his innermost being.

The word 'soul' in this sentence means the intuitive-soul or spiritual-soul, as the term Neschamah is used. It is not surprising that little exists in literature about this third soul. It is an intuitive semi-conscious faculty; so few people would have ever strongly registered its presence or abilities. It is the nearest of the three souls to the spirit, and in its activity, it does become a shining light into the hidden will forces of the human being. It is also linked to the core of our being, on the one hand giving intuitions, when the higher mind is active, but on the other hand, it also creates the most potent self-awareness, and hence self interest. As Rudolf Steiner taught in his book Theosophy it is,

> " that aspect of the soul wherein one is so aware of one's freedom, of the capacity to make one's own decision, nothing is so closely connected to our personal wants and wishes as the spiritual-soul."

So the spiritual-soul is a name for the intuitive faculty we possess and through which we make those deeper decisions which are not produced from logic or emotions. It is also this same sub-conscious power that underlies the immune system or digestion. (The conscience also manifests in an intuitive way, but it is a separate phenomenon; its origin is in higher spiritual realms.)

Now the psychological force operative in the will, especially in deeper decision-making is **intuition**, it is not emotion nor is it logic. This power of intuition is the soul power which has given us 'insight' into the situation – and it is this same capacity of insight which makes our third soul. Indeed this **is** our third soul, the '**spiritual-soul**'.

It is this same soul that gives to us – in rare moments – spiritual insight. Such insights into deeper spiritual truths need not be rare and unpredictable, they can become ever more frequent. And this is what the meditative life is all about – giving us a stronger, more vivified spiritual soul, which becomes a bridge across to the Spiritual-Self and the ability to function consciously in the true higher spiritual realms. Hence the reason why he preferred it to be called, in English, the spiritual-soul and not 'consciousness-soul'.

The view of spirituality and the goodness that is invoked into the soul by the spiritual-soul, functioning at its best, is beautifully expressed in a poem by the great German poet, dramatist and sensitive nature researcher, Johann Wolfgang von Goethe (1760-1832). In a wonderful outpouring of the intuitive insights that the spiritual-soul can give, he describes how the negative attributes of self-centredness, self-interest and self-will, 'shudder away' as the <u>heart's purity</u> manifests. This accords very clearly to the threefold human soul as explained in anthroposophy, and how the spiritual potential arises in the soul, as its triune nature is transformed.

One can see here how this verse affirms the anthroposophical perspective that spirituality (called 'piety' by Goethe back in the 1820's) is the polar opposite to self-centredness. It is precisely this self-centredness or debased ego-sense which is eradicated from one's attitudes and emotive responses through the condition of attaining to spirituality, or at least of sensing its approach. In 1823 Goethe had written his famous passionate love poem, *Elegy* in which he grieves over the loss of the relationship with a young woman, Ulrike von Levetzow. But partway through the poem he arises to a beautiful contemplation of the spiritual-soul,

> "...in the purity of our heart, there surges a striving, born of gratitude, to freely surrender oneself to a higher, purer, Unknown Power; thus resolving the enigma to oneself of the Eternally Un-named;
> we call this – being pious !
> In such blessed heights I feel
> myself partake, when I am in its presence –
> before its gaze, as if facing the power of the Sun,
> before its breath, as if before springtime breezes,
> melts away what has lasted so long in icy rigidity –
> self-centredness, deep in wintry tombs;
> No self-interest, no self-will, lasts;
> before its dawning presence they have shuddered
> away."
>   (translated the author)

In his comments on this passage from *Elegy*, Steiner describes these insights as being an expression of the spiritual-soul. It is just this condition of spirituality which Steiner, already in his thirties, laboured to demonstrate as a fact, perhaps the most important fact about humankind's nature. He argues that such a potential for truly selfless goodwill does exist in us all. In his book, *The Philosophy of Freedom*, written in 1894, Steiner argues that this spirituality is also the condition which is true freedom. That is, in true freedom, all actions are carried out from an inherent ethical quality, which has now been attained. Hence these actions occur in the realm of divine love in the human soul,

> "...the realm where the human being is no longer compelled to any deed, rather where everything, which lies in the realm of human knowledge and development, happens through freedom and devotion, from deep love...where

every compulsion, every arbitrary act, becomes transformed through a spiritual alchemy, where all actions flow into the realm of freedom." [89]

To Rudolf Steiner the condition of personal freedom (not to be confused with political freedom) is an ethical state, the final goal of spirituality, and is crucial both for the fulfilment of the human potential as well as for the future of civilisation. This condition is one in which a person has the above qualities of a spontaneously ethical nature as an inherent quality.

Moral intuition or inherent ethics
To Rudolf Steiner it is also a state of exceptional spirituality, because to him 'freedom' is not simply a condition bestowed upon the human being, rather it is a condition which, developed through specific esoteric soul-exercises, is the truest manifestation of the human spirit. To Steiner, 'love' is primarily a capacity developed in the volitional powers of the soul; in effect, love is 'good will'. In the poem *Elegy*, Goethe writes about this exalted state of 'freedom' as a result of his profound reflections upon romantic love.

Further, the attainment of such spirituality is seen by Steiner as the fulfilling of the actual intention underlying the creation of humanity; that is, humanity has the mission to become the bearers of spiritual, selfless love. He elucidates his idea in lectures on the Gospel of St. John, where he explains that Christ is the being of spiritual love, or good-will in the finest sense. The Buddha manifested these qualities of good-will and compassion, whereas the cosmic Christ is the source of this actual quality. He concludes that the result of the Incarnation of Christ, fulfilled through the Passion and Resurrection, is that human souls have the very real potential to achieve this state of freedom, or ethical intuitiveness. [90]

Finally, we can note here the striking words in Goethe's poem,

> "….to freely surrender oneself to a higher, purer, Unknown [Power]; thus resolving the enigma to oneself of the Eternally Un-named; we call this – being pious !"

Goethe is here very radically re-defining the meaning of being pious – which in today's language means being 'spiritual', in the sense of having reverence for the sacred. He has removed the scene of action for piety from organized religion to the spiritually striving person's inner life.

In doing this, Goethe is again pre-figuring the teachings of Rudolf Steiner, who taught, as we have noted earlier, that through the events that occurred at Golgotha, in every human being the highest ethics can arise – and this is true freedom. This is a condition which is also one of feeling reverence for the sacred.

---

[89] Lecture, 4th April 1904.
[90] GA 112, The Gospel of St. John, lecture three.

The Spirit-self
As one strives towards higher wisdom and compassion, one is invoking the presence of one's 'spirit'. Just what does this 'spirit' really mean? Today it has almost no meaning, and is therefore confused with the word 'soul'. This brings us to the three aspects of the human spirit which we listed above, but did not explain in any detail. The '**Spirit-self**' (or Spiritual-self) is Steiner's term for that part of our higher self which is brought into being, and ever more structured and strengthened, as the **spiritual-soul** becomes more prominent in a person's soul life. The term 'Spirit-self' in anthroposophical literature replaces the Hindu term, Manas, used by the Theosophical Society.

As the higher insights are experienced more and more, this means that there is a purified sentient-soul (or emotional/desire nature) and then one's heart is able to assist the intellect to achieve a more spiritualized intelligence. At this point the slumbering human spirit – in its first of three aspects – is awakened. Our **sense of self** becomes a spiritual one, so we have begun to develop the '**Spiritual-self**' (or Spirit-self). There is a 'soul-realm' from which the soul comes and there exists also a 'spiritual-realm' from which the human spirit derives; **the seven spiritual realms are of a higher, eternal transcendent quality than the seven soul realms**. See Chapter Nine for more about the nature of the spiritual realms.

We could say that the Spirit-self arises as the personal self, with its emotions, intelligence and will, is refined and uplifted. Hence in anthroposophical language, we could say that as the soul (or soul-body) is spiritualized, the Spiritual-self arises. This is the fifth part of our nature. A special instance of a hindrance to the developing of the Spiritual-self occurs when the student of anthroposophical ideas lets the intellect grasp the spiritual wisdom in Steiner's teachings, but does not make the effort **to absorb this wisdom into their heart, and thereby experience feelings of awe, wonder and reverence**. That is, when the student of anthroposophical wisdom lets their intellect predominate, and makes no effort towards a higher emotional life, a much more profound compassion and empathy for everyone else.

Rudolf Steiner once told an audience that then anthroposophy becomes an unwholesome thing. This, he said, leads to the student encountering the ideas "with too strong a self-sense (too strong a focus on one's self, one's mind) and this arouses the interest of luciferic beings, who then wrap illusions around the student's head."[91] These words will refer to illusions of self-grandeur.

The Life-spirit
But as we develop even further towards spirituality, it is possible for our ethereal energies, our 'ether-body' to be spiritualized. If that occurs, exceptional creative powers arise in the artistic field and in healing, and in higher consciousness and seership. This Steiner calls the '**Life-spirit**'. The term 'Life-spirit' in anthroposophical literature replaces the Hindu term, Buddhi, used by the Theosophical Society for this part of the human spirit. Rudolf Steiner once described this mysterious spiritual part of us in this way,

---

[91] Reported by Ernst Lippold, in *Friedrich Rittelmeyer*, Mitteilungen aus der Anthroposophischen Bewegung, Nr. 55, Easter, 1974 p.5.

"Visualize the usual life-forces now conserved by a pure, restrained harmonious life-style, and then made to resonate, to respond, to the utterly outpouring, selfless compassion of the Spirit-self." [92]

The Life-spirit is a spiritual force that is inherent in the artistic capacity ! On one occasion Rudolf Steiner describes it from the viewpoint of the artistic gift,

"But we can raise ourselves to another condition of consciousness than simply that which reproduces the experiences of our intelligence…There are certain conditions of a creative activity, where the human spirit becomes a creator, and can create something new, something never seen before. Such an instance is that of the soul-condition of the sculptor in the moment of conception, where he sees before his spirit in a sudden flash, the form of a statue, the like of which he has never seen before, but which he creates. Of such kind is also the soul-condition of a poet, whom in one draft, in one creative vision of his spirit, conceives a work." [93]

On the subject of spirituality, inner freedom and life-forces it is relevant to mention that in his book The Philosophy of Freedom, Steiner writes very briefly about the theme of human sexuality. The context there indicates that this aspect of human nature is viewed by him as an expression of un-freedom.

It is known in anthroposophical circles that someone asked Steiner why he did not give lectures on this theme, and he answered earnestly and simply that, "he would not give a lecture on such a lowly topic". On another occasion when he was asked the same question he replied that, he could not do this unless the audience were objective about this theme. [94] And in effect he was saying that the people who are objective on this subject are those who have overcome this impulse. [95]

The Spirit-human
Lastly, the third aspect of our spiritual potential called the '**Spirit-human**' can develop, but for most people this will only become tangible after many lifetimes of spiritual development. The term 'Spirit-human' in anthroposophical literature replaces the Hindu term, Atma, used by the Theosophical Society. As Steiner explains, this third aspect is derived from the spiritual forces which are hidden within the design and dynamics of our physical body. These forces exist in Devachan. This is a far-off lofty goal, which brings a kind of communion with the Father-God to the human being, who achieves it.

---

[92] GA 54, lecture 15th Feb. 1906, p. 289.
[93] GA 94 'Cosmogony', p. 91. (German edition)

[94] The dialogue occurred in 1907, the enquirer was Alfred Meebold from Heidenheim, as reported in his unpublished manuscript, „Erinnerungen an einen Geistesriesen." p. 80.
[95] He also commented in terms of linguistics, of word-formation, that the expression, 'love-making' is inaccurate. He means only the gods can do this, can make {the capacity for} love (agape) in the human soul. Whereas human beings can make or arouse a state of desire and yearning.

It is something which we can scarcely understand in today's world. In so far as we attempt to develop an active good-will towards others, and the ability to be in the moment with an intuitive moral alertness, then the Spirit-human is being slowly developed. So we can now look at the "sevenfold human being" again:

Spirit-human   (access to divine forces underlying the physical body)

Life-spirit   (access to the divine energies from which the life-
            force derives)

Spirit-self   (the result of the purified and enlightened threefold soul-body)

the Self or I

Soul (or aura)   (sentient-soul, intellectual-soul & spiritual-soul)

Life-force organism   (the ether-body)

Physical flesh body

See the diagram "The Sevenfold Human Being" again, which shows how the threefold spiritual aspects of the human being emerge as the threefold 'bodies' (physical, etheric and astral) are transformed. And also Illustration 12 which depicts the interaction of the sevenfold human being in a different way.

As we noted earlier, the elements of the human being are presented in the book 'Theosophy' as consisting of the threefold bodies (physical, etheric and astral), and the threefold soul (the sentient, intellectual and spiritual souls); and also a triune spirit. It is striking that in this list the ego is not mentioned. This is because the earthly ego is in effect the result of the interaction of the three soul qualities; and the eternal ego is derived from the interaction of the three spiritual aspects. A good way to further understand this threefold spirit is found in a fairy tale gathered by the Grimm brothers in Germany, called Allerleirauh or The Coat Of Many Skins. Many of these fairy tales have their origin in esoteric wisdom from medieval Rosicrucian thinkers.[96]

In this fairy tale the storyline is that of a feminine figure, which represents the soul, struggling to marry a prince, a masculine figure, representing the ego. She has to create three distinct dresses in the process, before encountering the prince. Firstly a golden dress which represents the Spiritual-self with its golden wisdom. Secondly a silver dress which represents the Life-spirit; silver symbolises ether forces and these are linked to the Moon. And thirdly a starry deep blue dress; this represents the Spirit-human.

The starry quality represents the zodiacal forces underlying the structure and subtle energies supporting the physical body. As a further help to understand these wonderful

---

[96] Note however that some of them are not of a high standard, and many are not suitable for children. It appears that some were created as a teaching aid concerning esoteric truths for adults, not children.

teachings, here is a note from a lecture by Rudolf Steiner on how these spiritual qualities can be subtly present in the two sexes, to the extent that they may have begun to develop in some people.[97]

in women	in men
Spirit-self : in speech	in features of the countenance
Life-spirit: in hand gestures	in the voice (speech organs)
Spirit-human: body refined over-all	hand gestures

Now again, what about the Ego ?
The personal pronoun "I" is an important word to Rudolf Steiner. He taught that the 'I' as the essential being of a person remains entirely invisible even to the seer and this 'I' is the human being itself. What does he mean by this? He points out that every person can call a table 'a table', or a chair 'a chair'; with the designation 'I', with this personal pronoun, this is not the case. No person can use this word to designate another person; each person only can call him or herself 'I'. Never could we hear the name "I" being used towards ourself by another person.

Through the fact that the human being designates itself as 'I', the person must be giving a name to themselves, from within their own self (or their inner self-awareness). Hence in anthroposophy, the personal pronoun 'I' is understood to be a name for the sense of self, which arises from within a sense of self. However, Rudolf Steiner emphasizes that the 'I' is not limited to the everyday personality; it has a deeper part to it.

The not-self or Anatta doctrine of Buddhism
It is said in Buddhism that the ego is an illusion, and the meditant seeking enlightenment should overcome the ego, should dismiss it, and seek an ego-less state. It is believed that only then is it possible for a person to enter into Nirvana. And once in Nirvana, one has escaped the so-called wheel of rebirth. (We shall see how Rudolf Steiner understands Nirvana in Chapter Nine.) This belief is derived from the conviction that the personal earthly ego is simply the impersonal karmic momentum of those energies which were active in the previous life's persona; this is the Anatta doctrine.

So the Self or ego as normally understood is only an illusory sense of self, derived from past lives on the Earth. But this doctrine is not actually stated anywhere by Buddha. It has been formulated by Buddhists who strive to develop a psychology based on his words, and who believe that they see the germinal beginnings of this doctrine in the Dhammapada (the authenticated words of the great Buddha).\

---

[97] GA 54, lecture, 15th Feb 1906, p. 292.

The initiate in the esoteric Christian stream considers this doctrine to be incorrect. The "I" which all human beings have cannot be dismissed as only an illusion. Certainly Rudolf Steiner affirms that there is much in the usual everyday self which is of no depth, having no roots in any eternal state of being. This includes trivial ideas, sensual wishes, self-centred intentions and so on. In anthroposophy another aspect of the ego is seen reflected in the word "I", quite apart from the somewhat illusory everyday aspect. This is a core spiritual element that transcends the personality. See Illustration Eleven, which shows the contrast between the Anatta non-self idea and the anthroposophical view of the dualistic ego.

Rudolf Steiner emphasizes that there is another aspect to the ego, an aspect which also implies the presence, or at least indirect influence of, a transcendent spiritual element in human consciousness, this is the Eternal-self. But what is this? It is the germinal beginnings of the threefold spiritual aspects of our being, which we have just been exploring. Rudolf Steiner regarded the ego as dualistic, comprising the conscious everyday sense of selfhood; he emphasizes that it can be influenced continuously by the germinal eternal ego. And very importantly the nature of our personality (our everyday self) is deeply connected to our Individuality, using this word to mean our eternal spiritual nature, or higher ego.

Now we can ask, what is this eternal self or higher ego, also referred to as the eternal ego? It is our still developing Spirit-self and our developing Life-spirit, and also, our germinal Spirit-human (Atma). But what is this triune higher self, from the viewpoint of the hierarchies and the cosmos? It is a divine spiritual reality originating in high realms <u>beyond</u> Devachan; and it derives from the triune Godhead. (Devachan refers to the realm into the human spirit goes after death, once it has journeyed across the lesser realm, known as the Soul World.

In Chapter Nine these realms are explained). Our higher, spiritual self was brought into being through an interaction between the Logos (referred to in St. John's gospel) and the Holy Spirit, or the third of the sublime triune Godhead. These two powers interacted in mid-Lemurian times, in the 7th sphere of Devachan, and brought forth this threefold human spirit.[98] However, our eternal self as a potential, was already in existence long before then; but the 'meeting' of the two divine powers transformed this entity into an active or more tangible reality.

We mentioned earlier that the use of the term 'Christian name' for the personal name came from a vague recognition of a deeply esoteric matter. What is this esoteric secret? Rudolf Steiner taught that it was the intention of the gods, and this includes the cosmic Christ, that the people in the Greco-Latin world, and on into European civilisation, should pioneer the development of this earthly ego-sense.

It is a process that the cosmic Christ wished to nurture, the reason for this being that without such a sense of self, the higher self or higher sense of self, of ego, cannot be born. Hence the teachings and deeds of Christ were designed to be in harmony with the sense of personal ego-hood, and this includes the purpose behind the Golgotha events.

---

[98] From an archive document, a question and answer session in Sept. 1908, unpublished.

The cosmic Christ anchored that spiritual energy into the Earth's aura which would enable the higher ego to develop, from out of the earthly ego-sense.

The higher ego and Christ
The Greek text of the gospel does affirm Steiner's view that these documents teach a cosmopolitan spirituality, in a veiled way for those with the 'ears to hear', centred on a cosmic being from whom the human spirit derives. For example in a well-known passage in the gospel of St. John, Jesus tells his disciple Thomas, "I am the way, the truth and the life. No-one comes to the Father God except through me".[99] However this passage includes an unusual Greek phrase, 'ego eimi',[100] which in everyday ancient Greek could mean 'It is me', or 'I am the one'.

But this phrase also had a sacred usage; it was used for the name of God, and then it could be said to mean "the I, I am." In other words, "I am the "I". One only has to recall the biblical passage where God told Moses, in a statement that has awed and puzzled scholars ever since, that His name is "I am that I am". As Rudolf Steiner points out, this emphasizes the ego or sense of 'I', which is intriguing as the expression 'I' is the name we humans give to our own sense of self. Rudolf Steiner then explains that the words spoken to Moses mean, "I am *the* I am (your sense of your self)."[101]

This same sacred usage occurs in an incident in the gospel of St. John (18:6) when some soldiers are hunting for Jesus when, not God but Jesus, in confronting them says, 'ego eimi'. This actually causes them to fall over, indicating that it was not used here as an everyday emphatic statement of oneself, but used by a divine being, manifesting its nature. The soldiers would have known that this expression was used as the name of God in the Hebrew Scriptures, and in the rites of Isis and of Mithras.

In other words, here Jesus, or rather Christ, is saying that he is the "I am" (the I-sense in human beings.) Thus when the cosmic Christ through Jesus says, "I am the way, the truth and the life", he is saying in effect, "The sense of 'I' which has I myself (Christ) within it, is the way, the truth and the life."

To the anthroposophical meditant this suggests that the self or ego of any person (of any religion) which is spiritualizing itself, also has spiritual forces in it from this cosmic being. So the self or ego which has spirituality has the divine spark awakened in it; and it receives that quality from Christ. Such an ego is actually the Way, the Truth and the Life, because within this person the threefold spirit is developing. This ego therefore has the Way, or the spiritualized will or Atma (the Spirit-human); and it has the Truth, or the spiritualized intelligence or Manas (the Spirit-self). Thirdly, it also has the Life or the spiritualized sentiency and life-forces or Buddhi (the Life-spirit).

---

[99] John14:6 λέγει αὐτῷ [ὁ] Ἰησοῦς· ἐγώ εἰμι ἡ ὁδὸς καὶ ἡ ἀλήθεια καὶ ἡ ζωή· οὐδεὶς ἔρχεται πρὸς τὸν πατέρα εἰ μὴ δι" ἐμοῦ.

[100] In Greek ἐγώ εἰμι which is literally, "I, I am" or "the I, I am".

[101] In the Hebrew, 'asher'(אֲשֶׁר) in the Hebrew, is an ambiguous pronoun not a definite article; we don't have the space here to examine the validity of Steiner's interpretation which factors in the highly complex grammar underlying this apparently simple phrase.

Illustration Twelve: The Nine or Ten Aspects Of The Human Being

This illustration is designed as a meditative mandala to help clarify the ninefold human being and the relation of these to each other. The astral body is in red, and hence so are the three souls, as they are an integral part of the astral body. So, please note that actually the three souls, shown in pink, are within the astral body (shown on the lower rung). Below on the left is the etheric body, which has an impact on our capacity for thinking, so above it there is the intellectual-soul. And as our thinking has an impact on the etheric body and thus on the development of the Life-Spirit, it is placed above the intellectual-soul. The ego is shown as an actual tenth aspect, but it derives from the other nine aspects, the earthly soul in its body and the germinal spiritual qualities.

Below in the centre is the physical body, above it is the ego (twofold) which affects and sustains our earthly ego-sense. And above the ego is the spiritual-soul which is enabled or disabled by the qualities of the physical body, and above that the Spirit-human. On the right below is the astral body, above that the sentient-soul which is the basic strand of the emotive life, and above is the Spirit-self which arises when our emotional nature is ennobled.

The threefold spirit
Above, the three spiritual aspects are golden, though each has the colour of a lower part of our nature, to which it is connected. There is an arrow from the spiritual-soul to the Spirit-self, this indicates that as one strives towards spiritual attitudes and intuitive insights, which is in effect the spiritual-soul, then we attain the Spiritual-self (or Spirit-self). It is not attained by the logical intellect nor the personal emotions and desires. The path to the Spirit-Self, the first of the three divine strands of our higher nature is via the development of spiritual awareness and insights. Hence there is a path from the spiritual-soul to the Spirit-self.

The intellectual-soul has a green outline because there is a connection between the etheric body, shown as green, and this soul. The more lively the life-forces (etheric body) the more capable the intellect. The more deadened the etheric body becomes by de-natured foods and excessive exposure to electro-magnetic fields, lack of exposure to beautiful art, then the more earth-bound will be the thinking and general awareness. In addition to exposure to beautiful art, the Life-spirit is helped in its development by a lively spiritual thinking.

The highest of the spiritual aspects, the Spirit-human, is directly enhanced by intuitive insights in the spiritual-soul, and this in turn is affected by the state of the physical body. A subtly hardened physical body hinders the development of the spiritual awareness and insights of the spiritual-soul. It is hardened by excess protein and chemicals in the diet, but also by coarse entertainment, and also by earth-bound attitudes, and low desires etc. The ego arises from the three souls, hence the pathways linking them to the ego. But the physical body also plays a substantial role in the development of the ego-sense during infancy and childhood and in maintaining the ego in life. In the diagram the ego is both a pink circle and also a golden circle; the former refers to the earthly ego-sense and the golden circle refers to the higher ego.

101

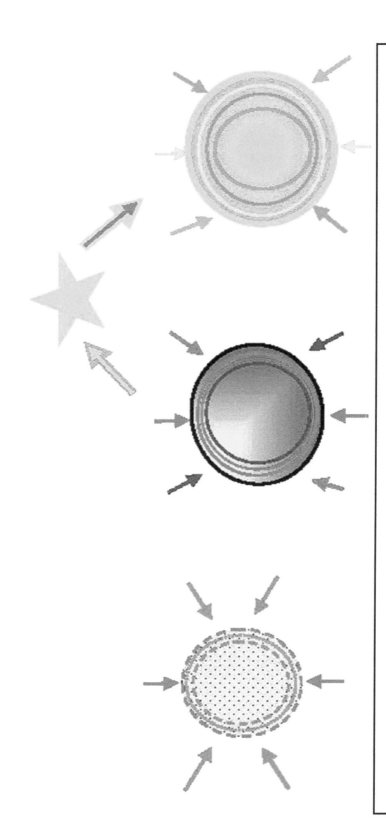

11 The ego as a twofold entity, not an illusion

Left: The Anatta doctrine: the 3 soul strands from a past life create the illusion of a centre, a real being; but the personality has none. **Middle & Right:** The complex dual ego of anthroposophy: below is the personality, above the eternal Ego. The eternal ego is both the star and active in the person (gold shades). The past life strands, via the action of the Higher Ego and divine beings, metamorphose meaningfully into the next personality. The eternal Ego constantly interacts with the personality, and thus (far right) in the personality of the next life more of the Individuality or Eternal Ego can be present (increased golden glow).

The auras of the three spirit aspects

Finally, it should also be mentioned that our three **spiritual** aspects also have auras. There are, confusingly, only two auras for our spiritual nature; these contain as it were, our threefold spiritual being. Such auras are not usually visible even to the psychic person; they are composed of spiritual energies which derive from the divine archetypal realm of the spirit, far beyond the soul realms. The lower spiritual aura contains the Spirit-self and also the Life-spirit, whilst the Spirit-human has its own aura. This latter aura is called the "Spirit-sheath" in Steiner's book *Theosophy*.

Note that there is what appears to be a printing-error in Steiner's book, *Theosophy*. The book states that "the sentient-soul extends beyond the soul-body" (or astral body or aura). But it is impossible for the sentient-soul to extend beyond the soul body as some kind of separate entity, because as part of our soul, it is totally inseparable from it. What is meant is "extends beyond the **physical** body." As Rudolf Steiner taught elsewhere, "... one cannot, when gazing with clairvoyant vision, perceive the sentient soul and the soul body as separate entities...they permeate each other and form a unity". [102]

The Path to Spirituality

A major part of Rudolf Steiner's work was to teach people the pathway to developing the three-fold spiritual potential. An ancient Greek text, attributed to Plato (ca. 350 BC) expresses the mood of a person who has successfully travelled along this path,

> "Thou gazest up to stars, my star; would that I had been created {as} heaven, that I may look at thee with {my} many eyes." [103] (trans. the author)

Rudolf Steiner described the Spirit-self as appearing as a star above the soul and it was his deep interest to offer people advice on how to bring this radiant, germinal part of our being into fuller life. During his two decades of publicly teaching his spiritual worldview, Rudolf Steiner also conducted private classes for selected students on spiritual development. He gave about 220 lessons in meditation and associated issues, such as the first clairvoyant experiences, the nature of the Lower Self, etc. He also published a small book in 1904 entitled, *Knowledge of Higher worlds; How is it Attained*.

This book was compiled from a series of articles for Theosophists which he had published in a Theosophical journal shortly before. It is essential reading for information about how Rudolf Steiner presents the path to spiritual development. [104] The introduction in my book, *The Way to the Sacred*, is useful to note here,

---

[102] GA 53, „Die menschliche Wesenheit", 13th Oct 1904, ps. 56 & 58.

[103] Plato's Greek: ἀστέρας εἰσαθρεῖς ἀστὴρ ἐμὸς · εἴθε γενοίμην οὐρανὸς ὡς πολλοῖς ὄμμασω εἰς σὲ βλέπω.

[104] *The Way to the Sacred*, is designed to be a companion volume to this book, it draws extensively on private lessons by Rudolf Steiner about the practical and esoteric aspects of meditating.

"Within the heart of every seeker for the spirit lives the inspiring knowledge that the very advanced meditant achieves a Spiritual Enlightenment, unbroken by the journey beyond death – so childlike in its awe before the good and beautiful, saintly in its purity, familiar with both earnestness and joy, pulsing with selfless love – yet always seeking to help and refine our limited earthly reality. The question that arises for every person who glimpses the spirituality of a truly great person is: How can I so live that this kind of consciousness gradually blossoms within me, replacing my ordinary self? How did the earlier students of the path to initiation transform this illusory, unfree, even potentially ignoble self into a spiritualized higher self?"

The word 'meditation' is widely used today for many different mind exercises. Rudolf Steiner's advice for the meditative path is designed to assist the serious student to walk the path of self-initiation. So what kind of path is this? It is a path in which meditation is undertaken, after preliminary spiritual study, designed to awaken higher consciousness abilities in the person. Meditation of this kind is different from older oriental techniques, which seek to help the acolyte escape the ego or sense of self. The path given by Rudolf Steiner does not seek to dissolve the normal ego-sense but to ennoble this into awareness of spiritual realms.

Here the twofold ego is clearly held in mind, and hence in the meditative practice taught by Rudolf Steiner, the personal self is to always be present, so that it can monitor and cognize what is being experienced, as the higher self starts to draw near to the person. Certainly the everyday self becomes gradually transformed, but never is the soul left without a conscious monitoring ego-sense. When earnestly followed with real enthusiasm and commitment, meditation can gradually enable the meditant to transcend the personal ego and achieve an eternal consciousness, the kind of consciousness that occurs in the higher spiritual realms. The Luciferic tendency to flee the Earth and enjoy personal bliss is not the goal of this path. The spiritual path that arises for the student of anthroposophy consists in the first instance of a study program, as Rudolf Steiner wrote in his booklet, "A Way to Self-Knowledge",

"Higher consciousness with its 'clairvoyant' perception begins with a thinking in which the soul has been inwardly illumined and has been mastered by its own will. From this kind of self-disciplined thinking the soul develops the clairvoyant perceiving referred to here. Such thinking is a prototype for higher vision."

The reason for this has to do with the need for the meditant to develop the ability to grasp spiritual truths conceptually. The books to read are primarily from Rudolf Steiner since he presented high spiritual truths in conceptual form, not as emotive or fascinating but unclear impressions. His books, whether those written by him or the notes of his lecture cycles, present the nature of the spiritual realities in clear, logical form. A study of the 'laws' and dynamics of the spiritual realm is vital, for in doing this we are not just intellectually learning about higher realms, we are also acquiring the ability to attune our thinking and our ego-sense to spiritual reality. Hence it is essential that the student strive through such preliminary study to develop the ability to understand higher spiritual realities intellectually. That is, to first approach the spirit in the form of ideas that can be grasped by the logical mind. Then when meditation brings about transcendent experiences, the ego – which is so strongly present in the logical processes – will be able to integrate the new perceptions.

It is also the case that if fascinating 'spiritual travel stories' are provided, the students' emotional energies are captured and then a subtly self-centred yearning can arise in the student for a blissful experience. Rudolf Steiner wanted people to be able to comprehend clearly in inner freedom the structure and dynamics of the higher worlds. Only after having attained some comprehension of this, can one feel in freedom how inspiring and significant these spiritual truths are. In this way, the student does not become directly emotionally excited by exposure to sensational statements and from that mood become committed, without really intending to, to an idea or organisation. As I wrote in The Way to the Sacred,

"The self will be able to maintain itself, to retain its inner integrity. In addition, if we have learnt to maintain our alertness in the process of conceptually grasping spiritual truth, we will be able to maintain our ego-hood, our sense of self-hood when actually experiencing higher realities. If you nearly fall asleep when trying to study the teachings about higher worlds, then how will you have the inner power to assimilate and assess higher experiences?"

See Chapter Sixteen for a guide to the basic books of Rudolf Steiner. In Rudolf Steiner's teachings on the inner path, there is also a second aspect to the preparatory stage. This involves something quite different, namely our emotions, moods and attitudes. I refer to this as the Path of the Four Moods. Again from my book on meditation;

"It is essential to realize that one reason for meditation not being successful is that the underlying attitude which one brings to this activity may not be appropriate. In other words, the attitude or mood prevailing in the soul of the meditant needs to be attuned to the spiritual realms. After all, a spiritual experience is the result of some aspect of the spiritual realms becoming perceptible to the soul. However it won't be perceived if the person's background mood is not attuned to the divine qualities of such realms, where love, beauty and goodness are interweaving continually like three 'substances'."

The soul moods in question are; awe, wonder, reverence and devotion. In addition Rudolf Steiner gave a series of soul exercises for developing a higher tranquillity, perseverance and general self-control which enables the student to successfully undertake meditation. These are described in the book, Knowledge of Higher Worlds.

The three clairvoyant states
It is a particularly valuable aspect of anthroposophy that one can learn of the three specific stages of higher clairvoyant consciousness which meditating can cause. In

earlier chapters we learnt about the triune spiritual potential that each human being has. These were the Spirit-self, the Life-spirit and the Spirit-human. But now we need to be clear that each of these as they are developed also create a state of consciousness, and these are clairvoyant states. The first stage of higher awareness brings about a **psychic-image consciousness** in which, as the term implies, you begin to have some images appear that are psychically received, they are not mental images from our memory or normal mental activity. The meditant is perceiving images which derive from spiritual realms.

The next stage, when more advanced meditating is achieved, leads to **cosmic-spiritual consciousness**. This faculty opens perception to the true spirit realm; referred to as the Devachanic realms, or the Realm of Archetypal Ideas, to use a phrase from Plato; see Chapter Nine. It is in this realm where our spirit, our divine essence has its existence. Hence when we can consciously experience elements of this realm, we are breathing in real, living wisdom. For the meditant striving towards the spiritual world, who has achieved to some extent **cosmic-spiritual consciousness** it is as if one does not only see in this realm, but rather, that one also **breathes in** the spiritual wisdom, so to speak. During perception of spiritual realities through this second faculty, musical notes are also inwardly heard, as if sounding forth from everything in the Spirit realm.

The third stage of higher awareness is very advanced; it can be called **high initiation consciousness**. With this third faculty, one **enters into** the spirit of the being or object being viewed. One looks into the very core of what one observes, becoming one with it. And then, from within it the meditant gazes outwards into the world, almost as if one has become that being. It is through this deepest perceiving that the highest level of wisdom is attained; however the initiate does not become one with the being in the sense of losing one's own integrity or independence.

The three names given here for these states of higher cognizing are what this author uses. In Rudolf Steiner's teachings they are given Latin names. This works well in the German world, where they are foreign terms; so they can easily have the specialized meaning that Steiner gives to them. These terms are Imagination, Inspiration and Intuition. But in English anthroposophical texts, these terms can cause misunderstanding, because in English these words each have a specific meaning – which is not the meaning that Rudolf Steiner gives them.

Often English and non-English students (e.g., from Asia) are bewildered at the use of 'Imagination' used in Steiner seminars or books. Because they encounter it as a term there for a spiritual perceiving, but to them this word just means 'fantasy', because that is precisely what this word means in the English world.

Another point with regard to correctly understanding the teachings of Rudolf Steiner in this area concerns the word 'thinking'. It is important to note that Rudolf Steiner used the word 'thinking' very often, but as he was not 'an intellectual', he was not focussed on clever philosophical ideas. Various anthroposophical books show a misunderstanding of this point. Steiner applied this word 'thinking' to the above three

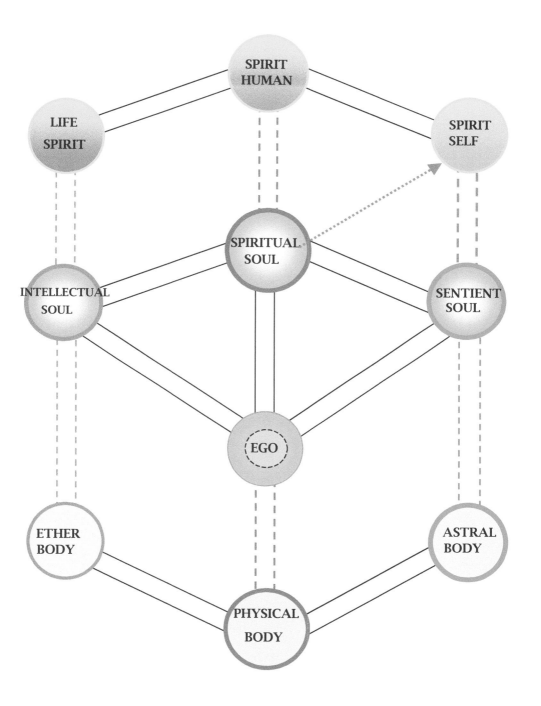

12 The Ten Aspects of The Human Being and Their Interrelatedness

© A. Anderson

clairvoyant states, not only to logical intellectual thoughts! So when you read the term 'thinking' in his works, remember that he could well be referring to any of the three clairvoyant initiatory states of mind. One good example of this is a poetic sentence from a 1924 meditative text concerning how over the past two millennia our consciousness has been changing. It usually incorrectly reads,

> "....because you are losing the capacity for thinking in the annihilating flow of time."

To convey the actual meaning this sentence should read like this,

> "....because you are losing thinking's higher capacity in the annihilating flow of time."[105]

In this form the verse now has a meaning, for it is about the loss of the old psychic awareness, which is defined as 'thinking' by Rudolf Steiner. Whereas it is precisely the capacity for logical, brain-bound thinking which is on the increase in modern times.

Some further important points need to be considered with regard to the path to spirituality as presented by Rudolf Steiner. He points out the unpalatable truth that the human being has a Double, or a lower self. This means the soul contains various unethical qualities, namely negative desires, thinking and intentions. And unless this Double is encountered and gradually transformed, the path to higher spirituality remains blocked.

The effects of Lucifer and Ahriman which constitute this Double need to be perceived and then worked on – they are hidden, but they are potent. The more pure and childlike (not childish) are the emotions, the more empowered is spiritual thinking, and the more unselfish the will, then the more blessed shall be the results of meditating. In his book, Knowledge of Higher Worlds, Rudolf Steiner presents information about a spiritual being who acts as a kind of guardian, preventing people from gaining higher states of consciousness until they have spiritualized their soul.

However through wrong techniques (ill-advised occult practices or drugs) people can come to clairvoyance and perception of spiritual realities without striving towards higher morality. This leads to an illusory view of spiritual realities, distorted by hidden Luciferic or Ahrimanic influences. Rudolf Steiner's approach encourages a genuine effort towards sanctification of the soul, because uncleanness or lack of spiritual wisdom within, leads to delusions perceived 'without' (in visions).

Absorbing the higher ego into the personality
A second and allied feature of the anthroposophical view of spirituality is that it is the union of the cosmic Christ-impulse to the Earth that has made available the spiritual energies that become absorbed by the meditant, forming the awakening Spiritual-self. And this feature of the anthroposophical view of Christology is reflected in some

---

[105] In my planned book on the 19 verses from 1924 where this sentence comes from, it will be translated in this way.

extraordinary words of Christ, as recorded in ancient Greek, but often translated poorly. It is about the mystery of the ego or self, and how the cosmic Christ-light becomes the substance of the new ego, so to speak. Here is a usual rendering of a sentence; it has the qualities of a Zen koan, and is found in the Gospel of St. Matthew 16: 25. In the excellent NIV Bible it reads like this,

> "For those who want to save their **life** will *lose* it, but whoever loses his life, for my sake, shall **find** it."[106]

And here is how it can also be translated:

> "For whoever wills to safely preserve his soul shall nullify it (shall have it pass away), but whoever nullifies their soul for my sake, shall encounter it."

A similar teaching is recorded in St. John's Gospel, 12:25. In the usual version,

> "Those who love their life shall lose it, and those who hate their life, in this world, will keep it for eternal life."[107]   (NIV)

And this is what it is saying, more precisely translated, for the esoteric aware reader,

> "The person who is fond of his soul, nullifies it (loses it), and the person finding abhorrent his soul in this world, shall retain custody of it in aeonic existence (heaven)."

In other words, these two passages are about how the fading away of this darker aspect of the earthly ego directly enables the higher ego to come into being. This statement is not about denying life, or indulging in a disturbed self-antipathy. It is for those people who have begun to see the possibility for a wonderfully higher spiritualized soul-state, and who then can say clearly to themselves that there are elements in their personality which are not compatible with high spirituality. Such people are becoming aware of the Double or lower self; whether from immoral impulses or the superficial desires and ego-centric attitudes that ensnare the soul.

These two passages are also about the need for the spiritual student to work on transforming her or his current personality, aware of the spiritual light being available to them. This is process is made easier by contemplating such passages as those above.

The Double
Acknowledgment of the Double or lower self is crucial. Many New Age groups owe their existence to someone who has indeed gained some clairvoyant perceptions, but without firstly ennobling their core soul qualities. And then falsified visions appear, appealing to their deeply hidden spiritual conceits or personal ambitions. Lucifer and

---

[106] The Greek text is: ὃς γὰρ ἐὰν θέλῃ τὴν ψυχὴν αὐτοῦ σῶσαι ἀπολέσει αὐτήν· ὃς δ" ἂν ἀπολέσῃ τὴν ψυχὴν αὐτοῦ ἕνεκεν ἐμοῦ εὑρήσει αὐτήν.

[107] The verb used here (Miso) does not only mean hate, but also 'turning away from' or repugnance: ὁ φιλῶν τὴν ψυχὴν αὐτοῦ ἀπολλύει αὐτήν, καὶ ὁ μισῶν τὴν ψυχὴν αὐτοῦ ἐν τῷ κόσμῳ τούτῳ εἰς ζωὴν αἰώνιον φυλάξει αὐτήν.

Ahriman take hold of such situations. The lower astral qualities derive from Lucifer and Ahriman that have accreted within the astral body, and the etheric body, during previous earth lives.

Awareness of this solemn truth existed with initiates in the great Mystery Centres of antiquity. The ancient Mesopotamian and Grecian sphinx, a human-headed creature with parts of a bull, lion and eagle symbolize this situation. And research by this author into the greatest ancient Celtic site, which is in north Germany, called the Externsteine, reveals that the same stark truth was pointed out dramatically to acolytes of the Druids.

The Externsteine
On approaching the site about 3,500 years ago, one would note the stark scene of two people ensnared by a large dragon. A solitary scene, but all the more impressive for being alone on the otherwise huge bare rock wall. It appears to represent the given human condition, as seen from the stern and lofty perspective of the priesthood. This depicts the challenging attitude of the senior priests towards that person, whether man or woman, who has not yet become spiritually renewed through the processes that they offer.

The features of this site are to some extent explained in the stories handed down from the Druids; these were preserved in Iceland, in the myths of the Edda. In these texts we discover a reference to the extraordinary natural stone towers which is the Externsteine, with its carvings,

> Easy it is for those who come to Odhin
> to recognize his hall –
> an outcast* is placed   (*literally, a wolf)
> to the west of the door,
> and an eagle hovers above. [108]
>
> (Author's translation, *Grimnismal* 10)

At the Externsteine, the figure of Nidhoggr, the dragon, is to the west of the entrance to the main chamber, and an eagle shape has been carved above it.[109] Often in sacred texts, the writer uses a veiled way of saying something; a kind of second meaning is interwoven in the words. Something very intriguing occurs here in this verse from the Edda. The Druidic priests who composed these verses used a word here for 'wolf' which is different to the ordinary, everyday term in Old Icelandic for wolf (*ulfr*). It is the word, *vargr*, which derives from the term for <u>warning</u> or <u>an admonition,</u> (*vara*). So here the word means 'outcast'. And so this scene was an admonition about the lower self or Double to the acolytes who had not yet been through the spiritual processes, offered by the Druids. (For more about the Externsteine, see Chapter 12.)

---

[108] The old Icelandic text: Mjög er auðkennt, þeir er til Óðins koma salkynni at séa: vargr hangir fyr vestan dyrr ok drúpir örn yfir.
[109] The Icelandic texts and the artwork's details, indicate clearly that the interpretation of the carving as medieval Christian or as the Teutonic hero Siegfried is incorrect. The otherwise excellent book by Speckner and Stamm (Das Gehemnis der Externsteine) is in error at this point. See the book, *The Externsteine*, by D. Pryor, for a detailed exploration of this site.

Inside the Goetheanum at Dornach, Rudolf Steiner has taken up this dynamic, so graphically depicted at the Externsteine, at Lalibela in Ethiopia and found in the Divine Comedy by Dante and elsewhere. [110] What we could call the Nidhoggr theme, but metamorphosed, is found in one of the magnificent stained glass windows. This scene is in the left side of the huge red window located at the top of the stairs inside the building. As at Lalibela, it portrays a threefold lower self. This window also indicates that once the lower self has been substantially reduced, then spiritual energies begin to appear in the soul.

The theme of spiritual development, and how we need to absorb from divine sources outside our own astral body the energies that become our Spiritual-self was explained by Rudolf Steiner in an exceptional lecture, early in his lecturing work. [111] The following extracts will be helpful here. My explanatory comments are placed in brackets, and in italics.

> "For we are, in our current existence {as a personal self} only a transit-point[112], a section of a passageway; and we could and shall attain nothing, if we seek to make this current transit-point the essential thing of our existence.[113] For then nothing would occur in the world through our own being, except what we have already done. You would be an infertile fruit on the human tree of life. For everything of which you are capable has already happened, if you remain with your own normal self.

> Only once you make the personal self fertile and creative by the higher-self, which exists in the cosmos, can you bring something <u>new</u> into the world. Then from your inner being an activity occurs which does not only have the past, with its {karmic} effects, within it. Indeed the only way at all for us to have the power to bring about something really new and productively creative is to have a {special} connection with whatever occurs in the world; {this special connection is something} <u>that is actually higher than ourselves</u>. It is solely through this connection {to an inspired activity which transcends our normal abilities,} and the fully humble consciousness we have discussed earlier, that we can have this creative power {at all}……

---

[110] For more about Lalibela see the book: *Lalibela* by D.Pryor. This is the only English language book written about the esoteric meaning of this site.

[111] Self-knowledge & God-knowledge, 16th Oct. 1905 it is available on www.rudolfsteinerstudies.com, "Two Gems from Rudolf Steiner". It is otherwise unpublished.

[112] In German, „wir sind nur ein Durchgangspunkt."

[113] A closer translation here of "den Wirksamen" which I have translated as "the essential thing" is really the scholarly expression, "The efficacious (formative) reality". Further this sentence is <u>not</u> denying that a divine spiritual reality is part of every human being's nature. Rather it is saying that the spiritual 'spark' is normally outside the functioning personality; it is not integrated into and efficacious within it.

...when we detect in us that we no longer wish to say something, but now simply yearn to be a vessel {for wisdom}, and have surrendered all of our narrow, personal-self qualities, then higher individuals {or higher beings} may speak to us. But for this to occur, there is still much more that we must achieve. Above all, we need a more thorough consideration of the precept, 'It is through Self-Knowledge, knowledge of our so-called inner nature, that the Will develops for perfecting of one's own being.' This attitude also implies recognition of the fact that through our normal self we can learn nothing. For truly, through this personal-self the human being surrenders itself to the most intractable illusions.

.....

What is this true self ? Consider it more closely. Is it to be found in our external life, our daily activities? Are you this self, when you go to the meal-table? Are you it (your true "I"), when you go about your daily work? Clear self-knowledge shall say to you, 'No, this is not the case', for our activities are from the normal, natural personality and natural urges or needs.

One is carried along and impelled {not compelled} by the personality. Natural urges and natural drives, which have also fashioned the physical body, push and press-on your inner being. It is the greatest illusion when someone says, {of deeds required through earthly life} "I am eating", or "I am going for a walk" or "I am taking care of this or that business activity". For then one is not the cause of the action, but one is driven by something. .....
To the person who immerses themselves in self-knowledge {by going within} the normal soul life is not the source of Truth. Such a meditant does not find the real self within, rather one notices that in the self, one finds forces which derive from the external world.....

These exterior forces are experienced as pressing and pushing on one's inner life. Indeed even if you are very strongly interconnected with your present individuality, what are you? You are the result of your karmic development, from earlier life-times. In other words, that which we in this life, think and feel, we do so think and feel, because we were driven in an earlier life to this or that inner activity. {And this now echoes on in us}
{Now here we see Rudolf Steiner making a direct reference to the Buddhist idea of the Skhandas or astral tendencies (soul qualities) that derive from the past lifetime.}
The earlier lives have an influence throughout our current life. If you ask, with some self-knowledge, why I do this or that, you do not come in this way to your true Self, rather to the earlier causative factors in the earlier life-cycles {And which are a part of the personality, not the Individuality, however the Individuality has in conjunction with the divine beings, created this new personality. Here Rudolf Steiner seeks to emphasize that the true self, the higher-ego, or the Individuality, is outside in effect, and needs to be awakened and incorporated}

112

If you still test yourself further as to what you have acquired inwardly in this present life, you find the same thing. Take for example, the faculty of speech. Is speech your self? You speak; you believe that you yourself are speaking. But can the human being speak from out of her or his *self*? If the answer were, 'yes' then each human being would have to be able to form {entirely} new words. That is, each person would have to bring-forth speech out of her or his own self, each time they speak. But the language itself {is what} speaks, the language of the nation, that is. The entire nation speaks through the language, the entire nation is our own language-basis, and speaks to us, and through us.

{Of course, we can also say that we do speak as individuals, but Rudolf Steiner's point here is more about the great degree of immersion in a unifying, non-individuated background.}

We can push on ever further towards self-knowledge *{in the sense of our personality}*, but we will find that the Self moves ever further ahead of us.
But when *{at last}* we begin to understand *{the Indian maxim}*, 'Tat twam asi' – thou art that - we will thereby begin to see that our true-self is spread out, over or behind the external world; at this point then we will be living in Self-knowledge.
{This means: when we grasp that our threefold spirit is linked to the spiritual realms which are the origin of all the beings and things in creation.}

But to achieve this stage one must be quite clear about, and have at some time felt inwardly what it means, to be hollowed-out in the way I have indicated here, and to stand, in this way before one's own personal self. The person who has attained to this normal *{but very important, initial}* self-knowledge will experience her/his own being as if hollowed-out. If we wish to attain the goal of Self-knowledge we must first experience a desolation and darkness within our being.
Desolate, dry and hollowed-out is our state of mind, it is the result of that self-knowledge which wills to seek only in the current self.
But once we have attained to this awareness, and understand that our Higher-Self is to be found entirely in Creation {spiritually}, then we have developed sufficiently to meet the first step on the path…to allow the teachings of the initiates *{as instruments of divine beings}* to speak to us, for they are the Keepers of the Seal of our Higher-Self. [114] They may then speak to us, once we no longer want our Higher-Self to be us, as we now are." *{When we no longer want to identify our Higher-Self with our current personality.}*

So in this lecture extract, various points are being made, including a rejection of the idea of literally "being in the spirit right now, just as you are, right now, just be in it !" This is in effect describing a Luciferic illusion, that is, a subtly indulgent illusion. It so

---

[114] This remarkable expression, in German, „die Siegelbewahrer unseres höheren Selbstes" has an echo of the initiation wisdom from the Hellenistic Mysteries, and is a meditation in itself. It appears to mean that the Initiates and the divine beings are in effect those who hold the key which opens up our access to our own Higher Self.

comfortably allows the entire journey of engaging with the lower self, and of studying to acquire real understanding of the spiritual in our minds, to be avoided.

Steiner's words here are not at all opposing the correct decision to be in the moment with courage and initiative and trying to sense the spiritual significance of a special moment. It is about deceiving oneself that by having this wish, one can be highly evolved and profoundly attuned to high spiritual realities. This is a real stumbling block to the seeker; Rudolf Steiner once referred to the quest for spirituality by the medieval Beghards or Beguines as an example of such a Luciferic striving. When such people reincarnate, it is possible that they would be drawn to modern versions of the same tendency.

Further Reading
As for Chapter Two plus,
Rudolf Steiner: Knowledge of Higher Worlds, how is it attained?
                The Stages of Higher Knowledge
                The Threshold of the Spiritual World
                 A Way of Self-knowledge

Adrian Anderson: The Way to the Sacred

7: THE FOUR ETHERS & THE LIVING EARTH

When we talk of the Earth as alive, or of anything as 'living', we are really pointing to the existence of the etheric realm; to etheric energies which sustain life. The human etheric body as we briefly noted earlier is an invisible energy organism which maintains the life of the physical body, as well as enabling healing and reproductive powers. And we noted too, that Rudolf Steiner taught that it is also the mediator of all sensory impressions to the soul, and it is involved in thinking processes, too. The subtle role of the ethers and of our etheric body is especially emphasized in anthroposophy. The primary reason in the Steiner schools for the delay in teaching children to read and write is connected to the pivotal role of the etheric body in the child's life. (See chapter 13.)

The life processes in plants, which differentiate plants from minerals are due to the efficacy of this invisible life force, the plant's own etheric body. In anthroposophy, the chemical processes that science identifies as sustaining the plant, or our human body, are themselves viewed as responding to the influence of etheric energies. In anthroposophical knowledge, the etheric body is a life-force organism, efficacious within the biochemistry of any living body. The DNA, or genetic substances which are now regarded as causing the multitude of life-processes in any living thing, are themselves in turn responding to etheric energies.

The role of the ether body in perception
Rudolf Steiner taught that the etheric body is a real, independent entity which calls forth physical substance into being. The ether body is an organism which preserves the physical-body from dissolution every moment during life. But the existence of this etheric energy field is even more directly crucial to our existence. You may be aware of the philosophical idea (presented in the area of philosophy called 'epistemology') that we can never be sure that we are ever seeing or hearing or smelling or touching anything.

The argument is that when scientists research what happens when we see something, the image that our eye sees goes inside our eye and it then becomes chemical and nerve processes which occur along the optic nerve and then on into our brain. And all of this seems to indicate that we can never really see anything. Rudolf Steiner taught that this discovery by science is of huge significance, if rightly interpreted. Because it tells us that some other process must be enabling us to experience the external world via our senses. For we do indeed perceive our environment; the ether body absorbs the sense impressions images, detected by the sense organs in the ambient environment, and conducts these further into the brain. (For more about this, see Chapter 13). The sense image does not change into chemical and nerve processes, it just brings these about in the physical body, but is itself carried along by the etheric body.

We shall see later that our etheric body is a tiny replica of the Earth's own vast etheric field. The etheric body also is the medium for our inner perceiving, not just our outer, sensory perceiving. In other words when a human being becomes aware of the presence of a thought, an idea, a memory, then it is the etheric body that is bearing these to the soul. It is the function of the life-force organism, the ether body, to mediate these as well as sensory objects, to consciousness.

Very significantly, hallucinations and clairvoyant or visionary imagery are also imprinted into the etheric body, and only then seen by the soul. Whether a human being registers the presence of a sensory stimulus or an element of their soul life, or a spiritual being, these are experienced via the intermediary function of the ether body. So the ether body registers an intuitive idea, a flowering bush, a flash of anger or a non-physical (spirit) entity.

Therefore, quite definitely hallucinatory images (sounds, odours) may be considered as objectively perceived, whether induced by schizophrenia, drug addiction or psychic exercises. Certainly these are deceptive products of an unwell mind. But they exist as images in the aura, or outside the aura in the soul world; and the ether body brings these images to consciousness. An hallucination is a real image manifesting unhealthily in the network of energies which constitutes the life-force body, and there it is cognised by the soul. (However, a disembodied soul sees spiritual realities directly, without the need of their etheric body.)

Four kinds of ether energies
Rudolf Steiner taught that there are actually four kinds of etheric energies, and these produce four states of matter. (A related worldview of various etheric energies is also found in some texts from India, used in Theosophical literature.)[115] There is an etheric energy that brings warmth and flames into existence, called the **warmth ether** A chilli tree or a fire is produced by the action of the warmth-ether.

Gaseous material and physical light is produced by the **light-ether**; the jagged-edged plants such as the maple have a strong light-ether influence. The fascinating glow-beetles have a strong concentration of light-ether in their abdomen, which enables them to glow brightly in the summertime, when the sun's in-streaming ether is at its strongest. (The sulphurous and phosphorous compounds in the abdomen which chemically produce the light are the products of the light-ether.)

Moist plants and mists and rain are produced by the **water-ether**. The water-ether is also known as the tone-ether or chemical-ether. And dense solid states of matter are produced by the **life-ether**, which also produces the denser, more compact plant types, especially the pine trees with their hard needles instead of leaves. So the states of fire, air, water and earth are the results of these four ether types.

Before we look further at the effect of the ethers, we need to note a few points about our familiar energy, electro-magnetism. We can ask ourselves, what are these energies? Rudolf Steiner taught that electricity and magnetism are actually coarser forms of energy; in fact an unpleasant, decayed by-product of the ethers. The decayed form of the light-ether is electricity, and magnetism the decayed result of the water-ether. So these electro-magnetic energies are closely related to the ethers. To try to discern how these energies sustain our planet and ourselves is an important task for modern

---

[115]Rama Prasad, Nature's Finer Forces, T.S. publications 1894, Adyar.

humanity. Until the ethers are actually seen, one has to be content with discerning their influence in agriculture, and in health and illness. One way to live into the feeling for the etheric energies is through bio-dynamic farming and gardening, which is based on the importance of the ethers for the growth and health of crops. Another approach to these subtle energies is through a more holistic approach to healing and medicine. In anthroposophical medicine the interaction of the physical body, the etheric body and the soul is pivotal to understanding wellness and ill-health.

But we can also try to become aware of their role in the actual life of our planet; this is both a fascinating experience and a powerful way to begin to develop a sensitivity to the influence of this all-encompassing energy field with its four aspects.[116] In this chapter I shall amplify some indications from Rudolf Steiner about some ways in which the presence and activity of the four ethers in the Earth's bio-sphere can be approached.

The ethers can exert a tangible effect upon the more tenuous subtle aspects of the material world. In particular, in the air with various light phenomena, and in ionized gases (these latter are substances whose molecules and atoms are fragmented and also almost in an energy form, rather than in solid matter). Another example of the way in which the effect of the ether can be indirectly seen, is in the strange shapes formed in a fine powder spread on a drum, when a musical note is sounded. These shapes are called the Chladni figures. The science of acoustics can present mathematical formulae which reveal that these figures arise from the intersecting of sound waves produced in music.

But as so often with the scientific approach to unusual phenomena of this kind, the assessment does not answer the deeper aspects; namely, the reason for the figures. This is only an explanation of how the motion of sound-waves must result in certain shapes, which still leaves unanswered just why the motion of sound waves has the impetus within itself to manifest in such geometrical ways. Rudolf Steiner taught that the water ether or tone-ether creates the shapes of physical objects, and that dynamics present in that ether, (impressed into it from the planets or zodiac) become manifest in the form of objects. Because these dynamics, placed in the ether, create the impetus in the physical sound-waves towards geometrical motion when music is played.

So, although the ethers are invisible to physical sight, their influence can be detected or inferred, when one contemplates many phenomena in the natural world with a sensitive, awakened consciousness. One could call this a kind of Goethean awareness, which indirectly senses the influence of the ether in its effect upon living things. In anthroposophy, the ethers are understood to be vital to our existence, actively sustaining all life, and our sensory processes, and also have a huge role in maintaining our health.

---

[116] But once the meditative life brings perception into the ethers, then they can be seen, even if not clearly distinguished as four separate energies, raying out from trees, and around people, beautifully around the sun and in a milder way around the moon. And on floors, there are etheric after-images of footsteps to be seen in the carpet or wood, etc. But above, they are seen in the atmosphere, darting constantly through the air.

We have noted how in seeing (or hearing, etc) objects, the object becomes as it were, a quantity of chemicals and also electrical nerve signals inside the brain; and yet we do see or hear the actual object. We noted that this is because the etheric body actually carries the image, or sound, etc to us. Scientific observation, not limited only to analysis but extended to a contemplative insightfulness, can start to give an observer the impression of an etheric energy behind sensory images. But as we mentioned above, tenuous physical things, namely the air or clouds or the glow of ionized gases (the northern lights, St. Elmo's fire, a flame), can indirectly reveal the influence of an etheric energy. An ionized gas is understood to be similar to a plasma state; plasma is a very tenuous state of matter, wherein molecules of a gas have become partially disintegrated (or ionized), so they exist more as energy than as solid matter.

In anthroposophical understanding, such tenuous, glowing energy fields are nearer to the ether than to solid matter. It is where such tenuous strange light phenomena occur that the influence of the ethers is less obscured by material substances. A related example is that of clouds which in some parts of the world, often have strange shapes, like primordial creatures. Rudolf Steiner affirmed that where this occurs the clouds, being themselves formed out of the water-ether, are reflecting the etheric forms of long-extinct animals.

The ether layers in the atmosphere

Rudolf Steiner taught that these four types of ethers encircle the Earth's atmosphere at some height, in four distinct bands or layers, and direct their influence down here in the air layer, see the accompanying diagram. In 1920 Rudolf Steiner described the Earth's ether body as having a structure formed of five layers, reflecting the four ethers. He indicated the existence of at the top of the Earth's ether body, of a second warmth layer; a kind of cosmic warmth layer. His statements appear to be confirmed by upper atmosphere research undertaken in the second half of the 20th century. In Rudolf Steiner's sketch, there is firstly a layer of warmth-ether above the air, and then a layer of light-ether, then a layer of water- or chemical-ether, then higher up, a layer of life-ether. And above that a layer of warmth he termed a cosmic-warmth-layer.

Through a study of recent scientific research papers by this author about the structure and nature of the atmosphere (Aeronomy), it has been possible to correlate Rudolf Steiner's indications regarding these ether bands to the discoveries about the very strange phenomena occurring in atmospheric layers. In-depth scientific research into the upper reaches of the atmosphere has really only been possible since the 1960's because of the difficulty of obtaining data from this region.

It has become clear in recent decades that the continuation of life on this planet depends on the thin skin of the air layer (the troposphere) that encompasses the earth, a layer of life-giving gases only about 15 kilometres high. And since the middle of the century, it has been known that above this air layer are further areas of the atmosphere which occur in distinct bands or layers, and these are also vital for earthly life. Let's first just clarify these four ethers again; the warmth-ether is responsible for reproduction, hence seeds (in plants and mammals) and also plant oils are derived from this energy, and this ether also exists 'behind' flames and glowing heat.

The light-ether is related to gaseous material and supports the production of light. The water-ether (also known as chemical-ether or tone-ether) brings about the liquid state of being, is particularly present in water, is affected by the moon's cycles, and brings about sounds or tones. (Hence water is a better conductor of sound than air.) The life-ether is the most subtle, the most tenuous, of the four ethers, and is present 'behind' oxygen; it literally sustains life. It streams into the human being via the solar plexus, renewing our etheric body.[117]

The warmth-ether layer

We can now review and update the research provided in my earlier book, Living a Spiritual Year, about this subject. We find that the higher one ascends in the air layer, the colder the temperature becomes; and the gases are sparser, more dilute. At the upper boundary of the air layer (at an altitude of 15 kilometres), the temperature falls to about minus 55 degrees Centigrade. But above this altitude, the atmosphere is chemically different; it is simpler. Above the air layer we enter the stratosphere, and an interesting phenomenon occurs: the temperature starts to rise and continues rising up to an altitude of 50 kilometres. At the top of this band of warmth, the temperature reaches approximately 18 degrees Centigrade in summer.

Demarcated by its warmth, this is quite a separate layer from the air layer below; there is very little interaction between the two layers. The increased temperature is understood to be due to the way that ozone (which exists here) absorbs certain energy waves from the sun which cause warmth in the ozone. Scientifically it is understood that in higher layers, there is simply not enough oxygen around to create ozone, and quickly unite with the sunlight. But still the question arises, why only here is this possible. Why are there not enough (incomplete) oxygen molecules present in higher layers, since other gases or water vapour are certainly carried up to great heights.

In view of Rudolf Steiner's description of the bands of ether, it appears that the warmth feature of this atmospheric band, extending from 15 to 50 kilometres above the ground, is caused by the warmth-ether in this layer. For above this band, the temperature once again falls, and other intriguing phenomena occur. There is another phenomenon that occurs here, perhaps indicating the influence of the warmth-ether. Inside this layer there occurs a mysterious light phenomenon, called the mother-of-pearl clouds, or nacreous clouds. But they are not clouds at all, as we understand this word.

Nacreous 'clouds' are formed from extremely tiny ice particles about 10 microns[118] across, forming between 15 and 30 kilometres up. Seen shortly after sunset or after sunrise, they are caused by water vapour in this layer being forced up from the

---

[117] GA 93A, p.18.
[118] A micron is 0.001 millimetre in diameter, a human hair is about 75 microns thick.

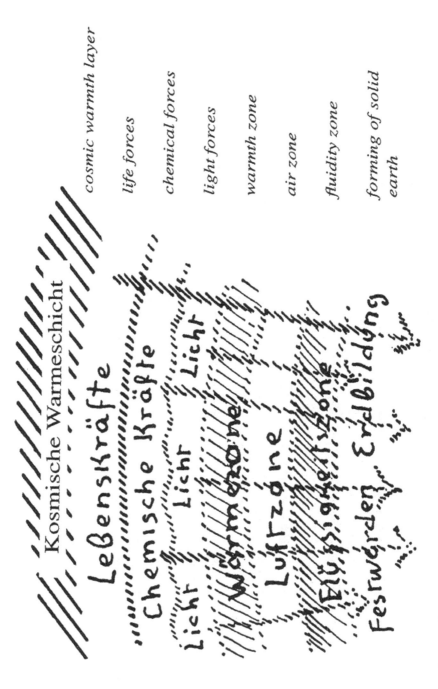

cosmic warmth layer

life forces

chemical forces

light forces

warmth zone

air zone

fluidity zone

forming of solid
earth

Diagram by Rudolf Steiner : indicating the existence of the ether layers in the atmosphere

120

troposphere, when winds encounter mountains. But the warm, burnished colours are striking, and difficult to explain physically. Their iridescent colours are presumably due to the light being refracted through different sized particles, but why they have mainly warm orange-red colours is intriguing. They are also far more brilliant than true clouds, slowly curling and uncurling, see Illustration Thirteen. From the above scientific data, we can ask, are these burnished clouds an indicator of the warmth-ether forces? (Chemical pollutants can also appear as very thin clouds in this area.)

The light-ether layer

Beyond 50kms height another specific band of the atmosphere exists, called the mesosphere, it extends from 50kms to about 100kms up above the Earth. In this band we encounter some interesting features; it is very cold, the warmth of the layer below retreats and the temperature sinks far below freezing, to about minus 150° C, at its coldest. Now this band correlates to the light-ether layer in Rudolf Steiner's research. So what are the physical and chemical features of this band?

There are several strange and brilliantly radiant phenomena here, with qualities that indicate a potent etheric force. Firstly the so-called shooting stars occur here and only here. And these are extraordinary, for the shooting star's brilliant trail of light usually occurs between 70 and 100 kilometres above the ground, and will be seen by observers up to 500 kilometres apart, see Illustration 14, for the over-all view. This area corresponds to the light-ether layer and so one can ask, is the brilliant light we see due only to basic physical forces? For the material object that causes this visual phenomenon is about the size of the head of tiny pin ! And has a weight of about one hundredth of a gram or at the most, in some cases, just one gram.

Furthermore, mathematical calculations indicate that the density of this tiny particle is about that of water ! The extraordinary radiance produced by such a tiny, semi-soft object is explained by science as the result of the speed with which it enters the atmosphere, about 45 kilometres per second, many times faster than a bullet. But the question arises whether the radiance of the shooting star might be enhanced by an ether force.

Meteors

This possibility gains credence when we consider that no solid rock has ever been produced by a shower of meteors. For these meteors are not solid objects, they never fall to the ground (it is the meteorites which do this, never a meteor). The meteor or shooting star is more energy (etheric energy) than matter. Is the light-ether here enhancing the radiance; would you see a firecracker rocket even weighing five kilograms, from 500 kilometres away? Since light intensity fades with the {inverse square of the} distance from the light source, it is raises the question whether the brilliance of a tiny shooting star is enhanced by the etheric energies forming the matrix of this layer.

In addition, in this band a very strange phenomenon was discovered. Whenever there is an electrical storm down here on the Earth's surface, then for a fraction of a second, far up in the light-ether layer, a huge and bright red shining tower of energy appears, called a storm sprite. And even more amazing, above this tower of red energy, a bright circle of light appears too; this is actually called an elf-ring, see Illustration Fifteen.

This link between these strange light-forms and the lightning produced in a storm is a mystery scientifically. Even the process causing production of electricity in a cloud remains scientifically unclear.[119] We have noted that the light-ether produces electricity as it decays, so the creating of an immense electrical charge, which is decayed light-ether energies, would have an impact upon its own matrix layer, the light-ether layer. It is interesting that scientists have decided to use terms which refer to nature spirits, for these are the spirits who make active the ethers. Modern attitudes have resulted in the choice of electrical energy, the decaying phase of the light ether, to power our world. This situation appears questionable as it has a negative effect on the ethers, and in many cases, as electromagnetic radiation, it can be harmful to human health.

Noctilucent 'clouds'

But also in this layer, at the border of the next ether layer, there also occurs the fascinating and rare phenomenon of noctilucent clouds, see Illustration Sixteen. These are brightly shining fields of tenuous energy (or 'clouds' for want of a better name) that are only rarely seen after dark in the summer, at an altitude of 80-85 kms.[120] At such a height and being so tenuous, in an area where very little material substances exist, they eluded scientific definition for many decades, and despite recent research projects, still remain unknown today.

A predominant theory is that very tiny ice particles, perhaps with tiny dust particles from meteorites, enable a perceptible but very thin cloud-like structure to form. And then the sunlight reflects off them. In this theory, it is believed that ice particles are carried up there by strong, upward surges of the air in the lower atmosphere. However, alternatively, other academic experts have formulated the theory that tiny dust particles from meteorites (called meteor smoke) become these glowing 'clouds' by absorption of plasma material existing naturally up there.[121]

Remember, plasma is semi-energy, semi-material atoms of various gases, (or 'ionized gases' in technical language). This theory provides a basis for understanding how such tenuous, semi-ethereal plasma fields could easily be affected by the light ether, enhancing

---

[119] As with the semi-diurnal pressure wave and the osmotic rising of sap in springtime, so too the 'mechanics' of this process in the clouds remains unknown. Various theoretical models exist. For electricity, one model is that of cloud 'charge separation', utilizing a postulated electron collision process. Rudolf Steiner explained the electrical component of lightning as a by-product of the friction resulting from an intense heat-energy release in the air.

[120] The slight creeping up of 1% of these clouds to 88kms height, at the border between 2 regions is of no significance since these clouds straddle both layers; Megner, Khaplanov, etc. Annales Geophysicae 2009, *Large mesospheric ice particles at exceptionally high altitudes*; Megner, Khaplanov, etc.

[121] A. Mahmoudian &W. Scales, *Investigation of Dusty Space Plasmas in the Near-Earth Space Environment,* Oct. 2011 paper given at the *LPMR-10 Layered Phenomena in the Mesopause Region,* conference, USA.

13 Nacreous energy-fields : indicating the warmth-ether layer

their radiance. But there is more to these fascinating glowing 'clouds' which indicates their origin in etheric energy fields. This layer has at times so-called 'wind' speeds up to 500 kms per hour, but the mechanism that creates this motion amongst the tiny energized particles there is unknown, as there is insufficient air to form winds. Present studies suggest that this is caused by the presence here of complex electrical energies patterns.[122]

And this is a significant feature since it is here that the light-ether layer exists, which produces electricity as a by-product. It is important to look at Illustration Fourteen; it will make these descriptions easy to understand. But the noctilucent 'clouds' can move at 650 kms per hour (!), so they are energized beyond the normal background energy fields. But they also have internal crests, just like waves (see below) which can actually move backwards, against the enormous forwards speed of the 'cloud'. Do these tenuous, brilliant semi-material clouds (plasma fields) exhibit such potent features because they are a specific, localized manifestation of the etheric energies here?

Now, another fact very relevant here is that these clouds occur at the border of the light-ether layer and the water-ether layer. And in addition to this radiance, they also have a watery feature, namely the crests. For these are wave-like crests, and therefore both crests and dips exist in them, just like the ocean waves. In fact one of the earliest scientific articles about them invited readers to look at the photos supplied, turned upside down, because after 30 seconds one notices a distinct quality of three dimensional depth.[123] And another early scientific paper included special images, when observed with a 3D-viewer, this also enables one to see this three dimensional feature.[124] So again this indicates these features are due to the influence of the water-ether layer, which is the next layer !

The water-ether layer
This next band of the atmosphere as scientifically defined, corresponds to the water-ether layer in Rudolf Steiner's diagram. And this layer certainly exhibits further fascinating features that are very suggestive of the influence of the water-ether (or tone-ether). It is here that the famous Aurora, known as the Northern Lights or Southern Lights occur (although a fainter, upper part of an aurora can reach up higher). The Aurora is understood in science as a glowing energy field caused by the Earth's own magnetic field becoming energized at various times, see Illustration Seventeen.

In this magnetic field are atoms of oxygen and nitrogen which glow in this energized state. The oxygen causes the green colour, and nitrogen the violet-purple colours; and nearly all auroras are green or violet-purple. It is understood that these magnetic energies of the Earth are brought into an energized condition by impact from energized particles (plasma) streaming in from the sun. So here in this band of the atmosphere which corresponds to the water-ether layer, the beautiful magnetic energy field, called

---

[122] It is also believed that upwards moving air-surges from the air layer and from other (longitudinal) surges, encompassing the entire atmosphere, may play a role.
[123] Robert. K. Soberman, in Scientific American, Atmospheric Phenomena, 1963
[124] Georg Witt, *Height, structure and displacements of noctilucent clouds*, Institute of Meteorology, Univ. of Stockholm, 1961.

the Aurora, lights up. But we noted earlier that magnetism is the by-product of the water-ether ! The aurora then is a strong indicator of the water-ether layer existing here in this band. (There are also some red coloured auroras which occur higher up, at about 240 kms, as the Earth's magnetic field itself does extend up beyond this layer.)

 Another indicator of the influence of the water-ether in this band is that water vapour is present here, and it is otherwise only present way down in the air layer. As we noted earlier, the water-ether is considered the originating matrix of water and rain. But furthermore, we noted that the water-forming ether is also called the tone-ether, as it produces and sustains physical sounds. And it is a fact that many people, but not all, who experience an aurora also hear strange sounds coming from it. It is also true that very sophisticated listening devices, especially deployed for this purpose in scientific research, have failed to detect any sounds at all from the aurora. However, the people who hear these sounds can demonstrate that they are hearing a sound because, from inside a building, without being able to see an aurora, they can hear its sound !

This indicates that the aurora, as a manifestation of the water-ether, also has its own etheric resonance, which people who have a slight psychic capacity can hear. Many people in the remote northern latitudes, such as Scandinavia, often have this psychic tendency. Technical instruments, attuned to electromagnetic frequencies, would not detect this kind of resonance. Above this water-ether layer, which corresponds to the upper part of the Mesosphere, is the layer of the life-ether. In this area the Thermosphere band of the atmosphere begins.

And indeed here we find, on coming down to the planet from space, the first presence of oxygen (in a semi-energy or ionic state). And in anthroposophy, it is understood that the life-ether generates oxygen. So, summing up, there are many phenomena in the upper atmosphere which are indicators of the four ether energies. In Rudolf Steiner's anthroposophy, many fascinating references are made to these energies, and how they radiate down into the air layer. Here in the air which all living beings breathe, these life-forces conjure forth and sustain life on Earth. This theme is explored in detail in my book "Living a Spiritual Year".

Finally, to finish this exploration of the etheric energies that sustain the living Earth, we can note that the thermosphere continues on beyond the life-ether layer. Rudolf Steiner back in 1920 referred to a layer of the atmosphere, beyond the life-ether layer as the 'cosmic warmth-ether layer'. This is actually an appropriate designation for this area because it does have a very slightly warm quality. Scientific texts state that this layer is fiery hot, with a temperature of $1,500^{oC}$. As this author suggested in a discussion on this theme with a senior meteorologist of the New Zealand National Meteorological office in the 1980's, this statement is wrong; a fact that many experts now acknowledge.

The so-called hot temperature is only referring to the energized state of the oxygen and nitrogen ions, which exist in such extremely small numbers, as extremely tenuous tiny things.[125] But these are themselves so tiny and so few that to a human being, the area is not hot at all. It is, as Rudolf Steiner's research established a century ago, a neutral state with only a subtle warmth. There have been various responses to Rudolf Steiner's initiative in presenting the ethers as an important level of being, amongst people familiar with his work. These include attempts to develop etheric energy technology, and new therapeutic models where weakened etheric energies in patients are strengthened. And of course, new, environmentally sensitive agricultural and ecological procedures have been developed, too. We will briefly note these at the end of the book.

Here it is relevant to note that in the 1970's two science graduates at Birmingham University, D. Milner and E. Smart, with the help of their electronics engineering professor, and using the university's facilities, set out to try to scientifically detect these four ethers. They presented evidence in their book, The Loom of Creation, in which they provided persuasive evidence that they had succeeded. This book is long out-of-print. The evidence was in the form of extraordinary images, showing four various types of energetic fields.

The book met a poor response. It is understood in Steiner circles that the ethers are too subtle to be photographed, and hence the book was dismissed, unfortunately. These scientists had photographed pockets of air that were subject to an electro-magnetic pulse. So it can be argued that the images obtained by the two scientists do indirectly reveal the ethers, through the electro-magnetic pulse 'frictionalizing' against the ether in the air. The electro-magnetic pulse thereby faithfully traces out the form of the ethers in itself. It is these indirect images of the ethers that the camera detects.

An article reviewing this book was published in the respected science journal *New Scientist* (27 May 1976). It did reluctantly acknowledge that their work had uncovered something of interest, but then concluded that these are perhaps just another kind of electro-magnetic field. However this conclusion leaves unanswered many questions, including why did the electromagnetic pulses take on these strange, ethereal patterns. Rudolf Steiner's research has indicated that these four ethers are each associated with a particular leaf-shape in the world's plant life. In other words, in plants that are primarily sustained by the water or tone-ether, leaves are formed which have a half-moon shape.

Whereas the life-ether produces leaves of an angular, lineal shape, such as the pine-tree needles. The light-ether produces the zig-zag, lightning-shaped edges of leaves; and the warmth-ether produces very rounded, almost globular shaped leaves. What is especially interesting is that the patterns of these etheric energies, as filmed by the two scientists, in relation to different plants, correspond precisely to the above situation. Another very good way to see the influence of the ethers active here around us in nature, has been developed by bio-dynamic experts; originally with the help of Rudolf Steiner. It is a form of chromatography, often called capillary dynamolysis. This

---

[125] Technically, the spectrum lines of atoms are analysed (the Doppler broadened resonance), but then the outcome is not placed in a living context of the upper atmosphere.

technique, briefly and simply put, allows one to indirectly vividly see the etheric forces, through the patterns that result when a solution of various extracts from plants are allowed to dry on a blotting paper.

The seasons and their significance for humanity
The seasons are a major rhythm in the life of the earth; and the cycle of the year is a reality for the entire ether body of the globe, not only amongst the flora and fauna on the ground. Rudolf Steiner taught that two processes are responsible for the seasonal cycle, one known to science and the other involving changes in the etheric energies and spiritual processes of the hemisphere. The scientific explanation that the earth is tilted a little on its axis, so one hemisphere is more exposed to the rays of the sun than the other hemisphere at certain times during the earth's orbit.

Thus in December, the northern half of the globe is pointing away from the sun, while at the same time the southern half is pointing toward the sun and is therefore having its summertime. The reverse is the case in June. In the summertime position, the hemisphere receives the sun's rays more directly, more intensely. The sun will also rise higher in the sky than at any other season, so the more direct rays are also permeating the atmosphere for a longer time in each 24 hours.

In anthroposophy, another cause is considered to be involved in the seasonal cycle. It is called the 'breathing of the earth', a process in the ether and astral auras of the hemispheres, which is similar to our inhaling and exhaling. This breathing process affects the earth's soul: as new growth develops in spring, the ethereal and soul forces in the springtime hemisphere begin to ascend out of the earth. They are exuded or exhaled into the atmosphere. This exhaling of subtle energies continues into the summer; then in autumn the hemisphere begins to inhale its forces, and by the winter these forces are again drawn down into the physical body of the earth.

Earth's breathing-in and breathing-out
The spiritual significance of the seasonal 'out-breathing' and 'in-breathing' of the hemispheres as presented in anthroposophy, is that the tangible, sense perceptible processes of nature are brought about by living beings. These are the so-called nature spirits but these are being directed by much greater beings. For when the ethers and the aura of the hemisphere tends to ray upwards, or be 'breathed out', certain kinds of spirits ascend with it up into the atmosphere, arising ever higher on into the summer.

They then begin to descend back down to the soil during the autumn, as the currents in the ether and astral body of the hemisphere reverse. During this ascending and descending, the altering of the consciousness and functions of these beings contributes considerably to the changing inner moods of the seasons, to the seasonal influences upon us. To Rudolf Steiner the subject of how these changing influences subtly affect human consciousness and how cosmic energies are brought into the hemisphere's aura during the seasonal process was very important. He hoped that a new cycle of seasonal festivals would arise, based on the seasonal cycle of each hemisphere. For more about this, see Chapter 12 where various themes in anthroposophy are briefly noted.

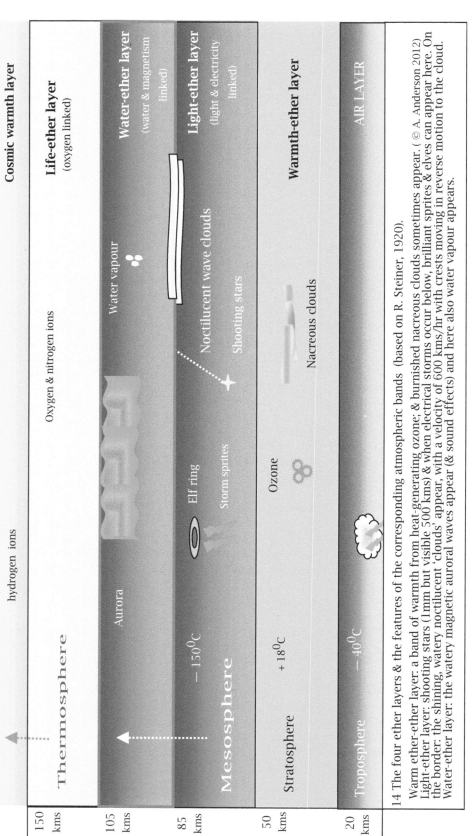

150 kms				Cosmic warmth layer
105 kms	hydrogen ions		Thermosphere	
	Oxygen & nitrogen ions	Aurora		Life-ether layer (oxygen linked)
85 kms		Water vapour	−150°C	Water-ether layer (water & magnetism linked)
		Noctilucent wave clouds	Mesosphere	Light-ether layer (light & electricity linked)
	Elf ring	Shooting stars		
	Storm sprites			
50 kms	Ozone	Nacreous clouds	+18°C Stratosphere	Warmth-ether layer
20 kms			−40°C Troposphere	AIR LAYER

14 The four ether layers & the features of the corresponding atmospheric bands (based on R. Steiner, 1920).

Warm ether-ether layer: a band of warmth from heat-generating ozone; & burnished nacreous clouds sometimes appear. (© A. Anderson 2012) Light-ether layer: shooting stars (1mm but visible 500 kms) & when electrical storms occur below, brilliant sprites & elves can appear here. On the border: the shining, watery noctilucent 'clouds' appear, with a velocity of 600 kms/hr with crests moving in reverse motion to the cloud. Water-ether layer: the watery magnetic auroral waves appear (& sound effects) and here also water vapour appears.

128

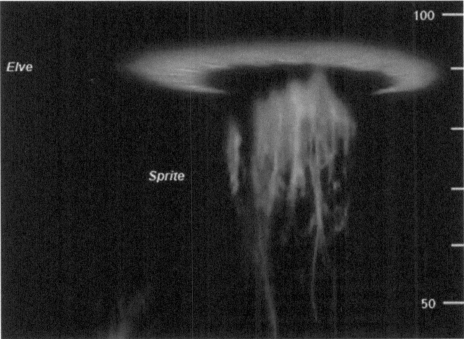

15 The elf-ring and the flaming red sprite: two mysterious energy fields that appear in the light-ether layer, at 50- 85 kms height, when an electrical storm occurs, down in the air layer. Above: elf-ring, an actual black/white photograph.
Below: elf and sprite, an enhanced composite image using actual photographs

16 Noctilucent 'clouds': Appearing at 85kms height, these radiant high velocity energy-fields indicate the light- ether layer.

17 The Aurora: Magnetic energies indicating the presence of the tone-ether layer. The northern or southern lights move wave-like, mainly in the tone-ether layer of upper atmosphere. Above: a NASA photograph shows how it appears in a specific layer, following the Earth's curvature.

Another way to feel the ethers active in the Earth is given in my book "Living a Spiritual Year" and concerns the so-called semi-diurnal pressure wave. Each day a phenomenon occurs in the atmosphere that is not explained by science. It happens twice every day and is an expression of a kind of breathing process occurring for the Earth. What is this semi-diurnal or twice daily pressure wave?

Twice-daily air pressure surge
There is, as one would expect, during the day a response to the sun's energies, in the course of which the air heats up and a wave of high pressure moves through the atmosphere. However, the daily timing for this response is irregular, as is its intensity. And our perception of this response is obscured by other atmospheric processes occurring in the air layer closer to ground level, on the surface of the Earth. So we cannot experience this once-a-day surge of high pressure.

But some other activity, some unknown surge of energy, causes a maximum of air pressure, a wave of high pressure, twice daily, always at the same times – between 9 and 10 am, and between 9 and 10 pm. This remarkable rhythm would appear to derive from some force not connected with that once-a-day heating up of the air by the midday sun. This is called the semi-diurnal pressure wave; and it was studied by such great pioneers of modern science as Laplace, Lord Kelvin, Goethe, and also Humboldt, who remarked that this development of high pressure each morning and evening was so regular that his barometer could serve as a clock.

At midmorning, a surge of energy manifests in the atmosphere of the eastern side of the earth, the side facing the sun. The wave of energy arises at this time in both northern and southern hemispheres (even though each is in a different season) causing physically, higher air pressure and consequent wind currents and other effects throughout the atmosphere. Then again in the evening, with clocklike regularity, the same energy surges in the western side of the Earth or evening sky of both hemispheres.

Because the sun's influence is minimal at midmorning and late evening, researchers over the last two centuries have naturally considered that this semi-diurnal energy wave cannot be due to the daily heating of the atmosphere by the sun. What then is causing it? The answer was intuitively grasped long ago by that outstanding scientist, Johann Wolfgang von Goethe, who thought that it derived from an activity occurring within the living Earth. He said the Earth is undergoing a similar process to breathing in and then breathing out at these times.[126] The major current scientific theory about this proposes that this event is part of the complex response of the ozone layer to the midday build-up of heat in the atmosphere. However, it is acknowledged that this theory is not viable because the mathematical modelling upon which this explanation is based cannot account for important aspects of the pulsing; for example, its seasonal variations, which researchers describe as 'remarkable'. The pressure wave is stronger

---

[126] In 2013 a brief film clip was posted on the Internet by a computer programmer, J. Nelson of IDV Solutions using NASA 'Blue Marble Next Generation' project images. These photos from space showing the changing weather patterns and ice over the Earth, and reveal a intriguing breathing dynamic: globalnews.ca/news/751154/watch-earth-breathe

in the hemisphere experiencing winter, than in the one experiencing summer.[127] This pulse of life is a phenomenon which is not explainable through scientific models. As we noted above, in anthroposophy it is seen as an example of the efficacy of the ethers which have their own daily rhythm.[128]

Until a few decades ago, this phenomenon was regarded by scientists as a tropospheric process – that is, as a process occurring just in the air layer (which extends up to 15 kms). As it makes these actions, it does exert a very slight effect upon the air pressure; the effect is so slight that it can only be detected by scientific instruments. But since the 1960s it has been discovered that this process – the twice daily pressure waves and the energy which they generate – takes place from ground level right up to an altitude of approximately 120 kilometres! And as we have seen, this area encompasses the four ether layers in the atmosphere. Rudolf Steiner confirmed Goethe's conclusion that an etheric energy is released in the morning, and then drawn back down in the evening. This is what causes the mysterious twice-daily pressure wave.

Summing up
In this chapter we have seen that in anthroposophy, life-processes have their origin not in chemical or electrical processes but from the activity of four etheric energies. These energies exist high up in the atmosphere in four bands, and through their activity all life on Earth is created and sustained. Various upper atmosphere metrological phenomena are indicative of the presence of these life-forces up there: nacreous energy-fields of the warmth-ether, noctilucent energy-fields, storm elves and sprites and shooting stars of the light-ether, and the aurora and water vapour of the moisture-ether, etc. The moisture-ether is active especially in the springtime, the light-ether and warmth-ether are intensified in the summer time, and the life-ether in the wintertime.

The human etheric body is composed of these four energies, and it is the etheric body which provides us with the capacity to register our sense-perceptions and our thoughts. It also makes reproduction and healing possible; the plants are a direct expression of these energies. Electricity and magnetism are the unpleasant decay by-products of the ethers; hence the harmful nature of electro-magnetic radiation (EMR). To become aware of these etheric processes and the spiritual energies that are active in them was an important part of Rudolf Steiner's teaching; see the entry 'seasonal festivals' in Chapter 12. We also noted that our planet has its own life-pulse; namely the twice-daily surge of energy throughout the atmosphere. The area affected corresponds to the area permeated by the four ether-layers. This surge of energy is derived from its own etheric body responding to the sun's motion.

Further reading: A. Anderson, Living a Spiritual Year.

---

[127] Namely, its amplitude twice as large, and its phase tends to lag.

[128] Many theories have been put forward in the last 140 years, starting with a 'resonance' theory from Kelvin (and later, Taylor/Perkeris) and through to such factors as semi-diurnal cosmic ray intensity (1948), and then back to models based on horizontal versus vertical gravity-wave activity (D. Randall 2007 / Covey et al, "Surface-pressure signature…"2010). Proceedings of International Astronomical Union symposia continue to put forward interesting models from time to time.

8: ZODIAC AGES, END-TIMES AND HISTORY

We shall explore the anthroposophical view of various phases of history and in particular the dynamics occurring from the 19th century through to about 2350AD. An important emphasis in anthroposophy is the understanding of the underlying spiritual dynamics that occur throughout history. This was offered by Rudolf Steiner to provide a deeper understanding of the purpose of human life by reflecting on the purposes that the divine-spiritual beings intend for each epoch. Understanding the special features of a phase or epoch in history helps people to align their life-purposes to these higher intentions, and also to be aware of unwholesome influences active in a given phase. We have already seen in Chapter Two that in anthroposophy, history unfolds in various Ages and that our souls (our ego-sense) evolve further as we incarnate in each of them. What Rudolf Steiner emphasises regarding history is that each epoch brings out a different quality in humanity's soul-life. In this chapter we shall see that these Ages are created by a zodiacal timing system.

We will consider briefly the basis to this zodiacal concept, but above all, we shall explore the nature of the potential spiritual battle being played out in our times between the forces of good and evil. In earlier chapters we noted that since the 15th century we live in the age of the spiritual-soul, and this creates both a potential for spiritual renewal and for hardened egotism. But we also live in a time when many people have heightened expectations or anxieties, awaiting a violent end of the world, or the golden age of Aquarius or the Second Coming of Jesus. Rudolf Steiner's explanations about what is happening spiritually in the modern era are very striking.

Firstly though, what is the zodiacal basis of the anthroposophical Cultural Ages that we explored earlier? We need to note that Rudolf Steiner's teachings also encompassed the creation of the planet Earth, and how this occurred through spiritual beings, over vast epochs of time. In a later chapter we shall explore this further, but for now let's just note that he speaks of historical events and civilisations existing prior to 3,000 BC, which is currently viewed as the dawn of civilisation. The evidence of civilisations existing long before 3,000 BC is actually very substantial; but the academic world has been unwilling to assess this.

Pre-Flood civilisations
Rudolf Steiner taught that prior to the ancient Sumerian and Egyptian peoples there were two earlier civilisations; and before these, a great Flood occurred. Prior to the flood, there existed the Atlantean peoples, and before them another civilisation on a landmass in the Indian Ocean. This is the ancient, now submerged, continent of Lemuria. He called the cultural epoch prior to the Atlantean age, the Lemurian epoch, and taught that it commenced about 26,000 BC. But we need to note that the landmass itself had existed for millions of years before that. People did live there long before 26,000 BC; but it was then that a specific series of seven cultural ages commenced. These had a similar time-frame to the seven cultural ages that developed during the Atlantean epoch.

In recent years mainstream archaeological research has uncovered some tremendously important discoveries of relevance here. The remains of towns have been found that are dated to about 9,000 BC or earlier. Evidence of advanced civilisations have been off the coast of Japan and the coast of Yucatan. There is also in Turkey the remains of a civilisation at a site called Gobekli Tepe; it flourished about 9,000 BC. This means that there were people living in such far-flung places who were contemporary to, but quite separate from, the Atlantean peoples. No doubt in future centuries, evidence of the Atlantean and Lemurian epochs will also be found (and also, evidence which is already known, will be allowed to be recognized as such).

Each of these two pre-flood civilisations is seen in anthroposophy as having seven distinct phases or smaller cultural epochs to them. Then comes the large epoch referred to as the 'Post-Atlantean Age', which commenced about 7,000 BC after the great Flood, and it too has seven small cultural epochs in it. We are currently in this large epoch, the 'Post-Atlantean Age'; and we are in the fifth of the smaller cultural epochs, which started in 1413 AD.

Atlantis

So we have here another striking feature of anthroposophy, namely that the fabled island-continent of Atlantis is taken seriously and is not considered a myth. This is because in Rudolf Steiner's research into the past of the Earth, he observed this land-mass in the Atlantic Ocean, and the role it played in humanity's evolution. In his presentations on history and pre-history, he speaks of a terrible nature catastrophe that occurred about 7,200 BC when Atlantis was destroyed.

Plato famously writes about an account of this event in his treatise "Timaeos", the records of which are said to come from the venerated Egyptian mystery centre of Heliopolis in the Nile delta. It is mainly due to Plato's account that the modern world still knows about this idea, although his account is not usually regarded in academic circles as historically valid. However, some historians do regard Atlantis as referring to an historical fact, but as referring only to a civilisation in the Aegean Sea, which was destroyed by a volcanic explosion a few thousand years ago.

However in anthroposophy the town of Heliopolis is regarded as a place which was once a sacred site, developed as an important Mystery Centre, before the Old Kingdom of Egypt, by Atlantean colonists.[129] There esoteric knowledge was recorded, and spiritual wisdom attained. So although one needs to be alert to such old records being distorted over many centuries, what Plato records can be regarded as a report of valid historical knowledge once stored at Heliopolis.[130]

---

[129] Reported in the private memoirs of Count Polzer-Hoditz.

[130] For example, part of the text on the famous Stele of Thothmes IV at the sphinx on the Giza plateau, "... at that sacred Place of the Creation, the sacred path of the gods towards the western horizon of Heliopolis." And in the mysterious Old Egyptian text, the Papyrus Westcar, it is said that the secrets of how the Great Pyramid was so superbly engineered is contained in a document in Heliopolis.

There is also a large body of evidence around the world for Atlantis, existing as a kind of folk memory, but of varying quality. Much of it strongly supports Rudolf Steiner's own research. In anthroposophy, Atlantis existed in the Atlantic Ocean, encompassing the Azores Islands (today the submerged peaks of Atlantean mountains) and also extending far beyond these islands. In Chapter Ten we shall explore statements from Rudolf Steiner about the Atlanteans.

Geologists are generally sceptical about the concept of Atlantis, that is of a landmass having until relatively recently existed in the Atlantic Ocean. However, this attitude is a reflection of the long-standing view of geologists that there have been no recent catastrophes on the Earth. One geologist examined the concept of Atlantis in the Atlantic Ocean and concluded it was not possible. His reason is that in his model, the islands in the Atlantic ocean were formed in short bursts of volcanic activity, but the time between each island forming was geologically very long.[131] This is an affirmation of the disputed geological conviction that no recent upheavals have ever happened. But other researchers point to evidence of geological upheavals that have taken place relatively recently in various places.

Consequently there are geologists who argue that Atlantis could have been a landmass above the water until fairly recently. These geologists point to the fact that deep rock cores drilled in the Atlantic Ocean seabed contain remains of freshwater plants. Opponents argue that plants and sea-shells from the shore must have been washed far out to sea and then became incorporated deep inside the ocean floor. But the geologists who present this data in favour of Atlantis point out that this is a very weak argument.

There are many phenomena in the natural world which scientific theories have not allowed, but which nevertheless have been found to be valid. Much evidence suggestive of Atlantis exists in world literature, in linguistics and in folklore, and in the records of many peoples around the world. It is not unreasonable to consider Atlantis to be factual.[132] Part of this evidence is in fragments preserved from ancient Greece and Rome. The Roman writer Marcellin states that "in the Atlantic Ocean is a more worthy (larger) island". But this idea is more potently expressed by Avienus (4th cent. AD), "Fruitful in the ocean stretch lands, and beyond, backwards, other shores stretch to another world." This is a reference not only to Atlantis but also to the Americas. And the ancient Greek historian Theopompus (4th cent. BC) has a vague statement that "beyond islands in the Atlantic ocean, there was {is} a continent situated beyond this."

In the 19th century dramatic evidence suggestive of Atlantis was encountered. A small portion of Atlantic Ocean floor actually was raised up to the surface, caused by a huge volcanic eruption, a little to the west and south of the Azores. It is a geological fact that portions of the ocean floors can and do rise up to the surface as islands, for a few days or weeks, before subsiding again. In March of 1882 various mercantile vessels encountered a long, sweeping drift of suddenly warm water which covered an estimated 7,500 square miles.

---

[131] This is the theory of Zdenek Kukal, *Atlantis in the light of modern research*, Earth-Science Reviews, 1984.

[132] And this means in the Atlantic Ocean, not in the Aegean Sea.

The waters were filled with millions of dead fish. The fish were edible, having just recently been boiled, evidence of a volcanic eruption in the seabed which had forced up an amount of land to the ocean surface. In this disturbed area of the Atlantic Ocean various mercantile vessels noted an uncharted island, and made entries in their log-books about it. According to newspaper reports in Louisiana, the captain of a British mercantile vessel, S.S. Jesmond, decided to explore this new island. A search party went ashore onto this dead, treeless land mass. They were the first people to walk on an area of land which had been on the Atlantic seabed for long ages. It is possible that this small landmass was literally a part of Atlantis, and had been submerged for about 9,000 years. Some weeks later it sank again beneath the waves.

The most thorough research into the news article reporting this event, published in New Orleans where the ship docked several weeks later, was undertaken by Lawrence Hills, Ph.D. (Hons). His research was published in May 1956. Hills was an internationally respected journalist and writer, as well as a British horticulturist. He was founder of the H. Doubleday Foundation for organic farming.[133] His research, undertaken in the Lloyd's Register and in the British Hydrographic Office established the veracity of the ship's movements, and the details of her captain as reported in the American press.[134]

The newspaper reports in the USA also state that the crew gathered up artefacts, including a statue of a woman, and a sword of yellow metal, skull and a sarcophagus.[135] However, there are no photos of these alleged artefacts, and no one has yet been able to trace them, although the British Museum did conduct a search for such items. Until some of the alleged artefacts are found, the incident remains only partially verified.

Rudolf Steiner in a 1905 lecture also mentioned an ancient Mayan text telling of a catastrophic submergence of a large landmass in the Atlantic Ocean.[136] The translation of this codex in the 19th century records a sudden submerging of a landmass with millions killed, about 8,000 BC. But soon academic translators denied this was the true interpretation; but one suspects this was mainly because they objected to the allusion to Atlantis.[137] For in recent decades, academic experts on Mayan texts have established that the earlier versions of the Troano codex are basically correct.[138] It is now affirmed that the Troano codex is about the submergence of an ancient civilisation, and that the Mayans in fact made several other records of a catastrophe of this nature.[139]

---

[133] His report was published in May 1956, ps. 72-75 of the Egerton Sykes Atlantis Journal, for research into evidence of Atlantis.

[134] The boat was an iron screw schooner, built by Wallsend Slipway Co. of New Castle; launched in Dec. 1878.

[135] For example in the Times Picayune (New Orleans) of April 1882.

[136] The stenographer was unable to record the name of the codex in full, being a foreign word, but an analysis of the archive text establishes it was the Troano manuscript, now properly called the Madrid codex.

[137] The translator was the learned Abbé Brasseur de Bourbourg.

[138] E.V. Garcia, lecturer at The National Autonomous University of Mexico.

[139] In particular, this is to be found in the Books of Chilam Balam and in the Dresden Codex.

The Zodiac Ages

Now to the theme of the Zodiac basic for these Ages. Rudolf Steiner taught that there are periods of cultural influences which commence and cease on a precise date, according to a certain zodiac influence. When the Vernal Point, that is, the spring equinox day occurs, (the 21st March in the northern hemisphere) in the following years, a new zodiacal Cultural Age began, or will begin:

7227 BC the Age of Cancer began
5067 BC the Age of Gemini began
2907 BC the Age of Taurus began
747 BC the Age of Aries began
1413 AD the Age of Pisces began
3573 AD the Age of Aquarius will begin
5733 AD the Age of Capricorn will begin (and so on)

So there is a kind of cosmic clock operative here: the passage of the sun through certain zodiac signs. But it has remained an enigma amongst his students what kind of zodiacal dynamic Rudolf Steiner is referring to here, as these dates do not relate to the years when the sun on the vernal equinox would enter the constellations.

Furthermore he taught that the religious leaders of earlier cultures were aware of these Ages. So, for example at 2907 BC on the spring equinox morning, the new Age of the Bull occurred as the sun entered a sector of the heavens associated with Taurus. This phenomenon is based on the astronomical fact that the sun appears to slide very slowly backwards through the zodiac when viewed where it rises on the same day year after year, for centuries. This is called the Precession of the Equinoxes. And Rudolf Steiner also indicates that this occurrence was noted by leaders of the ancient priesthoods. So, many centuries later the sun entered Aries on the spring equinox of 747 BC. And again it is implied in anthroposophy, at that time the main sacred symbol of deity was changed from that of a sacred Bull to a sacred Lamb (or Ram), because the initiated leaders were aware of this.

But the suggestion that ancient people perceived this spiritually, and formally responded to it, is rejected in most academic circles, because of the following problems. There is little historical evidence of any change in religious symbols as the sun 'precessed' or passed from one sign into another (this may or may not be true, but is only a secondary objection). This 'precession of the equinox' means the slow movement backwards of the point on the horizon where the sun is seen to rise on the spring equinox morning, when compared year after year. The primary objection from historians of astronomy is that no evidence exists of the precise, long-term astronomical observations, and the accompanying complex mathematical records that would make knowledge of this possible. Nevertheless some academics think that ancient cultures did indeed somehow have knowledge of the precession of the equinox point.

But in anthroposophy, whilst such scientific evidence and conclusions are taken seriously, these scientific objections are not seen as strongly relevant. This is because knowledge of the Zodiac Ages in ancient times, indeed knowledge of cosmic rhythms in general, is viewed as something acquired by initiatory (clairvoyant) research, and not by empirical mathematical studies and observation.

However, the further fact is that the Cultural Ages zodiac is only **indirectly** linked to the Precession of the Equinoctial point, because its dates create epochs each of which are precisely 2,160 years, whereas the precession of the equinoctial point of the sun is actually irregular, not a precise number of years. That is, the backwards motion of the sun around the zodiac over many centuries is irregular; it speeds up and slows down erratically.

So in this sense all objections to Rudolf Steiner's viewpoint here are not applicable, because he cannot be indicating a zodiac process known to astronomy. But for students of Rudolf Steiner's worldview, the question nevertheless arises, just how can this be so? What kind of zodiac sector is the sun entering on these dates, so regularly? Certainly it is not the constellations of the zodiac, as they are of various sizes. So the Cultural Ages would also have to be of various lengths of time, as the sun takes different lengths of time to go through them. Nor can it be said that it is due to the sun entering the signs of the zodiac used in horoscopes (called a tropical zodiac). For the dates of the sun entering those sectors or signs are quite different.

One could theoretically place the positions of these signs of the Inherent Zodiac onto the stars of the heavens and then see when the sun would enter them, in a time-flow chart. But the dates when the sun enters these 12 signs or sectors would be entirely different to the dates given by Rudolf Steiner. So the mechanism by which these Ages come about has remained unknown to students of anthroposophy. But recent research from this author suggests that it is caused by the movement of the sun through an etheric reflection of a zodiac known to ancient Babylonian initiates.[140] This movement results in a new cultural age precisely every 2,160 years. This process is not subject to the irregularities affecting the precessional motion of the Earth.

Zodiac Ages in Babylonia

Is there any evidence to support this zodiacal Ages theme? There is a body of research, to a great extent built on the work of Sir Norman Lockyer, which claims to have discovered evidence of architectural changes made to the orientation of ancient temples in Egypt, to keep them aligned to the vernal equinox sunrise as it slips backwards around the heavens. But mainstream experts remain sceptical of this. However there is also an indication from old Babylonian sources. It concerns reports about a Babylonian king, Nabonassar (or Nabu-nasir), who ruled 747-732 BC.

A ninth century Byzantine Christian chronicler, George 'Syncellus'[141], reported an important event from fragments of historical documents that he possessed, which were written by two Hellenistic writers some centuries earlier. He reports that in 747 BC king Nabonassar decreed that a new era had begun; an interesting statement in this

---

[140] The research is presented in detail in the e-booklet, *Rudolf Steiner and the Tropical Zodiac* available from www.rudolfsteinerstudies.com

[141] As people by now had no family names, this word simply means the monastic cell-mate.

context.[142] Going through the hundreds of pages of the Byzantine Greek of this vital document that George Syncellus wrote, we find that he writes,

> "As from Nabonassar the times of the stars' motions were diligently recorded by the Chaldeans."[143]

And in further on in the same book he writes,

> "King Nabonassar asked for the collecting up of the annals of the kings before him in order that the Chaldean kings before him become purged (from the historical records)."[144]

Now the order from the king for the 'collecting up' of the records of earlier monarchs is understood by some scholars as an order to have them destroyed; but other scholars, including this writer, conclude that it is more likely that the purpose was to have them locked away, to make a fresh start. For the Byzantine Greek verb used here means to collect up, and <u>not</u> to destroy. The significance of these two reports together, about what Nabonassar decreed in the year 747 BC, is intriguing. The two reports do not exactly constitute proof of a royal decree designed to usher in the new age of Aries, yet this Age did begin in this same year, 747 BC.

However these reports do strongly suggest that this is the case. Namely, that king Nabonassar, a monarch in a culture which had for millennia been studying the night sky, was indeed proclaiming the start of a new zodiacal Age. These reports from the Byzantine chronicler George are quite objective, as he himself apparently did not even believe in the zodiacal precession. For in his book he refers to "...the mythical retrograde of the zodiac its original position, from the beginning of Aries, and its return again to the same point."[145]

Another historical event may constitute support for the zodiacal ages system taught by Rudolf Steiner, and this is the founding of Rome. For in anthroposophy, 747 BC is the year when the Age of Aries began, which is also called the Greco-Latin era. Rome's first historian, Quintus Fabius Pictor, wrote that Rome was founded in the year 747 BC. Such an event as founding what would become a very powerful city, could be seen as indicating that this was a special year to the ancient priests and rulers of that part of Italy.

---

[142] Namely Berossus, active ca. 280 BC and Alexander Polyhistor active around 90-70 BC.
[143] ΧΡΟΝΟΓΡΑΦΙΑΣ page 207; 20-21 (p.389 Byzantinae 1832, Bonnae) ... απο δὲ Ναβονασάρου τους Χρόνου της τῶν ἀστέρων κινήσεως Χαλδαῖοι ἠκρίβωσαν ... (translated, the author).
[144] ΧΡΟΝΟΓΡΑΦΙΑΣ page 207;3-5 Ναβονάσαρος συναγαγὼν τὰς πράξεις τῶν πρὸ αὐτοῦ βασιλεων ἠφάνισεν ὅπῶ ἀπ᾽ αὐτοῦ ἡ καθαρίθμησῖς γίνεται τῶν Χαλδαιων βασιλέων. (translated, the author) (p.390, Byzantinae 1832, Bonnae).
[145] ΧΡΟΝΟΓΡΑΦΙΑΣ ...τὴν παρ᾽ αὐτοῖς μυθκὴν τοῦ ζωδιακοῦ ἐπὶ τὰ ἐναντία κίνησιν ἀπὸ τῆς ἀρχῆς τοῦ χριοῦ καὶ πάλιν εἰς αὐτὴν ἀποκατάστασιν... page 30,V.14;17 (translated, the author) (p.40, Byzantinae 1832, Bonnae).

However today most historians use the date of 753 BC, but in fact this mainstream date is only a convention, the date has no solid basis, it is just one of several dates put forward. So again, all this is only vaguely supportive of Steiner's viewpoint. Another fact which may indicate the awareness of the zodiac ages in ancient times comes from ancient Egypt. Between the paws of the great sphinx on the Giza plateau, there is a stele (a carved stone tablet), with a very significant inscription. The text was written by Pharaoh Thothmes IV (ca. 1400BC). The inscription begins with these words,

"{It happened in} the first year, the third month of the inundation (Athyr), the 19th day, under the majesty of the Horus, the strong bull who produces the risings (of the sun), that his Majesty paused to rest….." [146]

This text is speaking of the union of Taurean energies with the sun's rays. In 1400 BC the sun was rising amongst the <u>constellation</u> of the Ram (Aries), but at this time the sun **was rising in the Sign of the Bull** (2907 -747 BC). And we have seen that it is the sign, not the constellation, which is important. But again this is possibly an irrelevant situation, because throughout much of their long history the ancient Egyptians likened the sun god to a bull, (representing a god called Apis).

So, again supportive evidence from historical documents for this core theme in anthroposophy is vague, but future investigations may substantiate it. [147] So it is now time to consider the main points of what Rudolf Steiner taught about the nature of life and consciousness in the various post-Atlantean epochs. He taught that there are seven minor cultural ages which together constitute the Post-Atlantean Epoch.

The key to this is Illustration Eighteen: **The Post-Atlantean Large Cultural Epoch.** It is useful to look at that now. It shows the flow of history from the end of the large cultural epoch of Atlantis on to the end of our current large cultural epoch, known as the 'Post-Atlantean' epoch. [148] A large cultural epoch has seven smaller cultural epoch within it, these epochs, with their dates are as follows:

7227 BC the Age of **Cancer** began. It is referred to as the primal-Indian epoch, located in northern India. The word 'primal' can also be replaced by 'ur' which has the same meaning. Rudolf Steiner taught that in **ancient India** the first cultural progress occurred after the downfall of Atlantis, so it is the first of the Post-Atlantean epochs. In this epoch the main focus of evolution of humanity was a consolidation of the **etheric body**. The etheric body was far less densely drawn into the physical body than in later times, and they consequently had a natural clairvoyance. And perceiving through the

---

[146] My English version is formed from the English version of D. Mallet and the German version of Christine El-Mahdy (www.meritneith.de traumstele-thutmosis.htm).

[147] A full examination of this inscription and the mystery sites at Giza is available in the book, The Great Pyramid and the Sphinx.

[148] The indications given here are drawn from many volumes in the Complete Works, including GA 62, 97, 99, 108, 113, 105, 106, 158, 226 and also an unpublished archive document from 1917.

etheric body lead to a direct sensing of the cosmos as permeated by divine thoughts of gods.

There was a predominating feeling of fleeing from the physical world, and a yearning to return to the old spirit-rich ways. This meant to those people, the spiritually vibrant environment that once existed in Atlantis. Hence they sought through artificial means, to find ways to again attain to union with the old gods and the spirits. They felt that the physical body was an impediment to inwardly sensing the spiritual energies within Nature. This was a kind of blockage to perceiving these higher things. But when they were asleep, the dream life was very vivid and very real. And during the day-time everything which they gazed upon was permeated by a fine misty-cloud of etheric energy.

There are no artworks from this period which we can identify. But it is back to this ancient time that the mysterious term 'religion' actually refers. Rudolf Steiner taught that the origin of the word 'religion' is from 'religare' (as Lactantius asserted) and hence means 'to bind-back people to the spiritual aspect to life'; an aspect which was previously very present, but is now slipping away'.[149]

5067 BC the Age of **Gemini** began, referred to as the primal Persian epoch. There was progress in human consciousness in the area roughly equivalent to present day Iran. In this epoch the main focus of evolution of humanity was a consolidation of the **astral body**. For example, a person now felt that on the physical plane there are some opportunities for nurturing their soul's higher potential. Through the power of the elemental energies within fire the ancient Persians found a way to form a connection to the divine Sun-spirits; and their fire cult was started.

Through the initiate Zarathustra they were given an understanding that a kind of battle is occurring between powers of light and darkness inside the soul. At this time things of the sense world were embedded in a radiant auric glow, like a shadow, and one's body seemed like a dark shadow amidst this radiance. They felt that the body was always drawing them back into the dark-realm of matter, and this feeling was especially strong each morning, upon awakening. But the physical world was felt to be a much more real thing than in the earlier Age; the spiritual realms of light were actively compared with the physical world of darkness. The wish to go back, away from the material world, was weakening.

So in the religion of this time, which was developed by Zarathustra, there was a God of Light (Ahura Mazdao) and a demon of darkness (Angra Mainyu, later called Ahriman) who created matter. Consequently there was a dualistic religious view of life. But also people were now moving towards a settled existence, cultivating various grains and livestock. As Settegast observes in her excellent book, *Plato Pre-historian*, in Persia around 5,500 BC there was a rapid and crucial cultural transition which resulted in the

---

[149] The origin of the word religion is unclear academically. Three ancient authorities gave their ideas. Cicero concluded it was from relegere (to treat something carefully); Lactantius thought religare, and Augustine thought religere (to recover something). Thomas Aquinas mentions all 3, without concluding which one (Summa Theol. Article 1; quest 81).

nomadic tribes-people there becoming urbanized and developing cultivation of grains.[150] Zarathustra is mentioned in some Hellenistic documents as a great teacher around 600 BC. Rudolf Steiner explained that he was publicly active a second time, in another incarnation, in this later era.

2907 BC the Age of **Taurus** began, the Egypto-Mesopotamian epoch, located in Egypt and the empires of Akkadia, Sumeria, Assyria and Babylonia. In this epoch the main focus of evolution of humanity was the sentient-soul. Rudolf Steiner taught that in this Age the physical realm has become an object of interest because the laws and dynamics which derive from the spiritual can be seen to be active in it. To these people the imprint of the gods was to be seen in the movements of the planets and stars. So one could calculate and create buildings on these geometric patterns; what one could call astro-architecture arose in this Age.

To these people the world was no longer alien and hostile, but a source of interest, to study and meditate upon and from which to learn sacred geometry. And being focussed on the feeling life (sentient-soul) they felt deeply what they experienced of the spirit. But also it was just before the beginning of this Age, in the Orient, that a potent Luciferic force entered the spiritual life of humanity, deeply influencing the spiritual quest towards a disinterest in the earthly life; it lingers on especially in India and other eastern lands.[151]

747 BC the Age of **Aries** began: the Greco-Latin epoch. This encompasses the Greek civilisation with its interests in the Mysteries and art, and the Roman world with its focus on power and civil order. In this epoch the main focus of evolution of humanity was the sense of ego and the intellectual-soul. In this Age, through Aristotle, the science of logic came into being. The physical world was becoming the main focus of awareness, although initiation into spiritual reality was still offered in the famous Mysteries, at places such as Samothrace, Eleusis and Ephesus.

Rudolf Steiner explained too that when the person, spiritually striving, sought for a high spiritual light from above, it was more an experience that the soul exists, rather than the higher worlds exist. So now it was the soul itself becoming a soul-experience, and also the feeling that the soul permeated the body. In effect **the body and the soul now belong together!** [152] The body was understood as the external vestment of the soul, and this tended towards body identification, as gradually the soul-life began to be identified with the bodily life-vitality.

And a direct result of this dimming of the old deeper spiritual insights was the feeling of only a vague existence after the death of the body. Furthermore in earlier times the most important, most insightful ideas had always been experienced as slipping into one's mind from the spiritual worlds, and this was still the case, but now in this Greek-

---

[150] Mary Settegast, 'Plato Prehistorian', Lindisfarne Press, 1990.

[151] It is called an 'incarnation' of Lucifer, meaning an over-shadowing of a human being by Lucifer.

[152] R. Steiner, lecture 15th May 1917.

Latin epoch, people began to feel that they could work out the implications of such insights and ideas by their own inner effort.

1413 AD the Age of **Pisces** began; the current epoch, which Rudolf Steiner called the Anglo-Germanic epoch; it could also be named the Central European/Anglo-American epoch.

In this epoch the main focus of evolution of humanity is the Spiritual-soul and also its shadow-side. So it is also referred to as the Age of the Spiritual-soul or the Age of the Consciousness-soul. Already before this time, the Europeans with their one personal name, had developed the personal ego-sense strongly. Consequently, already in medieval times and then on into the Renaissance, they explored in religious thought and in philosophical enquiries the nature of the individual human being and its ethical responsibilities.

People in this era have a mission to enter totally into the physical world and mould and shape it, learn its dynamics, and then re-apply them in a metamorphosed way. Lofty spiritual ideas arise (especially in central Europe), and the impetus to technological progress and political power (especially in the Anglo-American world.)

3573 AD the Age of **Aquarius** will begin. It is also called the Slavic epoch, as this will occur in the Slavic part of Europe.[153] In this epoch the main focus of evolution of humanity will be the Spiritual-self. As the Spiritual-self becomes an active features of that age, a cultural blossoming should occur. Note that in the anthroposophical view, the Age of Aquarius does <u>not</u> begin in 2012 or 2300. These are incorrect dates, based on the sun's motion through the constellations. This is clearly shown in my e-book, Rudolf Steiner and the Tropical Zodiac.

5733 AD the Age of **Capricorn** will begin. It is referred to by Steiner as the American epoch, as it will occur in North America.

In this epoch the main focus of evolution of humanity will be the Life-spirit, but only for a smaller number of people. For with many people it will be a time where the outcome of the Ahrimanic technological impetus, starting in the 20th century, brings about ethical decay and nature catastrophes.

Those people who are not required by the karma guiding powers in the spiritual world to experience this War of All against All, will not be incarnate in the final part of this Age.[154] These people will have overcome their lower self and hence have no inner link to the activity of malignant beings on the world stage. Life shall re-establish itself and a new, better large cultural epoch begin. It could be called the Manichaean large epoch.[155] It is important to note here, after this survey of the anthroposophical view of

---

[153] Or according to a statement made in the Dornach Michaelmas Conference in Autumn 1979, Rudolf Steiner stated that if this area is too 'ahrimanized' by negative influences beforehand, then this cultural flowering may occur in Brazil.

[154] Actually a small number of spiritualized souls shall be there, but as Rudolf Steiner once stated (archive lecture 1904) "these people shall be protected by spiritual means".

[155] This is author's designation from the fact that Rudolf Steiner stated once that Mani will then be the leading spiritual inspirer of humanity.

cycles of time and the ages of history, that there is some criticism of Rudolf Steiner's view of history, as being racist. Critics say that some areas of the world, or some ethnicities, are being favoured over others, as it were. For the above views on history also imply that as one zodiac age ends and somewhere else on the globe a new cultural age arises, then the previous culture must have declined. This criticism derives from not seeing what underlies Steiner's ethics and work. He reports what his spiritual research has revealed. The arising and dissolving away of plant or animal species, of organs inside the body, of civilisations, of ethnic groups, of the entire solar system, is seen as part of the reality of existence. He reports in his lectures what he beheld in spiritual realms.

For example, he also reported how in the astral realm the group-soul of the mountain goat species is heard uttering a kind of groaning sound. This is an indicator that this spiritual being knows that its time of 'incarnation' on the Earth is drawing to a close.[156] Hence the number of mountain goats will gradually decline. But this is not said because Steiner was prejudiced against, or discriminating against, the mountain goat species. This was said because this is what he observed in his spiritual research.[157]

The Archangelic Regencies
A second historical element in anthroposophy, shown in the same illustration, concerns what we could call 'the Golden Ages' of cultural flowering, each lasting about 350 years, which occur approximately every 2,500 years. This process is connected to the influence of archangels in human cultural development. There are seven of these beings who are associated with the seven planets of astrology. Rudolf Steiner taught that the era of the sun-archangel brings about a time of cosmopolitan spiritual renewal.

The system of alternating regencies or cultural rulership by seven archangels is also an Hellenistic esoteric idea. And it became the subject of medieval Christian esoteric texts, such as that by Abbot Tritheim of the German town of Spanheim, as Rudolf Steiner mentions. In his introduction to his treatise on *'The seven regencies of the archangels'* the Abbott states,

> "According to a general view of antiquity, God, the highest Intelligence, guides the lower world through the mediation of lesser Intelligences, the spirits of the seven planets…these spirits or Archangels regulate the course of the world in a sequence of 354 years and 4 months…."

He tells how these beings each give a nuance to society, in accordance with that being's nature (they are each allocated a planet, whose astrological qualities they embody). It appears from what he says about the seven archangels, that each time their 'regency' comes around, they exert their own specific influence. Taking his calculations of about 354 years per archangelic being, we find that there was a sun-archangel age around 3,100 to 2700 BC (the time of the Egyptian, Babylonian and Megalithic cultural renewal), and again about 580-250 BC. And the Abbot says that

---

[156] Archive document, answer to a question, from 2. Feb. 1908, not yet published.
[157] For a detailed critique of these and other criticisms see the author's ebooklet, "Opponents and Critics".

"he will rule again from 1879 to 2233 AD". The medieval esotericist Tritheim of Spanheim believed that when a sun-archangel age occurs, it specifically brings about cultural renewal, by stimulating the arts and higher knowledge in general. This sun archangel is the archangel Michael, which we mentioned in earlier chapters. Although the next sun archangel era will be ruled by a different archangel, as Michael is moving up to the next stage of evolution, to that of the Principalities, as St. Paul calls these beings (see next chapter). Abbott Tritheim, writing about an earlier Michael age, says that then,

> "Various Arts were invented by men, namely the Arts, Astronomy, Magic, and
> …..knowledge of the true God; so little by little the superstitiousness of people
> became forgotten." [158]

The first of these eras occurred in the first post-Atlantean epoch, and there is no evidence of civilisations in northern India at that time. The second era occurred in the Ur-Persian epoch, and also here evidence of a special cultural time is not forthcoming. But we note that the great initiate Zarathustra is dated to this era in anthroposophy and also in some Hellenistic esoteric literature.

The third of these eras occurred in the Egyptian-Mesopotamian era, and historical records commence about now. Great spiritual-cultural initiatives occurred at this time which is about 3,200 - 2700 BC in various lands. In Egypt the great initiate Hermes established the magnificent wisdom of ancient Egypt and this resulted in the Great Pyramid and other centres on the Giza plateau. In Babylonia the mysterious initiation quest of Eabani, accompanied by the conqueror Gilgamesh took place; in Britain the greatest megalithic site ever, Stonehenge, began its initial phase, and in Ireland, Newgrange was begun.

The fourth of these eras, occurring about 650-300 BC, during the Greco-Latin Age, brought about a much better attested, and strikingly rich cultural age. In Greece Socrates, Plato, Aristotle, Pythagoras, Heraclitus and the immortal dramatists flourished. In the Hebrew world Isaiah and Jeremiah worked. And in China Confucius, Mencius, Mo-ti (or Micius), Chuang-Tzu and Lao-Tse (Tzu) lived. In India, the great Buddha appeared; and in Persia the great Zarathustra reincarnated, creating Zoroastrianism.

The fifth occurrence of this era is in our epoch, from 1879 until approximately 2340 AD. But in the modern world with vast numbers of people, it is harder to name just a few individuals; and the era still has about two centuries to run. However if the renewal of the esoteric wisdom of the Mysteries is a factor to emphasize, then the major focus is the work of Rudolf Steiner. In a lesser way, the works of Richard Wagner and the impulse behind Blavatsky also need to be mentioned.

Future intrusion of Ahriman

---

[158] Iohan Tritemis, Abbatis Spanheymen. De Septem Secundeis, Impressum Francoforti apud Cyriacum, Iacobum Anno Domini 1545. (for an English translation, see www.renaissanceastrolgy.com/heavenlyintelligences)

Now another significant historical dynamic involving Lucifer and Ahriman is to be seen in Illustration 18. Just before the beginning of the third millennium before Christ, there was a potent intrusion of Lucifer into the cultural affairs of humanity. And Rudolf Steiner revealed during the last days of World War I, that "early in the third millennium" after Christ, Ahriman shall overshadow a sinister human acolyte of his, in his efforts to introduce a deeply unwholesome influence to modern humanity. (He will become 'incarnate' so to speak.)

This event is said by Rudolf Steiner to occur "early in the third millennium" and that means in effect, any year from 2001 through to about 2350. He will seek to encourage a soul-darkening abstract mindset in people, weakening the capacity in the soul to sense their spiritual potential. This new mindset will seek to undermine the development of spirituality, of the divine potential slumbering in the soul, and push people into technological directions (the android human, for example). He will also establish a college for clairvoyance, in which the visions given are inherently misleading. But Rudolf Steiner revealed that a very positive and powerful spiritual dynamic is also active as from the 20th century, and this is linked to the religious topic of an expected return of Jesus, but in an etheric form. But before exploring the ideas around this theme, it will be helpful to get clearer about the core dynamic in the current era: the spiritual-soul era.

The Modern Era
The ego state of modern humanity, the spiritual-soul state, brings about a kind of a perilous dance with Ahriman, and often a hardened ego state with callous disregard for the living inter-connectedness of reality can result. Rudolf Steiner pointed out that ego-endowed individuals can metamorphose this acute ego-sense, this 'spectator consciousness', into an intuitive sensitive state of mind, even high spirituality. It is this activity that transforms the soul, and makes it into an instrument of the higher self. In other words, in this current Age, the fifth post-Atlantean Age, or Piscean Age, people have the karmic mission so to speak of metamorphosing the acute sense of self. This means in effect, rejecting self-centredness and learning to actively bring about community with others.

In earlier chapters we explored how the spiritual-soul is the part of our mind where we most intensely experience our own separated self. It is able to grant wisdom, intuitive insights, but it opens the door to a hardened self-centeredness if not spiritualized. In 1916 Rudolf Steiner spoke of how it isolates people, unless we act to prevent this:

> "In the Greco-Latin epoch it was still the case – unlike today – that when two people met, a mutual impression was made about the other person's character. But now, in order that the more withdrawn or introverted spiritual-soul may develop, things have changed. This immediate understanding of the other person will no longer arise; life will require of us that we make an inner effort to relate to the other person, to understand them. Indeed it is only in this effort to understand the other person that the spiritual-soul can be developed. In our present cultural epoch it will become ever harder and harder for people to find the right relationship to each other because to do this will require an inner development, an inner effort. The difficulty will intensify in the future,

18   The Post-Atlantean Large Cultural Epoch

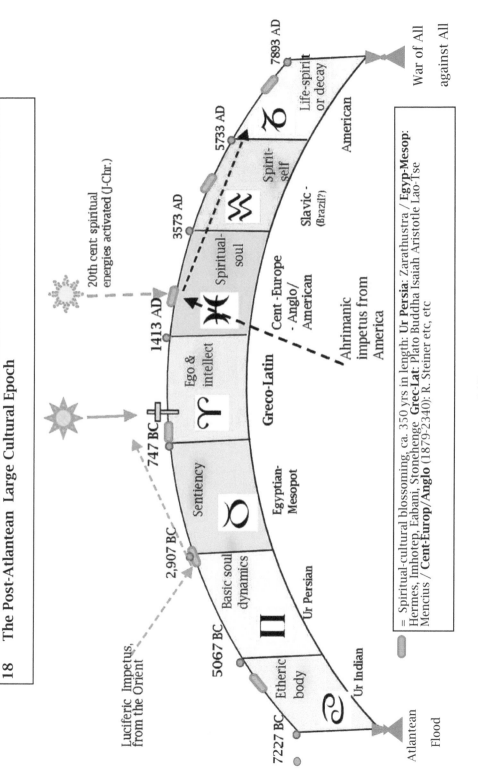

= Spiritual-cultural blossoming, ca. 350 yrs in length: **Ur Persia**: Zarathustra / **Egyp-Mesop**: Hermes, Imhotep, Eabani, Stonehenge **Grec-Lat**: Plato Buddha Isaiah Aristotle Lao-Tse Mencius / **Cent-Europ/Anglo** (1879-2340): R. Steiner etc, etc

and not only will it become a problem for colleagues and friends, but even for the family. It will become difficult for sons and daughters to understand their parents, and for the parents to understand their children, and indeed for the children to understand each other.

This is in some ways, a negative perspective for our times; but we must become clear about what our times demand of us. This new situation is necessary for the spiritual-soul to be able to develop. If this next evolutionary step were not to take place, then humanity would have to live within a less advanced, primitive group-soul structure.

A society formed ever more upon the basis of the spiritual-soul without, at the same time, the effort being made to understand each other, by conscious inner effort, would result in strife and disagreement permeating even the closest relationships. And so we see that in the Age of the spiritual-soul, understanding must be awakened ever more and more for social relationships.

Every social structure which we have inherited and continue to use, from previous cultures, structures suited to a humanity which had not yet developed such an individualized ego, such a spiritual-soul, will gradually lose all meaning, and dissolve away. Therefore in our times real social understanding, which is in effect a deeper understanding of the individual human being, must arise in a conscious way."[159]

Since these words were spoken, a great deal of work has been done in regard to improving human interaction skills by researchers from many walks of life, to enhance our capacity to communicate with significant others in our lives.

More about the spiritual-soul

But the spiritual-soul, as we saw earlier, is also the doorway to real spirituality, to higher intuitive insights; the path to joy and harmony between people. This is clearly but briefly pointed out by Rudolf Steiner in his book *Theosophy*,

> "Everyone knows how at first he regards as the Truth that which he finds agreeable, preferable. Such truths however are fleeting, are subjective; only that Truth is permanent or real, which exists in the soul, free of all traces of liking and disliking. And the same is true of morality; real higher ethics is quite independent of personal inclinations. Through causing this self-existent True and Good to come to life in their inner being, a person raises herself or himself above the mere sentient soul. Then the eternal real spirit shines into our being. A light is kindled in the soul then which is imperishable...By spiritual-soul is meant the kernel of human consciousness; that part of the soul in which Truth and Goodness and Beauty lives, is the spiritual-soul."

The idea that we are living in an era where very special spiritual forces are active was taught by Rudolf Steiner in respect of the idea of the Second Coming of Christ. He taught that this holy human being, who became the vessel of the cosmic Christ, and permanently united to this deity, is reappearing to human awareness. And this will be assisted by the development in humanity of a sensing of the ethers. To Rudolf Steiner

---

[159] GA 168, p. 395.

this dynamic was especially important; in fact the key dynamic spiritually in our Age, dramatically interlinking the popular idea of a new Age of Light with that of malignant forces from the approaching Ahriman. We shall explore briefly what the teachings of Jesus himself were in regard to this, and see how this relates to what Rudolf Steiner taught. There are several indicators of the "Second Coming", which Rudolf Steiner referred to as the 'Reappearing of Jesus' (to human perception).

The Second Coming of Jesus (The Reappearance of Christ in the Etheric)
Whenever the 'Reappearing' is mentioned in the scriptures, it is placed at a time of wars, and imminent outbreak of wars, "Ye shall hear of wars, and rumours of wars; but be ye not troubled…" (Matt 24:6, Mark 13:7, St. Luke 21:8). We can of course fairly accurately say that this omen places the time of the event in our century or later centuries. For there have never been so many wars - and of such destructive nature - in any earlier century. However, it is also true that a future century may have even more warfare than ours; so we may say that as regards this first omen, the 20th and 21st centuries are the most likely time for it to occur, so far. It is important to note that this sign or omen, like a number of others from the Gospels, is an indication of especially negative circumstances, not positive ones. This indicates that the Reappearing will occur at a time when additional spiritual light will be needed.

Another statement is, "Then many shall be *offended*" (or, "turn away from the faith" in other versions) Matthew 24:10. This sign is little known, yet crucial; it is somewhat obscured by the translations, which at this point don't convey the full meaning of the original Greek. The word 'offended' here seems odd to us - what does this sentence really mean? Translated in a more expanded way, yet true to the meaning of the original text, Christ is giving the following sign: "Then, also, many people will become uncertain in regard to ethical matters."

These words are significant as they again place the time of the Reappearing in the 20th century and in later centuries. Never before has humanity been faced with such a large number of such earnest moral-ethical dilemmas. Nor did we face so strongly in prior centuries, the real possibility of failing to meet ethical dilemmas. In the past, responsible moral behaviour was hardly discussed, since people were quite clear as to what constituted an ethical or unethical behaviour code.

But as from the 19th century, a serious dilemma arose in regard to ethics, that is, the moral implications of actions undertaken by Governments or individuals in commercial, technological or military decisions. The inner sense which tells us whether something is wholesome or harmful began to fade. Through the difficulty in even becoming aware of the ethical dimension to these actions, let alone finding the right approach to them, we have indeed experienced "uncertainty in regard to ethics". The dilemmas posed are now so numerous; such as by genetic engineering, nuclear energy, privacy and freedom being traded for efficient processing of data, and for the control of crime by government, the increasing merging of electronics into human nature, and so on.

Another indicator from the New Testament is contained in words of Christ spoken after the Sermon on the Mount, where, in connection with the arising of false prophets, he warns that although some persons may use his name constantly, they may well be opposed to him. "Not every person that says; 'Lord, Lord' shall enter the Kingdom..." Rudolf Steiner spoke of the souls who become fanatical Christians as constituting a kind of group who would be blind to the incarnation of Ahriman. Another statement in the Gospels is, "Be alert, that you are not deceived; for many shall come in My name ...and deceive many... saying; 'I am He'; and saying, 'The time is at hand !' Do not follow them." Luke 21:8 & St Mark 13:6 (combined)

Here we note that all physical persons who come forward as the Saviour are defined as false, they are to be avoided; and yet no identifying characteristics of His own appearance is given. This warning against every (physical) person is strengthened in the following: "And then if any person shall say to you; 'See, here is the Christ; see, there He is!', do not believe it. For false Christs and false prophets shall appear and perform signs and miracles in order to deceive the chosen ones, if that were possible."

> Mk 13:21-22, "Behold, I have forewarned you. Therefore, if anyone tells you: 'Look; He is in a remote place'; do not go out (seeking him). Or, if they say... 'Look; He is in the secret rooms'; do not believe this.[160]   Matt. 24:25 - 27

Now, what is intriguing here is that these words seem to identify all and every special, charismatic person as fraudulent. So the question arises, how would Christians know that the Reappearing has occurred? This question of what to expect in regard to the so-called return of Jesus has baffled people over hundreds of years, and led to innumerable false prophets. And this enigma deepens with the next statement by Jesus about this subject,

"Take heed, that no person deceives you, for many shall come in my name, saying, 'I am He'...take heed and watch."   (St. Mark 13:5 & 33,37)

So what or whom are alert Christians to watch out for? A clearer version of the Greek text helps one to find the answer to this question. "Let no person deceive you, for many shall come in my name, saying: 'I am He'...be inwardly alert and perceptive". The Greek words used in the Gospels for "watch" imply striving to perceive in an attentive, conscious way; that is, focussing one's inner vision, rather than simple physical looking. And, this hint of something transcendental grows stronger when we discover that the words of Christ seem to indicate that no tangible, physical person will return. For, he warns, "take care, that **no person** deceives you...for many will come in my name..." The following words from the esoteric texts of the Gospel of Thomas also indicate that the event shall not be a physical reappearing, but rather a more subtle reappearing of this saviour,

> "The disciples said; 'When will the kingdom come'? Jesus said; 'It will not come (simply) by expectation; they will not say; 'See, there' or 'See, here'; for

---

[160] It was announced in full-page global newspaper advertisements by the Benjamin Creme group, back in 1980 that the 'returned Christ' is on Earth, and that he will soon step onto the world stage. But then we were told shortly thereafter that he decided to retreat to a 'secret chamber'. Thirty years have gone by, and still no sign of him – except the false sign, that he is now in 'a remote place'.

the kingdom of the Father is spread out upon the Earth, but people do not see it." (Gospel of Thomas: verse 113)

These various statements together actually seem to affirm the view of Rudolf Steiner about this subject. He taught that as of the mid-twentieth century humanity shall start to gradually develop an interest in spirituality. This will include the tendency towards what could be called a slight psychic awareness. The old clairvoyance of previous pre-Christian millennia will re-emerge, but in a new form, wherein people start to see etheric energies moving in the air, and shining around people.

Rudolf Steiner taught that Christ Jesus has specifically undertaken to clothe himself in an etheric form, at this time; that is as from the mid-twentieth century. So that amongst the various ethereal forms and energies that the new vision shall reveal to people, this sacred person shall be included. Various reliable reports exist of people in fact having this experience (not caused by emotive problems or religious attitudes. Rudolf Steiner taught this etheric reappearing would become a source of especially high spiritual renewal for society, in a subtle way. But he does not associate this etheric reappearing of the saviour with apocalyptic ideas of a catastrophic end of the world.

Summing up, Rudolf Steiner taught that as of the twentieth century there will be an enhanced interest in spirituality and social conscience as people develop a sensing of the ethers. For this sensitivity enables inspiration of an esoteric Christian kind. But also, many ahrimanic tendencies will arise in the world. And so people shall be encountering an enhanced goodness and spiritual renewal, but also an enhanced temptation to soul-impairing technological devices and a moral decadence.[161] As he once stated, a decade of life in the modern era, brings the experiences and challenges normally encountered over a millennium, in earlier times.

Further reading
References to the zodiac Ages in this chapter are scattered throughout Steiner's Complete Works. And Steiner's book, "The Reappearance of Christ in the Etheric".

---

[161] It is as if in our times, the parting of the ways is subtly beginning.

152

9: AFTER DEATH: THE COSMOS & SPIRITUAL BEINGS

This chapter explores two themes which Rudolf Steiner regarded as important to modern humanity; namely, the structure of the cosmos and the beings involved in this, as well as the experiences of the soul after death in these realms. Just what kind of existence do we enter once the body has died?

Rudolf Steiner investigated these questions extensively, and through his clairvoyance was able to follow the journey that the Dead undergo. His teachings on these themes re-introduce to western civilization a very significant body of knowledge. In older religions the cosmos was understood to be multi-layered and filled with many kinds of deities. However in the western world, often there is not much said about spiritual realities between God and humanity, apart from Christ and the Holy Spirit of course. Angels and perhaps archangels are admitted, but seldom commented on. Life after death is a veiled mystery, apart from a general idea of a Hell and Heaven.

The Hierarchies

What is the nature of these beings who dwell in the higher realms, and what is our connection to them? A great deal of Rudolf Steiner's work involved discussing the activity of the hierarchies from various points of view. Here we can only give a brief over-view of this key theme in anthroposophy. But just before we consider the Hierarchies, it is important to note that to Rudolf Steiner, the word 'God' is an abstract term which often is better applied to one of the divine hierarchies. For these beings bring about the dynamics and events that people think of as carried out by God. We saw in an earlier chapter how different is his view of God to the usual cultural viewpoint.

In Steiner's teachings, the term God does not refer to a being that can be clearly identified experientially, as a being separate in nature from the great numbers of other lesser but sublime beings. Consequently a westerner can regard God as the cause of a wide variety of events, virtually all of which are however, caused by a much lesser being, for example an Angel. But it is also true that through these hierarchical beings the will of the true, ineffable, uncaused God becomes manifest. For example, Rudolf Steiner told one audience,

> "God is never a completed Being, he is [in existence] as the ongoing development inside all living beings, in all things... Each one of us is, so to speak, a ray or a reflected image, of God. The relationship of God to humanity is like that of the Sun to its own reflection in a multitude of drops of water...If one asks a Theosophist about God, about what is behind Brahman, he says nothing, for about this being one cannot speak. Everything which people say in this direction are indicators only."[162]

Rudolf Steiner developed a phrase to refer to 'God' which attempts to express the profound and sacred nature of this being: "the Allwelten-Urgrund", which in English

---

[162] GA 52, p. 44.

is, "the primal fundament of all worlds" (or "the primal foundation of all worlds". And in this connection, he taught that,

> "The human being has been created by the Primal Fundament of All Worlds, which exists deep in all of our souls."[163]

But nevertheless Rudolf Steiner also taught that every person should become aware (as an idea) that the human spirit does proceed from the Father God,

> "The soul, which dwells in every personality, must be able to feel at one with the eternal Cosmos-Foundation, who is called the "Father-God", and who dwells in every soul."[164]

Rudolf Steiner stated that this same realization was what Christ Jesus wanted humanity to achieve. And historically it is from Christ's words in the Gospels that the idea became so widespread that there is a spark of the divine from God in every human being. If Christ had not emphasized this point in his teachings, then still today there would probably only be a sense that we humans may have a connection to a planetary spirit or some other deity.[165]

But on the other hand, it is also true that the widespread idea of our link to God has been applied in a superficial way, regarding events as brought about by 'God', or mystical experiences as revealing of God, when actually, another lesser being was responsible or perceived. This very limited viewpoint arose because western Christendom developed in a context where the spiritual perspective was fading away. So the various ranks of spiritual beings were left out of consideration. And so, in this void people naturally associated everything with God.

There are various esoteric or religious traditions stemming from the Hellenistic era about these beings, with varying sequences listed. The sequence that Rudolf Steiner teaches is the same as that found in the writings of Pseudo-Dionysos and John of Damascus and also of Dante Alighieri. But in Rudolf Steiner's case it derives from his direct perception of these beings, not from his choice as to which historical listing to choose. Steiner taught that Pseudo-Dionysos was actually Dionysos the Areopagite, a student of St. Paul, and that his writings were handed down over the centuries.

Let's now consider briefly the nature of the hierarchical beings, but this can only be a sketch, drawn from a large body of material from Rudolf Steiner who presented the very numerous ways in which the hierarchical beings ate interwoven with the human life-wave.

---

[163] GA 54, p. 174.

[164] GA 105, p.114.

[165] In this regard a valuable service was rendered by the mediaeval Scholastics, lead by Thomas Aquinas. They fought to preserve the sense of an eternal individual ego, in the face of incorrect ideas from Arabian influenced people like Averroes who denied this.

The Nine Hierarchies

<u>Biblical name</u>   <u>R. Steiner term</u>   <u>Meaning of name</u>
                                Greek term

The highest group: the First Hierarchy, are:

Biblical name	R. Steiner term	Meaning of name
Seraphim[166]	Seraphim	inflaming, noble (Hebrew)
Cherubim	Cherubim	grasping (Hebrew) [167]
Thrones	Thrones	throne, seat Greek: *Thronoi* (referred to 2x in New Testament)

The middle group, the Second Hierarchy are:

Biblical name	R. Steiner term	Meaning of name
Dominions	Spirits of Wisdom	dominion Greek: *Kyriotetes* (4x in NT)
Mights	Spirits of Movement	inherent power Greek: *Dynameis* (3x in NT)
Powers	Spirits of Form	active power Greek: *Exousiai* (7x in NT)

The lower group, the Third Hierarchy are:

Biblical name	R. Steiner term	Meaning of name
Principalities	Spirits of Personality or Primal Beginnings	beginning, or origin Greek: *Archai* (8x in NT)
Archangels	Spirits of Fire	chief of the angels Greek: *Archangeloi* (2x in NT)
Angels	Spirits of Twilight	messenger Greek: *Angeloi* (about 200x in NT)

---

[166] In the plural they are more correctly, the Cherubine & Seraphine.

[167] The references to Cherubim & Seraphim in the Bible can refer to lesser beings, but these names have been used for the 2 highest ranks.

We shall now briefly consider the nature of the individual ranks of divine beings, and their sphere of influence in the solar system.

The Angels
Their location is the Moon sphere, considering the solar system in the geo-centric model. They have the Spirit-self as their central consciousness dynamic, and their further evolution is accomplished via an interaction with the human being. Every human being has an Angel, and this has become known as the Guardian Angel.[168] As Rudolf Steiner taught,

> "We know that the eternal essence of man's being, his Individuality, endures from life to life. But the majority of people have, as yet, no consciousness of having lived in a life upon the Earth. There would be no continuity, no relationship between these lives, if certain beings did not establish continuity from life to the next. Every individual is endowed with a being who, because he stands one stage above humanity, guides him or her from one life to the next. These beings do not arrange one's karma, they are simply guardian spirits who preserve the memory of one incarnation until the next; these are the angels. It is the task of the angels to stand watch over all the threads that human beings weave from one life to another." [169]

The Archangels
Their location is the sphere of Venus. These beings have advanced one step beyond the Angels, and their central consciousness dynamic is the Life-spirit, which as we noted earlier is in effect the divine devachanic source of the ethers. This results in them having a central role in the producing and sustaining of the ethers, of the Earth.

But a small number of archangels are also the Folk-spirits; these are beings who hover above each nation, providing the national cohesion of a nation or tribe. This they achieve via the subtle energies (ether forces) in the atmosphere permeating the landscape. These archangelic beings are of differing degrees of greatness, and hence of lesser or greater power. Their destiny follows that of the tribe, and they attempt to exert some power over the destiny of the people involved. But conversely the most advanced people of a nation can assist the Folk-spirit in its efforts to ennoble the nation.[170]

Four of the archangels are especially important and are referred to in old sacred writings from the Hebrew and early Christian cultures. These are Michael, Uriel, Raphael and Gabriel; they guide the nature spirits in the seasonal processes of each hemisphere, under the guidance of the Earth-spirit (the cosmic Christ). Michael is active in the autumn, becoming the regent of the nature spirits in that season. Gabriel is the regent in the winter, Raphael in the spring, and Uriel in the summer.[171]

---

[168] GA 105 lecture, 6th Aug. 1908.
[169] GA 110, 15th April 1909 & GA 101, lecture 27th Dec. 1909.
[170] GA 121, The Mission of Individual Folk-souls.
[171] They also have other roles, including causing a subconscious influence in the human soul in the opposite of the season in which they are the predominant regent. This minor influence is not relevant to any seasonal festival themes.

The Principalities (in Greek, the Archai)

Their location is the Mercury sphere. These beings are also called the **Time-spirits**; that is they are the regents of the 2,160 year zodiacal cultural epochs, for example the seven post-Atlantean epochs. They have in earlier ages manifested through high initiates, to help influence the cultural epoch.[172] A small point of confusion could occur here, as some <u>archangels</u> are also referred to as Time-spirits. Those are archangels which govern the much shorter, approximately 350-year periods which we referred to in Chapter Eight. For example with these shorter periods, whenever the sun archangel is the regent, there is a global spiritual-cultural blossoming. The Principalities over-see the activity of the seven archangels in their smaller cultural age.[173]

The Powers (in Greek, the Exousiai)

These great beings are in the sun sphere and are regarded as the same beings as the Elohim of the Book of Genesis. They are manifest within the sunlight, spiritually experienced. Hence in anthroposophy that divine being in the old Hebrew world who was referred to as God, is understood to be of this rank of being. It is from these beings that the human being has received a germinal seed-bud of the higher self; this was placed in our astral body in the Lemurian times. Hence the holiness of these beings to ancient spiritual leaders.

The reverence for the Elohim or Powers or Spirits of Form in olden times was also due to the perception that they have fashioned the form of earthly creation. So the actual form of the mountains, rivers, hills and valleys, is due greatly to them. As Rudolf Steiner taught, when we behold the splendor of a sunrise from a high mountain top, this is a reflection in the mineral realm of the creativity and cosmic thoughts of the Elohim.

The Mights (in Greek, the Dynameis)

These beings, called the Spirits of Movement in anthroposophy, are in the sphere of Mars, and are active in the shape of the Earth's surface. They form its evolving contours. The animal group-spirits have their origin from the creative powers of these beings. These beings are also called the Virtues. They are, spiritually considered, the cause of the planetary motions; they bring about the movement of the planets through the solar system.

And since flower and plant forms are, to a great degree a reflection of the motion of the planets around the Earth (geo-centrically viewed) these forms are due to the actions of the Mights or Spirits of Movement.[174] In the second Aeon, the sun aeon, it was these beings (at a lesser state of evolution then) whose activity began the process that eventually lead to the crucial action that underlies the circulation of our blood.[175]

---

[172] GA 110, lecture 7.
[173] GA 121, lectures 1 and 2.
[174] GA 136. p. 174.
[175] GA 266b, p. 260.

The Dominions (in Greek, the Kyriotetes)
Their sphere is that of Jupiter, and they are involved in developing the form of the human being and of plant species. Called by Rudolf Steiner the Spirits of Wisdom, their influence in the human soul assists the development towards the Spirit-self.
These beings are the spiritual matrix of the plant species; the Earth's flora are derived from spiritual forces coming from these beings. The over-all nature of the world's flora, that is, the inner feeling of Earth's forests and meadows, derives from these beings.

The Thrones (in Greek the thronoi)
The location of these beings is in the Saturn sphere; they have a deep connection to the subconscious will of the human being. It is these beings who gaze into all that which occurs in the will-life of humanity on the Earth, and it is their consciousness which thereby creates and sustains the Akashic Record. It is also these beings, or more accurately, the highest of these beings, who is meant, at least initially, in various sacred texts by the term God, (or Father-God). From them the Spirit-human or Atma initially derives. They regulate the orbits of the planets and they seek to manifest the intentions of the Cherubim. In the process of doing this they establish the foundation for the next phase of development in the solar system.

Cherubim
These beings exist beyond the Saturn sphere. They coordinate planetary movements of each planet with the other planets. It is their task eventually to work towards redeeming evil. The essential nature of their consciousness as sublime gods is one of an immensely <u>illumined awareness,</u> so that every thought experienced becomes immediately radiant light, giving profound understanding.

Seraphim
The essential nature of their consciousness as sublime gods is that of <u>being all that actually exists</u>. With these beings, "the cosmos is, and I am the cosmos, and the cosmos is I". The tone of their consciousness is an enormously enhanced form of what we humans call enthusiasm.[176] They receive the purpose of a new solar system from the Trinity and pass this down to the Cherubim.
All the First Hierarchy beings are active together, in an intricately interwoven divine creativity, as Rudolf Steiner describes it,

> "...the **Cherubim** interweave their powers into the foundation for a new impetus for the cosmos, formulated by the **Thrones** (the essence of which the Thrones received from them in the first place).
> The **Cherubim** allow this foundational element to stream forth from them, strengthened by their light, and then the **Seraphim** take this up into their being, enveloping it with their immensely radiant, joyous affirming creative inspiration." [177]

---

[176] GA 291, lecture, 4th Jan. 1924 p. 219.
[177] GA 291, lecture, 4th Jan. 1924 p.221.

The relationship of Christ to the Hierarchies

Rudolf Steiner explains, in harmony with the great Alexandrian sage Origenes, that the term 'Logos' can be applied to either the sublime spiritual being who created the zodiac system, or to the leading spiritual being of the sun. And since the zodiac becomes relevant and efficacious for us through the motion of the sun across the starry background, these two realities, sun and zodiac, are therefore closely interlinked.

The solar logos aspect of Christ is the one which is the more understandable and closely linked to the great religions of the past. For awareness of, and reverence for, the solar logos or sun god is very much part of ancient religions. Humanity's need to revere, and become attuned to, the great sun spirit was a common fact of life; it was the focus of core religious rites of antiquity. This idea that the Christ has a cosmic dimension, in fact consisting of two distinct, but interrelated beings, the solar Logos (or sun god) and the zodiacal Logos, is alien to modern religiosity. But it was once mainstream Christian theology in some parts of the early church. However, the idea that Christ was somehow associated with the sun is a theme that sometimes is explored in contemporary religious writings. The usual conclusion is that in the past, pagan ideas have intermingled with those of the early church.

Mainstream theological writers today reject any idea of Christ as a cosmic being, with a location in a specific part of the solar system. So how can people of today approach this idea? Firstly, we note that as its basis is the idea that behind the physical universe there are other levels of being. In earlier chapters we saw that Rudolf Steiner enumerates these as firstly the etheric realms of life-force, then the soul realms (or astral energies) and finally the divine Devachanic realms.

A similar understanding held sway for millennia in ancient times, but gradually died out. It started to die out with some people in the Hellenistic Age already, and then as from the time of the Renaissance a scientific, humanistic attitude dominated. (But Eastern Orthodox Christianity has maintained awareness of hierarchical beings.) Consequently this spiritual perspective was never incorporated in western Christianity, which significantly was pre-destined to be born and also to mature in an age where ancient more psychically sensitive attitudes were dying out. And therefore the idea of finding a location where Christ belongs in the universe quickly became alien, and still appears very alien to us today.

Rudolf Steiner taught that the universe is multi-layered, just as each human being has an etheric body, a soul-body and a spiritual aspect. The greatest celestial body in our solar system is of course the sun. We are intimately interlinked in our soul to the astral energies which fill the planetary spheres around our planet, and this includes the sun. The view put forward by Rudolf Steiner regarding the activity of the hierarchical beings and consequently of humanity in relation to the primal Trinity can be expressed, somewhat simplified, this way;

God is reflected in the foremost Principality
The Logos is reflected in the foremost Archangel

The Holy Spirit is reflected in the foremost Angel[178]

In many books of Rudolf Steiner's the following association of the Third Hierarchy with the human being is taught,

The Principalities are active in developing our Spirit-human
(the spiritualized will which manifests via our limbs)

The Archangels are active in developing our Life-spirit
(the spiritualized life-energies/creativity)

The Angels are active in developing our Spirit-self
(the spiritualized soul-life in general)

The interaction of the hierarchies with the human being is extensively explained in Rudolf Steiner's life's work, and this chapter gives only a brief overview. For example, after death, the hierarchies take up, and then work with, the subtle after-echo of our thinking-life. Our thoughts are intimately connected with our etheric body, whilst we were alive. The etheric body receives our thoughts from our soul (whether self-produced or insights from beyond) and makes them perceptible to us. What the divine-spiritual beings in the higher worlds receive as the effect of our thinking, they weave into the cosmic ether, and this etheric energy-force then becomes a factor in the forming of the etheric body for the Earth in a future evolutionary phase.

A feeling for this kind of activity is reflected in a passage in Goethe's Faust, Scene One, lines 447- 454,

> O, how everything weaves itself into a unity,
> Each in the other is living and active !
> O, how heavenly forces ascend and descend,
> and pass on to each other the golden amphorae !
> Moving through the Earth from Heaven,
> their wings fragrant with blessing.
> Harmoniously each one pervades the All ! [179]

An aspect of Steiner's anthroposophical cosmology is that various hierarchical beings have fallen behind in their evolution, and from these beings comes what we know as evil. We note that both Ahriman and Lucifer are of the same rank of being as Christ, namely a Power (or Spirits of Form in the term developed by Rudolf Steiner), but they are fallen beings of this rank. However there also exists, up above, beyond the nine hierarchies, the Logos Christ-being, as part of the Trinity. This being created the zodiac system, and is obviously a much higher being than the Spirits of Form. And this

---

[178] GA 99, lecture, 2nd June 1907.

[179] Goethe's German has a poetic quality and a metrical structure not captured in my translation; „Wie alles sich zum Ganzen webt, Eins in den andern wirkt und lebt !Wie Himmelskräfte auf und neider steigen und sich den goldnen Eimer reichen ! Mit segenduftenden Schwingen Vom Himmel durch die Erde dringen, Harmonisch all das All durchdringen !"

ensures that the will of the Father-God is predominant over the will of these fallen entities. But Rudolf Steiner also indicated in various lectures that within the nine hierarchies, the great Logos has manifestations of itself in beings higher than those in the Sun-sphere. For example, the Gospel term, 'The Lamb of God' refers to a Christ-being so to speak, in the rank of the Mights or Spirits of Movement; it is the most sublime of this rank of being. So again the influence of both Lucifer and Ahriman are limited.

There are also realms beyond Devachan, such as Nirvana, which is understood in anthroposophy to refer to a realm or state of consciousness in which there is no longer any impetus in a human spirit existing there, towards an earth life. All the life-lessons that the Earth can provide have been learnt, the lower self has been extinguished. It is a misunderstanding to consider Nirvana as a state in which the human being has become extinguished. It is the need for, and striving for, an earth-based, incarnate state of being has been extinguished.

The impulse for this non-earthly state can be derived from a premature subtly self-centred wish to obtain bliss for oneself; it is only a valid impetus if the soul has attained to the Spirit-self and the Life-Spirit. The beings who attain this state first amongst human souls are the Bodhisattvas, understood in anthroposophy to be Spirit-Self initiates who are reaching towards the Life-Spirit stage. Once the initiate has attained to the Life-Spirit stage, they become what in the east is referred to as a Buddha.

Life After Death
In the 1960's individual near-death experiences began to be published and the idea of a more involved, complex situation after death became well-known. Rudolf Steiner's teachings had already communicated virtually all these facts to the few who read his books. He went much further than what these accidental experiences reveal, or what psychic people had communicated.

We saw in Chapter Three that the soul returns to the Earth many times in a process designed to assist the higher self to develop. And as we make this journey we enter the spheres of nine ranks of divine beings. Each night the sleeping human being makes this same journey, even if the sleep is only a brief nap. Now let's consider in outline what Rudolf Steiner taught regarding the experiences of the soul after death.

The Call for friends
According to Rudolf Steiner when a person is dying, they know in advance and are preparing. So they unconsciously or consciously send out a call to a loved one, to meet them when they are free of the body.[180] Many a nurse working in palliative care has witnessed the joyous calling out by a dying person of a loved one's name, just before that person breathes out for the last time, and leaves their body. The next experience of

---

[180] This point is confirmed in the important six volumes of extensive research into life after death experiences published in the 1960's by academics lead by R. Crookall, on behalf of the UK inter-church research group. Their work confirmed many of Rudolf Steiner's basic teachings on this subject.

the dying person is that of becoming aware of seeing all of their life, in vivid images, which they gaze at entirely unemotionally no matter how potent the images may be. These images are stored in the etheric body.

The three-day memory transfer
These memories of one's life constitute the actual substance of the ego, the sense of self. So shortly after death these images are transferred from the etheric body into the astral body. The following statements about the after-death experience are relevant to an ethical person of today who has kept an open mind about the after-life. The circumstances are different for people who are not ethical or highly spiritual. The dying person is unaware that this is what is really happening; the gods have arranged the death process in this way so that as we journey on in soul realms, we may experience the memories of our earthly life.

The Awakening
Meanwhile the etheric body dissolves away into the cosmic ether.[181] This process takes about three days to complete. Above us, shining like a star is the Spirit-self, to the extent that it has been developed. This moves away ever higher, and as it does so the yearning arises in the soul to follow that star. But there are major experiences awaiting us before that star can be re-discovered. There is of course the momentous and joyous experience of realizing that one has survived the death of the body. In a radiant light-form a being appears and makes the soul aware of the multitude of moving images that are all around it. The soul strives to interpret the significance of these images for its journey through the Soul realm.

The Ptolemaic solar system
So where are we in this journey? There are two models of the solar system. One model is based on looking at it from out in space as if from a space ship; in this one the sun is in the centre and the planets revolve around it. This is the Copernican model. The second model is ancient and it's derived from human experience; in it the Earth, where we live, is the centre. In this model called the Ptolemaic solar system, the Earth is in the centre because this corresponds to our life experience, and around the Earth the moon, sun and planets all revolve.

The geocentric or Ptolemaic solar system is much more real and important to the soul, whether alive or disembodied, than the Copernican solar system model. In the after-life there are important tasks waiting for the soul. There is a journey through the solar system, viewed geocentrically, that is, in terms of the Ptolemaic solar system. Knowledge of this journey was part of Hellenistic esoteric wisdom, but Rudolf Steiner provided clear knowledge from his own research. [182]In other words, the soul journeys through the planetary spheres. So we arise from the Earth and move upwards to the moon sphere, and then on into the spheres of the planets. And in view of what we noted

---

[181] The etheric body of malignant people or those killed in their prime can linger on and become the so-called 'ghost'.

[182] In Book 10 of Plato's *Republic* and in fragment 31 of Numius, and in texts of Lucius F. Philostratus for example.

earlier, the soul will be journeying up through spheres or realms in which specific divine beings are active. In this process we have, above all, the task of <u>disengaging</u> from earthly impulses, that is the earthly thinking, sensual desires, and earthly concerns.

And this process can be painful depending on how earthly or how spiritualized is the soul. As a second, associated task, the soul now has to become <u>objective</u> about the life that has just ended. This means seeing the truth of the three soul qualities – the nature of one's feelings, thoughts and will. In particular, the extent to which the triune soul harbours qualities that are not in harmony with spirituality, and what that now means with regard to the realms in which one is now existing.

This process occupies a third of the time that the lifespan lasted; so about 25 years for a person dying in old age. And it occurs in what Rudolf Steiner calls the Soul-World or the astral realm.[183]

The Seven Soul Worlds
This realm has seven aspects to it, the lowest two of which are approximately what is known in Biblical language as Hell. But people do get released from it, and can ascend up into the higher spheres, eventually to return to the Earth. So there is no eternal Hell as such. The remaining five of the seven realms of the astral plane correlate to what is called Purgatory in old traditional language.

This is what the time in the astral plane is about; a phase of consciousness in which souls are being purified of earthly desires and values, so that they can move on to the next higher plane. The soul moves on through the planetary spheres toward the sun; but now it is the spiritual sun, not the physical sun. But to get beyond the fourth realm of the astral plane the deceased has to become aware of just how subtle was the way in which the personality identified itself with the body. One is so used to saying 'I' or 'me' to the body. This deeply ingrained attitude has to be fully rejected. Naturally for those who have adopted a consciously spiritual life-style, this is not such a problem. These various realms through which the soul journeys are in fact places where souls stop, or rather stop over, until they can move further on. It is knowledge of this deep mystery which enables an otherwise puzzling passage in the New Testament to be correctly translated. The sentence is in St. John's gospel, chapter 14, verse 2,

"In my father's house there are many mansions"[184] (King James version)
   or "In my father's house are many rooms" (NIV)
   (en te oikia tou patros mou monai pollai eisin)

The puzzle here has been that the word for rooms or mansions (monai) means either

---

[183] Steiner recommends not using the term the astral "plane" as this word gives the wrong impression, namely that of a flat, linear state of being. The Latin root word here, planus, was originally used for the spirit realm, the sense of an architectural plan, not a plain or flat surface. (GA 97, p.223; lecture of 22nd Feb. 1907.)

[184] In Greek, ἐν τῇ οἰκίᾳ τοῦ πατρός μου μοναὶ πολλαί εἰσιν.

permanent abodes or temporary stop-over places ! And this presents a stubborn riddle to most theologians. Also the word oikia means not just a house, but also the house and its grounds. In the light of the Greek and Rudolf Steiner's research, the meaning becomes clear to the meditant,

> "In my father's inclusive realm (the multi-layered cosmos) there are many permanent abodes (planetary spheres of different quality) and these also serve as temporary stop-over places for souls on the journey after death."

All kinds of human beings find an appropriate place to be, according to what their current truth is.[185] So what is happening then to the dead? They are undergoing a journey through the planetary spheres, in the Soul-World (or astral plane), towards their own spiritual origin in a higher realm. Those qualities in the soul that are not compatible with the higher divine-spiritual worlds are drawn out, and also personally renounced.

This process was known to early Christians, as an inheritance from the Hellenistic Mysteries, before Christianity entered the phase of western humanistic theology. As the great church father, Origenes of Alexandria said in the third century,

> "...just as people on the Earth, when they die in the way normally people all do, are allocated places according to the deeds they have done, and perhaps judged worthy of admittance to the better soul realms (as distinct from Tartaros (the Greek Hell)" [186]

There is a significant implication here about what happens to us, namely we change; indeed our very being changes. The lower qualities are burnt off or drained away, and in a manner which is determined by the demands and the dynamics of the soul world. This leads to the same result as spiritual striving whilst alive on the Earth, but it has been attained through the external agency of the soul world, and therefore is not an inherent eternal truth of the individual.

It is a much more joyous situation if, before our life ends, we have put away sensual pleasures, earthly values and focussed on spiritual values. But eventually a purification is brought about and in earlier times there was knowledge of this transformation. It is revealed in an old English phrase, "O my sainted aunt" ! This old expression is born from an awareness of the fact that departed souls do become spiritualized, (but importantly, not through their own ego-based striving) some years after leaving the Earth.

---

[185] In the more holistic attitude of eastern Christendom, this passage is actually quite well understood. A commentary by the early church father Ireneaus (ca. 170 AD) suggest both these meanings in one.

[186] Origenes Greek in ΠΕΡΙ ΑΡΧΩΝ ΤΟΜΟΣ ΤΡΙΤΟΣ IV, 3, 255 Τάχα δὲ ὥσπερ οἱ ἐντεῦθεν κατὰ τὸν κοινὸν θάνατον ἀποθνῄσκοντες ἐκ τῶν ἐνταῦθα πεπραγμένων οἰκονομοῦνται, εἰ κριθεῖεν ἄξιοι τοῦ καλουμένου χωρίου ᾅδου...

Another example of this insight is of course the worship of ancestors in various older cultures. They are regarded as sacred beings, to the bewilderment of modern humanistic people. This attitude was shown graphically in an incident involving a Japanese war shrine, in the 1980's when Australian officials refused to place flowers at it, because some war criminals were buried there. But the Japanese officials explained that in their view, these departed souls are no longer criminals, these ancestors are now semi-divine beings. Underlying this partially correct attitude is a sensing of the dynamic mentioned above, wherein the soul (or astral body) does become cleansed and spiritualized.

Why do we human beings die? Because we are born. For just as there is an intention to us being born, so too there is an intention behind the fact that our lifetime does not last forever. For long ages people have been experiencing life times on the Earth. We have been on a journey over millions of years towards the realization of our spirituality, our potential for divinity. So the physical Earth is not our permanent home. But this process requires many life-times on earth, and it is important after each life that we assimilate and integrate into our soul, the results of that life.This becomes purity and wisdom. And eventually in future time-cycles we shall live in spirit realms in a higher state of being where there is no longer any need for a flesh body.

Our experience after death brings into sharp focus that which is the concern of the spiritual-religious-esoteric life. It ceases to be what it often is for modernity: a resented or irrelevant aspect of life. Consideration of life beyond death brings into sharpest focus the connection each person has with **purity** or lack of sensual desires, with **wisdom** or lack of materialism and clever intellectuality, and **good-will** or selfless will, that is, lack of aggression and selfishness. **For what our inner being is, becomes our external environment after death.**

The transformed cognitional abilities
It is worthwhile here noting a passage in a Psalm (146:4) which has caused some people to conclude that after death we are simply in a kind of sleep state, unable to think, "The Dead: his breath departs, he returns to the soil…in that very day his thoughts are no more." Rudolf Steiner explains that soon after death, we find that gradually our thinking ceases, that is, thinking as we know it here. These are concepts derived from analysis of the sense world.

Instead we learn to relate to the brilliant radiant thought-forms, or images with their inner qualities that are all around us, because these are the astral equivalent to thinking. Shadowy silhouetted earthly concepts are replaced by very alive, pulsing forms, and one begins to sense that these are linked to a divine cosmic background.

What lives in us, as our inner truth, in our feelings, thoughts and will, becomes forces which determine how we proceed along the journey the dead undergo. These inner truths become our external environment across the threshold, too. Rudolf Steiner gives a name and a brief description of the main dynamics in the seven realms in the astral plane, and mentions that the person's Guiding Angel assists them in the journey up into the higher realms.

The astral realms and the names given to them

1 *Burning desires* - here self-centred desires that cannot be satisfied predominate, and there is an antipathy towards anything else in the environment now. This realm is inside the Earth and correlates to the idea of Hell, except that the soul does eventually leave here. The burning lusts and potent ego-centric energies keep repelling anything or anyone who would try to get through to them.

2 *Flowing stimulus-susceptibility* – here the glitter/glamour mentality is overcome, the soul is neutral to the environs. This realm also correlates the idea of Hell, but is not as horrid as the lowest stage. The soul now has a small possibility to experience something beyond its own desires.

3 *Wishes* - here empty trivial desires and wishes are overcome, and some attracting power in the soul now appears, opening up the environment to the soul. The soul can actually attract some of the environment into its orbit; that is, it can start to have some companionship.

4 *Pleasure and dislikes* - here active sympathy or empathy is learnt, the body-identification is overcome, and there is some passive interest and acceptance of whatever is perceived in the environment. Here at the moon sphere, the soul can begin to look up to the increasingly splendid realms above. A greater degree of interaction with others becomes possible.

5 *Soul-Light* - here sympathy and empathy is stronger, an active interest/liking develops, and the soul may now be illumined or affected by various other beings.
This is a much brighter place, a delightful realm. Ancient Hebrew initiates taught that this realm is illumined by the spiritual goodness of the souls here. Rudolf Steiner taught,

> "…here a wonderful new quality emerges…a creative power of soul…as this increases a soul light begins to radiate out from one; one begins to illumine the beings and gods around one, like a pre-dawn light on the Earth"[187]

He also emphasized that moral-ethical development is needed when the soul is in this region, or else one feels here in as if in isolation, and somewhat cold.

6 *Active Soul-power* - here the inner life of the soul now rays out, illumining others.
This is an even brighter place, a delightful realm. **Religiosity** is needed here; that is a capacity to feel reverence before the holy, or else one feels here in isolation, and somewhat cold.

7 *Soul-Life* – the now ennobled soul lets its radiance ray out for the benefit of others around it, and the last subtle materialism is overcome. Also needed is a reverence for the divinity within the human spirit and deriving from the sun; this is connected to the sun god Christ. The more of this quality the soul has incorporated into itself whilst incarnate, the greater is the joy experienced here, and the sooner one attains to this realm. Rudolf Steiner taught that souls having attained to this realm revere and worship

---

[187] GA 153, p. 57.

the divine beings, and then they behold in utmost reverence what he calls the spiritual sun.

The Egyptian Book of the Dead
A passage from the Egyptian Book of the Dead, which Rudolf Steiner several times affirmed as to its deep esoteric insights, echoes what he revealed about this realm,

> "I am pure at the great boundary place...of the passage of soul. I have done away with my sins, I have put off my offences...I have destroyed the evil which was in my limbs on the earth...Hail ye divine beings who guard the doors, make for me a pathway
> Behold, I have become like unto Ye ! Osiris, lord of the aeons, king of gods, thou who art the hidden soul in human beings, the son of Ra, the Sun God.. all mankind makes offerings to thee..."

There is another passage from the Egyptian Book of the Dead about this realm, which is very important, "I am the **boy** in the city....in the city my name is now: " the **young person** in the plains." Rudolf Steiner revealed that the soul by now has re-attained the innocence and purity of the little child, and that this is what is meant by the words of Christ, "Unless you undergo an inner transformation, becoming childlike, you can not at all enter the Kingdom of the heavens."

The Harrowing of Hades
At this point, it is very relevant to mention another aspect of Steiner's Christology, namely that during the time that the body of Jesus was hanging from the cross, Jesus, permeated by the cosmic Christ, descended down into the lowest of the astral planes (which are inside the earth). There through his presence the astral darkness was illumined, and the worst of evil beings disempowered. This extraordinary process (known in earlier times as the Harrowing of Hades) also wrought a wonderful change, somewhat higher up in the astral plane.

The spiritual radiance enabled the souls to find their way towards the divine devachanic realms. This concept was in fact taught by the evangelists and others in the Gospels and early epistles. Meditative encountering of the New Testament unveils some of these secrets. A key text here is from the first Epistle of Peter (1Peter 4:5-6). When this text is more correctly translated than is usually the case (translators have often agreed to insert a word or two to allow them to give it a less esoteric nuance) it reads,

> "For this is the reason the gospel was also preached to dead persons {in Hades}, that they may be judged indeed as to the flesh, according to human nature, but {that} they may live as to the spirit, according to God."

It is the case that every tradition in the New Testament affirms this teaching that Christ Jesus also helped those whose body had died and were languishing in the less pleasant realms of the astral plane.[188]

Whilst journeying through the astral and higher realms, we are within the realms of the divine-spiritual hierarchies. There are nine ranks of these spiritual beings; and they have brought creation into being, in response to the impulses from the triune the Godhead. As Rudolf Steiner taught;

> "If we on the Earth here pluck a flower then it is quite correct to say, I am plucking a flower. But this kind of expression would be quite wrong regarding our inter-connectedness in life after death with the divine-spiritual beings. If we do something over there in conjunction with these beings, then we must say, well, we are in a condition in which we are continuously impelled to call the activity in which we are sharing, not "our" deeds, but as the activity of the hierarchies.
>
> Just as we here on earth feel inside us the lungs, the heart, etc, so do we feel over there within us the cosmos, but it is a realm of the divine-spiritual beings. And everything that occurs there occurs through an activity in which we ourselves are also interwoven."[189]

See illustration 19 regarding the fading and the re-appearing of light in the soul realms. A further lecture extract from Rudolf Steiner reveals clearly the nature of the interaction of the soul in these realms and the importance of seeking spiritual thinking whilst alive,

> "What we need in order to form again our life on the Earth is acquired in the time we spend between death and rebirth. During this time we approach step by step so to speak, the spirit beings appropriate to the particular realm that we are in. These beings can bestow upon us the faculties or forces of the higher hierarchies which, once we are incarnate again, shall be needed. But we can pass them by or interact with these beings in two ways.
>
> We can pass them by in such a way that we recognize and understand their inner nature; and if this is done then we can be receptive to that which they would grant to us. It is a receiving from Beings of the higher hierarchies of that which they can bestow upon us, that which we shall need in the next life. We need to be in the condition of understanding, even of just seeing that which is offered to us. For there is a second way that we relate to these divine beings.
>
> We could fail to be receptive to what is offered to us, because all around us everything is dark, spiritually speaking. Now the way in which one does proceed through these spiritual realms will be determined by the nature of the

---

[188] Although with St. John this is only briefly indicated. For more on this theme, see the author's book, "The Hellenistic Mysteries and Christianity".
[189] From GA 219, p. 60.

life that we have just lived. A person who has in their last life been antagonistic and unreceptive to thoughts and ideas which come towards us as teachings about the spiritual worlds passes through the spiritual world as if in darkness. For we need light, spiritually speaking, in order to perceive how these beings approach us so that we can perceive what gift a spiritual being can give us for our next life. The light of understanding which we need we cannot gain in the spiritual worlds; this we need to develop whilst on the Earth. The understanding of the spiritual worlds which we gain here on the Earth becomes transformed into the light that illumines our pathway in the journey between death and a new life." [190]

Entry into Devachan

Eventually the soul reaches the seventh realm of the astral plane, with only those qualities of thinking, feeling and will left to it, which are spiritual. Now it needs to cross over another threshold into a glorious, divine spiritual world: the Devachanic realms. The spiritual core of the human personality, closely linked to his or her own Guiding Angel, and now enveloped by the germinal Spirit-self, now enters this realm. Rudolf Steiner describes Devachan or Heaven like this,

> "Heaven consists of that from which thoughts are created. In this realm are the archetypal thoughts from which all things in the lower realms are created." [191]

This realm is the true Heaven. Heaven is filled with living archetypal Ideas, and these are living things. Everything here resonates with tones. The human spirit with its finest soul qualities feels itself as if immersed in a glorious ocean of light and tones. (This is the experience of the initiate during life.) Music resonates for the human soul-spirit here. But the great challenge here is for people entering this divine realm to still have a clear alertness as to their sense of self; this requires some development, whilst on the Earth of higher wisdom, purity and good will. The archetypes of all things in the astral, ether and physical realms are found here, as well as all things created by humanity.

Such was Rudolf Steiner's spiritual attainment that he was able to describe the nature of these realms. This realm is that inferred in the writings of Plato: the realm of the Archetypal Idea. A realm where sublime deities bring forth the idea of the vast variety of life that exists on the Earth. See Illustration 20 for a diagram of the journey from one life and back to the next life.

The Seven realms of Devachan

The First Realm is where the archetype of the physical plane exists. One beholds in this realm, like an enormous panorama, the geographic formations of the planet spread around one, appearing like a photographic negative. One's own previous physical body is also perceived, but as an Idea.

---

[190] GA 140, p. 247.
[191] From his book Theosophy, p. 178.

169

The Second Realm is where the archetypes of the ethers exist; hence for us the archetype of our ether body, from which our temperament derives. In the **second** realm of the archetypal Spiritual Worlds is that of Universal Life, which means in effect the Life-spirit. The life-force which in physical life is bound up with the forms of human, animal and plant kingdoms, and in which each being is delimited, flows here like the waters of the sea on Earth. One sees this universal life flowing there. It is pinkish-lilac in colour, from plant-form to plant-form, from animal-form to animal-form, as if embraced in the unity of life.

Third Realm is where the archetype of the soul qualities of feelings and emotions exist, and also to a small extent our thoughts and will. From the more elementary feelings up to the most noble emotions. And that means for us the archetype of our astral body, hence also our personality. The yearnings of the human being appear like a gentle sighing. Wars occurring on Earth reflect in the equivalent of stormy weather, it is as if the atmosphere there reflects the emotions, it is alive, responding to feelings of all beings. The equivalent to the sunlight here is bliss and blessedness.

Fourth Realm is where the archetype of our creative insights and wise thoughts exist. These are the highest aspects of our ego in normal life; in effect they are a reflection of the higher ego. A strong self-consciousness in this high realm is not so easy to attain; one must have striven to think clearly, especially in a spiritual, wise, sense. For example, those who have put the effort into attaining wise ideas about new social systems, or technical inventions of real benefit to humanity, and of course scholarly thinking; in essence, work of a deeper spiritual kind.

The **fifth realm**, for nearly all people, is experienced for just a brief moment. There, the Intentions which underlie the existence of our cosmos are to be found. There exists in the higher Devachanic realms the so-called Akasha Chronicle wherein the memory of all events in human beings' lives is maintained. This is in effect, the basis of the karma of humanity and is formulated through the reciprocal interweaving of divine beings. As Rudolf Steiner wrote in his book, Theosophy,

> "Here are the creator-energies behind the archetypes themselves....they exist as living germinal points in the archetypes...there the heavenly music of the spheres resounds in exquisite manner...each creature resonates a tone-colour ...each thing resonates its secret name...here the Intentions which underlie the existence of our cosmos are to be found..."[192]

One can conclude that the human being needs the spirit-aura to be reasonably developed to be conscious here. All karma is held in the consciousness of sublime divine beings. The active pursuit of spirituality in the deeper sense lead to the development of the Spirit-self and when this has been achieved whilst on Earth, then one may venture forth in to the divine higher realms. As Rudolf Steiner told one audience,

> "The true self of the human spirit now can expand itself and live in totally

---

[192] GA 88, lectures from Feb. 1904.

untrammelled freedom on all sides. In an indescribably exquisite and living radiant light, the human spirit, within its spirit aura, unfolds its wings, so to speak."

But then the very highly developed person may soar into higher divine and holy realms interwoven with the consciousness of the higher hierarchies, as the revealers of the love and wisdom and power of God. These are the **sixth** and **seventh** realms. Rudolf Steiner reports that the nature of the realms is even more remote from the power of earthly words to describe. But where are we, as we journey onwards, after death? We are in our solar system, and later we journey amongst the zodiac stars. The astral realms extend across the cosmos, as do the Devachanic and the etheric levels. The deceased person begins their journey on the astral level. But upon reaching, or rather venturing beyond, the sun-sphere, then they 'step up' into the devachanic level of the cosmos. So the first four levels of the astral plane commence from deep inside the Earth, and extend up to the Moon sphere.

The 5th, 6th and 7th spheres of the astral plane, which we explored earlier, occupy the sphere of Venus, then Mercury and then the sun, respectively. We need to note here that Rudolf Steiner reverses the order of the realms of Venus and Mercury when he lectures the theme of life after death; so Mercury is the realm near the earth and Venus is the realm nearer to the sun, (see entry under 'astrology' in Chapter 14.) The first level of Devachan occupies the sphere of Mars, the second sphere that of Jupiter, and the third sphere that of Saturn. The fourth sphere of Devachan extends from beyond the outer edge of the Saturn sphere up to the edge of our solar system. The remaining realms of Devachan take the human spirit up into the zodiac stars, see illustration 20.

The spirit in Devachan
In Devachan, the human spirit works on its next incarnation metamorphosing its previous soul qualities into something higher. Steiner taught regarding this,

> "The human being realizes I can now compare how I was at the end of my previous life, and how much I have developed in this latest life, and what can be developed in the future, as a result.' Then the human being is impelled to bring into being the Idea of the next body…this is done in untrammelled activity and the human being feels, in doing this, the sheer bliss of being creative…
> Love (good-will) becomes there the inexhaustible fountain of all life…"But each person's work is also being done on behalf of other loved ones…this work is the element which unites the human beings there.

Rudolf Steiner taught that over the many centuries the human spirit remains in Devachan, it moves through the zodiac constellations, that is, their spiritual equivalent. This means the hosts of divine beings who manifest in those star groups. In this way the connection is re-established with the spiritual beings there, and the nature of the new astral body is slowly formed. This is reflected in the horoscope. The human spirit whilst doing this is integrating the planetary energies with those that are raying into it from the zodiac. Hence the horoscope of the soul upon re-birth will have for example, Mars in Libra or in Taurus, etc.

19 The after-life journey: from 3,100 BC the length of time in the astral realm increased, the time in Devachan decreased. From 1900 a new time-cycle began, the Golgotha events started to exert an influence, so the time in Devachan increases for those who will, and a radiance re-develops in astral realm, for those rising above materialism.

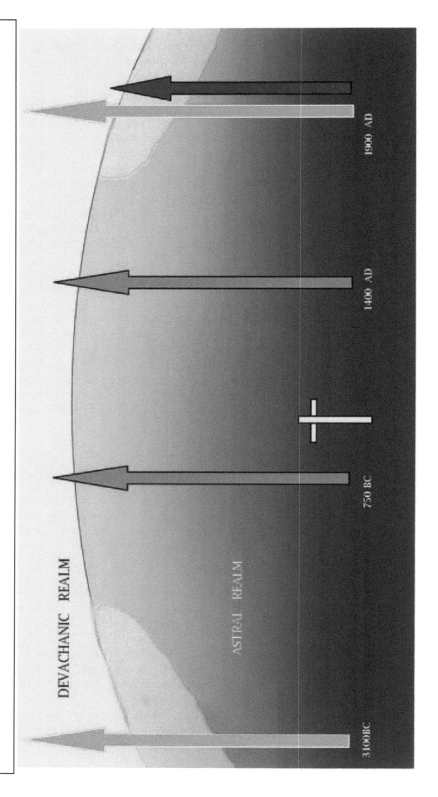

DEVACHANIC REALM

ASTRAL REALM

3100BC   750 BC   1400 AD   1900 AD

Eventually in Devachan, the human being, interwoven in its consciousness with its Angel and responding to the activity of the hierarchies, sets out to prepare for the next incarnation,

> "Just as here on the Earth we are perpetually under the influence of the environment, and the atmosphere...so too we are under the influence of the environment in Heaven...But there, the environment is formed of soul and spiritual qualities...these derive from ourselves, from other human beings and from the gods.
>
> All these soul forces exert an influence upon us continually...and precisely through this interaction process, those qualities are formed which become our new talents...our new gifts.
>
> That is, our own incipient qualities, our own characteristics draw into us forces which are similar to themselves from the living environment around us in heaven.
>
> Thus was Mozart able to be born with his immense musical talents, because he had harvested experiences and tendencies throughout many lifetimes, tendencies which were designed to instil musical talents. We experience the refinement of our inmost being through the outer environment in Heaven, and also by drawing on the events and lessons of past lives... all of which become transformed by the time we spend in heaven...

What we today are capable of achieving, we have incubated slowly and gradually in heaven. The feeling which arises from such incubating of higher abilities, stronger talents is one of infinite joy..."[193]

The Midnight Hour

But eventually the time arrives for the descent to a new life. As the human being reaches the end of its ability to journey into the divine spiritual cosmos, it is also finalizing what it can achieve in preparation for rebirth. This is called the "Midnight Hour" by Rudolf Steiner, and is usually the Saturn sphere, or the third realm of Devachan. The Midnight hour he says "is the most distant place into Devachan that the human spirit can move with some degree of awareness." And he also describes it as, "This is where the human being has the strongest and highest spiritual consciousness in its inner being, but no longer has the creative soul power within it, to illumine its spiritual environs." He also gave an invaluable, more detailed description of the Midnight Hour,

> "As the time for another earthly birth again draws near, the human being enters a state which can be compared, if we try to describe it by means of an earthly comparison, to that of a person who is beginning to experience loss of some memories. A person who is searching, as it were, for some memories, but cannot find them. So to, does the person as a new earth-life is approaching, search for a state of being which is filled with reality, **which is filled with reality.**

---

[193] GA 100, p. 60 and GA 108 p. 64.

The human being feels that it wants to become a real person again.[194] For at this point in the cosmic journey the human being cannot achieve any inner substance to its conscious understanding (thinking). However, its feelings and will <u>are</u> intense. But the person is searching for its concepts, which are becoming dimmer and dimmer. And in fact the will is becoming mightier and mightier. This begets within the person the wish – which now impels them on towards an earthly incarnation – for an earthly body. By the spiritual powers overseeing this process, this is then affirmed to the human being, via incorporation into an hereditary stream." The 'spiritual seed-bud' of its next body begins to become incorporated into a particular sequence of ancestors."
[195]

So, how do we return to the Earth? Many cultures have some knowledge about the initial stages of life after death. And since the 1960's experiences of near death and dying are now widely known. But little is known in old traditions or modern spirituality of the process whereby we return to a new life on Earth.

Returning to birth
Rudolf Steiner's initiatory consciousness was able to provide knowledge of this veiled process whereby the human being returns to rebirth. The human spirit in Devachan is drawn down towards a new life when the gods indicate that the karmic needs require this. As we saw earlier, this will be many centuries after the previous life, and we have reached the Midnight Hour.

There are two ways that the soul returns. One is the long-term way in which the new parents and locality of birth are planned. The other way is when the soul has not been able to arrange this, and has to seek out the best compromise possible. In the first way, a kind of seed-bud or germinal essence of the new physical body is sent earthwards, centuries before birth, and is incorporated into the male ancestors. (In the second way this incorporating has to occur in the current generation.)

Down through the spheres
The spirit, with a germinal essence of its new astral body, descends from the zodiac down into the solar system and then into the sun sphere, all on the devachanic level of being. In the sun sphere the new astral body attracts astral energies from the planets in the solar system (especially from the sun). This takes only a few hours (in the earthly time sense). The astral qualities in that new soul should be replicated by those prevailing upon the Earth at the hour of birth of the baby. (Hence one tries to choose the right place and time of birth, allowing for some variation, as the birth can be delayed or speeded up depending on medical conditions.)

In the Sun-sphere there comes a moment of temptation. We are approached by Lucifer, whose wish is to hold us back from incarnating, to delay our incarnation. He tempts us with the urge to try to evolve onwards with only that measure of spirituality which we

---

[194] Behind this soul-mood lives precisely the incapacity to truly seek an on-going devachanic sense of self.
[195] GA 211 p.15.

have already achieved, and to renounce going down into the world. Actually, we also had to face Lucifer on the way up to the sun sphere after death, where he offers the soul a false Paradise to enter for a while, delaying our entry into the divine realms. Living in a self-centred form of spirituality, or in a re-vamped form of ancient spirituality from cultures that historically have had little interest in the Earth, can predispose a people to his overtures and entry into his realm. The soul now descends towards the Earth, and passes through the spheres of Mercury and Venus. Here it has to absorb the residue of its lower self which was drawn out of its astral body on the journey upwards.[196] But since the soul has been further evolved by its own spirit in Devachan, the power of these negative astral energies will be weaker than in the preceding life.[197] It then moves down towards the moon sphere, guided by higher beings, and this occurs on the astral level of being.

As it nearly reaches the moon sphere it pauses, and waits for the winter solstice of whichever hemisphere it will be incarnating into.[198] As we saw earlier, as the winter solstice comes, the hemisphere 'breaths in' its energies, turning the etheric currents earthwards. The souls due to be born between that time and the next winter solstice, then descend down into the moon sphere. And in a few seconds after so doing, the soul's new etheric body forms, from the four ethers.[199]

Conception

At conception, the spiritual seed-bud of its new physical body unites to the ovum, and at this moment, the astral body (in the shape of a bell) is also enveloped by its etheric body.[200] After 21 days the etheric body begins to directly influence the tiny embryo.[142] An then at seven weeks the etheric body becomes much more active in it.[142] As the embryo develops its future central nervous system and its sympathetic nerve system the astral body almost splits into two, for a while. At two months the rudiments of the future brain form and during this process the radiant star of the person's germinal spiritual self shines brightly.[201]

At seven months both the astral and the etheric bodies fully unite to the embryo. For months already the soul has been raying its energies down into the embryo, forming the structures of the body and the internal organs. As this occurs, the complex, beautiful shapes moving inside the aura fade away. But some sparkling star-like forms shine on in the aura of the little child, and especially the one above the head. Shortly before birth the person has a brief preview of what the primary karmic experiences will be in the coming life. (From this, there derives what we call dejá-vu experiences.)

Verses for the Dead

---

[196] GA 141 p. 78 and GA 218, pp. 45-8, 125 and GA 226 pp. 31,40, 109.

[197] Although with criminal souls, the opposite may become true.

[198] GA 229, The Four Seasons and the Archangels, lecture, 13th Oct 1923. Steiner here and elsewhere when discoursing about the seasons confines his remarks to the northern hemisphere, but makes it clear that it is a seasonal phenomenon.

[199] GA 95, p. 48 & GA 100, p. 68.

[200] GA 94, p. 154.

[201] Archive lecture 18th Sept. 1903.

And what is the relationship of those living on the Earth to those who have died? Rudolf Steiner emphasized that the living are very important to those who have passed on into the spiritual realms. The dead whilst in the astral plane very much need our loving feelings and thoughts. For their existence, without us even thinking about them, would be similar to what life here on the Earth would be for us, without any beauty, without beautiful music or paintings. It is also a somewhat sad existence for our loved ones, if they discover that we have discarded them, so to speak. He gave a number of meditative verses that can be used to assist and comfort the dead, for example,

> May my love be the sheath that envelops you,
> cooling your warmth,
> warming your coldness,
> interwoven into your being
> as a freely given gift to you.
> May you exist with this gift of light
> into the heights, borne aloft by love.

Underlying this verse is the perspective that each soul has at times whilst incarnate either failed to carry out ethical actions when they were called for, or at times manifested lower desires and intentions. (Various small books are available from Steiner publishers with verses to help deceased loved ones.) As the soul encounters that episode in their life when either of these occurred, they find themselves in a state which resembles what we know on the Earth as unpleasant heat or coldness. Rudolf Steiner also taught that every night our deceased loved ones like to meet us and if we have been thinking about spiritual themes, they gain a great deal of help and uplift from us.

Further reading
Rudolf Steiner: Life between death and Rebirth
                Life beyond Death
        Anonymous   Bridge over the River

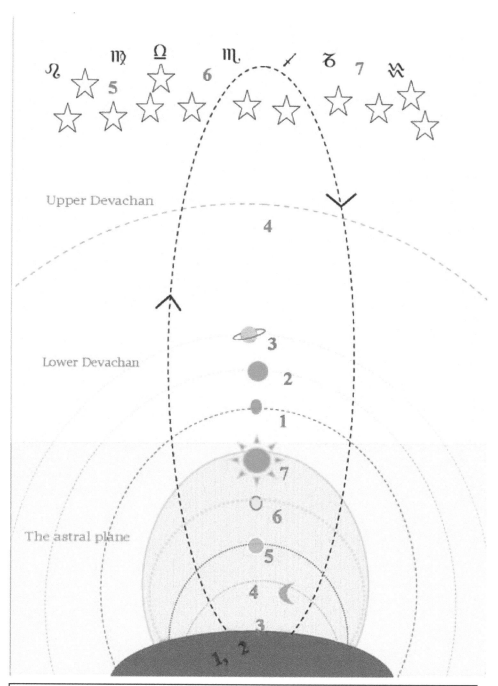

20 The journey after death: pink area = on the astral level,
blue area =   on the Devachanic level

10: ORIGINS: THE ANTHROPOSOPHICAL VIEW OF CREATION

In Rudolf Steiner's book 'Esoteric science: an Outline' (1910) the theme of cosmogony or the origin of the universe is the major focus. One chapter in this book is about a hundred pages long, and in it he provides a fascinating and graphic description of creation, from the spiritual perspective. In his early years of lecturing he focussed very much on this theme. He presented a view of creation which is in stark contrast to, but not incompatible with, that of modern science. He starts from a point above and long before physical creation started. He describes how the divine hierarchies formulated and moulded their intention to bring humanity into being. This will be a humanity that eventually develops its sevenfold nature, and then continues on the creative impulse from its creators, becoming creators themselves.[202]

So anthroposophical evolutionary teachings do not commence at a material level with such agents as sub-atomic particles producing the Big Bang, but within the creative will-forces of the Thrones, who are in the first hierarchy, and act as agents of a primal Trinity. Eventually, three-quarters of the way through its narrative, anthroposophical cosmogony arrives at the point where, after three vast aeons of evolutionary activity have been described, the solar system condenses down into the material level. This is where the scientific model starts, and the Kant-Laplace nebula appears.

There is some precedent for the spiritual cosmogony that Rudolf Steiner brought. This includes ancient creation myths, the Indian Vedas, and more especially the large book compiled by H.P. Blavatsky, 'The Secret Doctrine'. However, despite some parallels to the work of Blavatsky or ancient texts, what Rudolf Steiner taught was achieved by his own spiritual research, and entirely independent from the writings mediumistically channelled to Blavatsky. Madam Blavatsky wrote down the detailed and huge evolutionary processes in her book, without direct perception of these realities.[203] Rudolf Steiner directly perceived these remote and sublime primordial states of being; and he could comprehend and actively assess the dynamics involved. It is especially important to note here, as we consider an outline of anthroposophical cosmogony, that only by reading the book "An outline of Esoteric Science" can you really appreciate the contribution of Rudolf Steiner to this subject.

The First Aeon (the Saturn aeon)
In his book Rudolf Steiner begins with an appeal to one's imagination, to imagine moving as a spiritual being with clairvoyant capacity somewhere in the universe, going back to a very distant time. In a particular region one detects an area of warmth, but this warmth is devachanic warmth, not physical warmth. This means it is the fiery energies of a divine will, of latent intention becoming stirred. So it is not enthusiasm, desire, anger, etc (that is, astral warmth) nor even etheric warmth.

---

[202] His teaching is vast and provides a wholesome counterpoint to the New Age theory which asserts that Jehovah was a UFO technocrat.

[203] Consequently she was not always clear as to the meaning of some passages in her book. This becomes apparent in the proceedings or transactions of the Blavatsky Lodge, where a group is discussing their esoteric evolutionary ideas on April 25th 1889; published in the *Aquarian Theosophist*, Sept. 17th 2002.

What a person with Devachanic clairvoyance, which we have called Cosmic-spiritual Consciousness, would notice when experiencing this primordial event, would be differentiated regions of warmth, with their own pulsing, flowing structures. This seer becomes aware of a potent divine Will, a Will focusing on the unfolding of a vast pulsing living solar system. And the seer gazing back, then cognizes that this Will emanates from sublime beings, the Thrones. The Thrones are beings whom today manifest through the Saturn sphere; they have, as we do, seven aspects to their nature. The lowest of their seven aspects starts one level of consciousness above the Spirit-human, and consequently the highest element of their nature towers up some eight levels of evolutionary development, beyond the Spirit-human.

After some time, this spherical warmth area becomes a more tangible area of astral energies; and as other divine beings send their energies into it, the warmth field differentiates into numberless units of warmth. Gradually these individual units of warmth become more structured, and there is even towards the end a flickering etheric radiance.

The energy in these billions of units reflects back a resonance into the cosmos towards their creators. And from this the Principalities (at that time four stages of existence behind where they are now) experience their own inner nature. Hence a kind of self-sense awakens for them. All this has been occurring through a sequence of seven cycles of evolutionary processes. Then the Thrones become active again, and the entire sphere fades way, breathed back into the bosom of the godhead. A phase of non-time, and of non-creativity occurs (called a pralaya in theosophical language).

What has happened in this vast aeonic process? From what was originally a divine fiery will existing in the higher Devachanic realms, a tenuous energy-field has been created which becomes partly physical and partly etheric. This results in the first rudimentary form of a human physical body being formed. And associated with each of the billions of these bodies, there is also a subtle energy-template for the body, which sustains it. This is an invisible spectral form, called the 'phantom', meaning an invisible subtle template of the body.

The Atma or Spirit-human emerges
Before the rudimentary physical body was formed, an archetypal idea (or archetypal form) of the body has been developed, in the first level of Devachan. And from this the 'phantom' template (itself directly linked to the devachanic archetype) was fashioned. And also the seventh highest part of our nature, the divine 'Spirit-human' has been created. This was resting within the Thrones, not yet linked to an individual ego. So in effect it is unawakened, and this already indicates the purpose and highest future outcome of creation, namely that human beings may awaken within their ego-sense the Atma or Spirit-human. This is the highest aspect of our spirit.

A series of profound meditations were given by Rudolf Steiner on the theme of the four aeons. Yet these are also reverential verses in regard to the Logos, for behind the activity of the hierarchical beings is the Logos (and the Logos is understood to be directly expressive of the Father-God). This is the meditation for this first aeon,

179

Great, encompassing Spirit,
Thou who en-filled endless space,
when of my body's limbs
nothing was as yet existing.
     Thou wert.
I raise my soul to thee.
I was in thee.
Thou didst emanate forces from thyself   *
and at the Earth's primordial beginning
was mirrored the first archetype of my bodily form.
Within the energies sent out from Thee was I myself.
     Thou wert.
My archetype intuited thee;
It intuited me myself,
I, who was a part of thee.
Thou wert.

              (*via activity of the Thrones)

The spiritual depths of this verse evokes comparison with the grandeur of the Vedas, and provides a valuable perspective on the mystical concept of "Thou art That" of classical Hinduism. Earlier English versions of this Steiner verse don't allow the deeper implications to be seen.[204]

We have just gone through a brief over-view of the first aeon, which is the first of four such evolution eras. Each aeon occupies vast phases of time, and starts in the Devachanic realm, gradually descending down to the physical plane. There are seven aeons altogether. They have the names, Saturn {aeon}, Sun, Moon, Earth, Jupiter, Venus and Vulcan.[205] But the Earth aeon is seldom called that, as it is divided into two halves; the Mars half and the Mercury half.

We can also note here, as the diagram shows, that there are some technical terms which need to be known. I have found it better for my students to update these, as many were borrowed by Rudolf Steiner from 19th century theosophical literature, since many of the audience were Theosophists. Some of these older terms are prone to negative connotations; and the term 'planet' is used, which is confusing unless an explanation is provided.

Rudolf Steiner	New suggested terms
Old planet, (*thus*	Aeon *(thus 1st Aeon,*
old Saturn planet, etc)	*or Saturn Aeon, etc*)

---

[204] The latter part reads, "...On thee did my archetype gaze, it gazed on me myself, I who was a part of thee..." However, the verb anschauen used here also means to intuit.

[205] The term Vulcan was chosen because of its association with fire. Vulcan or Hephaestos in Greek myths, was a deity associated with subterranean, elemental fire. And Rudolf Steiner indicated that after the 7th aeon there shall arise a new cosmos, as if from a primordial cosmic fire. (GA 60, p.473).

Rounds	Cycles
Globes	Phases
Root-races	Large Epochs
Minor races	Cultural Ages (= zodiac ages)

Rudolf Steiner refers to this first aeon as "Old Saturn" or the "Old Saturn planet", but I have found an alternative term, the 'Saturn Aeon' or the 'First Aeon' very helpful, as the term 'planet' here can be confusing. Rudolf Steiner uses the name Saturn because the present-day planet Saturn exerts an influence upon the human soul similar to that which was emanated from the Thrones in this first aeon.

The planet Saturn is the sphere of the Thrones in our solar system and consequently it exerts an influence on that same aspect of our human nature which the Thrones created back then, namely our deeper will impulses, these are today mainly subconscious. There are similar deep interconnecting links of the present-day planets with the aeons that bear their names. Except of course for Vulcan, which is a stand-alone name and does not refer to a planet.

Illustration 21 may help to provide a feeling for the entire concept. It shows a mosaic from the 12th century Monreale cathedral in Sicily. It depicts God creating the solar system, and He is seated on a replica of the solar system, however this is a counter-image of the actual solar system. The mosaic is suggesting that from the archetypal realms of Devachan, God via the hierarchies, has created the archetypal Idea of the solar system and is then occupied with the task of bringing the Idea down into material reality. So there is an aspect of ancient Greek initiatory wisdom to this mosaic that echoes the esoteric insights of Plato.

Now, Rudolf Steiner's teachings are in effect describing the creation of our solar system, not the entire universe or the galaxy. In his lifetime, people in general did not know that galaxies existed, and consequently he did not attempt to present his perspective on the origin of things cosmic with reference to galaxies, just to an amorphous universe. The cosmos or universe which is the scene of the evolutionary processes in the book is gradually understood by the student of anthroposophy, ireading his book, to be in fact our solar system, and its associated zodiacal 'sheath'.

The Sun Aeon
The next event in creation is the Sun Aeon. And here already one meets in Steiner's cosmogony an indication of the transcendent nature of his teachings, because he points out that in the intervening situations between aeons, where God has 'breathed-in' so to speak, time actually ceases. So his descriptions are approximations of processes beyond the capacity of earthly concepts and words to correctly describe.

Seven cycles in each aeon
And this aeon also unfolded in a sequence of seven cycles; and within these cycles there occur seven phases of manifestation. The first phase starts in higher Devachan (we noted in the preceding chapter that there is Lower and Higher Devachan), the

181

second phase of its creative activity occurred in Lower Devachan. By the third phase, creation is now manifesting in the astral realm, and at the pivotal fourth phase it is in the physical plane. However the environment during the physical plane phase in any of the three earlier aeons was not as dense or as material as in our current aeon. We shall see later why evolution proceeds in a sequence of seven cycles and also why the fourth cycle or phase is so pivotal.

The Second Aeon

In this second aeon, all that which was achieved previously is rapidly recapitulated and then a lower rank of divine beings, the Dominions, emanate their energies into the sphere (which will become our solar system). And consequently the billions of units, which are the primordial beginnings of the physical human being, become endowed with warmth of an astral and etheric kind, but also with etheric energies. Together, they have an appearance vaguely like a blackberry, many tiny parts forming a larger body. The human being acquires the first rudiments of the etheric body. At its densest stage the solar system now is physically perceptible, a warm, dully shining cloudy oval.

 The vast primordial devachanic-astral-etheric oval now has some physical warmth, some light. But to the clairvoyant gaze, behind this light there exists a vaster, brilliant etheric radiance and an increasingly active, condensing will-energy which is felt as a kind of warmth. As this process develops, gaseous material is created. And also a satellite body forms, after a portion of the central sphere moves out to the periphery and then is spun off, away from the core cluster of spiritual beings, taking with it the ancestor of the present Earth with its vast multitude of primal human forms.

A prototype of the present day solar system has emerged; a sun (a central radiant body) and a satellite (a planet) have emerged. The dwellers on the satellite absorb energies from divine beings in the sun. As the etheric forces reach a certain peak of interaction with the physical bodies of these primordial humans, this gives rise to a form of animating, almost reproducing, power within them. But then soon the entire cosmic oval gradually fades away. The primordial physical-etheric body of human beings had emerged. But now once again, the solar system is 'breathed-in' and time ceases. The achievements attained in that aeon are brooded upon or assimilated by the creator gods, and when creation re-occurs, the physical-etheric human being will be consolidated and ready to meet the next step. As this aeon ends, and the solar system is drawn back into Higher Devachan, a period of inactivity occurs again.

Moon aeon

A third cosmic day dawns, the Moon Aeon; the vast cluster of divine-spiritual beings now re-emerge. The previous cosmic achievement – physical and etheric bodies – is quickly recapitulated. The shining central Sun, now etherically very potent, re-emerges as the core of the system, and within it there are the ancestors of the human life-wave. Now the Mights or Spirits of Movement, from within the cluster of divine beings in the Devachanic aura of the Sun, emanate creative powers from their being. And as a result, a degree of sentiency arises for these primordial human beings; tenuous astral energies swirl around and within the physical-etheric body of human beings. As this happens, a denser element arises now: the fluidic. And again, as during the previous aeon, a satellite moves off from the central sun. The Earth-dwellers become aware that the Sun-beings move out, leaving the Earth as a satellite.

So the primeval ancestors of humanity now dwell on a satellite which gradually begins to orbit the central cluster of divine sun beings, with its extraordinarily radiant etheric and astral powers. On this ancestor of the planet Earth there were also the antecedents of our animals and plant species. Many less evolved spirit beings, below the rank of Powers (or Spirits of Form) have moved out of the central body (the sun) to exist with Earthly humanity on the ancestor of our Earth. These are the Principalities, the Archangels and the Angels. As millions of years pass by, in this third aeon, humanity gains the ability to experience sentiency. This is the capacity to be aware of one's environment. Within the warmth/gaseous/fluidic physical body of the human beings, a nervous system develops.

The third Aeon brings forth the astral body
Human beings now possess a rudimentary astral aura, which hovers above the planet's surface, and is linked to the tenuous, dissolvable physical-etheric body down below. But these astral auras (or astral bodies) are devoid of any real individual human ego. These primitive humans gather in vast numbers into one of four groupings of human souls; some resemble present-day ruminants, and others appear somewhat like birds, other feline animals, and others more like a standard human form. These four primary types have their origin in the zodiacal influences from Taurus, Scorpio, Leo and Aquarius.

The satellite (the primordial Earth) now absorbs and responds to the spiritual impulses surging out from the sun gods. Then gradually once more, as the integration of the sentiency capacity with the life force and very tenuous, non-fleshy physical body reaches its highest capacity, the cosmic oval begins to be breathed back in. We are still vast time periods before the Kant-Laplace starting point of astronomical cosmogony. (As Steiner taught that the etheric stage of creation slowly condensed ever more until the physical world emerged,[206] he would not be supportive of the Big Bang theory.)

But let's now go back over the previous aeon, the Moon aeon in a way that shows the reason for the number seven figuring so prominently in evolution.

Cycle 1: The evolutionary development attained in two previous aeons is recapitulated.

Cycle 2: The Mights (Spirits of Movement) allow forces to stream out into humanity, who are clustered inside the sun. And in this interweaving with the rudimentary human physical-etheric body the first stages of sentiency arises for the human being. Or one could say, it is added to the physical-etheric, as it is now capable of being imbued by a rudimentary astrality.

Cycle 3: The Powers begin to be active now, and as their energies permeate the human being, and only whilst this happens, a vague astral nature of wishes, desires, dislikes, arises in the human being.

---

[206] GA 106 (Egyptian Myths) 5th Sept 1908, p. 54.

21 God creating the solar system, from the basis of a Devachanic archetypal Idea. A twelfth century mosaic from Sicily; revealing a Platonic Christianity.

Cycle 4: As the human being imbues itself with the desire nature, or astrality which is flowing all around its being, the vast solar system of the third aeon begins to form a somewhat vaporous wateriness, in parts. These denser parts are drawn together and then cast out of the central sun, forming a satellite around the main body. This satellite is the ancestor of the planet Earth. (The central sun is now smaller than it was back in the previous aeon.) The human being's bodily form was subject to a regular dissolving and re-forming, its consciousness that of a dreaming state, filled with awareness of the gods.

The activity of the angels on this primitive human life-wave has been considerable; they are deeply interwoven in the soul-processes of these early human beings. And this is the factor which has enabled human beings to achieve their dream-image psychic consciousness state. It is a pivotal event.

Cycle 5: As the human beings experience the inner imagery arising in response to all the potent, colourful, phantasmagorical beings and energies of the planet, they begin to vaguely sense the presence of the angels. This process allows the angels to develop further and to consolidate a form of ego-hood or self-hood.

Cycle 6, Cycle 7: These attainments for all the various hierarchical beings and for the human beings are now consolidated and the solar system is once again 'breathed in' and disappears from physical, etheric and astral sight.

Now before we consider the current aeon, the fourth one, we need to answer the question, why are there seven stages to evolution. It is slightly evident in the description of the seven cycles in the Third aeon that we have just explored. In essence it is because the godhead is triune.

So in the first stage, 'being-ness' arises into existence (via the Father God).
In the second stage, life arises into existence; that is being-ness becomes animated, vivified (via the Logos or active principle).
In the third stage, consciousness arises into existence (via the Holy Spirit or deity which meditates the spirit to humanity).

Then in the fourth stage **a new element enter**s into the cosmos. The three preceding stages, now actively interrelating, bring forth this new element.
Then in the fifth stage that which arose in the first stage is brought to an enhanced condition, and that which arose in the sixth stage is likewise enhanced. And in the seventh stage, what was manifested in the third stage is enhanced.[207]

And why does Rudolf Steiner take so much trouble to explain all this? It was his conviction that the great challenge that human beings are facing is to understand themselves, in other words **to gain self-knowledge**. And real self-knowledge has to include an awareness of how deeply embedded we are in the aeons of evolutionary processes sustained by divine hierarchies.

---

[207] Explained in a lecture of 25th Oct. 1904, in *Beiträge zur Rudolf Steiner Gesamtausgabe*, Nr. 67/68, 1979.

If we have contemplated our inner life, we have seen how when faced with something beautiful, a liking, or a delight arises. Or when faced with something ugly, sinister, or malignant we see how antipathy, fear and rejection arises. We have experienced how, when our interest is engaged, our energy levels increase. And how when we do a bad deed, an inner voice tells us that it was bad. And we have observed how a tiny infant, who has not yet learned of good and evil, naturally feels delight at its mother's love. The question arises, where does all this come from? What is the origin of the qualities which we take for granted in us?

In Rudolf Steiner's evolutionary teachings, all these inner qualities come from the energies within the divine beings who have directly or indirectly created us. In his words, the purpose of the cosmos itself is – humanity ! We have seen that in the preceding three aeons the human being has been given its physical body, etheric body and soul (astral body). Now the sense of self, the ego is needed. This becomes the task of the higher beings in the next aeon, the fourth aeon.

The Earth Aeon
There is much more information given by Rudolf Steiner about this fourth aeon than the other earlier ones, but we will only briefly consider it here. As this fourth aeon, the Earth aeon began, the spiritual beings called by St. Paul 'the Powers', called Spirits of Form in anthroposophical literature, became the primary instigators of the evolutionary impetus in this aeon.

So in the fourth aeon (the Earth Aeon) the first 3 cycles (each of which has 7 phases) recapitulate the achievements of the previous aeons. Little is said about the processes occurring during them in The Outline of Esoteric Science, however there was a lot of explanatory material given in various lectures from 1904-1909.

At this point it is important to refer to Illustration 22, which goes beyond the simple branching-out sketches usually used for this theme in anthroposophical literature. Here you can see clearly the various sequences of sevens that are involved in the evolutionary process.

The fourth cycle begins with the first of its seven phases about which Rudolf Steiner says little, because the major new developments in this aeon will occur with the 4th phase of the 4th cycle. So we will consider this fourth cycle, beginning of the fourth phase of this cycle (see illustration 22, this shows clearly what is meant). The first Large Epoch of the first phase of this fourth cycle called the **Polarian** large epoch as the diagram shows. This is followed by the **Hyperborean** large epoch. The large epochs are shown as green lozenge-shape features. The next large epochs are the Lemurian and then the Atlantean, and so on.

In the Polarian large epoch the events occurred which are briefly mentioned in the Bible, Genesis1:1. This was the time when in the devachanic realms all the previous development of the aeons is recapitulated and the archetypal Ideas of the future physical Earth with its four realms of minerals, plants animals and human were consolidated. Rudolf Steiner taught that if an initiated priest of ancient times, perhaps a Hebrew or Druid, were to write a poetic brief description of the creation of the world, such a person would start with the first three phases of the Earth Aeon. Then they would refer to the Polarian large epoch of the fourth phase, wherein this consolidation process, occurring in Devachan, was being undertaken by beings of the hierarchies.

And then such an initiate would say to himself, such a description is not complete, I must also include a description of how all of the higher energies actually became gradually physically real, in the condensing, material Earth in the course of the next few large epochs. These are the large epochs of Hyperborea and Lemuria. So such a person would need to write two creation stories, and thus the book of Genesis provides us with a second creation account, which many people see as duplicating the first account in Genesis in many ways.

With regard to this current, fourth aeon, it was back in the Hyperborean large epoch, which existed before Lemuria, that there occurred the separation of the sun from the Earth. Other, other outer planets had already spun off into the solar system. Human beings existed as aquatic creatures, but with a very tenuous body which actually dissolved and re-built in response to the rhythms of the sun and Earth. Above this bodily form, on the etheric and astral level, there hovered a very refined, somewhat chalice-shaped, human countenance. This astral-body indicated the nature of the potential for the rudimentary bodily form down below, to one day be shaped in likeness to the evolved human being of the future.

Lemuria

In the Lemurian epoch, the Earth became gradually firmer whilst still hot and subject to volcanic action. On the planets Venus and Mercury fallen luciferic spirits are located, the consequence of their inability to remain in the sun. The human being, with a soul now more connected to a more dense physical body, has become subject to the luciferic stimulus towards ego-centric deities and thoughts. But the human being also became exposed to ahrimanic influences active from within the material substance of this turbulent, primal Earth. Forces from Taurus are active in developing an ahrimanic or brain-bound thinking life. And the more this occurred, the denser the soft body became. So humanity is starting to experience personal desires and earth-bound will impulses and logical attitudes, and these are the basis of the earthly ego-sense. Human beings still existed in the aquatic environment, but this would gradually condense into a more solid form.

The sentient-soul has in effect become empowered; the human being is awakening to itself. Luciferic beings in Venus and Mercury enhance this, but a group of sun spirits (Powers) or Elohim as the Old Testament calls these beings, prepare to both enhance this primitive self-sense and to ensure that there is a link between the earthly ego and the future potential for a Spirit-self, see Illustration 23. Rudolf Steiner calls this process the bestowal of the ego; actually it attempts to depict the human being a few million years after the moon has been cast out, when the human body was more dense. Yahweh in the moon sphere assists the soul to feel its earthly human nature and as regent of many elemental beings this deity also regulates the heredity and fertility of nature and humanity.

187

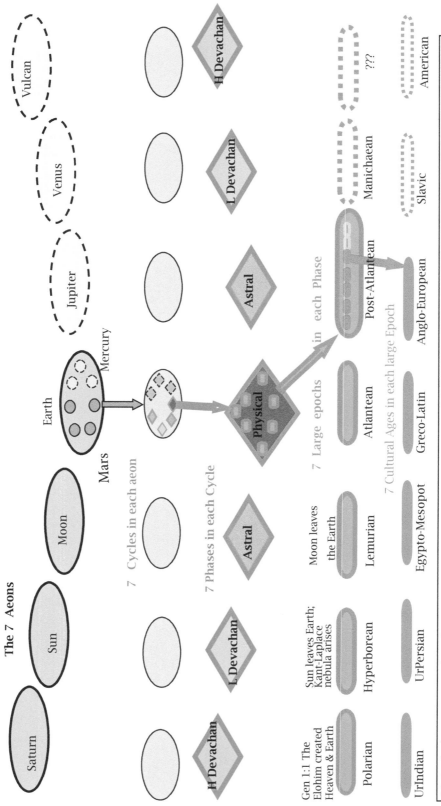

The 7 Aeons

Saturn | Sun | Moon | Mars | Earth | Jupiter | Venus | Vulcan

Mercury

7 Cycles in each aeon

7 Phases in each Cycle

H Devachan | L Devachan | Astral | Physical | Astral | L Devachan | H Devachan

7 Large epochs in each Phase

7 Cultural Ages in each large Epoch

Gen 1:1 The Elohim created Heaven & Earth | Sun leaves Earth; Kant-Laplace nebula arises | Moon leaves the Earth | | Post-Atlantean

Polarian | Hyperborean | Lemurian | Atlantean | Post-Atlantean

UrIndian | UrPersian | Egypto-Mesopot | Greco-Latin | Anglo-European | Slavic | American

Manichaean | ???

22 Evolution We are in the 4th Aeon, in its 4th Cycle, in the 4th phase of this, in its 5th Large epoch, & in the 5th cultural age of this

188

As we saw in earlier chapters, in the works of Rudolf Steiner, the ego is a dual organ. So the processes described here relate to both aspects of the ego. At this crucial mid-Lemurian time, the luciferic spirits helped humanity to develop a sense of selfhood in their astral body, and thereby at the same time, with influence from Ahriman, they created the lower, earthly self. This event, the so-called Fall of Man, occurred some 18 million years ago.[208] Whereas the great sun spirits, who had provided the general 'material' of the soul or astral body in earlier evolutionary cycles, ensured that the newly developed earthly sense of ego would be of such a kind that in the future it could be accessed by noble spiritual influences deriving from the sun sphere, thus forming the eternal, higher ego.

The Genesis stories

The reader will have now noticed that the reference to the Bible in the anthroposophical view of creation refers to a plurality of divine beings, called the Powers or the Elohim. These beings are referred to as our Creators, rather than the single being, 'God' as mentioned in the Bible. Rudolf Steiner taught that this term, the Powers, refers to a group of beings from the sun sphere.

In earlier chapters we noted how in anthroposophy the term God is often really a way of referring to the hierarchies. So it is relevant here to briefly consider what evidence there is, if any, in the Bible itself that supports his viewpoint. To do this effectively we need to note the actual original Hebrew text (see foot-note). The usual translation is "In the beginning God created Heaven and Earth…" The question is whether the term God here and the associated verb are singular or plural. The term Elohim, translated as 'God', is a plural noun.[209] But the verb 'created' is actually in the singular. Consequently most scholars regard the plural term for God here as a kind of royal plural, indicating the majesty of God. And with the verb being singular, this seems quite correct.

However a singular verb can be used for a plural thing, such as, 'the crowd was delighted'. So the scholarly argument is not necessarily correct; there are other references to God being a plurality of beings in the Hebrew. And there is one reference where Elohim occurs where the verb too is <u>in the plural</u>. So it is possible to conclude that Rudolf Steiner's viewpoint is not in contradiction to the Biblical account.[210] And there is a special feature to the Scripture here which tends to be supportive of the anthroposophical view. Steiner taught that there were six of these great sun gods, working as one, who undertook creation. But he also taught that actually there are

---

[208] Stated in archive lecture, 18th July 1904 and indicated in GA 189, p.145.
209
This is how the beginning of the sentence looks in Hebrew (NB, it goes from right to left),

אֱלֹהִים   בָּרָא   בְּרֵאשִׁית

(plural) the Elohim   (singular)created   the-beginning In
[210] Statements in Deuteronomy, chapter 4, that Yahweh is the <u>only</u> Elohim, is then seen as not an absolute about the number of deities in existence, but about the call for reverence and loyalty from the Hebrews to this especial deity.

seven of these beings. The seventh one separated off from the sun sphere and exerts an influence on humanity via the moon; and this one is the revered Bible deity, Yahweh. There are some indications that the great Hebrew sages thought that there was a sevenfold aspect to their deity, for example in their commentary on Deuteronomy.[211] Rudolf Steiner differentiates between the Elohim and Yahweh (or Jehovah). They are from the same rank of hierarchical being, but the former are a group of six deities in the sun sphere, whereas Yahweh has left the sun sphere and taken up activity within the moon sphere, to guide the life-processes on Earth.

This anthroposophical view also provides an answer to the notable enigma in the book of Genesis, for those who know the Hebrew. Namely, that in the first Creation story the term for God is 'the Elohim' but in the second story, it is Yahweh. Anthroposophically this is understood as the result of the account in the second story being especially focussed on the activity of the seventh of the Elohim, Yahweh. For now the Earth is in existence as a physical reality and its genetics and heredity dynamics, which are the especial province of Yahweh, need to be established.[212]

If Yahweh or Jehovah were to be active alone in humanity's consciousness on Earth, we would never have felt able to develop an inner independence, from which freedom eventually arises. Whereas Luciferic powers, without actually seeking to allow freedom to arise in us, brought about the pre-conditions for the development of a personal ego-hood.

The way that the book of Genesis was written provides some supportive evidence for Rudolf Steiner here. When the original Hebrew here is worked with in a meditative way, it is possible to write it out in such a way as to mean 'Six divine beings created, the Elohim created, Heaven and Earth'; see the Appendix about this.
This event, the creation of the world, as described in Genesis, was depicted in a scene painted in the large dome of the Goetheanum; the Elohim and archangels ray down their creative energies to the Earth, nurturing the development of humanity, and also the flora and fauna, (see the entry in the next chapter, *Goetheanum Cupolas: their paintings*).

Middle to late Lemuria
The planet condenses further, but for some millions of years there was an aquatic, gaseous fiery environment where physical life manifested in ahrimanic primitive forms.[213] As the Earth cooled and hardened, the ancestors of the dinosaurs arose; this is

---

[211] In Deut. 10:8 "...and to bless His name..." the verb used there, shaba, to bless or praise (שָׁבַע) is very similar to the word for 'seven', sheba, (שֶׁבַע). On this the Zohar (Fol.1: 204a,) comments, "...as we are taught, cleave to the secret of the heavenly continuum of seven gradations, placed over all things, to the secret of the completing of this continuum." This appears to refer to the interweaving of creative impulses from the seven Elohim.

[212] The New Age depictions of the Elohim as spacemen, is an idea that chains people to a materially-based view of creation, deleting the spiritual matrix from which we derive.

[213] A comprehensive study of Rudolf Steiner's many lectures on the creation of the solar system, shows that he presents these primordial stages as occurring over several million years, and not as previously thought, over some tens of thousands of years.

in the Lemurian large epoch. Less and less pe\ople can descend to the Earth, as the soul cannot incorporate itself in the denser bodies.

In early Lemuria, we humans existed within the semi-aquatic turbulent environment, with bodies that were denser than ever before, but still soft by our standards today. They were watery and gelatinous, and gradually developed a musculature system. But we still had no skeleton, therefore no trace of these human beings remain from the Lemurian epoch. The human body only gradually hardened, forming a skeleton by the Atlantean epoch, but animals had hardened bodies long before this time. We modern humans don't have our skeleton fully ossified until we are 18 years old; it is in part still cartilage until then. (The African rift valley skeletons are of a degenerate, quite separate quasi-human species whose skeletons hardened much earlier than did human bodies.)

The next event is that in mid-Lemuria the **moon is extruded** in an enormous upheaval, taking with it on an etheric and astral level, the more ahrimanic energies that were hardening the Earth. But the moon from out in its orbital path also regulates the fertility of our planet. The planet gradually settled down and cooled further, and the excessive hardening tendency ceased, allowing humanity to return and to live on it, in life after life. Over some millions of years, throughout the Lemurian epoch, the basis for a preliminary ego-sense is brought into being in humanity.

The Elohim have wrought this great deed, so that now divine forces maintain a presence in the primitive human soul, and also luciferic and ahrimanic powers have their sphere of influence. The influence of these powers, especially the luciferic beings, brought about a sensing of desire in the sentient-soul, and also a faint sense of self, or an inner independence.

The Fall of Man
It is the effect of these processes, culminating in the extrusion of the moon, that brought about what is called the Fall of Humanity, described in Genesis (Gen. 2:18, 21-22, 3:1-7). This term really refers to the inevitable and indeed pre-ordained descent of the human soul (devoid of an ego) into the material plane. Hence we came into a flesh body, and no longer existed in the ethers. But it is precisely this process which resulted in the gift of the earthly ego. This is the meaning behind the Biblical story of the serpent persuading Eve to get Adam to eat of the fruit from the Tree of Knowledge of Good and Evil.

The animal species have various origins. Some animals exist because through their It is in the Lemurian epoch that the vast variety of animal life-forms begin to emerge, and on into Atlantean times new animal species appeared on the Earth. The animal group-souls derive from the great hierarchical beings, known as the Mights or Virtues; these deities are one stage of evolution beyond the sun gods or Spirits of Form. Humanity's own spiritual source however, derives from the primal Trinity, the Godhead. existence, they incorporate their unique astral nature into themselves, and hence drain it away from our astral body. For example, if foxes did not exist, we humans would be potentially more subject to viciousness in our predisposition. Other animals by their existence, alter the astral energies in the Earth's aura in such a way that we humans can develop essential qualities.

For example the horse species, which arose in the later phase of the Atlantean age, enabled us humans to develop our frontal lobe and thus our individual intelligence capability could emerge. From this role of the horse, comes the mystical association of them with mastery and freedom.[214] The group-spirit of an animal species is often a high spiritual being. In the next aeon, which will be the fifth of these great evolutionary times, the animal group-spirits (not the individual animals) will evolve up to approximately the state of a human being.

The land mass known as Lemuria was located in the Indian Ocean but it was destroyed in a nature cataclysm about 26,000 BC.[215] At this time the Lemurian large epoch came to an end. Madagascar is a remnant of this land. Late Lemurian human beings were still not fully hardened as our body is today; they had cartilage rather than bones, and they established primitive dwellings and large rock temples. They also carved out dwellings from caves, and became very skilled at doing this. There were also some Lemurian-age buildings outside of the Lemurian landmass. And people still had a flexible body in that time; they could increase its length and its
actual muscle power.

The Atlantean large epoch
Then came the Atlantean large epoch on various large and small islands in the Atlantic Ocean. We noted this in an earlier chapter. This landmass existed for millions of years, but as the Lemurian large epoch ended, the Atlantis became the place where, for the next seven zodiac ages, humanity progressed further ahead. This civilisation itself was destroyed about 7,500 BC. But prior to this catastrophe the landmasses and ocean currents were quite different; for example, the Siberian plains were vast inland seas.[216] The air was filled with vast wet clouds, and a misty vapour. So the sun was not seen clearly, nor the moon, and there was a vast, coloured auric glow around them.

A far memory of this is contained in the Druidic wisdom, preserved in the Edda, of a region called Nifelheim or Misty land.[217] The stars were not visible at all. In early Atlantis, stones were shaped to form rough buildings, with growing trees interwoven with these. The night-time brought dreams that were felt to be as real as the experiences of daily life. The language of the Atlanteans was a unified common language which was oriented towards the sounds of nature. It was an imitation of the sounds of the babbling brook the sighing winds, the rustling of the trees, the roll of the thunder, the breaking of the waves.[218] Steiner taught that in the earlier stages of this large epoch there were no codified ethical guidelines.

---

[214] This may be the reason for the Uffington white horse carving in the UK.
[215] GA 205, lecture of 10th July 1921.
[216] GA 98, p. 94.
[217] GA 97, p. 290.
[218] GA 101, p.70.

If someone needed to know how to act in relation to their neighbour, that person did not have recourse to a precedent or a code of ethics, they listened to the waves and then they knew {what their soul-spirit nature advised them to do}.

An after-echo of this state of awareness is found in a passage in the ancient Epic of Gilgamesh, where the boatman Utnapishtim, speaks of how he heard in the whispering sounds of the reeds the intention of the great god Enlil, to build the Ark in preparation for the great Flood that ended the Atlantean epoch some 9,000 years ago.[219] In this epoch initiatory and religious sites were developed, which were similar in general intention to the Hellenistic Mysteries. These Atlantean Mysteries were guided by semi-gods, that is, more evolved angels who overshadowed the leaders of the Mysteries. By mid-Atlantis, a more noticeable sense of self was developing. And as this happened the ugly sloping forehead filled up and out, to encompass the frontal lobe of the brain.

Rudolf Steiner taught that the people lived in this moist air environment on islands in the Atlantic Ocean, and they gradually developed a simple form of natural technology. In brief, the main points of his description are as follows. Over some thousands of years, the people flew over the stretches of water between the islands in their rudimentary flying vessels. The airships were powered by etheric forces, but the Atlanteans needed to be able to access their own etheric energies to make them fly.

In last third of Atlantis (about 15,000 BC) the air thinned, as the water vapour descended and also the ether body of the Atlanteans shrank in towards the body, no longer raying out as far as it used to. The result of this was that the ability to use etheric forces in airships dwindled; and so they had practical reasons to learn to use mechanical land-based technology. And the air was now beginning to actually rain, to rain down water instead of just a thin vaporous mist.

Later in Atlantis, as Rudolf Steiner describes, some Atlanteans began to feel interest in navigating on the water, and this was felt to be a sensational development. To do this however, boats had to be invented, and they were. This was the single most significant achievement in the minds of the people of that time. People were directed by the initiates to do this, and once boats were invented, and the rain continued pouring down ever more, people were required by initiates to live within the boats. This enclosed way of living also assisted them to feel a sense of selfhood. Long before Atlantis was destroyed, there was extensive trade and other interaction, made possible via these boats, between the Atlanteans and the lands to the west and to the east. People from the 5th Atlantean cultural age had emigrated to northern India, for example. Hence in the great Indian epic the Mahabharata there is a reference to seven great islands in the western ocean, where there was an empire with the city of the three

---

[219] Steiner comments that this episode in the legend is a flash-back to the Atlantean era, lecture 28th Dec. 1910.

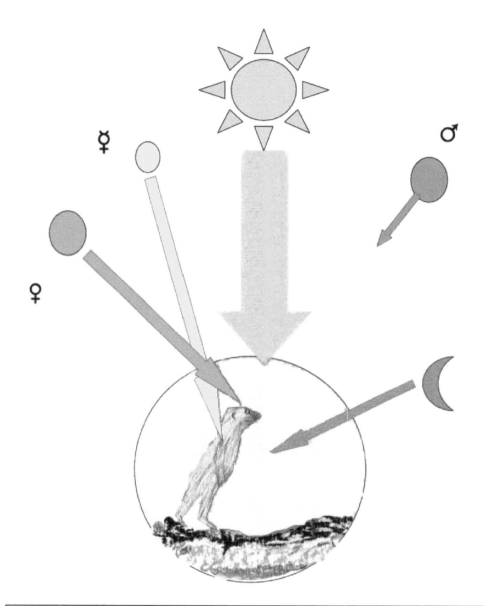

23 Fall of Man or the earthly ego state: 18 million years ago, with the moon extruded, the Elohim enhanced awareness in the human soul & linked it provisionally to the Spirit-self. But Luciferic spirits from Mercury (intellect) and Venus (heart), influence the soul towards a separated ego sense. Mars forces prepare to permeate the soul, enhancing its inner life. Lunar forces govern fertility.

mountains as its capital. Atlantean trade with Mediterranean peoples began in later Atlantean times, and so there are still today some ruins of temples around the Mediterranean, which were built before the great flood which brought Atlantis to an end.

From around the world, ancient legends preserved by nations and tribes tell of a mighty flood which long ago nearly exterminated mankind. From Iceland and the Eskimos, across to North America, to the central American lands, down into South America. Across into Mesopotamia and the Mediterranean peoples, over in Persia, Sumeria, Babylon, India, Tibet and China these myths recall the Atlantean world. And in all of South-east Asia, Indonesia and Australia, New Zealand and Hawaii one also finds similar ancient legends.

At this point anthroposophical history then starts to merge with the conventional flow of history. Although the epoch from the Atlantean Flood onwards is referred to as the Post-Atlantean large epoch. In an earlier chapter we considered the nature of these cultural ages, each lasting 2,160 years.

Further Reading
Rudolf Steiner: Atlantis and Lemuria (also called Cosmic Memory)
               An Outline of Esoteric Science.
               (also called An Outline of Occult Science)

Appendix

Six divine beings created, the Elohim created, Heaven and Earth

Without having to know Hebrew you can see to some extent how this other meaning is veiled within the first sentence from the Book of Genesis. The Hebrew sentence but now with the English going from left to right is,

בְּרֵאשִׁית בָּרָא אֱלֹהִים

Elohim bara Be'Reshith

= In the-beginning the Elohim created …..

But it can be written this way:

בָּרָא שִׁית בָּרָא אֱלֹהִים

Bara-shith bara Elohim

= Six created, the Elohim, created….

All that has occurred here is that the first word has been split into two, and it also starts with a different vowel. And one <u>can</u> change the vowels because they were not written down originally, only the consonants were written down. To see the possibility of such different meanings veiled inside the original text is a profound feature of the great Hebrew writings. This is a deliberate feature of the book of Genesis.

So now this altered sentence means, 'Six divine beings created, the Elohim created, Heaven and Earth'.[220] And this of course, does echo the perspective taught by Rudolf Steiner. But he provided his knowledge on a wide variety of subjects from his spiritual research, independently of texts. However, he was always interested in finding textual evidence for his research, if this was possible. Hence we provide this brief look at the Hebrew text here.

---

[220] The Pentateuch commentary, The Zohar, Mantua version, vol. 1 paragraph 3a/b speaks of this.

11: Various Themes: The Arts

Architecture of the Goetheanum,
Art: its spiritual value, Colours: their soul-mood
Eurythmy: a new kind of dance
Goetheanum Cupolas: their paintings,
The four Mystery Plays, The Group sculpture
Paintings valued in anthroposophical circles,
The Planetary Seals,
The Windows of the Goetheanum,
Voice (acting, recitation).

Architecture of the First Goetheanum

With regard to the First Goetheanum's unusual architectural forms, Steiner emphasized that these were not drawn from nature. The curving surfaces were not an imitation of nature. Instead the forms derive from a shape intuitively arrived at, independent of any forms in nature, (although similar) and their shape metamorphoses itself throughout the building,

> "The architect has to be able to find such forms for a building in an entirely inherent, original way....and the forms that arise must correspond to the *energy-layout* of the building."[221]

One notes in these words a resonance with the feng-shui approach to architecture. Rudolf Steiner had hoped that in the 1980's the organic architectural style which he used for the First Goetheanum would become a catalyst for a large number of buildings using such organic styles, late in the 20th century. But with the arson attack on that building at the end of 1922, the possibility of such an outcome faded.

This building consisted of two cupolas, the smaller one seeming to emerge from the larger cupola. The entrance to the large cupola was located to the west, so the small cupola was towards the east. Rudolf Steiner wanted this building to continue the idea behind the symbolic Temple of Solomon, namely that the building in its design and relative dimensions, should symbolize the human soul;

> "What did the temple of Solomon want to be? It wanted the same thing as the temple of the future wants and can only want....the soul must be able to be a temple, a soul that can receive into itself the spirit...The temple, that is the human being, the human being who can receive the spirit into its soul !"[222]

At another time he explained the dome or cupola shape in this way,

> "If a human being could lie down on the ground, as if firmly anchored onto the earth and then with the hands spiritually feel out into space, seeking to feel

---

[221] Lecture, 23rd Jan. 1920 in, Architektur Plastik und Malerie des Ersten Goetheanums, Dornach, 1972.
[222] Lecture, 12th Dec.1911, in Wege zu einem neuen Baustil, 1982.

what is up above, then such a person would dimly sense the spiritual worlds above, as if he or she were in a mighty dome, a building that was in every way symmetrical." [223]

Rudolf Steiner explained to a visitor that the large windows made of stained glass, set in the walls, were designed to let the walls of the building open the interior space up to the cosmos, not close it in.[224] In fact Rudolf Steiner had also hoped for such people-friendly architectural elements, intuitively grasped, to develop in the general area around the Goetheanum. A small colony of houses and buildings, to be organically in harmony with the geographical features of the landscape was his hope. It was known that the plans for the building had been submitted to the Munich council authorities, but they rejected it. As Rudolf Steiner wrote to a young architect, Walther Schwagenscheidt, in 1922, who had been pioneering the same sort of architectural ideas,

> "The speed with which the Goetheanum had to be relocated from its original site in Munich to Dornach, made that impossible". And as individuals requested designs for their own private houses, the possibility of an over-all organic village design had to be laid aside".

He had in fact explained in a lecture that the proposed private dwellings should all seek to incorporate this new approach to architecture and not remain in the older approaches to house designs.[225] Apparently the members had drawn up plans for buildings that were not consistent to this ideal. Steiner also wrote to the architect that, "his ideas for a 'Raumstadt' resonated with himself very much".[226] The Raumstadt idea is about a city having its residences and civic buildings and industrial buildings integrated into a parkland environment, with spaces organically alluding to the terrain which would encourage a community spirit of sharing it together. To read more about the details of the architectural concept of the Goetheanum, see The Goetheanum: Rudolf Steiner's Architectural Impulse, by Biesanz and Klingborg.

Spiritual value of Art
Another aspect to attaining a higher spirituality and a finer social life involves the arts. Rudolf Steiner was himself an artistic person, gifted across a range of artistic activities. These included pastel and water-colour paintings (although as he said, he was not trained) and in architectural design, poetry, plays, sculpturing, choreography for eurythmy, jewellery design and acting. He taught that a balanced spirituality includes the capacity to value beautiful and ennobling art. Or even better, to learn to create works of art for oneself. As he told one audience,

---

[223] Lecture, 24th Oct. 1914, in Der Dornacher Bau, als Wahrzeichen geschichtlichen Werdens und künstlerischer Umwandlungsimpulse, 1985.
[224] The memoir of Professor Bergmann in, Blätter für Anthroposophie, 10. Jhrg. Basel, 1958, March, p.106.
[225] Lecture, 23rd Jan, 1914.
[226] "Ein Brief Rudolf Steiners über ein Architekturproblem", published in Blätter für Anthroposophie und Mitteilung aus der Anthroposophischen Bewegung. 7. Jhrg. 1955, Nov. Nr. 11.

"The great spiritual truths do influence the astral body, but in addition, the sensing-feeling life should also be influenced. The great truths shall not only be spoken but also painted, built (architecturally) and sculpted."[227]

And in another place, to emphasize the importance of the soul being influenced by beauty, he declared,

"I am convinced that when the artistic element ever more draws into our ranks, then it will also be possible for our friends to overcome the difficulties involved in attaining to actual spiritual vision. The artistic element shall become an elixir of life for the anthroposophical movement."[228]

To emphasize this point, he told one audience about one-sided spiritually minded people who in previous lifetimes devoted their minds to deep truths and religious teachings but neglected the task of refining their sensory capacity and their emotive responses to the environment.[229] Such people when returning to the Earth will find themselves in a difficult situation; they will be consciously committed to higher ideas and deep thoughts, but their predisposition will be sadly inferior. In other words, their way of being, their general habitual tendencies, will be coarse and incompatible with the person's higher qualities.

The underlying reason for this is that the etheric body receives and holds our sensory impressions. So exposure to an image or music etc, in the environment, constantly or repeatedly reinforces the effect in the etheric body. If it is something of beauty and depth of meaning, then its constant presence in the etheric body means that the soul or astral body will be uplifted. This is because the soul is constantly registering subliminally the images present in the etheric body. Rudolf Steiner radically expressed this perspective in this way,

"My dear friends, regardless of how much people contemplate getting rid of criminality in the world by means of outer institutions and arrangements, for human souls in the future, true redemption – the transformation of evil into good – will happen {only} when art permeates human souls and hearts with spiritual substance."[230]

He repeated this perspective in another way in a 1907 lecture,

"...in the normal external life with its material themes and its cultural interests, ethical ideals exert an uplifting effect. But what a person receives in the way of art and religion exerts a transformative and refining influence upon the etheric body. Through these the human being has an intuitive glimpse of the Eternal. The social impulse of the Arts exerts a stronger influence than a {specific-intellectual} moral education, and stronger than the influence of legislation, for

---

[227] GA 93a, p. 164.
[228] GA 277, p. 426.
[229] GA 94, p. 164.
[230] Lecture: Buildings will speak, 17th June 1914.

through true artworks, there shines through the Eternal and the true, unchanging Spirit."[231]

The kind of artwork implied here are works of beauty, not discordant or sinister or fragmented imagery; and since this lecture is particularly referring to architecture, then organic forms will be in question, not cubes or lineal or haphazard minimalist shapes.

The spiritual origin of artistic gifts

A few brief sentences from Rudolf Steiner present his view of the link of art to the spiritual realms,

> "The arts are in a certain way the herald of the spirit revealing itself in the sense world…through Art humanity secures a dwelling place for the gods in the earthly world."

This is given a deeper perspective when he reveals that the various artistic gifts themselves are a reflection of the divine 'devachanic' world; namely the realm where divine beings exist, above the Soul-World. As the sleeping person leaves their body and journeys forth each night up into the realms of spirit, these realms leave a kind of imprint in their soul.

He speaks of the **painter** as someone in whom the divine realms echo on in his or her **sentient-soul**, that is, in the feelings.
The **musician** is described as someone in whom the divine realms echo on in the **intellectual-soul**, in other words, in the intelligence.
And the **poet** is described as someone in whom the divine realms echo on in the **spiritual-soul,** that is, the intuitive mind.
And he describes the **sculptor** as someone in whom the divine realms echo on in the **etheric-body**, as they awaken.

It is also noteworthy that Steiner valued the art of puppetry very much. It is known that he and Marie Steiner went often to classical style puppet shows (Hohnsteiner puppets), in Berlin. He spoke to the friends accompanying him, of the need for this art form to be preserved and developed.[232] (Further aspects of the Arts are treated under 'emptiness of soul', 'eurythmy', 'colours and painting', 'architecture', 'paintings'.)

Further reading
Rudolf Steiner: The Arts and their Mission
               Art in the Light of Mystery Wisdom
               The Spiritual in Art (a compilation of lectures)

---

[231] GA 96, lecture 25th March 1907, p. 255.
[232] Memoirs of Clara Geister, published in *Mitteilungen aus der Anthroposophischen Arbeit in Deutschland,* Jhrg. 19, Nr. 74, Weihnachten, 1964, p. 270.

Colours and painting

Colour was very important to Rudolf Steiner and he lectured extensively on this theme. He gave an explanation as to how each colour speaks to the soul, how it affects the soul. And he also gave indications to a medical doctor for the use of a colour therapy cabinet.[233] His own hardwood furniture was painted a purple colour.[234] He painted or drew with pastels about 100 works of art; and his blackboard drawings, using coloured chalk were often deeply evocative. New ways of using colours in painting and in art therapy were developed from his lectures. And new ways to imbue a painting with deep meaning drawn from spiritual insights arise for those who seek to take up his teachings on this.[235]

A note has to be made here of an error in the English translations of nearly all German texts about colours, from Steiner and his students, when the colours correctly known as "violet" and "purple" are concerned. Wherever you read the term in English, 'violet', **what is actually meant is purple**. In the works of Liane Colot D' Herbois, and in Hilde Raske's book, "The Language of Colour", in books of lectures by Rudolf Steiner himself, etc, the term 'violet' is almost always wrong and should read 'purple'.

This is because in German the word for 'purple' is borrowed from the French language, namely 'violette'. And this is often incorrectly understood to mean 'violet' to translators. When red and blue are mixed in equal parts, purple arises; but if there is more blue then violet forms. If there is more red added, then magenta or cerise is formed.[236]

And you may encounter the strange term, 'blue-violet' in such books; the correct meaning here is 'violet'. Likewise the term 'a pinkish-violet' can be encountered; such a colour is impossible. (The bluish colour 'violet' can never be pinkish.) What is meant by 'pinkish-violet' is pinkish-purple which is actually magenta, also known as cerise. In other words, a purple which has more light red in it than purple does, and thus cannot be considered similar to violet at all.[237]

Colours: their soul-mood

These brief remarks are drawn directly from Rudolf Steiner's books. They consider the general significance that a colour has on the soul; the keynote impact when we see it, and what it says about a person when that colour is present in the aura.

---

[233] This subject is presented (in German) in Beitrag (supplementary volume)#97 to the 360 volumes of Complete Works, (1987).

[234] Assia Turgenieff, Erinnerungen an Rudolf Steiner, 1973, p. 35.

[235] There is for example, the respected Sienna Academy, in Queensland, Australia.

[236] Hence there are three nuances of lilac. Pale purple produces lilac, but pale violet produces bluish lilac and pale magenta produces pinkish lilac.

[237] Note that often you cannot determine if an object is violet or purple when it is looked at under an electrical light, the light will falsify the appearance. And even some colour charts of artists' paints can also be incorrect here.

RED
General impact is: satisfaction in activity, happiness in a particular moment, or in events in general.
* Keynote, as sensory stimulus is: liking of activity.
*Auric quality is: will/libido, liking action, strong wishes (or anger).
GREEN
General impact is: Our earthly incarnation is strengthened or affirmed, our normal every-day ego is enhanced.
* Keynote as sensory stimulus is: restful, inducing contemplative state.
*Auric keynote is: empathetic to the environs, intelligent understanding of other beings.

BLUE
General impact is: peaceful, in blue rests the yearning for the spirit.
* Keynote as sensory stimulus is: it encourages the overcoming of earthly egoistic qualities.
*Auric keynote is: piety, devotion.

PURPLE
General impact is: it speaks of the soul, hence of the spiritual worlds.
* Keynote as sensory stimulus is: I affirm life and my existence, from a spiritual perspective.
*Auric keynote is: accustomed to immersion in prayer, "a soul who is immersed in prayer experiences inwardly purple".

YELLOW
General impact is: one is inwardly consolidated, so that one may indeed be a human being within the natural world; yellow transports back to the beginning of all of my earthly lifetimes, and speaks to me of earthly life.
* Keynote as sensory stimulus is: "yellow changes me, I must accept/absorb something into myself". (Hence one could say, stimulating to active receptivity.)
*Auric keynote is: clear thinking,

ORANGE
General impact is: you sense your own inner pulsing warmth; you feel the defects and virtues of your character.
* Keynote as sensory stimulus is: it is empowering me as I go through the world; I want to be merged with the things of this world.
*Auric keynote is: pride, self-aware, ambitious.

PINK
General impact is: for every little child, it speaks of gentle, selfless love.
* Keynote as sensory stimulus is: "I feel the source/fountain of life" (Rose-pink).
*Auric keynote is: the colour of caring love, unselfish love, and affection.

Painting (water colour)
In October of 1922, Rudolf Steiner gave a workshop on painting technique to mainly younger artists. This was followed a week later by a lecture on the same theme. In the

workshop he painted as he taught, but unfortunately no stenographer was present to record his words. However the artists gathered in a studio after these sessions and wrote down key statements that Steiner made.[238] For example, he told his audience that,

> "The starting point for painting is a surface. What is a surface? In a surface the human will cannot come to expression because the will is three-dimensional. The will is active in a three-dimensional manner; the feelings express themselves in a two- dimensional manner. A surface is two- dimensional; I can only experience something from a surface to the extent that I have a realm of feeling in me. Thoughts I cannot paint, as they are one-dimensional."

He painted a matt blue across a large part of a white art paper and then in the centre, which was left blank, he painted a pinkish-yellow colour. He commented, "this is too noisy or hectic, it needs some support", then below he painted in a pinkish area, across the lower section saying,

> "From the blue, which is brightened in the middle with a pinkish-yellow which sends its influence out and around, and which is supported from below – in this way a sunset is experienced, from the viewpoint of its colours."

Later he referred to a copper engraving by Albrecht Dürer, who was famous not only for his great artwork, but also his interest in esoteric themes. Steiner referred to Dürer's 'Melancholie' from a deeper artistic perspective saying that,

> "…it was not a study of the melancholic temperament but of how the darker coloured nuancing aspect is conquered by the light; the word itself meaning (in its original Greek roots), 'dark-bright'. Dürer wanted to study the play of light in the four realms of nature."

He then put the task to one of the painters to count how many brightness-darkness nuances are used in the polyhedron shaped rock in the middle left field. The student, Maria Strakosch-Geisler, reported that she had found twelve, which were in effect throughout the painting. Rudolf Steiner affirmed this discovery and then suggested that she 'translate' the engraving into colour, but then he said,

> "She was to be aware that there are two separate sources of light in the picture. One source comes from outside and brightens the objects in it, the other source breaks forth from the picture itself."

He then indicated to her that the sphere at the feet of the angel was illumined from a source beyond the painting, whilst the rest of the lighter nuances derive from the sky (the sunlight, through the clouds).[239] He also pointed out to his audience the value of

---

[238] Maria-Strakosch-Giesler, *Erinnerungsbilder aus zwei Vorträgen von Rudolf Steine über Malerie...* in Blätter für Anthroposophie, 7. Jhrg. 1955, März, Nr. 3, ps. 97-102.
[239] It is interesting to note that a bat is shown fleeing the light, a theme also found discreetly placed in the First Goetheanum's cupola.

Goethe's colour theory, telling them that it is a treasure trove for insights about the effect of colour especially the chapter, "the sensory-moral effect of colour".[240]

It is useful here to note that in Steiner books you may come across paintings of a rainbow in which the colours are actually wrong; they are the reverse sequence of what occurs in nature. A rainbow starts with a red band, then orange, yellow, green, blue, violet (or indigo) and finally purple; this latter band is often hard to see. (This description omits one or two transitional colours such as turquoise.) But in the graphics from Rudolf Steiner, surprisingly, the rainbow will start with a (pale) purple, then a thin violet-indigo then, blue, green, yellow, orange and finally red. The various illustrations deriving from Rudolf Steiner are all of spiritual or astral scenes, not of rainbows in nature. Research by this author with anthroposophical groups and publications has not resulted in any clear answer; but can conclude that this reversal depicts how a rainbow is seen in the astral world.

Further Reading
Rudolf Steiner: Colour

Eurythmy
Eurythmy is defined by Rudolf Steiner as an art of movement, rather than a dance form. It was developed by Rudolf Steiner and has two unique qualities. Firstly, it makes cosmic energies visible; energies that stream in from the planets and the zodiac. Secondly, it conveys artistically to the audience the deep truth that these cosmic energies are embedded in the human soul and come to expression in us, especially in our faculty of speech.

So the goal of eurythmy is quite different to the goal of various forms of dance. Take for example ballet. In ballet, the dancers after years of training, reinforced and sustained by hours of daily practice, strive to present sensitively a wide range of human feelings. Feelings of delight, disappointment of romance, of sadness, of hope etc. And so ballet companies have thrilled audiences for several centuries through their stirring performances and technical prowess.

With eurythmy, which also requires years of arduous training, and constant practice, the goal is different. It is to show, to make visible, various invisible forms by the use of the arms and hands in particular. These forms are specific and yet very alive, mobile, metamorphosing. And these forms are precisely what arise in the ether whenever a human being speaks. Every vowel and every consonant, when spoken, create their own unique gesture, their own unique living form in the ether around us.

---

[240] For further information, see his lectures, in his book "Colour". A look on the Internet will reveal many courses and books on Steiner's approach to colour and also some courses in colour therapy.

Regardless of what language we may have as our mother tongue, every vowel and consonant when spoken in whatever language, has the same form, deriving from the same cosmic influence resonating in the etheric body.

Rudolf Steiner taught that in the vowels there comes to expression inside our soul the reflection of the planets. In the consonants there comes to expression in our speech the reflection of the 12 zodiac energies. The concept that the vowels and the seven note musical scale can be correlated to the seven classical planets was known in antiquity. The esoterically informed early church father Clement of Alexandria (155-220AD) wrote, "…of the sevenfold creative elements of the solar system, the forms of these which are audible to our soul, are the seven vowels."[241]

Each vowel has its own unique quality; if we speak the same vowel to an infant from Iceland, New Zealand, Brazil, Japan or Italy this will bring forth the same response, the same feeling in every infant. And the elements of music also create their specific ethereal forms whenever music is played. Eurythmy can bring these ethereal forms to visibility. As the audience experiences these forms, they are given an opportunity to feel the cosmic energies that have created the musical tones, and the sounds of language.

It is these same cosmic energies, radiating out from the zodiac and the planets in primordial times that created the human soul and has given specific shape to the body itself. These eurythmy movements can also be applied in a therapeutic manner; further specialist training can be undertaken in therapeutic eurythmy (also called curative eurythmy).

So in experiencing eurythmy, the audience is given a wonderful opportunity to sense the activity of great spiritual beings who have brought forth humanity itself. Instead of making their muscles tight, eurythmists seek to let their limbs manifest, in relaxed, subtle movements, the living, metamorphosing etheric forms. They can also seek to manifest these in either a classically harmonious way or in a more vibrant, intense way (the Apollonian or Dionysian modes). To really appreciate what eurythmy has to offer, as a member of the audience, it is best to focus on the over-all scene and also on the movement of the eurythmist's arms and hands, but not on the face of the artist.

Further reading
Rudolf Steiner: An Introduction to Eurythmy

The Vowels and the Planets
The vowels in our speech are created in the soul (astral body) in response to energies raying out from the planets and resonating in the soul. Each planet produces its unique

---

[241] In the ancient Greek of Clement: "…οἱ τούτων αἰσθητοὶ τύποι τὰ παρ᾽ ἡμῖν φωνήεντα στοιχεῖα…" ΚΛΗΜΕΝΤΟΣ ΣΤΡΩΜΑΤΕΩΣ, Vol. VI: XVI; 141:6 Leipzig, 1905.

vowel sound. In brackets are some words or exclamations are given that indicate what sound is meant.

A = Venus (ah!)   **E** = Mars (eh!, not whee!)

I = Mercury (as in 'infinity')

O = Jupiter (oh!)   **U** = Saturn (oo !)

AU = Sun (ow !)   **EI** = Moon (eye, or I)

The Consonants and the Zodiac
The consonants in our speech are created in the soul (astral body) in response to energies raying out from the zodiac and resonating in the soul. Each zodiac influence produces a unique consonant or several similar consonants in human speech.

Aries = v	Libra = c (as in 'human' [242])
Taurus = r	Scorpio = z, s, sch
Gemini = h, ch	Sagittarius = g, k
Cancer = f	Capricorn = l
Leo = d, t	Aquarius = m
Virgo = p, b	Pisces = n

Goetheanum Cupolas: the paintings
The First Goetheanum had two cupolas or domes, and both of these were painted with scenes that presented various aspects of the anthroposophical view of life and the cosmos. We noted one of them earlier in regard to the creation account in Genesis. It is very hard to actually study these, as there are few books available which present these pictures, with a commentary. One reason for this is historical; Rudolf Steiner told the Waldorf teachers that he did not want these images to be available, separated from their context in the building.

The original task of painting them for the first Goetheanum was daunting. As one of the artists involved reported, each of the six artists chosen to do the work had to carry out their motif, but the over-all effect on the large cupola had to form a unity. And the paint used was based on plant-dyes, which had to be ground and mixed by hand; volunteers worked for many weeks doing this work. After four years of painting, the artists were not satisfied with the outcome of their work and turned to Rudolf Steiner for help. He then re-painted the detailed sections of the cupola, about 150 square

---

[242] And the Greek C (*X*) as in Χριστος (Christos) not the English 'ch'.

metres over-all.[243] But not all areas that needed to be re-painted were painted over; it was too time-consuming to do that.

However the building was destroyed by arson on Dec. 31st 1922 and many decades passed by until they were re-created on the ceilings of the new Goetheanum. So, copies of these graphics are regarded now as appropriate, since opportunities to see them and contemplate them in their location have been severely restricted. And this is still the case today, as one cannot spend hours in the Second Goetheanum; and if the curtain is drawn over the stage, then the scenes that were once in the small cupola cannot be seen.

The small cupola

Briefly, the images in the small cupola have a depiction of the Mystery of Golgotha as the centre feature. Above the figure of Lucifer is what appears to be the moon, and on the other side of the Christ figure is a cosmic radiance streaming into the Earth. And then proceeding both left and right there are two identical series of motifs. Firstly, there is a scene depicting the spiritual dynamics operative in an advanced person of the future, of the Slavic Epoch.

This epoch will start in the 36th century AD and is also known as the Age of Aquarius, or the 6th Post-Atlantean Age or the Age of Philadelphia. The next motif concerns the duality of Lucifer and Ahriman as powers hindering the spiritually questing soul. This was a dynamic in the old Persian epoch (the 2nd Post-Atlantean age) and is also a dynamic in our current age, called the Fifth Post-Atlantean age. The next motif relates to ancient Egypt; the next to ancient Greece and the last scene refers to the figure of Faust, from Goethe's play, as a symbol of our times.

The Large Cupola

The large cupola takes a more cosmic, long-range view of humanity's evolution, with scenes in the western end depicting the creation of humanity as recounted in the book of Genesis, and the forming of our eyes and ears, through which we perceive the physical world. In the Creation scene, there are seven Elohim or Spirits of Form, six of whom are more in the vertical plane, emerging from a field of strong red energy, and streaming their creative will into the Earth sphere, and from this arise the rudimentary bodies of both animals and humans (dark brown swirls). Lower down towards the horizon is the seventh of these great beings, possibly Jehovah, active from the moon sphere.

Their rays of in-streaming energy were drawn in a strong blue colour by Rudolf Steiner. His coloured sketches for these scenes were worked on by another artist, Hermann Linde, in preparation for the task of painting them onto the cupola; an activity that required the artist at times to make some interpretation of the sketches. It is unknown to what extent all the various changes made by this artist were affirmed by Steiner. But in the version painted on the ceiling of both the first and consequently in the second Goetheanum, the blue rays were changed to a pale mauve. In the illustration

---

[243] Reported by Natalie Turgenieff-Pozzo, "Aus der Arbeit am ersten Goetheanum-Bau" in *Mitteilungen aus der Anthroposophischen Arbeit in Deutschland*, Nr.6, Dezember 1948, p. 21.

here, this author has stayed with the original blue tone for these rays, because the pale mauve colour makes them very hard to see, (especially when seen in the great hall, 20 or 50 metres away from the viewer), and definite evidence that Steiner changed his thoughts as to the colour is not available.[244]

Also on the original sketch Rudolf Steiner drew another deity, positioned somewhat above the Elohim. The figure was not included in either Goetheanum cupola; because it is thought that this figure is an error by Steiner. That it was not included in the first Goetheanum is quite supportive of this view, but is not entirely conclusive. For one may conclude that Steiner would erase any erroneous figure, before passing on the sketch from which the artists were to work. This spirit being is partially within the aura of other beings or energies, a situation which is expressive of the interweaving of beings that occurs in spirit worlds. (That the artists could make a mistake in their work was not impossible; the same artist who did this same scene, through confusion, painted in an eighth Elohim (!). Rudolf Steiner reluctantly agreed that it was not practicable to have it removed.)

In our illustration here, this higher being has been included. This is because it may represent a higher deity, as it does not appear to be a Spirit of Form (Elohim) because its figure is drawn differently to those beings. So its presence suggests the impetus that the Spirits of Form are manifesting has its origin in still higher beings. Ultimately, the impetus does come from God, from whom all the hierarchical beings receive their creative impetus. If this interpretation were correct, it would lend a somewhat monotheistic quality to this 'polytheistic' scene. This scene is after all regarded as the western world's most famous monotheistic event: "In the beginning, God created heaven and Earth."

There are also archangels, seen here as emerging from an area of violet coloured energy; they are creatively active, in Devachan, developing the archetype of the Earth's plant species. Then moving towards the centre of the cupola, one finds depicted the Fall of Man through the intervention of Lucifer, an event which brought us into the physical world. Then there are scenes referring to Lemuria, Atlantis and also to the primal Indian, primal Persian, Egyptian-Mesopotamian age and the ancient Greek era. Finally in the eastern end there are several closely interconnected scenes depicting the spiritual archetypes of our earthly ego and spiritual higher ego. These depict Jehovah battling Ahriman who is entwined around the Earth, and below this, the seven planets, and further below, the twelve zodiac forces interwoven with the three vowels, I O A.

The Lemurian scene in the cupola is fascinating. It shows the primitive humans and animals emerging from the oceans, to become land dwellers. There are some similarities between the humans and some of the animal forms, but crucially, above the human beings are the individual Guiding Angels, from whom eventually each human

---

[244] The Goetheanum person responsible for its artwork documentation, Herr Dino Wendtland, has kindly pointed out to this author that Steiner did alter the colours of his original sketches in the process of finalizing a scene, and also sometimes did not have the right colour available when he made his sketches. For this reason the decision was made in Dornach, after careful consideration, not to use the blue colour rays, nor to include the other, higher deity.

shall develop an individualized eternal spirit. Whereas above the animals is shown a group-soul entity to which many animals all belong.

Further Reading
The Language of Colour in the first Goetheanum, Hilde Raske, Walter Keller Verlag, Dornach, 1983.
The Goetheanum Cupola Motifs of Rudolf Steiner, Peter Stebbing (editor)

The four Mystery Plays
From 1910 to 1913 Rudolf Steiner wrote four dramas which are referred to as 'Mystery Plays'. In the same year that a play was written, amateur actors performed it; one play was performed in each of these years. All four plays portray the influence of spiritual realities in the inner life of its characters, who are seeking esoteric enlightenment. It is obvious that these plays would be of interest to a limited circle of people, mainly students of anthroposophy. They are unlikely to appeal to wider audiences. But for those who immerse themselves in the teachings of Rudolf Steiner, they become highly valued because they portray in the form of personal experiences what is otherwise only presented as concepts in the many lectures.[245]

The first drama, The Portal of Initiation, was specifically termed "a Rosicrucian Mystery Drama", indicating that Rudolf Steiner considered this drama to be of the same genre as the ancient Greek dramas, but deriving its inspiration from a Rosicrucian stream of esotericism. By 'Rosicrucian' is meant here an esoteric Christian wisdom (in effect, anthroposophy).

> To see what Rosicrucian means in anthroposophy, see the entry in the next chapter, *Sacred Sites and Mystery Streams of Earlier Times*. As the titles of the plays suggest, the intention of each drama is to portray the challenges encountered by modern individuals, in their striving on the path towards the initial stages of esoteric spiritual development. The following lecture extract is useful to consider here, "… the development which has led to our contemporary theatre, had its beginning, its germinal form, with all that which was regarded as a Mystery. And one only attains the appropriate understanding of the dramatic art, if one goes back to the art of the Mysteries. In the Mysteries, the concern of art was to trace the primal form of all dramatic portrayals back into those impulses which penetrated into human beings from the spiritual world."[246]

In other words, these ancient dramas were performances designed to depict, for esoteric-pedagogical purpose, the spiritual dynamics occurring in the path to initiation. That is, the dramas were to assist in the training of the acolytes in the temple communities, and also to communicate elements of the mystery-religion to the community at large. Steiner's own dramas continue this tradition. They are set in the

---

[245] The author's Ph.D. thesis contains a detailed critique of the first play, the Portal of Initiation.This was published by Otago University, and is available from their German Dept.
[246] Rudolf Steiner, Sprachgestaltung und Dramatische Kunst, Dornach, 1969, p. 226.

early 20th century, and the character of the wise initiate, Benedictus, is similar to Rudolf Steiner's both in costuming and in his over-all role.

However, in the context of an English language appraisal of his texts, there is the translation problem as the original is in a sophisticated, poetic form of German. This has several characteristics that can cause difficulties. Firstly, in the poetic passages and in prose texts, there are often phrases which refer to an esoteric spiritual theme, which itself is not explained. This is because the audience is meant to contemplate such phrases and to thereby discover their meaning. Secondly, there is the use of remarkable 'neologisms', that is, words which Steiner created for the purpose (see the last chapter, *A guide to Rudolf Steiner's books* for more about engaging with Steiner's books).

These are the first dramas ever written that portray the nature of both the acolyte and the initiate's experiences in spiritual realms, and the re-birth in other earth-lives. The three remaining plays, The Soul's Probation, The Guardian of the Threshold and The Souls' Awakening, continue to follow the experiences of the students of Benedictus in their striving towards initiation. The plays also portray the metamorphosis of the personalities from one lifetime to another. The speeches are often very long and are not accompanied by the usual 'dramatic' actions of a theatrical work. The key to learning from these plays is to know that most of the dramatic action of the plays is in effect to be found in the inner life of the characters as they journey on their spiritual quest.

The 'Group' sculpture

This term refers to a wooden statue, sometimes called the 'Representative of Humanity'. It is a wooden carving, nearly ten metres high, which was intended to be placed at the back of the stage in the First Goetheanum. It was not harmed by the fire that destroyed that building, as it was still being finished in an outside building. This large statue was not named as such by Rudolf Steiner. How was it carved, and by whom? It is actually not a finished work of art; it was still being worked on as Rudolf Steiner died. Various sculptors worked on all parts of it, (except the Christ figure, which was basically carved in its entirety by Rudolf Steiner). But with regard to the specific beings depicted, a very accomplished English artist, Edith Maryon, proceeded to take over at an advanced stage, and then Rudolf Steiner himself completed the figure. However, the top left figure, a humorous sprite, was carved solely by Henni Geck, as Rudolf Steiner's death prevented him from completing the figure. He also could not complete the carving of a dove behind the upraised hand of the Christ figure.[247]

He wanted people to artistically feel its message rather than it being prosaically named. It is clear however, from his own comments that it depicts the moment in time when the Resurrection of Christ took place, and also the effect of this event upon Lucifer and Ahriman. It is as if the Christ is standing in front of a large mass of rock. It shows the moment when the Christ arose at the Resurrection and disempowered Lucifer and Ahriman, see Illustration 24. (There is reason to believe that there is another layer of

---

[247] Reported in *Nachruf für Henni Geck*, Blätter für Anthroposophie, 3.Jhrg. 1951, Nr.4, April p. 139.

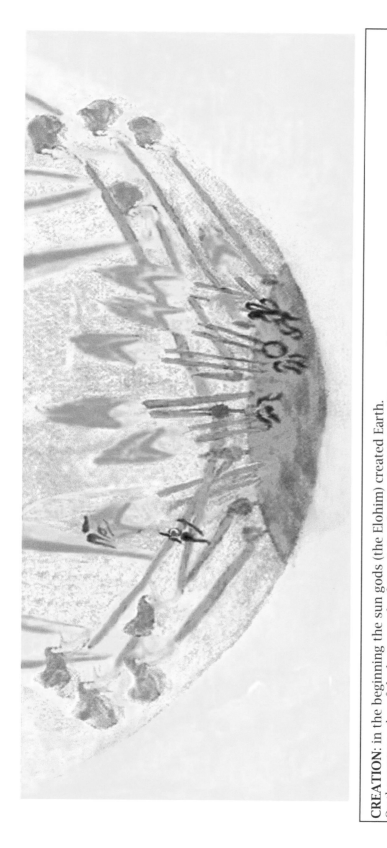

CREATION: in the beginning the sun gods (the Elohim) created Earth.
On the western edge of the large cupola, this painting depicts the 7 Spirits of Form or Elohim (or Exusiai) emerging from a red coloured field of energy, sending their creative powers down to the Earth in blue rays. Emerging from a violet field of energy are several Archangels, raying forth their creative powers in reddish-brown rays, forming the plant species for the Earth. Dark swirls may indicate primordial animal and human bodies. Above the Spirits of Form another deity is shown here, but not included in the Goetheanum; it may indicate another, higher rank of creative being.

211

meaning, hidden in the complex features of the carving.[248]) These two beings are displayed twice: once before their disempowerment, and once afterwards. Rudolf Steiner explains that at the Resurrection, Christ did not exert compulsion over these two entities. But rather Lucifer found himself shrinking back from Christ and in his vicinity, losing his power. Lucifer could not endure the sacred spiritual energies raying forth from the Christ, whilst the effect upon Ahriman of the Christ light raying forth, caused himself to become entangled in the gloomy depths of the Earth, enchained in a mass of gold rivulets.[249]

The hands of the Christ figure have the fingers in a special gesture. This is an allusion to the same hand gesture as used by the Jewish initiates of olden times.[250] There is also a small humorous sprite on the top left, which lightens the potency of the scene.[251]

Rudolf Steiner comments on how Lucifer has a wide, outspread upper part of his 'body', and a broad forehead. Whereas Ahriman has a narrow head and a wide, out-spread lower body, which has a bat-like quality. The association of Ahriman to bats is also discreetly found in the paintings on the small cupola of the First Goetheanum, but unfortunately not in the Second Goetheanum. Where Ahriman and Lucifer face each other, a bat face emerges.[252] The theme of this statue is then a dynamic, cosmic one.

The face of Christ is very striking and there are some words from Rudolf Steiner that are relevant here. He explained that this is how Christ Jesus appeared, as he saw him, in his spiritual research, looking back to the time of the Christ. And he also explained that,

> "...the carving was undertaken from the viewpoint of what you would see if you were to incorporate the underlying etheric energies, not just the physical body {of Jesus}. And this is why a strong asymmetrical element has been attempted here. Every human countenance has this asymmetrical quality, but not of course to such a degree as is presented here....[253]

It portrays a moment when a colossal event occurred and its impact surging out towards the two other potent spiritual beings. As such one can imagine that it requires the sculptor to capture the motion, the movement within realms of spirit. In this case, to capture or portray the core dynamics active in the interweaving of Christ, Lucifer and Ahriman around the evolving of the human life-wave. This is probably what was being referred to when Rudolf Steiner gave a kind of meditation about the statue to the architect responsible for the First Goetheanum. Steiner was showing him the carving in

---

[248] It is part of the oral tradition of the anthroposophical world that Rudolf Steiner told someone that he was meant to depict the Double of the human being, but such a depiction would be too potent for people to observe.

[249] GA 159/160, lecture, 13th June 1915 p. 192-95.

[250] Reported by Julia Klima from Prague, in her memoirs.

[251] But perhaps it also performs another, veiled function.

[252] It is above the Germanic-Persian initiate, but this veiled motif, painted by Steiner himself for the first building, was not included in the version painted for the Second Goetheanum.

[253] Lecture 25th Jan. 1920, in Architektur, Plastik und Malerei des ersten Goetheanum, 1972.

the workshop; "Here it has been attempted to bring forth this statue from an aspect of a high-spiritual movement."[254]

When the second Goetheanum was built, it was unfortunately decided that it should be entombed in a small room in the centre of the new building. Henni Geck was given the task of cutting it into segments and re-joining the pieces in the small room once the Second Goetheanum was completed.[255] It depicts at least six entities, and was meant to be seen by people at a distance. In this way it would have been noticed indirectly, so to speak. It contains a deeply esoteric hidden quality which speaks to the soul discretely when a person is cognizing it in a peripheral way, and not staring at it directly.

Paintings
In this section we shall have a brief look at some of the paintings highly valued in anthroposophical circles today. Rudolf Steiner recommended displaying artworks which have beauty and which depict a spiritual theme.

The Sistine Madonna by Raphael Sanzio
Rudolf Steiner commented on the high inspiration behind this painting. How the many faces in the clouds reflect the fact of the unborn babes crowding around awaiting their conception. (This occurs after they enter the hemisphere in which they are due to be born, at the time of its winter solstice.) And the exquisite nature of the Madonna here means that this painting serves as a kind of ideal for the expecting mother and for motherhood in general. In addition, it is of course a superb portrayal of the historical Madonna and her child. But Rudolf Steiner also referred to an inspiring quality in this painting that alludes to Sophia, the old name for the Spiritual-self; or one can also say, there is a nuance of Isis, a revered deity of ancient Egypt, holding Horus, who is a understood to be of pre-figuring of Jesus. (Isis is the same as Sophia, when this is viewed as the cosmic dimension to the Spiritual-Self.) So it is a painting that has become highly regarded in anthroposophical circles. And many other paintings by Raphael are also of deep spiritual-esoteric quality.

The Isenheim Altarpiece by Matthias Grunewald, ca. 1515.[256]
Rudolf Steiner referred briefly to the skill of this painter in his lectures on art history.[257] It seems likely that Rudolf Steiner recommended it in private conversations. Its depiction of the Christ mystery is unsurpassed for spiritual depth. The depiction of the resurrected Jesus and of the Crucifixion scene is of great esoteric depth. Its depiction of the cosmic Christ (above Mary and child) is unique, as is the hauntingly evocative rococo style magical temple, filled with various spirits beings and also portraying several ancient initiates from non-Christian cultures.

---

[254] Told to Hermann Ranzenberger, reported in *Blätter für Anthroposophie*, 13. Jhrg. 1961, Sept. Nr. 9, p. 344.
[255] Reported in *Mitteilungen aus der Anthroposophischen Arbeit in Deutschland*, Nr. 16, Johanni 1951, p. 51.
[256] His name is more correctly, Matthias Neidhardt.
[257] GA 292, p. 108; in English translation the title of this large 2 vol. work could be "The history of Art as a reflection of inner spiritual impulses", lectures given in Dornach, October 1916 & Oct. 1917.

But not all of the beings in this painting are beautiful, some scenes are too potent to be suitable for children. You can see the original in France, in the town of Colmar, which is not far from the border with Switzerland, about an hour by train from Basel. This author regards this painting as a candidate for the title of greatest painting of all time.[258]

The Polish Rider by Rembrandt, ca. 1650
This painting dates from about 1650; it was lost and then re-discovered in the 1880's. From Rudolf Steiner's comments one can deduce that it depicts the great leader of the Rosicrucian movement, Christian Rosencreutz, seated on the white horse. In the background is what Rudolf Steiner referred to as "the first painting of the First Goetheanum". You can see the original in the Metropolitan Museum of Art in New York.

Ninetta Sombart
For paintings of a religious nature from an anthroposophical approach to colour, the exquisite works of the artist Ninetta Sombart, are unexcelled. Some of her paintings are reproduced as art prints by Wynstones Press. And the book "Ninetta Sombart" by Volker Harlan, presents many more of her paintings. If you do study Steiner's lectures on the Gospels and the two Nativity stories, then a painting by Raphael Sanzio, *Madonna del Duca di Terranuova* showing the Madonna with three holy children will be inspirational.[259]

 The Triptych Grail, or "From Solomon across Golgotha to Christian Rosencreutz" by Anna May, ca. 1915.
Rudolf Steiner designed this important picture and asked the gifted painter, Anna May, to paint it. But this exceptionally esoteric painting does require some study of Steiner's lectures about the Rosicrucians and the old legend about the tree planted by Seth on Adam's grave which was used for the cross on Golgotha. Sadly, the painting was destroyed in World War II but copies were produced from a colour photograph taken before the war.

From the Love of the Light:
A painting by Nikolaus Gysis (1842-1901). This is Rudolf Steiner's name for it; it is actually known as "Vision from the Gospel", and also as "The Heavenly Bridegroom". An unfinished work, it depicts the adoration of the World Saviour by hierarchical beings. But unlike all of his earlier works, this one leaves behind the traditional, somewhat naturalistic style used for several centuries, for depictions of the Holy family and the saints. Ranks of spiritual beings gaze towards the Christ in the centre in a vibrant red colour, but the outer part of the painting is in indigo-blue, and some gold is used for halos. Above are several high beings associated with the Saviour.

---

[258] This is due to its unsurpassed technical skills, inspired thematic depths as well as the breadth and fineness of its emotive tonality. A book about this painting and some of the other paintings mentioned here is planned.
[259] A copy is on the author's website.

24 The Group sculpture: 9.5 metres high, carved in wood

There are also two faintly drawn spheres. Rudolf Steiner makes such comments as,

> "…It must touch us, when from the pure, chaste red, and the blue that speaks of veneration, the clear gold is brought in, partly glittering around the figures, partly enveloping them, and then we intuit, that this carrying in the gold into the closely linked red, and then into a blue which attunes one to reverence, brings to expression deep, deep secrets of the heart."[260] And we feel here the harmonies of the divine hierarchical beings, especially the great Thrones, painted with such correctness as to how they really are…" [261]

Redentore by Vincenzo Foppa

This is a painting of the risen Jesus. Jesus is between a golden arch and has his hand raised in blessing. This painting was recommended by Rudolf Steiner to the Christian Community church, but individuals can also use it privately. It is very hard to obtain and appears not be displayed on the Internet. It was described prior to the 1980's as by "an Unknown Master". It is in the Brera gallery, in the Italian town of Milan.

The Planetary Seals

You may come across this term, and find it a bit puzzling. The term actually refers to seven sigils or symbolic designs developed by Rudolf Steiner in 1907, and placed on display in a major Theosophical Conference in Munich of that year. These designs interpret artistically the key dynamics occurring in the evolutionary aeons, as we described in Chapter Ten. It is easier to understand what they are about if one thinks of them as **The Seals of the Aeons**. These designs have been carved in various metals, in round shapes usually supplied with a wooden or ceramic backing.

In Chapter Ten we saw how evolution proceeds in seven aeons (or 6 aeons and two half aeons) but are named after planets: Saturn Aeon, Sun Aeon, Moon Aeon and the Earth Aeon, (divided into Mars-Mercury halves) Venus Aeon, Jupiter Aeon and finally the Vulcan Aeon. Rudolf Steiner explained in 1907 that,

> "In these seals there is present something of the 'hidden script', and that the person who lives into the lines and figures with all their soul, will experience some inner understanding of the evolutionary circumstances important for knowledge of human evolution. This gives us a greater understanding of the evolution of ourselves and of the spiritual energies active within us – the essential basis for self knowledge."[262]

By this he means that contemplating these forms tends to give intuitive insights into the dynamics of the corresponding aeon. Note that these seven forms exclude the last, the

---

[260] From an address by Rudolf Steiner in Munich on 25th August 1910, published in *Blätter für Anthroposophie*, 3. Jhrg. Nr.12, 1951, p. 424-5.
[261] See Chapter 15 for more about this work.

[262] GA 34, p. 601, repeated in GA 284/85.

Vulcan, Aeon; instead there is one for each for the two halves of the Earth aeon. See illustration 25 for photographs of these seven graphics carried out in pottery. A study of the Steiner books, 'An Outline of Esoteric Science' and 'Inner Realities of Evolution' will be very useful when seeking to live into these forms.

The Windows of the Goetheanum

In both the first and second Goetheanum, there were (are) nine windows. These are large stained-glass window panes into which various scenes have actually been carved. There is one red window at the entrance to the Great Hall in the Goetheanum, and inside the hall there are eight other windows. These include two sets of windows in green, in blue, in purple and lastly, in pink. However, owing to the technical difficulty in achieving this delicate shade of colour, the last two windows in the second Goetheanum have a pale orange-pink colour rather than pink. In the time that the Goetheanum was being built, there was no known way to actually carve glass, so Rudolf Steiner invented a small grinding wheel device for the purpose.

The scenes speak of many aspects of the spiritual development process. They portray the teachings of Rudolf Steiner on this subject in a manner which is ideal for meditation. And as works of art they speak differently to different people. They are of immense value to those seeking to understand the process of developing higher consciousness. They speak of the threefold lower self and threefold higher self, and of the obstacles to achieving spiritual awareness in the thinking, and emotional purity in the sentient soul. They also have messages about the chakras, and the descent to birth and the release from earthly life. A blue window admonishes the viewer to contemplate the nature of the will in the human being who is unaware of the double; and to then contemplate the will of the hierarchies, as they work to create the human being, from within the zodiac energies.

One of the green windows alludes to the famous 'dark night of the soul' and then to the ancient concept of a temple as a symbol of the human being. Two windows allude to the high initiation stage of finishing one's earthly lifetimes. Another is directly echoing the initiation experiences of the ancient, true Manicheans (an esoteric Christian group from the third century). Another alludes to a modern version of the spirituality that was sought after in the ancient rites of Serapis, from old Egypt. This author is planning an e-booklet about the meaning of these scenes, as there is little available that explains the significance of the nine triptych scenes.

Further reading
The Goetheanum bookstore sells various reproductions of these motifs, and you may find on the Internet, the folio: *The Imagery of the Goetheanum Windows*, with a poem by W. Rath.

Voice (acting, declamation)

Rudolf Steiner gave a number of lectures on the nature of the spiritual forces active in our speech, and together with this, he gave indications for a new approach to the fading art of recitation. In doing this, he had the help of Marie Steiner who had brilliant multi-linguistic skills. She had also trained in recitation in Paris in the 1890's under the highly respected Madam Farvard of the Comédie Française. Marie Steiner also audited lessons in recitation and elements of theatre at the Paris Conservatorium.

She was then offered a key role in a Berlin production of Friedrich Schiller's play, The Maid of New Orleans.[263] For various reason this did not happen. But when Rudolf Steiner began to teach on eurythmy, recitation and drama, she became a co-teacher and eventually trained students in recitation, declamation and to some extent in theatre.

Rudolf Steiner gave a strong emphasis to the actor, or person reciting, of really living into the inner qualities of the elements of language: namely the vowels and the consonants. The inner life, the evocative power of a character's speech or of a poem, he taught, lies not in an intellectual grasp of the ideas being expressed, but in an inner feeling for the way that the breathing process and the blood circulation, assisted by the heart, come to expression in a word, and in the metrical structure of poetry.

These two bodily systems are referred to as 'the rhythmical system' of the human being He insisted it is an awareness of this interplay of the breath-stream and the pulse of the heart, which is the key to successfully speaking forth words in a performance. This approach becomes more readily understood when one recalls what we noted under the heading "eurythmy" about speech. Namely, that the vowels derive from our soul's inner perceiving of the energies streaming across the solar system from the planets. The consonants derive from a similar dynamic, but from the stars in the zodiac.

For actors and others who recite stories and poems from Steiner's approach, it is essential to live into the perspective he gave about speech and how cosmic forces are active in it. He refers to the breath-stream resonating with the sounds of speech and thereby embodying cosmic forces which are the origin of our soul. And these same forces have also formed the human body itself, over the ages. With regard to the training for actors, Rudolf Steiner gave a series of important, innovative exercises to help them in regard to this new approach.

Rudolf Steiner's approach was made more popular when it was taken up by Michael Chekhov, and explained in his book, 'On the technique of Acting'. But it was only when he re-issued his book, after deleting the references to Rudolf Steiner, that his career blossomed in the USA.[264] Other actors have taken up Steiner's indications and developed their approaches, independent of Chekhov, and became internationally respected for their achievements.[265]

---

[263] As reported by Tatiana Kisseleff in "*Aus dem Leben Marie v. Sivers in den Jahren 1867-1902*, in, Beiträge für ein freies Geistesleben, Nr. 38-41, Arlesheim, 1951.
[264] See the very informative article by Franc Chamberlain, "Michael Chekhov: pedagogy, spirituality and the occult", on the internet at WWW.utoronto.ca/tsq/o4/chamberlaino4
[265] For information about English-language actors in this Steiner tradition, see internet article, *On Rudolf Steiner's Impact on the Training of Actors*, by Neil Anderson.

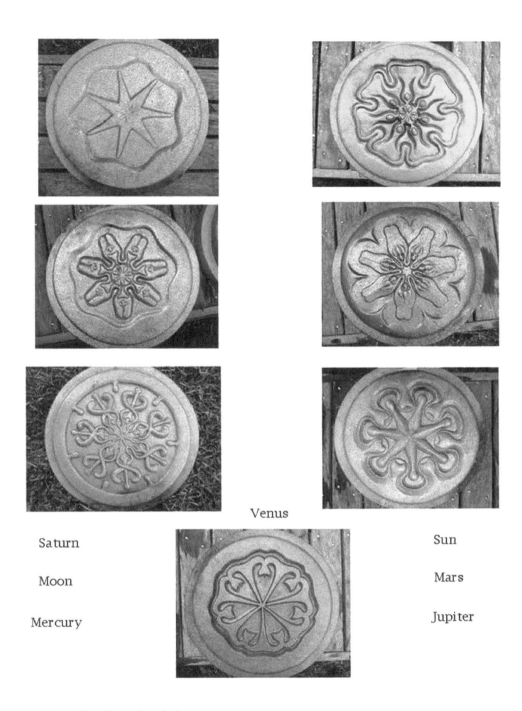

Venus

Saturn   Sun

Moon   Mars

Mercury   Jupiter

25   The 7 Seals of the Aeons: the dynamics central to each aeon

Rudolf Steiner's impetus in speech and acting has also lead to the development of therapeutic techniques. In order to work with clients however, the anthroposophical speech therapist (or their training college) will usually want or need some kind of state accreditation as well.

For those with a feeling for the easily over-looked, yet core human faculty – speech – Steiner's work in this area, aided by Marie Steiner, has brought new depths to the art of acting.[266] And it has also brought back from the brink the art of declamation, the role of the troubadour, the story-teller.

Further reading
Rudolf Steiner: Speech and Drama (lecture course given in 1924).
Dawn Langman: The Art of Acting

Rudolf Steiner and Music
Most of Rudolf Steiner's comments on music are to be found in his lectures on tone eurythmy; "The Inner Nature of Music and the experience of Tone." A concise overview of his teaching here is not really possible. He refers to the three elements of music, melody, harmony and rhythm and their correlation to the threefold soul. Namely that there is correspondence between the intellect and melody, of harmony with the feelings or emotive life, and thirdly, the rhythmical element of music and the will. A lecture from 22nd Aug. 1924 has a small but pivotal digression about music (in the book, "True & False Paths in spiritual Investigation"). Also lectures given on 12th Nov. 1906 and on 8th March 1923 are also important.

---

[266] Marie Steiner died in December, 1948; it is reported that her last words were "keep on going...work!" (Fred. Poeppig, *Schicksalsbegegnung mit M. Steiner*, in Beiträge für ein freies Geistesleben, Ostern, 1949, p. 33.

12: Various themes: The Spiritual Life

Akashic Record, Ancient Egypt, Chakras, Emptiness of soul:
the battle for meaning, The First Class,
The Foundation Stone meditation,
Festivals of the Seasons: spiritual ecology in action,
Freemasonry, Hierarchies and the human soul, Holy Grail,
Meditation, Religion and anthroposophy, Sacred Sites and
Mystery Streams of earlier times,
Vidar: inspirer of anthroposophy

Akashic Record (Akashic chronicle)
Anthroposophical literature refers to seeing things in the "Akashic Record", which is also called the 'memory of nature'. The word 'akasha' is Sanskrit and means a subtle spiritual essence. The phrase has several possible meanings. On a high spiritual realm – in the fifth stage of Devachan – the Akashic Record exists, in which there exists a memory of all previous events in Earth evolution. It is a manifestation of the consciousness of the great beings called the Thrones. In this realm the essential will impulse behind an action, or the thought behind an object, is preserved and can be perceived by the seer.

But there also exists a lesser manifestation of this in the astral realm. This astral reflection of the Akashic Record preserves not so much the inner will-impulses but the more tangible aspect of the past – their forms and colours. It is more easily seen by the seer, but it is less accurate, because it is somewhat distorted.[267]

However in the ethers there also exists a much lesser type of Akashic Record. This is in effect a reflection in the ethers of past events and people and other life-forms on the Earth; so it is even less reliable than the astral type.

Ancient Egypt
The high degree of interest shown by many people today who are drawn to spirituality in ancient Egyptian culture derives from a dynamic underlying historical evolution. There are seven cultural ages in each large epoch; the fourth era acts like a pivotal point in a balance. The 1st, 2nd, and 3rd eras will be reflected in the 5th, 6th and 7th eras. Our current epoch is the 5th post-Atlantean epoch, whilst the Egyptian time was the third epoch. So these two eras fall just before, and just after, the mid-way point, which was the Greco-Latin age. So our era mirrors the old Egyptian one. Much of the materialism of today is, in part, a result of the later, less noble phase of Egyptian times. But also much of the finest spirituality of today is, in part, a result of the successful

---

[267] Rudolf Steiner refers to a Theosophical book, *Atlantis and Lemuria* by Scott-Elliot, as an example of seership which provides both inaccurate as well as some accurate reports, because the author was seeing only into the astral reflection of the Akashic Record.

221

quest for initiation in ancient Egypt.[268] To Rudolf Steiner, the Great Pyramid and the great Sphinx are both ancient Egyptian creations, they are not pre-Flood relics. He gives the date of the building of the Great Pyramid as approximately 3,000 BC, contrary to some theories.[269]

The unusual Egyptian pharaoh Akhenaton is a prominent feature of this civilisation, arousing much interest. This pharaoh was in fact commented on privately by Rudolf Steiner. He was a person with a human-centred view of life, rather than the age-old cosmos centred view. Akhenaton sensed the development of a more earthly, body influenced individualism arising in his times. Crucially it was his actions which indirectly triggered off the events in Egypt that led to the exodus of the Hebrew people, and hence also to the mission of Moses.[270]

Chakras and 'the energy body'

When Indian texts on the 'subtle bodies' became available in English in the 19th century, in such books as The Serpent Power,[271] the idea of energy centres or vortices in the aura became known in spiritual circles in the west. Today the word 'chakra' is widely but loosely used in many spiritual groups. Much of what is thought about chakras in New Age groups is based on modern popular ideas, sometimes influenced by mystical views from old systems of spirituality. This often leads to incorrect views, which ignore the changes in human consciousness that have greatly changed the way to develop the chakras, and which also omit the need for a rigorous ethical development to be undertaken, prior to any attempt to influence the chakras. So what did Rudolf Steiner teach about this subject, and how does it differ from the popular view? He referred to seven of these or to fourteen, depending on what aspect of the human being is under consideration.

Rudolf Steiner explained that there are seven chakras in the soul (or aura or astral body). But from these, another seven eventually form in the etheric body. These seven etheric body chakras are in effect, a reflection or replica, of those in the astral body. In Hinduism these seven astral chakras are known. In traditional oriental medical texts, 21 chakras are referred to; this refers to 21 centres all existing in the etheric body or energy body. These centres are related to the energy flows in the etheric body. The many meridians referred to in acupuncture are likewise referring to intersection points within the etheric body.

The seven astral-body chakras exist already, but only in a rudimentary form; through spiritual development they develop into their full state and become active, rotating

---

[268] For further reading about the esoteric nature of the Great Pyramid and the Giza plateau, see the book by Damien Pryor, The Great Pyramid and the Sphinx.

[269] Notes taken after a private esoteric lesson in 1914, record "in the year 3,000 BC the great Pyramid was built", so his actual words were probably "in about 3,000 BC", for in 2907 BC the Age of Taurus began, and the building was more likely commenced then or shortly after.

[270] For a fuller treatment of this theme, the author is planning a booklet, "Akhenaton, the silent Isis and the Exodus".

[271] By Sir John Woodroffe.

clockwise. But these rudimentary parts can be forced into rotation by incorrect techniques such as mind-altering drugs. They then begin to rotate anti-clockwise, communicating distorted revelations of spirit to the unfree psychic person.

The seven astral chakras develop through the hard inner work that purifies the soul's desires, bringing compassion and wisdom. In anthroposophy, in contrast to the popular view on chakras, the use of different coloured foods or clothing has no effect on how they develop; but above all, they do not develop through some short-term soul exercises that are really just encouraging a change of one's attitudes. They develop only when the qualities in the thinking, the feelings, and the intentions are inherently noble and pure that is, spiritualized. When the aura of the soul is substantially transformed and the devachanic aura (or Spiritual-self) has also started to develop, and then the chakras become active. This takes years of persistent strenuous effort. Rudolf Steiner suggests that the spiritual seeker focus on the task of meditating and on high ethical development, and just let the chakras develop, as they naturally will. As I wrote in The Way to the Sacred,

> "The esoteric pathway presented in anthroposophy is based on the attitude of seeking sanctification of the soul first and foremost, for the gaining of clairvoyance is of secondary importance. It cannot be said too often, that the spiritual faculties are attained **through developing spirituality**, and not via ill-advised occult techniques which directly stimulate the chakras."

In the forehead is a chakra formed from two lines of energy and this, when developed, brings the capacity of seership, of seeing into the astral plane and hence of the divine beings there. It is this chakra which must be developed first– at least in a provisional manner – before the heart chakra is awakened. It is developed by acquiring spiritual ideas and higher discernment about spiritual truths in contrast to the illusions of the sensory world, all on the basis of an enhanced purity and wisdom.

In the throat area is the chakra with 16 lines of force, it brings perceptions of ideas of the concepts underlying creation, with all of its many life-forms. In the heart area is the chakra with 12 lines of force; it develops as chasteness develops in the feelings, and therefore a capacity to be in charge of one's mental processes. These capacities imply a genuine, resolute intention towards inner freedom. It reveals the inner warmth or coldness of other entities and also the enchanting world of Faery.

This subject does relate to the theme of magicians, psychics and initiate. As the book, The Way to the Sacred, explains, referring to three statements of Steiner (bold font),

> "**Constantly repeated practising of occult techniques makes a magician**": that is, someone who can perform magical deeds, and has wrongly endeavoured to have power over spirit beings, without having developed the high spirituality, that is so necessary, beforehand. **A clairvoyant is someone who has perception of the higher realms:** but not necessarily through enhanced spirituality or esoteric meditation. It may be simply through a variety of occult techniques, or because they possess unusual ether energies that cause

psychic abilities. Such a person need not have substantial spirituality or profound wisdom.

Thirdly, **an Initiate is someone who knows and deeply understands the laws or dynamics of the higher worlds**. In other words, an initiate, through meditation and contemplation, and in being willing to manifest the spiritual laws of creation, acquires such inner purity and wisdom that he or she becomes enlightened. So, an initiate is a person with spiritual wisdom who may not even have Psychic Image Consciousness but whose thinking is powerfully intuitive; their consciousness is attuned to the consciousness of the divine-spiritual beings who created and maintain the universe. This may not include direct perception of the spiritual world, but it will usually be present to some extent.

The spiritual energies needed for development of the seven chakras derive from the cosmic sun god (or Christ), and this sacred process, when undertaken by the acolyte is guided by Christ Jesus, as the initiation book of the New Testament indicates, "…listen to the words of Him who holds the seven stars in his right hand, and who walks amidst the seven golden lamp-stands…" Rev. 2:1. The seven chakras are linked to the seven classical planets of astrology.

Emptiness: the battle for meaning

A perspective on daily life that arises from Rudolf Steiner's anthroposophy is about the struggle for meaning in one's life. For people to whom earthly interests and pleasures are fulfilling, this is not a burning issue. But sometimes a person can 'step across the threshold' so to speak; that is, they have a life-changing experience which brings awareness of spiritual aspects to life. Once this happens, it has major implications for one's quality of life and many questions arise about the purpose of human existence.

This causes new and deeper life-priorities to arise, and often an interest in developing oneself spiritually, however that might be interpreted. And this means in effect that the ego or self is asking for inner content; that is for some wisdom, a higher spiritual morality, and a clearer sense of how to serve the common good.

But there is an additional point here; Rudolf Steiner taught that as of the year 1900, most people began to subconsciously sense the spiritual dimension of life. This is because the etheric body has ceased to become so strongly immersed in the physical body during the time in the womb, and this brings about a faint psychic capacity for the adult. So whether the interface with the spiritual is through this over-all change in humanity's evolutionary dynamics, and just faintly touching the soul, or the result of a specific incident, it invokes a specific dynamic in the soul.

As a result of this, there is a feeling of an inner emptiness to life, if we don't seek to find ideas and activity that transcend earthly pleasures and diversions. This feeling is active in the subconscious, at least. And many ways to achieve this inner depth are offered through the works of Rudolf Steiner. In most orientation courses into anthroposophy, there are modules designed to assist the students to develop their capacity for consciously discerning the world around them. This is the starting point of the journey – to be consciously discerning the nature of life and the experiences it offers.

And by taking up a spiritual and creative path, the ego becomes inwardly enriched; which means in anthroposophical terms, the spiritual-soul (the intuitive faculty) becomes stronger. As this happens, a wonderful feeling of enhanced meaning arises. But where no such effort is made, what happens to the ego then?

One's values and ideas become increasingly a reflection of the values of other people, especially from the mass media. But Rudolf Steiner taught that a strong sense of self is the key to a healthy mind, which forms its own conclusions. Without a decisive ego-sense, the feelings, logical thinking and the volition can gradually cease to have any real basis. So how we assess the world becomes more and more superficial. Rudolf Steiner commented that if this happens, then in the cultural life, trivial or worthless things will become valued, since people will not have a basis to assess things – but they won't want to admit this.

He taught that the requirement for people to provide genuine substance in offering someone a philosophy of life, or a mode of spiritual beliefs, or a musical composition, a painting, a sculpture or a poem, will become less and less.[272] He spoke about people then becoming 'people of phrases', where empty, trivial slogans replace meaningful thoughts.[273] And on other occasions he taught that it is a particular mission of anthroposophy to help humanity against this trivialisation.[274]

But as this emptying-out of the ego happens, it is constantly reinforced as purchasers of objects of art and art critics, or devotees of cults declare that a trivial, ugly or unwholesome thing is of great value. This is a social phenomenon linked to a solemn forecast by Rudolf Steiner about the future. He forecast that a vacuous, non-engaged state of mind would occur as the ego becomes 'emptied out'.[275] This phenomenon becomes a barometer of humanity's mind-set; and it appears to be edging closer to becoming a reality.

There is also another side to this phenomenon. It could be called 'the cult of ugliness'; this occurs because, as science tells us, 'nature abhors a vacuum'. This is where everything which is not kept consciously aesthetic, from shoes and clothes to artworks and entire buildings, does not stay in a neutral state, but descends into an actively repulsive condition producing an ugly environment. These have a negative affect on the soul, via the etheric body which stores up these images for the entire life. Rudolf Steiner spoke about how malignant elemental beings can start to influence humans to move towards this blindness in regard to ugliness.

In contrast to this, he spoke of how efforts towards beauty and inspired art works invoke help from beneficent spiritual beings. The production of an aesthetic

---

[272] GA 143, lect. 4th March 1907.
[273] GA 196, p. 288 & GA 302, p.150.
[274] GA 56, lect. 10th Oct. 1907, p. 33.
[275] GA 99, lect. 3rd May 1907.

environment does the opposite to that of disturbing sights. He speaks of how wonderfully beautiful works of art, for example the Cologne cathedral, will re-emerge in a future ethereal Earth as exquisite objects, similar to flowers in our physical world.

Concerning the artistic creative impulse, and new ways for the artist to be active, the following words of Steiner are quite relevant,

> "…when the artist can perceive spiritual realities and then imbue them with material substance, then in this way there will be created a renewal of art. The artists of earlier ages have created very great works. How have they created these? Firstly, they have attentively looked at the external physical substance, with their sense organs. Consider Rembrandt or Raphael, they have really looked at the external physical substances and indicated the spiritual element in material things, in their cultural era.
>
> They knew how to take hold of the spiritual from out of the external, sensory world and how to place this spiritual element into the material substances they were using in their artwork. The nature of their art consists of indicating the spiritual that underlies the physically real. Those who look at art in an unprejudiced way know that the hour of this kind of art has expired. Nothing new can be created in this modality.
>
> Spiritual science leads into a spiritual perceiving. Spiritual realities are then perceived in a way that is living, to our soul and our spirit. And with the same degree of reality, with the same sense of actuality, which was previously there in the earlier mode of artistic creativity, an artistic creativity is underway. But now it is an artistic creativity which is **bringing the spiritual into material expression**, just as earlier it was an **indicating of the spiritual** that **underlies material things**.[276]
> Earlier, the artist drew the spiritual out of the material; now the spiritual is carried into the material. But this is not done in an allegorical or symbolic way." [277]

This is the background to his suggestion that an environment of beauty and harmony is to be striven for. This advice from Steiner has substantial value to society; and is fully implemented in the Waldorf schools (their architecture and interior aesthetics wherever possible.) It is also shown for example, in the successful use of Mozart's music in railway stations to reduce vandalism.

The First Class
You will find this phrase mentioned, if you decide to take up a study of Rudolf Steiner's works, and become acquainted with other people with the same interests. It

---

[276] The key phrases in German here are *Idealisierung des Realen* (but clarified by Steiner as, 'aus dem äußerlich-sinnlich Realen das Geistige ergreifen'); and *Realisierung des Geistig-Spirituellen* (der Geist in die Materie hineintragen).
[277] From an archive lecture, 20th Feb. 1921; not for publication in the Complete Works, in *Mensch und Welt*, October 1967, Nr. 10 p. 343.

refers to the first of three intended Classes in meditation and the initiatory path. These classes each consist of a key meditative verse and Rudolf Steiner's commentary on it. But owing to the premature death of Rudolf Steiner he gave just this first of three classes, as he only started to offer these in 1924. He gave only one third of this First Class set of lessons, before his illness overtook him. The original intention and strict policy of the General Anthroposophical Society, also after Steiner's death, was to ensure that only those people who joined that Society could attend the lessons, which were read out by trusted anthroposophists, from the notes taken of Steiner's original lessons. And such people had to be involved in the Society for two years before getting access to this.

But this guarding of what is indeed profound spiritual guidance broke down soon after Steiner's death. The texts of these lessons soon found their way into other organizations and individuals who were opposed to, or only vaguely interested in anthroposophy. But it is still used as a valued private spiritual resource in the General Anthroposophical Society. Often individuals will endeavour to talk about the mediative verses in their own words and insights, and not read out the notes of Rudolf Steiner's own lessons. The translations into English can contain places where errors or poorly nuanced phrases occur, as the German originals themselves are very complex.[278]

Festivals of the Seasons: spiritual ecology in action

As we noted earlier in this book, the spiritual influences operative in each season could become the basis of a new cycle of festivals. From Steiner's extensive lectures on this subject it is evident that he was hoping such seasonal festivals would arise. He also emphasized that the cosmic being from the sun sphere (the cosmic Christ) after the events of the Crucifixion and Resurrection, took up the task of monitoring and sustaining these hemispherical life-processes. Rudolf Steiner thereby pointed the way to a new festival cycle, which is both nature-based, yet also associated with the cosmic being indicated in the gospels.

Rudolf Steiner taught that this seasonal awareness is not simply a matter of experiencing "something out there." The differing etheric and astral influences, subtly active in the seasons, form an ideal doorway to developing a sense for the spiritual. Our connection to these spiritual forces behind nature is quite intimate, as he taught:

> "Only the coarseness of our perceptions prevents humanity from sensing what, in themselves, is dependent upon this external cycle (of nature spirits ascending and descending) in the out-breathing and in-breathing process of the earth." [279]

In many lectures he expresses clearly that trying to meditatively sense this spiritual reality can re-unite humanity with the spirit. This can be an individual activity, but they can also become larger festivals with artistic and contemplative contributions. These

---

[278] The author is planning a new, corrected version of the verses, with a brief commentary.
[279] GA 223 1st Oct. 1923.

contributions would attempt to portray vividly the beings and energies operative at the season, and their significance for the community. For example in 1923 he taught,

> "Humanity must again learn to be able to think of the spiritual as connected to the natural yearly cycle. Today the power must awaken to directly link the sensory appearance of the world with the spirit." [280]

In effect he hoped that a re-awakening to the spiritual could be achieved by a feeling for the spiritual aspect of the Earth's ecology, not just the physical environmental aspect. In his introduction to the Soul Calendar he wrote,

> " Our inner {soul} processes are now less connected to time, to the cycle of the year, but if we bring our own 'timeless' soul activity into correspondence with the temporal rhythms of the year, then great secrets of existence will unfold for us. The year becomes the great archetype of humankind's own soul processes, and thereby a fruitful source of self-knowledge."

This author's book, Living a Spiritual Year: Seasonal Processes in Northern and Southern Hemispheres, is the most comprehensive study of this theme written from an anthroposophical viewpoint.[281] This book explores in detail the implication of the teachings of Steiner that the spiritual energies active in any of the four seasons had the same implications for the human soul, whether occurring in the southern or the northern hemisphere.[282] One of the implications is that any corresponding festivals would not be global, but hemispherical, unlike the traditional church-based global festivals.[283] For more about the difference between the ecclesiastical and the esoteric, see the entry in this chapter, *Religion and anthroposophy*.

To help people feel the subtle spiritual dynamics of each season for Rudolf Steiner was a very important task. To accompany the inauguration of the new anthroposophical society in 1912/13, he wrote the meditative booklet, The Soul Calendar, which has 52 verses to assist people to feel the spiritual dynamics occurring each week. Verse One starts in either hemisphere on the first Sunday after the first full Moon which occurs after the spring equinox has happened. So it starts in the southern hemisphere in September-October, but in the northern hemisphere in March-April.[284]

---

[280] GA 223 1st April, 1923.

[281] A smaller book on this subject is available in manuscript form, by Geert Suwelack, The New Dialogue with the Spirit of the Earth.

[282] He clarified this to a personal student, Fred Poeppig who was working in South America, specifically in regard to the Soul Calendar verses (Poeppig's book, Abenteuer Meines Lebens, Novalis Verlag, Schaffhausen, 1975) and in over-all terms in lectures given in Norway and elsewhere.

[283] The reception of this book was negative in some anthroposophical quarters, as this non-global quality, merging an esoteric Christian view with nature-based dynamics, was a radical new thought.

[284] This difficult point has been discussed in the author's "Living a Spiritual Year" and will be further discussed in his planned translation of the Soul Calendar.

Verse One is also called the Easter mood, due to Rudolf Steiner defining Easter as a springtime dynamic involving the movement of the sun and the moon in whichever hemisphere is in its springtime. For the sake of clarity, he sometimes uses the term, "the Mystery of Golgotha" when referring to the traditional Easter festival.

Rudolf Steiner integrates this expanded awareness of how the life of the Earth is sustained by etheric energies and their associated spiritual beings, into a fuller, spiritual ecology. He taught that the cosmic Christ or sun god, having become incorporated into the Earth's aura, is vitally involved in the monitoring and sustaining of seasonal processes. This being has the role of interrelating the activity in each hemisphere's seasons of a large number of deities who are part of our planet's spiritual life.

It was his hope that in these new seasonally aligned festivals for each hemisphere, Christ (understood as a cosmic being beyond narrow religious definitions) would be viewed as the spirit being who since Golgotha became the new guiding spirit of the Earth and its hemispherical life-processes. This cosmic being now guides the activity of the nature spirits and their guiding archangels. It is in effect a teaching in which both pagan and Christian viewpoints were to merge and dissolve to form a new festival cycle for the relevant hemisphere.

A core concept underlying the new festival concept from Rudolf Steiner is that the spiritual influences which are active in any season are the same in each hemisphere, regardless of whether it is the northern hemisphere spring or the southern hemisphere's spring. He taught that many of the nature spirits in the atmosphere move around the globe, bringing the same seasonal dynamics into reality in the two hemispheres; and thus bringing the same kind of spiritual energies into operation in each hemisphere.[285] And these influences subtly affect our consciousness.

Rudolf Steiner's teachings on this theme have been subject to confusion. A major factor has been the difficulty in separating out the traditional Church festivals from the seasonally-based (but subtly Christian) new festival concept of Steiner's. A prominent influence here derives from the activity in the 1960's -1980's by a cleric, Friedrich Benesch, in the church established with the help of Rudolf Steiner in 1921. This cleric wanted festivals by people in anthroposophical circles to stay in alignment with the global church dates. Thus they remain in this way globally celebrated and ignore the full reality of seasonal dynamics. His writings are the primary source for the arguments put forward today by this church.

His primary lecture on this subject is "Does one celebrate Christmas in summer?" (*Weihnachten im Sommer feiern*?), this was later expanded to full-size book. Early in his lecture Benesch declares that, "…this yearly breathing-in and out, which actually produces the seasonal cycle, is therefore in the soul (astral) realm {of the Earth}, <u>it is not at all in the etheric realm</u>.."[286] This one of many statements in his lecture which are incorrect to Steiner's teachings.

---

[285] GA 143, lectures 7th & 16th May 1912.
[286] The German text of this cleric, Friedrich Benesch,"Dieser Jahresatemzug, der eigentlich das Jahreslaufgeschen bewirkt, ist also das Seelische, es ist gar nicht das Ätherische..."

Steiner describes how the nature spirits who, as we saw earlier, carry out the seasonal processes of the in-breathing and out-breathing, <u>actually compose the Earth's etheric body</u>.[287] And Rudolf Steiner also described how the nature spirits and their plants exist within the astral aura of the hemisphere. So the nature spirits are within both the etheric energies of the planet and within its astral aura. As he once told an audience, "The plant's astral nature is part of the astral aura of the Earth".[288] The plant's astral aspects are manifested especially in its blossoms; this is the origin of the 'language of flowers' or how different flowers symbolize different emotions for lovers. One sees here that Steiner's research is pointing out the inter-twining of the planet's etheric life energies and the soul or astral aura of the Earth. This is to be expected; just as the interlinking of the human being's own etheric and astral bodies is a major factor in our life. The existence of stress (in the soul or astral body) can easily make the interlinked etheric body unwell, and it in turn affects the physical body, leading to an illness.

In a 1923 lecture, after explaining the nature of the spiritual influences from divine beings on humanity, Steiner taught that our etheric body forms a bridge to the divine worlds. For the etheric body receives astral influences out of the spiritual realms and, retained in the etheric body, they influence one's consciousness,

> "…the human being in his etheric body {not only in his soul} lives with that which spirits of a higher ranking intend, regarding the soul's moral qualities {astrality} … therefore the soul-life of the human being is dependent upon its existence within its etheric body."[289]

So too, the astral energies pulsing through the Earth-soul, from season to season, are living on in the etheric energies of the Earth, in its two hemispheres. As part of his description of the seasonal processes, Steiner taught that the nature-spirits absorb the changing spiritual influences and rise and fall with the astral energies of the hemisphere during the seasons.[290] Of course, each hemisphere has its own seasonal astral and etheric dynamics, and Rudolf Steiner describes how the etheric and astral dynamics that are operative in a season, "apply to <u>each hemisphere equally</u>".[291] Steiner also taught that, at Golgotha the sun god Christ united to the Earth's etheric body. So these nature processes and their associated nature spirits are deeply linked to the cosmic Christ.[292] The winter in-breath, of either hemisphere, creates the basis for the Yuletide or Holy Nights festival, which links the soul to Jesus and the cosmic Christ.

Benesch's many mistakes here are still not widely seen, and illustrate the difficulty people have in grasping Steiner's teaching that the seasonal processes have the same spiritual significance in either hemisphere and are directly monitored and nurtured by

---

[287] GA 136, pages 39, 46.
[288] GA 98, p. 143, & GA 60, p.172.
[289] From GA 218, lecture in London 19th Nov. 1922.
[290] GA 143, pages 156, 200.
[291] GA 145, p. 73.
[292] GA165, p. 136.

the sun god, Christ.[293] Summing up, each hemisphere in Rudolf Steiner's teachings has its own valid seasonal dynamics, of an etheric and also an astral kind. And these processes are subtly monitored and permeated by the new Earth-Spirit, the cosmic sun god.

The Foundation Stone meditation
During 1923 Rudolf Steiner laboured to re-invigorate the Anthroposophical Society after a major setback at the very beginning of the year had occurred: the burning down of the First Goetheanum. He announced a re-founding of the 1912 Society, to take place in a carpenter's shed, near the ruins of the Goetheanum. The intention was to place a 'foundation stone' of the future anthroposophical work into the hearts of the members. As a core part of this process he spoke a lengthy meditation called The Foundation Stone Meditation.

This verse enables the meditant to gain his or her own insights into many core aspects of anthroposophy. The primary intention of the re-founding conference of the Anthroposophical Society, which included a cycle of lectures, was to provide this verse, so that students involved in regular meditating, and using this verse, could attune their soul to the springs of anthroposophical wisdom.

This long verse has four sections to it. Three of these refer to the development of the Spirit-self, and the Life-spirit and Spirit-human, and indicate how deeply interwoven is humanity with the activity of the hierarchies in these three processes. The fourth section refers to the coming to the Earth of the 'cosmos-spirit' (the cosmic Christ). It also incorporates several Rosicrucian meditative phrases, deriving from the 17th century (or earlier.) The use of this verse was obviously regarded by Steiner as vital for those who wished to imbue themselves with the spiritual energies and insights that inspire and consolidate their anthroposophical work and spiritual development.

Further Reading
W. Zeylmans von Emmichoven, *The Foundation Stone*: an insightful booklet by a student of Rudolf Steiner's.
Michael Wilson (introduction) *The Foundation Stone Meditation.* (A compilation of several translations of the verse.)
The author's book on this theme, *The Foundation Stone Meditation – a New Commentary*, was written to provide an accurate translation of the verse into English, as this is otherwise scarce.[294] This book also provides a brief meditative commentary on the verse, as well as a new version of the main lecture given by Rudolf Steiner about it. This lecture provides an essential guide to the substantial verse.

---

[293] Benesch joined the church in 1947 and rose to become its most powerful figure over decades. But the competence of Benesch to represent anthroposophical ideas was rejected by many people after 2004 when Holocaust historians reported that he was a fanatical Nazi, participating with the SS who carried out the extermination of Jews and others. See the author's e-booklet *Opponents and Critics of Steiner.*

[294] This is available as an e-book on www.rudolfsteinerstudies.com.

Freemasonry
The question sometimes arises as to whether Rudolf Steiner was a Freemason. He never joined the recognized Freemason movement; but around 1902 there were some Theosophists who were Freemasons. They were interested in a renewal or esoteric deepening of their ritual ceremonies, and Rudolf Steiner obliged them by taking up the task of offering sessions, independent of the main stream freemason movement. He chose a form of freemasonry apparently originating with an 18th century Italian Freemason, and later lead by a brilliant English freemason, John Yarker.

This was known as the Egyptian ritual of Memphis and Mizraim, which was usually not regarded as authentic by the mainstream movement.[295] The authorization to use this material later passed into the hands of a disreputable occultist, named Reuss. Steiner never met this person; in 1904 he simply paid the fee demanded and thereby obtained the authorisation and texts needed to offer the sessions. In 1914 this activity ceased, as First World War began to devastate Europe.

Rudolf Steiner did lecture for the members of this freemasonry on some of the imaginative myths that are used in it, especially those concerning King Solomon and Hieram the builder. He also commented with regard to mainstream Freemasonry that its myths and dialogues are in effect preserving a noble spiritual heritage but that the freemasons today generally don't have the esoteric expertise to unlock the deeper meanings of these stories.

The Nine Hierarchies and the human soul
In Chapter Nine we considered the divine-spiritual beings from whom we ourselves derive, and their relation to the realms that we journey through after death. Another way to develop a feeling for these beings is to contemplate their own inner structure; that is, their spiritual constitution. We humans have a sevenfold structuring of our own nature, and so too do all the hierarchical beings. But of course they tower up far beyond our capacities. These beings are, Angels, Archangels, Principalities, Powers, Mights (or Virtues), Dominions, Thrones, and also the Cherubim and Seraphim (or more correctly in plural, Cherubine, Seraphine).

Beyond the Spirit-human state of being, Rudolf Steiner indicates there exists nine further states of cosmic consciousness. The hierarchical beings each have an aspect of these higher states of consciousness. He names the first three of these higher states, beyond the Spirit-human, as Holy Spirit, Son and Father. He says very little about these (or the other higher states), but it is reasonable to conclude that the above three states of consciousness are in some way a reflection of the Trinity.

The trinity is the so-called Godhead, the three divine beings who are above the hierarchies. Illustration 26 presents in a simplified way, these states of consciousness; those states beyond a certain level are not named by him, so here they are just numbered.

---

[295] See for example, Mackey's Revised Encyclopaedia of Freemasonry, Macoy Publishing, Richmond, USA, reprinted 1966.

The Holy Grail

This subject is perhaps the most sacred of the spiritual truths that Rudolf Steiner disclosed. There are several ways to understand the Holy Grail, for it has various aspects to it. Here we can only briefly note the aspect of the Grail which is related to personal spiritual development. In The Way to the Sacred, this description was given,

> When the meditant attains the ability to stand in awe before the starry heavens, to become immersed in wonder at an autumn leaf, to revere truth, beauty and goodness, to experience real spiritual insights, and to become selflessly loving, then a source of spiritual renewal is forming within the heart.

As the meditant earnestly strives to re-vivify the primal spiritual qualities that imbue the very young child, this results in deeply spiritual soul-energies accumulating in the heart chakra. These then rise up as sacred etherealized energies from the heart towards the throat. Such inner exercises, together with the constant effort at thinking spiritually – both in study exercises and through intuitive thinking (i.e. meditative activity) – **is creating a chalice to receive a divine light-substance into an energy centre near the throat. This light has been made accessible through the deed of Christ**. As Rudolf Steiner taught, if the human being has found himself in this innermost sanctuary he or she will also be allowed to enter the great temple of the Grail and find the Holy Grail. Gradually the sanctified acolyte will sense its holy content, so that the content itself shines for him in a golden radiance.

It is a central message in Rudolf Steiner's teachings, that this process of spiritualization, of finding the way to the sacred, has become possible for every person because the spiritual light of the cosmic Christ (united to the soul and spirit of the person, Jesus) **now exists as an ethereal life-essence in the Earth's aura**. Prior to the events on Golgotha hill, only a few select acolytes could attain to this.

The mention of the human vessel of the sun god, Jesus of Nazareth, occurs here, because when he became united to the cosmic Christ, he became the archetype of the fully sanctified (or initiated) human being. One could say, of the human being who has found the Grail. And this achievement is especially important, because it is essential that an archetype exists of the fully spiritualized human being. For once the archetype exists, then millions can take up this path in the same way that once a tuning fork begins to resound in the presence of many other tuning forks, they too can start to resonate. In recent decades a blasphemous obstacle was created which blocks understanding of the Grail. It is the absurdity of presenting the figure of Mary

Magdalene as a lover of an earthly Jesus. Mary Magdalene was <u>never</u> in France. But in about 810 AD Hrabanus Maurus, a Benedictine monk and archbishop of Mainz, a pupil of Alcuin, wrote a pious fantasy reporting her journey there.[296] Hrabanus by his nature was ready to go beyond the prudent limits of pastoral theological work that Alcuin had laid down. [297]

---

[296] The Life of Mary Magdalene, Hrabanus Maurus. Already by the 17th century, religious scholars established it to be a fiction, in articles appearing in the Analecta Bollandiana.
[297] A. West, Alcuin and the rise of the Christian Schools, Heinemann, 1893.

Very significant evidence of its fabrication at a late date is that the story was unknown to Gregory the Great and Gregory of the French town of Tours, back in the sixth century. These two church leaders would have made much of this situation were it true. The most accurate accounts about her tell us that she died at Ephesus. But Hrabanus was determined to Christianize the Teutonic people of Charlemagne's empire, stirred on no doubt by the creating of a huge Christian carving at their most sacred site, the Externsteine; he was probably involved in that audacious task.

Modern writers, drawing on his pious fantasy, falsely presented an extract of an ancient text, the Gospel of Philip, to create this slur. They presented Jesus as loving the Magdalene (passionately) and kissing her on her mouth. But the original text has no mention of 'the mouth', as there is a piece of the papyrus missing in the line; and anyway, the verb to love used in the Coptic text here means to have good-will.

Furthermore the spiritual teacher in Judaism followed an age-old custom of kissing his students, of either gender, on the forehead or the cheek. So in the missing piece of papyrus the word for cheek or forehead would have been written, not mouth. See the illustration for a brief extract of the ancient gospel relevant here. A very fine version of the Grail legend is from Wolfram von Eschenbach written in Middle High German about 1210 AD. In book 5, as Parsifal enters the Grail, this is described as,

> "...the fullness of Paradise. The core and circumference too. It was a thing, called the grail, the surpassing earthly blessing."[298] (author's translation.)

A significant feature here of Eschenbach's text is that this high state of spirituality requires one to be living on the Earth. It is a blessing that only becomes attainable through personal development whilst incarnate. For it is only here that the human being can encounter the sensual desires and, if they freely wish, find a way to overcome them.

The grail is also described as 'a thing' and yet as something which is the essence and the all of heaven; a statement that can become meaningful if one considers a spiritual radiance developing in the meditant's aura as an object, as something real, although not a material object, but an etheric-astral reality. It is also historically a cup used at the Last Supper, but that is a different aspect to this many-aspected theme.

Meditation
The term meditation is very often encountered today; but it is a word which has many different meanings. In an anthroposophical context, it refers to an inner soul activity through which the meditant is trying to perceive directly higher truths, and hence also higher realms of being. This kind of meditation enables one, in the course of time, to directly experience the divine spirit which is part of our human nature. Drawing near to this spirituality starts to bring into being within the meditant, spiritual wisdom, compassionate love, and a deeply selfless good will. It brings this about through a

---

[298] In Wolfram's German: Truoc sie den Wunsch von Paradis, bede wurzeln und ris. Daz war ein dinc, das hiez der Gral, erden wunschen uberwal.

merging of the personality with the human spirit. This means the Spirit-self (the spiritualized soul), the Life-spirit (the spiritualized etheric body) and eventually even the Spirit-human. As this occurs, higher (clairvoyant) faculties, also arise. Further, one begins to become aware of brief flashes of insight, concerning the theme of the meditative text on which one is meditating. And then, as I mention in my book, "The Way to the Sacred", these brief moments become deeper and more prolonged, and one becomes aware, that from spiritual realms, from a source of holiness, **my 'I' is being 'enlightened'**. The 'I' is now becoming illumined, becoming transcendent.

It is taking on layers of richness and depth that interface with a realm that transcends time, and space and the 'substance' of which is formed from God. This higher self is also permeated with the consciousness and creativity of a multitude of divine beings. One sees from this brief comment that unlike some eastern pathways, the sense of self is valued and therefore maintained, but one endeavours to widen and deepen it.

It is a question of so refining the soul, into a purity, a goodness, and a wisdom that the chakras naturally develop and become active. This underlies a New Testament statement, "The pure in heart shall see God". It is also a case of learning how to allow intuitive insights to become perceived in the mind as a result of focussing upon high spiritual realities. And then it is necessary to learn how to one aware of those insights.

For those seriously interested in this theme, and who have acquired a reasonable knowledge of Rudolf Steiner's teachings, this author's book, The Way to the Sacred, is available.

Further reading
Rudolf Steiner: Self-transformation, (a compilation of his lectures).
                    Verses and Meditations
But see also www.waldorfbooks.com/anthroposophy/inner-work, for a list of other books of relevance here.

Religion and anthroposophy
In the modern mind, religion is increasingly associated with fundamentalist attitudes, with political extremism, and in recent decades, with sexual abuse and with terrorism. Of course, there are many fine people in the great religions who are entirely genuine in their feeling of reverence for the divine. It is also understood that in earlier times especially, religion was an activity in which souls with a pious or mystical inclination found an occupation that was widely revered. It was for millennia from these religions, that society received its main ethical guidelines. This included moral principles, the encouragement to charitable deeds, to good-will and also reverence for the deity or deities involved.

But as the modern era arrived, a potent change occurred in relation to how people responded to a so-called sacred book. In the earlier times people were aware that to really comprehend these teachings, a great deal of sincere inner refinement would be

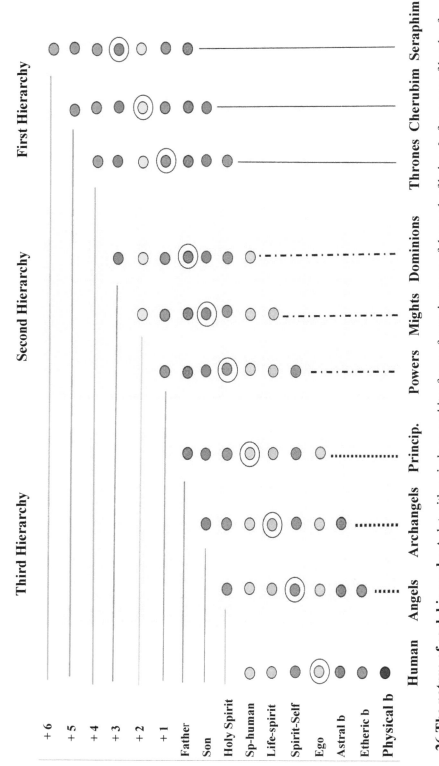

26 The nature of each hierarchy A dot with a circle around it = focus of consciousness of that rank of being. Left: names of levels of awareness above Spirit-human, from R. Steiner, not referring to the Trinity, but the Trinity is reflected in these levels of awareness.

required, along with mental effort. People were aware that the finest texts in the great religions derived from arduous learning and often from seership, attained through training in spiritual development. In modern times it seems that large numbers of people approach a text with a potent, but concealed ego-centric attitude. They have an attitude of what can I find in this revered book that I can use to gratify my own yearnings for power, for self-praise, for a sense of having an important mission in life. Since we modern people often encounter this type of false religiosity, with its negative social implications, the thought of Rudolf Steiner being involved in anything religious, and lecturing on Christianity, can be quite a negative outlook for some people today.

As we noted in a previous chapter, anthroposophy is not defined as a religion, but as a path of knowledge. But because Rudolf Steiner did help to found a church, and also provided a text for an optional religious instruction hour at schools, this has meant that anthroposophy is at times seen as a religion, and Waldorf schools are therefore at times incorrectly viewed as religious institutions.

Anthroposophy is not a set of religious doctrines, nor a new church, even though included amongst Rudolf Steiner's teachings are references to the spiritual beings who are worshipped in various religions. He provided valuable insights into Buddhist, Jewish and Hindu texts. These three religions were familiar to his audiences, who often had a background in Theosophy. Rudolf Steiner also spoke with deep respect for the Buddha; whom he described as a high degree initiate. He also spoke of Zarathustra, the ancient Persian initiate, and his profound perception of the nature of Ahriman and of the sun god, Ahura Mazdao. Steiner lectured on the Bhagavad-Gita, highlighting its profound depth and beauty. He spoke about the ancient Manicheans, who taught an esoteric, cosmopolitan form of Christianity. But he spoke as a spiritual researcher, or spiritual scientist, on these topics, not as a priest. However, as we noted earlier in this book, he is closely associated with a new Christian church.

Throughout this book we have not only considered Rudolf Steiner's worldview, we have also seen how his ideas relate to today's attitudes and to advances in general knowledge during the past century. So we have been noting the reception of his teachings by the wider public, and by those who consider themselves anthroposophists. And we have also noted how some of Rudolf Steiner's teachings appear in the light of more recent scientific work.

Now a question can arise here, how did Rudolf Steiner expect people to relate to anthroposophical ideas which include a cosmic, esoteric Christianity? How would this aspect of his work be influenced by his involvement in the founding of a new church? What did he advise concerning the relationship of the path of esoteric spiritual development to the religious life?

Christianity is not only a belief system focused on divine beings it is also, like any religion, a codified system of reverential practises, such as organised sessions of reverence and prayer and sacraments. This includes baptism, receiving the sacred host at the Sunday service and funeral services. Rudolf Steiner's main focus in regard to lectures on religion was Christianity. And as we saw in Chapter One, some pastors and

The Gospel of Philip: the actual Coptic text, the gaps and what it really says.

.ЄⲢO.[.].[..]Ⲙⲁ   ⲠⲈⲬⲀⲨ ⲚⲀ Ϥ ⲬⲈ

He   --ves   -----,   they   say   to   him
= Jesus lo{ves} [the Magdalene],   they   say   to   him"

Above: = Jesus has agape for her, the verb here is 'agape' which means spiritual good-will.
That is, Jesus has good-will, as traditionally shown by the Master to the student

Below: the fabricating of the word 'mouth', which is then used to create the slur used in the Da Vinci code. There is **actually a gap in the papyrus,** but since it is all about agape, the kiss was on the forehead.

ⲚⲈϤ]ⲀⲤⲠⲀ ⲌⲈ ⲘⲘⲞⲤ ⲀⲦⲈⳞ[.....Ⲛ̅ⳞⲀⳞ] Ⲛ̅ⲤⲞⲠ

{And} did he kiss her on her   - - - - {many} the times.

religious students in Germany did respond positively to Rudolf Steiner in the 1920's, and consequently asked him to establish a new type of Christian church. The new church was designed to have sacraments with elements similar to both ritualistic liturgy and Protestant rationality.

But Rudolf Steiner emphasized that he himself did not found a church, but rather he had responded to priests and theology students who came to him and asked for his help. And even though it was he who consecrated the initial clergy of this church, he had done this reluctantly, only after the founding clergy of the proposed church failed to find a suitable person to consecrate them. A few of these clerics were sent on a journey throughout central Europe to find an aged and deeply pious priest from whom they could receive consecration; but no such person was encountered. Aware that this situation could cause confusion, Steiner wanted the difference between anthroposophy and religion, and especially the new church founded in 1922, to be clearly seen.

A religion codifies ideas and feelings about spiritual beings so that a community can express their reverence for that being or beings. In the course of his lecturing work for anthroposophists, not for members of a church congregation, Rudolf Steiner explained the esoteric secrets of Christianity. As we saw in the previous chapter, his lectures provided a new and profound perspective on the terms, God, and Christ. His views were of course considered heretical by most theologians.

Steiner wanted to leave people free in the matter of religion. This is clearly shown in the following incident. A brilliant Stuttgart teen-ager, Erwin Birker, had read Steiner's book, The Riddles of the Soul" at eleven years of age. In 1919, now 14 years old, as the first Waldorf school was founded, Erwin wanted to attend, but his mother declined permission, telling her son that Steiner was 'not Christian'.

The young Erwin was determined to find out if this was true or false, as he wanted to go to the new school. By chance he saw a notice of a lecture to be held by Steiner soon, and on that day, he crept into the hall and then waited until the last person had spoken with Steiner after the lecture. He then approached and asked Steiner "What do you think about Christ, and can anthroposophy affirm the Christ?" Steiner answered in a manner that avoided people feeling unfree, "Certainly, certainly; you see, this Christ-impulse it has entered into the middle of humanity's development (historically), and it has its place within anthroposophy.[299]

So why did he help found a new church? To Rudolf Steiner, the action of renewing the role of the church in society was an important one because – in the time before there was any widespread interest in what we now refer to as spirituality – the church, at its best, provided access to sacred stories and ideas that supported decency and good-will towards others. Importantly it also provided a way for souls to become attuned, in their feeling life especially, to what he refers to as the Christ-impulse. He indicates that the effect of a sincerely held church ritual is beneficial in a subtle way, for the Earth's own etheric life-processes. (Naturally, he rejected enforced celibacy or males-only clergy.)

---

[299] In *Mitteilungen aus der Anthroposophischen Arbeit in Deutschland*, 20 Jhrg. Nr.77, Michaeli 1966, p. 206.

In the early 1920's awareness of his views on Christianity caused conservative religious organisations to attack him. In Rudolf Steiner's view of this religion, there is a cosmic dimension to Christ, with a specific association to the sun, and some aspects of the Hellenistic and Egyptian Mysteries. And there are many other facets to his explanation of the Gospels concerning the life of Jesus and the importance of the cosmic Christ which were viewed as seriously heretical and unfounded.

The worst attack led to the destruction by arson of the first Goetheanum, in the night of December 31st 1922. It is a significant fact that this crime occurred on the same night that he was holding a solemn lecture inside this building for anthroposophists, emphasizing to them the need to realize that, although a liturgical religious service was a valuable mode of seeking the divine for the general community, it was not appropriate for those people who may regard themselves as anthroposophists. For these people are ready for the self-initiatory path.

He emphasised that it would be counter-productive to try to engage seriously in the ritualistic church service, and to also become involved in the esoteric meditative path. The priestly work, he explained, is to stimulate the feelings of the laity by the sights and sounds of the ritual and in this way to let descend upon the congregation a palpable feeling of the sacredness of the Christ. This becomes the act of communion with Christ, formally celebrated as "the Lord's Supper" in the church service, where bread and grape juice (or wine) is consumed ritually.

Whereas the practice of regular meditation preceded by and combined with the study of anthroposophical texts, stimulates the development of the spiritual-soul. This then enables the chakras to become active and raises the consciousness of the meditant up to the astral and even possibly Devachanic realms. Hence he told his esoteric students that becoming able to cognize clairvoyantly the spiritual origin and nature of things and beings in the physical world by developing higher faculties, is the true act of communion of the human being.

He also expressed this in his book, Goethe's Theory of Knowledge" where he wrote, "Becoming aware of the Idea within reality is the true communion of the human being". And to his esoteric students he put it this way:

> "Whomsoever knows and understands spiritual truths – not only religiously feels them – no longer needs the Eucharist, because he or she daily and hourly celebrates the Last Supper with everything which they receive as physical nourishment or as food for the soul or the spirit."[300]

Consequently he taught that the new church's sacramental service would not be required at all for those people actively involved in an esoteric meditative life. Or more accurately expressed, of the seven sacraments that it offered, one of them, the Sunday service, would not be appropriate. The other sacraments, such as baptism, marriage, and the funeral service, are appropriate. Hence he emphasized that the new religious movement, which was eventually called the Christian Community, was not to give

---

[300] From an Esoteric Lesson given in Cologne (date unknown).

anthroposophists the impression that they were in need of its Sunday service for their own spiritual development. But he taught that anthroposophists could certainly be friends of the church and support its many functions.

Hence when a senior priest, Gottfried Husemann, reported to him with enthusiasm, that "in the previous Sunday service there were 100 people in the congregation in Hamburg, and only three were <u>not</u> anthroposophists !"[301] Rudolf Steiner replied gravely, "Then we must work to reverse that proportion." As he explained later in the same conversation, "The anthroposophists should experience their anthroposophy as something which goes beyond sermons and ritual."

In modern terms, Rudolf Steiner viewed anthroposophy as a path to esoteric spirituality through which eventually the meditant may actually cognize the divine realities in Devachan, whereas a church is a pathway to religious piety, to a devout reverence for divinity. The esoteric path includes a sense of piety but also requires the empowerment of the spiritual-soul, and then the person's chakra system, in the effort to allow the Spirit-self to unfold.

However, in later decades in anthroposophical circles the difference between the two activities became blurred. This resulted in anthroposophists erroneously concluding that they could participate in the esoteric meditative activity of the Anthroposophical Society and also fully immerse themselves in the church's Sunday Eucharist service. This has created a confusing situation for both new anthroposophists and for people outside the anthroposophical movement trying to define the nature of Steiner's initiative in this regard.

This confusion was deepened when the church itself obscured this situation, as reported in 2002 in the weekly journal, "Das Goetheanum Wochenschrift", the official publication of the Anthroposophical Society in Dornach, Switzerland. Steiner gave a number of lecture cycles on religion and theology for the clergy interested informing new church. But some decades ago these had been specifically altered in favour of the church, then printed and used in the training of the priests. These alterations gave the impression that anthroposophists should indeed be an integral part of the church.

One example of the alterations, given in the article is this sentence from Rudolf Steiner in the church edition; "If anthroposophists now ask, *how* they are to participate in the religious service…" Whereas in the correct, official Rudolf Steiner Archives edition it reads: "If anthroposophists now ask, *whether* they are to participate in the religious service…"[302]

A clear indication of Rudolf Steiner's view of the difference between religion and esoteric wisdom is reflected in the Creed which he gave to the new church. This document commences with a statement about the nature of God,

---

[301] Memoir manuscript of the founding priests of the Christian Community: *Erinnerungen an die Begründungsereignisse der Christengemeinschaft*, Stuttgart 1984, p. 296.
[302] *Goetheanum Wochenschrift* No. 24, June 2002, ps. 453-454.

"An almighty spiritual, physical Godly-being is the basis of existence of heaven and Earth....."

Throughout the history of Christendom, a church's creed has been designed to briefly formulate its theology and to help the feelings of the congregation to develop a reverential mood about deity. But the above Creed given to this new church by Rudolf Steiner directly contradicts his teachings on the nature of God, as given in lectures to anthroposophists.

As we noted in the chapter on Christianity, Steiner taught that in anthroposophy, God **is not almighty,** but instead has a much more complex nature. In this sense, Rudolf Steiner's teachings about God resonate with profound writings of the great mystics of earlier ages. And it is this more mature view of God in anthroposophy that releases the soul from the view that God is ruling almightily over our evolution.

The religions that espouse this traditional view of God have been losing their role in society for some decades, partly because people are confronted with all manner of atrocities and genocides, and cannot reconcile this with the church's view of God. The esoteric wisdom in anthroposophy indicates that there has never been a protector placed over our existence, at least not to the degree assumed in the naïve 'almighty' concept. But rather divine-spiritual beings strive to moderate the activities of Ahriman, who inspires cruelty and hardened egotism.

Evolution is a living encounter between higher divine beings and evil powers; the outcome of which in the various Ages is not always predictable. Poetically one could say that the cosmic train shall certainly arrive at its destination, after passing through its seven stations; but how many souls will be onboard and in what spiritual condition – that is the unknown factor.

In anthroposophy there is then, a substantial difference between the worldview appropriate for the religious world, and the worldview developed from esoteric wisdom. To Rudolf Steiner the ecclesiastical worldview is appropriate for people to whom the esoteric perspective on God, and an active interest in initiation, is not appropriate. Anthroposophy is not a religion, but a path of spiritual knowledge which offers an esoteric view of important truths about Christianity.

So, as regards both anthroposophy and the Steiner schools, there is an interest in spirituality, but not a concern with religious convictions. This point needs to be grasped. For example, an internet critic has written about how the use in Waldorf schools of moist paper for water-colour painting classes by children, is preferred over dry paper. He notes that this is due to the anthroposophical view that wet paper creates a gentler, more diffuse experience for the children.

He then declares that this is a religious conviction, and is an example of how Steiner schools are really disguised religious institutions.[303] Nothing could be more incorrect. The viewpoint here about the advisability of wet paper comes from an insightfulness, a

---

[303] Internet article, *"The delusional world of Rudolf Steiner"*, Ian Robinson.

living wisdom, concerning the sensory experiences of the young child, and their impact upon its soul. It does not derive from religious feelings nor religious dogmas.

Spirituality is valued today globally. For vast numbers of people it is considered a wholesome and important part of life. The use of delightful, simple verses about the sun, moon, plants and the stars for young children in the Waldorf schools helps to foster in them a sense of awe and wonder at the world they live in; it is a form of spirituality. From these attitudes, environmental responsibility arises naturally in the older child.

The two kinds of Stigmata

Here we can briefly note an unusual aspect of the religious life known as the stigmata. This is a strange phenomenon which mirrors the wounds on Jesus' body caused during the Crucifixion. It has occurred occasionally in the Christian church, since the time of St. Francis of Assisi. It produces an unpleasant medical condition that creates five wounds on the body, which often bleed throughout the person's life. These stigmatics also are subject to visions, strongly influenced by the religious convictions of the person, which reinforce their religious beliefs. It is one of two types of phenomena that could be called 'stigmata'. The second type is however an entirely different, wholesome phenomenon.

This second type of stigmata is one of seven strange temporary experiences of an initiatory religious life, which was carried out in medieval times. In stage four of this seven stage pathway, small red marks would temporarily occur at these same five places as the emotive stigmatics report; and as Rudolf Steiner comments, (as this is in contrast to the first form, "of course they only occurred during the time of the meditation".[304] For when the prayer session was over, these harmless reddish marks then <u>disappeared</u>, and only returned when the meditant entered into this spiritual exercise. There would be no bleeding and the reddish marks disappeared when the meditative prayer session ended.[305]

They occurred because at these places, he explains, because the physical and etheric body are especially closely interlinked there. And when the soul is undergoing intense spiritual exercises, wherein the higher self is beginning to manifest, this can energize the etheric body, and its increased energy condition in turn brings about these five small reddish marks on the physical body.

This second type of stigmata was a wholesome meditative religious experience; and was not due to the unhealthy emotive urge (consciously or subconsciously) to be immersed in the sufferings of Christ. It is simply an esoteric physiological process which brings this temporary reddening of the skin. The deeper reason for these places being depicted in art as the locations of wounds on Jesus is to subtly point out this dynamic that exists between the physical body and the etheric body. Such paintings emphasise the sheer power of the higher self in Jesus, and how it caused this same kind

---

[304] GA 97, p. 178, lecture of 19th Sept 1906.
[305] GA 97, pp. 47, 190, 221.

of energizing of his etheric body.[306] One can assume that this is also the reason in the first place for these five wounds to be inflicted in this special pattern on Jesus. If the Roman centurion had not been impelled to put his spear into the right side of the body, then there would have been only four marks on the body. In the esoterically inspired painting, the Isenheim Altarpiece by Grunewald, these five places on the risen Jesus actually radiate out a potent etheric force.[307]

Rudolf Steiner points out that the existence of these five intersection points of the physical and etheric bodies was well known long before the Christian era. So some of the pre-Christian initiates also manifested the stigmata, as it were – but only in one of these five places. These persons, being obviously of lesser stature than the Christ, would normally manifest only one of these marks. Rudolf Steiner description reveals that the other, long-term bleeding stigmata derived from a pathological condition of the soul.

The above perspective on the two kinds of stigmata is summarised by words of Rudolf Steiner about 'the stigmatas' in an unpublished archive document, from an archive lecture given in Rome about the mystical religious path, wherein the temporary reddening the skin in five places occurred. Then he comments, with regard to the stigmata that does not fit the esoteric type, and therefore does not give a temporary reddish spot, but medical conditions, that is a pathological phenomenon,

> "…but one has to be cautious in regard to any occurrence of this phenomenon as being the sign of spiritual development, because the stigmata can also arise through certain pathological conditions."[308]

A pathological condition results in all the abnormal medical conditions which are absent from the wholesome initiatory stigmata, which lasts only a hour or so. The unhealthy stigmata could occur to a person interested in anthroposophy (or various other esoteric movements) if they also had a strongly emotive religiosity. If such a person were also born with an atavistic clairvoyance, this could trigger off potent, but false, visions. A person who pursued this unwholesome religiosity as a religious extremist in their past life in medieval Europe could have this bleeding condition suddenly break out in this lifetime, without any known triggers. For others who are deeply emotive in their religious life, this emotionalism can trigger off the stigmata. It is often activated at religious festivals, such as Easter time.

Sacred Sites, earlier Mystery Streams
It is of value for those studying anthroposophical texts to become acquainted with the earlier esoteric streams, as this gives a feeling for how earlier humanity experienced the quest for spirituality. It can also give the serious student some indicators as to esoteric influences from the past that resonate with their own soul. There are various

---

[306] GA 139, The Gospel of St. Mark, lecture, 21st Sept 1912,

[307] The body of Jesus in this painting is his etheric body, but made more dense, to be more perceptible to the disciples.

[308] Unpublished lecture in Rome, late March 1909, (author's library).

texts from Rudolf Steiner about these earlier esoteric streams; he is uniquely able to lift the veil on what occurred in these sites.

With regard to earlier Mystery steams or esoteric groups, we can briefly note here in general terms, the perspective given by Rudolf Steiner on the Gnostics, the medieval Alchemists and the Rosicrucians. He points out that in the first centuries of Christianity there was an influence from the spiritual worlds upon some human beings; these are known as Gnostics. There were some Gnostics with a slight clairvoyance and an esoteric awareness who ignored the new religion of Christianity. Within these groups there were both decadent, and idealistic people. Other Gnostic texts indicate the existence of groups of Gnostics who were able to discern the significance of Christianity and became in effect, esoteric Christians. These latter were in a similar position to the students of anthroposophical ideas today. So the term Gnostic is rather multi-nuanced.

In the Middle Ages a variety of spiritual-esoteric groups existed. Amongst these were the alchemists, some of whom set out to magically create gold from baser metal for profit. Steiner differentiated between these materialistic alchemists, and other alchemists who applied the language employed in the transformation of metal, for the process of developing spirituality. During this time the original Rosicrucian society was formed in secrecy. This came about through the decision of the great and saintly person, who had been living at the time of Christ, who became a close disciple of Christ. This initiate commenced his work of inspiring people in Europe as from the late 14th century. His movement grew in numbers and it offered a deeply esoteric teaching based on an esoteric Christianity. Some of the truly spiritual-minded alchemists were attracted to this group. He became known by the mystery name of Christian Rosencreutz, and in 1616 this movement announced itself to the world publicly.

In the Middle Ages the Rosicrucians were in a similar position to the students of anthroposophical ideas today. They were responding to the most contemporary form of high spiritual wisdom. But by the 18th century this Rosicrucian impulse was fading out and its teachings betrayed into the hands of persons who were not capable of assessing them properly. The spiritual impulse then withdrew and re-emerged in modern times in Anthroposophy, after an initial expression in Theosophy. Finally we can see that the esoteric ideas of these earlier groups, by now outmoded, have been revived by various New Age groups of today.

It is also valuable to contemplate what remains of ancient sacred sites and to learn something of whatever might be known about these places historically. But it's important to note that these sites can not be re-activated, as their time is past. New mysteries are needed, and Rudolf Steiner's work was in part designed to help create such a renewal of the Mysteries.

In ancient Egypt for example, the process of initiation was carried out over many centuries, using the Great Pyramid and the secret underground Tomb of Osiris on the Giza plateau, not far from the pyramid of Khafre. (Rudolf Steiner mentioned that the Tarot cards are a remnant of old Egyptian esoteric knowledge.) He also taught that those who succeeded in obtaining a high level of spiritual wisdom in ancient Egyptian times could find that in modern times anthroposophical wisdom can really blossom in their soul. These are just some of the places where the striving towards the attainment of the Spirit-Self and Life-Spirit, and thus to the cosmic sun god, was carried out.

In the European world there are many sites sacred to a mystical Christianity, and these are generally well known. Although we need to especially note here, Chartres cathedral in France and Karlstejn castle, near Prague. We can note that at Chartres in the 12th to 14th centuries, some great teachers were active who had a Platonic, mystical Christianity; their souls belong to the spiritual stream behind the anthroposophical movement. At Karlstejn a Rosicrucian wisdom was active, designing the building to be a reflection of the mysterious Grail castle.[309]

A brief mention is needed regarding a site which is not well known, yet was once very important. It is called the Externsteine, and is located in a forest in northern Germany, not far from Detmold. Until the early medieval times, it was the greatest sacred site in all of Europe, serving the ancient Celtic people. Rudolf Steiner made only an indirect reference to it, as it is no longer a valid site for the spiritual life, and ancient sites can be the focus of modern mystical interests which run counter to the purposes of the anthroposophy. But this site is possibly the most impressive of all ancient sacred places (except the Great Pyramid). It was the chief site of the Druids, and played a vital role in the history of the Roman empire, the Teutonic tribes and Charlemagne's empire. Hence it is worthwhile knowing about the immense historical, esoteric, religious and cultural significance of the place.

Another site to mention is a remote site in Ethiopia, called Lalibela. It was the result of an out-of-body experience of a 13th century Ethiopian king. About ten underground sanctuaries devoted to an esoteric Christian wisdom were constructed here. One of the very unusual buildings in this site exactly meets the description Rudolf Steiner gave of how a temple would be constructed if one were to create in architecture a temple to the Holy Grail.

He told one audience "if you could visualize the entirety of human souls streaming towards a common point above the landscape then you would have these many, many souls forming a kind of dome." And then imagine the 72 disciples of Christ radiating out their spiritual energies, and then the gathered mass of humanity receiving this and then streaming this energy out towards the heavens. And then imagine all of this forming "a kind of cross-shaped temple, with three doors in the north, south and west; and an altar in the eastern side". It appears that here Steiner means the Holy Grail in terms of a society in which everyone has a yearning towards a social life, inspired by the Christ-impulse.

In Lalibela the sanctuary called Beth Medhanie Alem has precisely this esoteric shape; it has 72 pillars each of which are square and the three doors and the eastern altar. Another sanctuary at this site presents secrets of the quest for the Sophia, in its architecture and art.

---

[309] The emperor Charles IV who built it in 1348 was described by Rudolf Steiner as the last of Rosicrucian rulers in Europe. Reported by Julia Klima in memoirs manuscript.

Further reading

For more about either of these places, and also Stonehenge and megalithic sites, see the four books by Damien Pryor.

When you become familiar with Steiner's work, there are various books which reveal the deeper aspects of the old Mystery Centres, such as "Mystery Knowledge and Mystery Centres", "The Mysteries and their Wisdom" and "Egyptian Myths and Mysteries".

Vidar an inspirer of anthroposophy

In anthroposophical circles it has always been a question as to the kind of inspiration Rudolf Steiner was receiving from the higher worlds in his spiritual research work. From his various statements about the archangel Michael, anthroposophists have accurately concluded that this great being had an inspiring, guiding role in Steiner's life. This archangel has been revered throughout the history of Christendom, and before that, in Judaism, and appears also to have been revered under other names in other cultures.

Rudolf Steiner himself indicated that those people who take up an active interest in anthroposophy can be also inwardly helped by this same being. It is relevant here to mention that you might find, when encountering Rudolf Steiner's teachings, that they seem to 'ring a bell' in the mind; one feels as if one has heard this before somewhere, somewhere far away, or long ago. Rudolf Steiner revealed that this great Archangel held a kind of schooling process on several occasions in the Soul-world for those people and also spiritual beings who serve him.

These occurred from the 13th century, and around the time of the Renaissance onwards for several centuries, and also in the 19th century; they were designed to help humanity by ensuring that some people would retain in their memory an awareness of spiritual truths, despite being incarnate. This extra help was intended to reduce the power the ahrimanic materialism. What Rudolf Steiner brought is a reflection, in many ways, of these truths taught in this Michael School.

But in his 1911 lecture cycle on the Mission of the Folk-Souls, Rudolf Steiner also referred briefly to another inspiring being, whom he identified as Vidar. This is a deity mentioned in the Icelandic Edda. Such was the sacredness of this being, that his name was seldom used in the Edda. The following extract from the Song of Hyndla, when carefully read shows this reluctance to name him, and also how powerful are his spiritual forces,

> A noble one* came forth to us,　　　　(* Odhin) [310]
> greater than all others,
> the Earth empowered this son,
> He was declared the most endowed of rulers,
> Through kin, kinship had he with all the Powers. [311]

---

[310] Usually the text reads, "a man was born" but the old Icelandic verb here 'bera' often has entirely other meanings, such as 'to bring towards, 'raised on high towards', 'carried forth'.

One day another shall come forth,
Mightier than he,
But to name him I dare not,
Few now gaze further ahead than
when Odhin encounters the wolf.[312]   (trans. the author)

Here the Druid initiate is referring to a great change in the dynamics between the gods and humanity, and also how hard it was for the Druids to learn much about the secrets of Vidar. For this verse is about Vidar, a deity who shall be in effect greater than Odhin, (called the greatest of the gods). To the Druids, Vidar was awaiting his mission, which commences at the time of Ragnarok or the Twilight of the Gods. Rudolf Steiner taught that the time for his mission to start is now, the modern era, when Ahriman (the Fenris Wolf) becomes active in human consciousness. Much speculation has occurred amongst anthroposophists with regard to Vidar, trying to determine just who this being is in terms of other deities referred to in world literature. His spiritual importance, according to the statements of Rudolf Steiner, is extraordinary.

He describes that this being shall remove the old clairvoyance; and shall also give the ability to attain to the new clairvoyance. And further, that this archangel is also the one who is the bearer of the etheric energies needed for that lofty and mysterious process we examined earlier; the reappearing of Jesus Christ. And with particular reference to anthroposophy Steiner stated that,

> "Those who are called upon to elucidate, from the signs of the times, that which must come to pass, they know the new spiritual research (spiritual science) will re-establish the power of Vidar".[313]

Anthroposophical writers have put forward several theories about this being. The best known, but very erroneous theory which has led to associated incorrect ideas, is that the archangel Vidar is the biblical figure, known as "The Angel of the Lord". This theory comes from the Russian writer, S. Prokofieff. But Rudolf Steiner's taught that this deity was always an Archangel, and was never of a biblical nature. At the time of the life of Jesus, it was not yet even a Christian entity. Rudolf Steiner taught that it only became attuned to Christ after four or five centuries had elapsed since the events on Golgotha.[314] Hence this archangel could never have been the 'Angel of the Lord'.

---

[311] Usually "...kinship had he with all the tribes/families". But since Odhin was a deity, spiritual powers are intended here; and the word 'sjölum', old Danish for spiritual powers (or earthly dynasties) occurs as a reliable variant reading to sjötum (tribes) in the pivotal Codex Regius.

[312] The old Icelandic text here is: (40) Varð einn borinn öllum meiri, sá var aukinn jarðar megni; þann kveða stilli stórúðgastan sif sifjaðan sjötum görvöllum.

(45) Þá kemr annarr enn máttkari, þó þori ek eigi þann
at nefna; fáir séa nú fram of lengra en Óðinn mun ulfi mæta.
 (Urtext and variants in, Die Lieder der Älteren Edda, K. Hildebrand, Detmold, 1912.)
and, www.asnc.cam.ac.uk/resources/research/old-norse and www.northvegr.org/old

[313] GA 121, lecture 17th June1901, the Mission of individual Folk-Souls.
[314] These points were ignored or unknown to Prokofieff.

This archangel was, and is, deeply interwoven with the realms of elementals and nature-spirits, and also with higher beings. As Rudolf Steiner reports, Vidar would only take up his Christ-associated mission as from the 20th century "…after he has **converted himself to the Christ-impulse**", some centuries after the events of Golgotha.[315] Rudolf Steiner taught that just as human souls can gradually turn towards the Christian reality or not, so too spiritual beings can also gradually do this, or decline to do this. In an unpublished archive document a comment by Steiner suggests that this conversion process of Vidar occurred in early medieval times.[316]

Steiner also revealed that a statue of this deity was carved by ancient Celtic initiates. This statue, known as the Flame-Column, is a fascinating work of art, despite being somewhat damaged. A careful examination of photographs made of the statue under specific lighting conditions, was undertaken by this author. Carried out with the kind assistance of the Director of the Bonn Museum, this work revealed more of the symbolic features of the statue, see Illustration 27.[317]Rudolf Steiner stated, on the occasion of the first founding of the Anthroposophical Society,

> "Anthroposophy is consciousness of one's humanity, wherein one's gathering of knowledge, engaging of the will and living with feeling into the destined events of the time all have the intention of giving to one's soul a Sophia consciousness."

Since anthroposophy is connected to the quest for the Sophia or Spiritual-self and Vidar, as Steiner stated, provides the spiritual energies that "bring the core and living essence of all anthroposophy", [344] then one can conclude that the deity Vidar is also connected to the cosmic forces that bring about the Spiritual-self (referred to as Sophia). Vidar is an archangel has been involved for millennia with the majestic deities who sustain the life of the Earth. He also provides a way to the new spiritual consciousness and yet is also attuned to the intentions of the sun god Christ and the human vessel of this deity. A correct understanding of this mysterious being provides the possibility to align oneself to the spiritual inspiration behind Rudolf Steiner's work.

Further reading
The Edda texts
A. Anderson: Vidar and the flame column (e-booklet, due: 2016)

---

[315] GA 226, lecture of 21th May, 1921, p.120.

[316] This Steiner indication will be explored in the author's forthcoming e-booklet about Vidar.

[317] Prokofieff identified a burial headstone of a Frankish chieftain from the Christian era, carved many centuries after the Celts had vanished. But Steiner was referring to an ancient pre-Christian statue made by the Celtic priests.

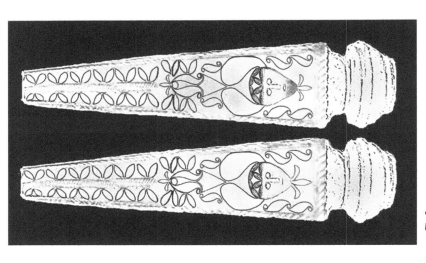

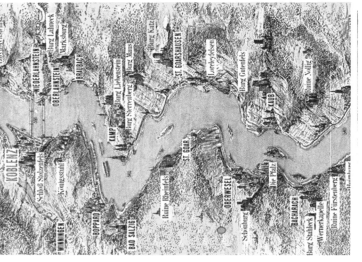

27   The Vidar Statue: an ancient Celtic carving, known simply as the Flame Column.

Above left: The statue today, damaged. It has four near identical sides and was considerably higher.

Above middle: A map of the Rhineland; the red spot indicates Pfalzfeld, where the statue was originally placed by the Druids.

Above right: reconstruction of its features by the author, showing : a young, silent god and an old god who now speaks.

13: Various themes: The Mind
Education: the Steiner schools, Philosophy,
Plagiarism, Psychology,
Seven Planets, their influences,
The Three-folding of society,
Twelve senses and the zodiac,
The 7-year Phases of life

Education, Waldorf

The Steiner schools are perhaps the best-known activity that is associated with Rudolf Steiner. There are now some 800 schools in the world, making this the largest independent (non-denominational) school movement worldwide. But first, just to clarify: these schools are co-educational and non-religious. The children are not taught the esoteric-spiritual worldview of anthroposophy; anthroposophy is for adults, not children. The children are taught normal and wholesome subjects, with an emphasis upon art and craft and also developing a feeling for the environment, especially in the junior school. But this is not to be undertaken at the expense of academic pursuits.

Underlying the curriculum and the standards required of the teachers is the thought that for the child from 1 to 7 years the motto "The Good" is central. That is, the young child has a natural inner feeling for the existence of a spiritual basis to creation. That is, the tendency towards reverence for an unknown Higher Power, who is the source of goodness, lives in the child's soul.

For the child from 7 to 14 years, the motto "The Beautiful" is central, as the child in this phase is responsive to beauty and harmony, and feels more vividly (not necessarily more consciously) than most adults the grandeur and beauty of the natural environment.

For the teen-ager from 14 - 21 years, the motto "The True" is central. In this phase the young person is aware of his or her own opinions and thoughts, and inherently assesses the ideas and attitudes of people as to whether they accord to their view of the truth.[318]

Here just two of the essential points that make this education system different from the mainstream will be touched on. Two of the most obvious differences are that children don't start school until they are in their seventh year, depending upon state legislation. (Note, **not** when the child is seven years old, but sometime after their sixth birthday, which is the seventh year of life).

Secondly, although they may be placed in a Steiner kindergarten before that age, they don't start to read until they are in their seventh year. The curriculum and over-all structure of the school is of course developed from Rudolf Steiner's teachings and advice. Although variations occur depending on the country and the requirements and

---

[318] The reader can access excellent books about Steiner education, especially on the associated topic of parenting in a manner compatible with the ethos of the school.

demands of its Education Department. A lot of work has been done in the last 30 years to adapt Steiner's indications to the needs of children in Asia, for example. The schools are usually run by the College of Teachers, not a principal. But this feature is also changing in some places, where a Headmaster or Headmistress is appointed. Steiner suggested on one occasion at least, that a principal was a good feature of a school; that is, someone who could take responsibility for the over-all direction of the school.[319]

A particular feature of the Steiner schools is that the main lesson teacher stays with the class for seven years. This has the advantage of creating a social link for the children to the older generation and to the wider community. This develops because the child forms a meaningful bond to the teacher over years, who represents the society into which it is find its place. This greatly reduces the feeling of alienation from society in school-leavers and therefore the risk of anti-social behaviour.

Critics say that if the College of Teachers lacks an over-all awareness of the standards of work of each Class teacher, then a poorly performing teacher can poorly educate for seven years. Supporters object that a properly functioning College of Teachers would be alert to and take action against such a teacher, and that the advantages of this system outweigh any potential disadvantages. (It remains a disputed point.)

In particular here we need to note that Rudolf Steiner made detailed suggestions as to the themes for each school year and other activities, based on his deep insight into child psychology. (This insight is presented in many books for Waldorf parents.) That is, the Steiner school offers a curriculum tailored to what experiences best suit the needs of the growing child in each year.

Now, let's consider the question as to why the delay in starting schooling and especially in learning to read. This is derived from a deep understanding of the interaction of the physical body, etheric body and soul, in the developing child. For the first seven years the etheric body has to meet the demands of the growing physical body. The future health and well-being of the child depends upon how effectively this is done.

As we noted in Chapter Two and Chapter Seven, the etheric body is also that part of us which receives and stores all sensory impressions, which then becomes the basis of our memory. It is also the underlying basis for activities of an intellectual, rational nature. The activity of perceiving and storing away data, so as to be recalled consciously later on, requires the etheric body to be very involved. The exercise of our intelligence, which also involves creating and storing up mental images from which we later form our ideas, requires the support of the etheric body.

According to Rudolf Steiner some time after the sixth birthday, the physical body has been formed almost completely as to its internal organs and general structure; it only needs to grow larger. In the seventh life-year, a kind of etheric sheath, derived from the

---

[319] He stated this to Margarethe Blass in Sept. 1924 at Torquay, in reference to the new school at Essen, in the Ruhr Valley of Germany. (Reported in the *Mitteilungen aus der Anthroposophischen Arbeit in Deutschland,* 26.Jhrg. Nr. 100, Johanni 1972, p. 151).

mother is cast off, and the child's etheric energies are now free to focus on the world around, and hence on what the child is perceiving. So the etheric body is now independent of its maternal sheath and also free of its previous substantial task, of over-seeing the correct contouring and structuring of the internal organs, etc.

Steiner then quite logically points out that if the etheric body is required to function in its other mode, by the child learning to read and then remember texts before its seventh life-year, then it may be impaired in its function as a sustaining organism of the physical body's health and its growth. (Although some small efforts by the bright child towards reading somewhat before attaining this age, won't create any serious problems.)

So in the seventh year, the child can learn to read and memorize letters and words, etc., yet Rudolf Steiner taught that it is better for even this to occur slowly, and to focus more on uplifting and inspiring stories. The capacity to form powerful images in response to stirring stories is at its peak, and if the adult has been able to store away memories of many such stories, then it will have an inwardly secure and stable soul-life.

And indeed Rudolf Steiner was particularly firm about this point. He indicated that since reading does have to begin by now, then make the encounter with the letters and words as artistic and as non-conceptual as possible. So the teacher presents artistic malleable forms which metamorphose to become the letters of the alphabet. The important point is that in a well-run Waldorf school, the children are not in any way impaired in literacy and numeracy skills. The children in the first two years are usually behind their non-Waldorf friends for a while, but soon they catch up, and catch up completely.

It is easy for some misconceptions to arise when one encounters these ideas. A common misconception has to do with the child being placed in a beautifully gentle, imaginative space at the kindergarten and in early primary school years. And also that children are not given access to computers until later school years. Some critics can feel that these two features of the schooling are making the child too soft and unable to cope with the harsh world later when he or she leaves school.

In fact, the opposite is the truth. If you give a six months' old toddler a diet of heavy adult food, it will become very unwell, but if given soft, mashed foods, it will be quite healthy. And it will develop for its later adult life a healthy digestive system and an over-all healthiness. It will then be able to cope as an adult with the stresses placed on the adult digestive system of having meals in a rush, etc.

And it is also understood in the Waldorf schools that if the little child is given a gentle environment, free of ugliness and discord and away from harsh electronic images, rapidly changing and flashing, then it is receiving precisely what it needs at that age. In this way, it will be given such a strengthening of its body and soul, that it will be resilient to adult stresses. And as regards exposure to computers occurring later than it does in state schools, senior executives of Google place their children in Waldorf schools, so they obviously find this a positive point.

Philosophy

Rudolf Steiner was also a philosopher; he was the author of a major text on epistemology, "The Philosophy of Freedom" published in 1894. This was in effect a continuation of his Doctoral thesis in which he challenged the 'limits to knowledge' concept of Immanuel Kant. He was appointed editor of the text-critical edition of the complete works of the philosopher Arthur Schopenhauer. This work was published in twelve volumes in 1894.[320]

After 1900, he began to speak of his spiritual research, and this then became his primary focus. However, in 1914 he published his large book, "The Riddles of Philosophy" and between 1908 and 1911 he gave some lectures on philosophy. Included in this work was a lecture delivered at the International Philosophy Congress held at Bologna.

His book 'The Philosophy of Freedom' is regarded by those who find it of value, as a particularly great achievement in philosophical thought. They conclude that Steiner has accurately shown the nature of the mental processes involved when a person cognizes his or her world. In showing the nature of cognition, Steiner has revealed the existence of a capacity in the human mind to carry out two processes. One is to accurately cognize sensory phenomena; the other is to experience intuitive insights, and this latter opens up the possibility of cognizing spiritual realities.

Not that Steiner refers to the perceiving of spiritual realities as such in this book; it does not refer to clairvoyant or mystical powers of perception at all. It is a philosophical book, although it does allow the existence of a spiritual being behind creation and also of the archetypal Platonic ideas. It is in fact an epistemological book; that is, it deals with the question of how do people actually cognize anything. Readers who are impressed by the book also conclude that Steiner has shown that the human soul can develop an intuitive morality. This means an inner awareness of, and access to, moral capacities pulsing in its will. In other words, the soul is able to cognize high spiritual intuitions as well as to correctly cognize the sense world.

But the reception of his book by the majority of the philosophical streams of his times was negative, despite Steiner discussing his ideas with the greatest philosopher of the times, Eduard von Hartmann, for over 20 years. Philosophers carried on with their conviction that perception of the sense world is itself inherently unreliable or at best inscrutable. To these thinkers the world is the result of one's own inherently subjective mental images, formed from sensory stimuli; from this Schopenhauer formulated the sentence, "The word is my mental image".

Consequently, as regards perception of anything spiritual, since the perceived world is regarded as one's own illusory mental picture, many philosophers would not agree that a capacity to spiritually perceive even exists. To them such an idea is seen as part of a belief system that has nothing to do with true philosophy.

---

[320] Arthur Schopenhauers Sämtliche Werke in 12 Bänden, herausgegeben von Dr. Rudolf Steiner, Stuttgart: Cottasche Bibliothek der Welt Literatur, 1894.

But Steiner in his 'The Philosophy of Freedom', in the chapter on the world as a perceived object, wrote about this from a very different perspective, "when thinking contemplates its own activity, then it makes its own innate being, which is also its subject, into a thing, into the object of its activity." In other words, here Steiner is revealing that thinking, in contemplating sense perception, makes its own innate core being, that is, <u>its subject</u> – for here the subject of the thinking and the self are one and the same – <u>into a thing</u>, namely <u>the object of its activity</u>. He then concludes that such thinking can never be considered as merely subjective; it lies beyond subject and object.

But here we cannot go into the details of the thinking presented in this book; the reader needs to encounter this extraordinary book in a contemplative way. As Steiner liked to recount in a humorous vein, about this theory of the world being an illusion, a Kantian philosopher once declared to him that, "The world is my mental picture and there is no way around that" (and therefore it is a subjective shadowy illusion). To which Rudolf Steiner replied, "The world is my mental picture, but a shoemaker made my shoes".[321] For Steiner taught that Kant was the last outpost of the earlier Nominalist school of thinking.[322] These thinkers since medieval times, had argued against the the reality of the Devachanic archetypal truths of which our concepts and nouns are a reflection. The Realists were on the other side of the intellectual battlefield; they knew that ideas and thoughts are spiritual realities contained within the phenomena of the world, but originating in spiritual realms, namely in Devachan.

There is a cultural basis for this predictable negative response to Steiner's work. As he comments, the term philosophy was commonly used in popular language as a word for those who were clairvoyant or at least spiritually aware, such as Plato. But as the western world developed its materialism, philosophy became a preoccupation for those who find a purely logical, non-spiritual intellectuality the only valid tool for enquiry into the nature of existence.

So where philosophical enquiry stops, spiritual science starts. Where philosophy finds the end of valid investigation, meeting a brick wall known as 'the limits to knowledge', spiritual science points to the capacity for new cognitive powers to arise which can scale the wall. For Steiner taught that higher faculties of cognition can be developed, dissolving the 'limits to knowledge' obstacle. These faculties transport one into the realms, and the states of consciousness, from which the answers to the great life-questions can be directly experienced.

Where philosophy finds no solution to the riddle of how we cognize, Steiner – in his spiritual scientific work, not in his philosophical book – describes precisely the solution to the problem. But first, we note that back in 1888, in a German encyclopaedic work, an article by Rudolf Steiner acknowledges the enigma philosophy encounters in regard to the reliability of sense perception. The enigma here is, can

---

[321] Natalie Turgenieff-Pozzo, "Aus der Arbeit am ersten Goetheanum-Bau" in *Mitteilungen aus der anthroposophischen Arbeit in Deutschland*, Nr. 6, Dezember, 1948, p.21.
[322] GA 108, p. 195. Notes from a lecture of March 20th 1908.

anyone actually perceive anything, considering that the sense impressions become simply chemical processes and nerve response inside the head?

> "It is impossible to build a 'living bridge' from the fact – at this point in space there exist certain movements of colourless material – to the other fact; the human being sees, at this place, the colour red. Only movement can be derived from movement. And from the fact that a movement becomes efficacious upon a sense organ and thereby upon the brain, it can only follow – from the mathematical and mechanical method – that the brain will be induced by the external world to make certain movements; and not that it perceives certain tones, colours, sensations of warmth, etc."[323]

But later on, in 1904, as he commences to speak of his spiritual research, he gives this answer,

> "You can never seek the sense perceptions in the sense-organs themselves. What happens when the light of a flame meets my eye? This light exists within external space; ether waves are set in motion {raying out} from the source of light into my eye, these penetrate my eye, there they bring about certain chemical processes in the rear wall of my eyeball, they transform the so-called retina {visual crimson}, and these chemical changes continue on in my brain. My brain perceives the flame, it receives the impression of light. If another person could observe the processes which occur in my brain, what would he see? He would see nothing else than physical processes {electrical nerve impulses and various chemical changes}; he would see that which occurs within space and time {on a material level}; but in these physical processes occurring within my brain he could not see the light-impression {*the image of the flame* in this case}.
>
> (So we may say,) This light impression (of a colour) is something other than a physical impression, which is the basis of the above processes. For the light impression, the image, which I must first create, in order to be able to perceive the flame, is (actually) **a process within my astral body**. Those who possess a capacity for seeing such astral processes, see exactly how the physical phenomenon in the brain {mediated by the ether forces}, is transformed within the astral body, into the image of the flame, which our ego {then} registers….A sensory impression of light is thereby made possible, because as I have already said, **ether vibrations enter into my eye**, and these are **transformed by my astral body into an image of the light**, and the ego cognises this light-image; it is in this way that I become aware of this light-image." [324]

In other words when the vivid, living etheric image in our etheric body reaches the brain, then the soul which interpenetrates the body, and is linked to the brain, perceives the sensory impression **within the etheric field**. Hence instead of concluding that

---

[323] Kürschners National Literatur, Goethes Werke Bd. 36, xii.
[324] GA 52, lecture 7th March 1904, p. 257.

sense impressions have no objective existence or no existence outside of an observer, Steiner concludes that their existence is indeed valid, but that they can not have any existence as such in chemical substances or nerve processes. But confronted with such teachings as these to resolve the riddle, modern philosophy shrinks back from having company with anthroposophy. It feels itself unable to accept the concepts implicit in such knowledge, or to accepting even the implications of attaining to it, despite the solid evidence for the validity of Steiner's cognizing.

Unlike those of some mystics, Steiner's perceptions, as we have seen in earlier chapters, can be applied to very grounded realities. This lead to his sophisticated and complex contributions to medicine, pharmacology and agriculture. However, the purely logical, philosophical arguments of Steiner in his earlier writings remain thoroughly appropriate for, and valuable to, philosophical debate. He insisted that the actual method whereby he cognizes and assesses spiritual insights are fully in accordance philosophically with the scientific method of research. The books by Rudolf Steiner to read for his philosophical ideas are: "Truth and Science", "The Philosophy of Freedom" and "The Riddles of Philosophy". The author's Doctoral thesis, which specifically assess the earlier epistemological writings and Steiner's transition to anthroposophical views, may be of use here.[325]

Plagiarism
Rudolf Steiner explained that when other people use his ideas in lectures or in their own books, it is important that his teachings are identified as his, and not merged with the other person's thoughts. Obviously, not to give credit to the originator of a creative work in any field of endeavour is dishonest; it is plagiarism. But Steiner was concerned that if the audience or readership were never informed as to the true origin of such unique revelations, then they will be cut off from any possibility of searching for more helpful guidance in his books. The other outcome of plagiarism is that the audience gets drawn towards the plagiarist, ranking them higher than is their reality. Several people have used Steiner's teachings without any acknowledgment, to build up a circle of followers.

Psychology
Very few lectures with the title 'psychology' were ever given by Rudolf Steiner; but he gave many hundreds of lectures on what we could today call psychology. In other words, as with astrology, he wished to avoid his teachings on this subject becoming associated with what was presented in the world around him as psychology. As he told one audience,

> "Let's consider psychology, the knowledge of the soul, in our times. It is as if a great incapacity has entered into this. You can go from university to university, from lecture hall to lecture hall. What you there encounter, as regards the soul and the intelligence is completely disempowered with regard to the most burning questions of our times."[326]

---

[325] Titled "Dramatic Anthroposophy", it is volume 19 in a series of publications available from Otago University's German Dept. www.otago.ac.nz/german/OtagoGermanStudies/home
[326] GA 52, lecture of 1st Feb. 1904, p. 220.

Elsewhere he commented that academic people wanted him to use the latest scientific research into physiology as a basis for his psychology. He commented that in contrast to this, he wanted academic people to use what his spiritual-scientific research had to say about the soul, when creating their theories on psychology.[327] For to Rudolf Steiner, the mind **is** the soul, it is an actual real entity, not a by-product of the body, called into existence by the nervous system and the brain. So in Rudolf Steiner's anthroposophy there is very much said about the soul.

Another major point of difference is that Steiner taught that it is necessary to first understand the nature of the soul, the soul's core dynamics, before trying to assess a dysfunctional soul-life. To do this involves factoring in the full reality of the astral realms that interact with the soul. On that understanding, one can start to research the dysfunctional modes of these dynamics. The three strands of feeling, thinking and will need to be cognized, and in particular their inherent dynamics need to be understood. The significance of the core dynamics needs to be considered. This we have already explored in Chapter Two, about the three souls and the ego; and in Chapter Six, the dualistic ego-sense and the spirit. The dynamics include the alert presence of the ego in the thinking activity, and the dreamy state of the emotions coming and going without any real impetus on our part. These dynamics also include noting the similarity of our will to that of the deep sleep state, wherein the ego-sense has disappeared.

Anthroposophical psychology also factors in the living interconnectedness of these three strands to an invisible, but very real, spiritual environment made up of the etheric and the astral realms. In the first instance, this is the fullness of our astral body or aura, pulsing with the thought-forms we consciously experience, but also many that we do not. However there are also thought-forms present in us which we have not created, they come from outside our aura. They derive from other beings. Additionally the soul is permeated by our emotions and the emotions of other people, both alive and deceased. Some of which we sense as they come and go of their own accord. Many of these influence us in a manner which we do not consciously cognize.

Finally there is our will or intentions, most of which is hidden from us and which is deeply interlinked with the stream of our karma. This is coloured by our past life's noble and ignoble deeds and thoughts; and it also resonates to suppressed guilt, traumas. In it is also active the yearnings of the deceased with whom we were associated. It also includes the specific goals and resolutions, which we make before we were incarnate. This is in effect a veiled awareness of the karmic duties that our higher self and the gods have decreed we need to encounter in this lifetime. [328]

There is also the role of our etheric body, containing all our sense impressions which, if cognized, are our memories, and if not cognized still do reside there and continue to exert a potent influence. But there is also as a substantial factor, our soul's environment, namely the wider astral and etheric realms. These are the realms in

---

[327] GA 73, p. 11.

[328] And in the subconscious are the main tendencies of our past life's zodiac sign; this is identified in the horoscope. The entirety of our soul life, both the conscious and subconscious elements, is revealed in the horoscope.

which the deceased and the unborn are dwelling, and in which both demonic and angelic beings exist. Once all of this is factored in, then the specifics of any dysfunctional dynamics can be more realistically grasped than a materialistic viewpoint allows. Then effort to create an appropriate therapy can be devised. In this book we can only make a brief survey of a part of Rudolf Steiner's contributions to a deepening of psychology. We can glimpse here the importance of the etheric body in anthroposophical psychology (or 'psychosophy' as it is sometimes called). The etheric body is the receiver of our sense impressions; it stores all of sensory stimuli for our life. These become what we know as our memories.

Steiner gave a series of lectures designed to assist his students to develop a new modality for practising the art of psychology. These are published in a book called "Anthroposophy, Psychosophy and Pneumatosophy". In these lectures he first provided his audience with a detailed assessment of the point of interface between a human being and the sense world. He pointed out that, first we have a sense impression, this occurs via the sensory organs of the physical body. This results in a sense-stimulus which is registered, or imprinted in, the etheric body. This results in a "sensory-sensation"; and in this way a sentient reality is experienced by the person (their soul, or astral body). So, this sentient experience, derived from the sense-world, Steiner calls a "sensory-sensation" (in German, Sinnesempfindung). Then the results of this are: we know that we have been impacted upon by a sensory thing which is cold or hot, gives pleasure or pain, abuse or kindness, etc.

Then in addition, we form an inner response to this; we either like it or dislike it. In the split second that we are aware of a sensory sensation, we also have an emotive response of like or dislike. Then our ego, our intelligence, makes an immediate verdict about it. Not a worked out or reasoned assessment, but a snap verdict (Urteil).[329] The rapid verdict identifies or tags it for what it is. So in every one of the millions of "sensory-sensations" which we experience, there comes about a response of the feelings and intelligence, and these factors make up every experience derived from the sense-world. But all of this generally remains subconscious, and yet this is still a significant factor. Obviously in really significant sensory experiences we **are** aware of how we feel and what our snap assessment or verdict has been. But for every one of those, there are thousands of others of which we are unaware.

Now, should the verdict or snap assessment be intense, and thus really noticed, then a **mental representation is formed in the mind.** In other words, we create a mental image of the sensory experience ! But otherwise we don't form a mental image. Rudolf Steiner focuses on the power of these mental images as the major factor in mental health or ill-health.

He emphasises that **in the etheric body** memory images stored in us as mental representations of what we have cognised, are in effect <u>**living** images or living forms</u>. These memories are not just 'flat' images, when in storage, so to speak. It is of course well known that in our subconscious all these mental pictures are stored. But in a

---

[329] The English translations have decided on "reason" for 'Urteil', but actually a quick judgement or assessment is meant.

spiritual-scientific psychology what this means is that our sense impressions are stored as etheric images; and as such they have a certain life to them. (For more about the involvement of the etheric body in sense perception, see the entry, "Philosophy".)

We don't think of them as living, or of much significance, because when we recall an image or concept, we experience it as a 'flat' thing. But Rudolf Steiner emphasizes all these mental-images are endowed with an elemental life. These images are **living forms, forms that have a rudimentary life** in the ether body. However, when recalled into normal consciousness, **they become again simpl**y a flat image, and this process is deceptive.

But we have not just registered various mental images; we have often devised various ideas or concepts, based on our mental images which form out of our sensory experiences. The etheric counterparts to these ideas or concepts are described as *especially malleable* living-forms in the etheric body. Steiner also points out that firstly, both types of etheric images, <u>even all those now forgotten,</u> **do** have an elemental life, they are not inert. Secondly, all concepts of a certain kind**, associated with a similar theme,** will build up an accumulative power, and these create an enhanced dynamic in the mind, or soul-life. These give to a person's consciousness a negative or positive nuance; they contribute a positive or a negative factor to the soul. And he emphasises that this occurs, even if this is not a factor which we consciously experience. So these images are not just abstract "things", in the subconscious.

Many of our thoughts are rather hazy, but whenever we really work out a concept, or when we really do understand someone else's idea, then the concept we ourselves make is strong and clear. In response to this, the etheric body makes a specific, **moving-mobile** form. So for example in terms of therapy, when a child perceives the idea behind the actions of an abuser (the evil intentional thought-form), or when an adult formulates an unbalanced conclusion about someone or life in general, then these ideas or concepts, built up from a mass of mental images, take on a living energy and seek out similar ones, reinforcing their own dynamic in the soul.

Rudolf Steiner points to these as pivotal in mental health issues <u>and</u> – since the client actually has brought into being a <u>concept</u>, not just a sense impression – its corresponding mobile energy-form will actually become a tangible 'habit' **in the etheric body**. In other words, it becomes a significant constituent element of our mind or psychology, in pre-dispositional dynamics, and not in the conscious mind. It will become a part of our temperament, and from this many psychological problems derive, such as addictions.

So firstly, all our mental images from our sense perceptions, or from our mental activity in general, result in living elemental energetic-forms in the ether body.

Secondly, all of our ideas, concepts – good or bad, encountered, or self-produced – will result in active, mobile energy forms. Most importantly, as a key element of anthroposophical psychology, the influences of these forms, the living, elemental energies from these 2 sources, **are <u>always</u> detected by, or always <u>impact upon,</u> the soul**, **they always exert an efficacy upon our soul-life,** even if mostly subconsciously. Steiner taught that our model of consciousness is incomplete if this is not in the picture.

Consequently, in lectures from 1922 he explored the human soul-life and its spiritual striving, showing that it is very significant that the soul is actually aware of the **disempowerment state** in which it has to live, in regard to the mental images and feelings which have sunk into the subconscious, or which have never risen up from it.[330] He concludes that one cause of a non-specific nervous problem is awareness of this inner disempowerment. It is the task of the therapist to offer ways that assist the client to empower their ego-sense sufficiently to enable the person to substitute a different and more efficacious set of values and ideals (which become images) and to consequently pull up out of the old dynamic.

Rudolf Steiner points out the difference between his anthroposophical view of psychology and that of Jung and Freud. He affirms that these men have some significant insights and made valuable discoveries – especially Carl Jung. But he comments that such efforts cannot create a fully viable psychology, unless the soul is considered to be a reality. That has to mean the soul, as a reality, (as an astral body), existing in the astral world, interacting with its own very real inner reality, and with spiritual beings.

There are many case Jungian studies that indicate the inherent difference between the Jungian view and the anthroposophical view in regard to the over-all context in which the soul functions. One such case, an unusual one, is given in a book by a leading Jungian psychologist, June Singer. She tells how a woman client, whilst on holiday with her pregnant friend and their two husbands, found herself in a hut with her friend as the baby was suddenly due to be born. The two men were far away, and unable to reach the hut.

The client reported later about how suddenly she was seeing and also hearing her deceased mother, who told her how to deliver a baby. This she proceeded to do successfully, despite her concerns and amazement. The Jungian explanation is that the 'collective image' of the Mother arose in the client's mind, due to a need to help a woman become a mother, and her wish for her own mother to be there, for she would know what to do. This abstract mental 'collective image' talked her through the procedure.

Steiner views the 'collective images' theory of Jung as an abstract materialistic theory in which the living spiritual reality is in effect avoided; and therefore really effective therapies are thwarted.[331] Steiner explained that the 'collective unconscious' theory is too abstract to serve as a good basis for counselling, because there can be no such thing as a storehouse of memories which is connected to lots of people, "Once we go beyond the individual, one can no longer speak about {a common} memory".[332] Rather, the individual astral body has an interface with a common astral realm, and people may subconsciously form similar images for a given motif in life.

---

[330] GA 83, 3rd June 1922, Vienna, 1922, & GA 212, 9 lectures given from April 29th to June 17th 1922.
[331] GA 206, lecture, 12th Aug. 1921 & GA 178, lecture, 10th Nov. 1917.
[332] GA 73, lecture, „Anthroposophie und Sozialwissenschaft" 14th Nov. 1917, p. 190.

So the anthroposophical view of the above incident is that the client became slightly psychic, her vision perhaps assisted by her mother in response to her daughter's fervent wish to help her friend. The mother, from the astral realm, then proceeded to communicate the necessary information to her daughter.[333] The avoidance by Jung of the actuality of the etheric and astral may be the reason for Jung's reported personal antagonism towards Steiner.[334] But it is the case that Steiner concluded that valuable insights into psychological problems are available from the work of Jung.

We cannot go into further details of the many sophisticated and complex contributions to psychology contained in Rudolf Steiner's anthroposophy. There are many detailed lectures on this theme. These include such elements as influences from the various spiritual beings with which we are connected from the time before we descended to Earth, and from whom the actual substance of intelligence, emotions and the will derive. Anthroposophical psychology also factors in the phases of life, wherein every seven years the personality undergoes an inner deepening, which we noted earlier in this chapter.

An important aspect also of anthroposophical psychology and medicine is the perception of how the body itself has three specific areas which are vessels of the three strands of the mind. Namely the heart and lungs (and the skin is connected to these) serve as the organs through which the emotional life is able to manifest. And the head (the brain and the sensory organs) serve as the organs through the intellectual life is able to manifest. But thoughts, as we noted in an earlier chapter are produced in the soul, not the brain.) [335] Thirdly, the will or volition is manifested through the five sets of bones or limbs. These are the obvious two sets of legs and arms (especially the hands) but also as a fifth limb-system, the lower jaw through which speech is made possible. Rudolf Steiner's contributions to the normal dynamics of the soul, and to unhealthy processes in the soul, provides a basis for an understanding of such problems as phobias, compulsive behaviour disorders, hysteria, hallucinatory phenomena, depression, and schizophrenia.

Seven Planets, their influences
In addition to the complex planetary dynamics that a horoscope can reveal, the planets also have a very significant influence in the grains, and in the creation of tree species, and in the internal organs of the body. They are also manifested in the vowels of all human languages, and are active in various metals. Illustration 28 presents the brief indications about this from Steiner in a table form. The order of planets in the table is: Moon, Venus, Mercury, Sun, Mars, Jupiter and Saturn. The days of the week are named after the planets. Various grains are each a vessel of a specific planetary etheric

---

[333] J. Singer, Boundaries of the Soul, p. 105, Anchor Books, N.Y. 1973.

[334] When asked about Steiner, "Jung said fiercely, 'I would like to put him in jail' ". Katharine Grant Watson in *A visit to Carl Jung* in the journal, *The Christian Community*, Jan-Feb. 1976, p.19; 32/34 Glenilla Rd. London, UK. Jung gave no reason for his attitude.

[335] However a few basic instinctive 'impulse-ideas' (such as the drive to surviving potential threats to existence) do have their seat in the etheric energies closely linked to the brain.

energy; as are a variety of trees and metals. Also the seven internal organs in the trunk of the body are formed with the influence of a particular planetary force.

The threefolding of the social organism

In the terrible aftermath of World War I in Europe, which led to the rise of extremist political movements, Rudolf Steiner took on the task of explaining how the governance of society could be much more wisely undertaken. He taught that 'the body social', just like our soul, is triune. By this he meant that it consists of three independent, but interrelated spheres, just as our consciousness has three faculties namely emotion, logic and will.

He explained that society consists of three sectors, which we can call either spheres or domains or sectors. These are the Economic Sphere, where goods and services are generated, and secondly the Legislative Sphere, which creates legislation providing a framework of rights under which groups and individuals may function. Included in this sphere are the police and the defence forces. There is a third Sphere, which Steiner called by a German term, 'Geist' (the Geist sphere). This is translated as 'the Spiritual sphere' in some anthroposophical books, but other books more accurately refer to it as the Cultural sphere. This third sphere is not a 'spiritual' sphere or sector; it refers to all activities not in the other two spheres. So this third sphere includes schools and tertiary education, hospitals and medical schools, entertainment, the Arts, and religious or spiritual activity and so on. Only a small part of this third sphere encompasses spiritual activities.

Rudolf Steiner pointed out that these three areas of the body social, once they are cognized as such, would have their own independent governing bodies; this is in essence the threefolding of society. (We shall call them 'parliaments' for convenience.) And the parliamentarians would draw up regulations relevant to the dynamics in one of these three areas of life. If this were done, the economic sphere would cease to be today's destructive element, wherein the pursuit of wealth and the power of the wealthy, determine the actions of the other two spheres of society. The sphere of the rights would draft legislation to protect people's rights, but these laws would not determine the activity of people in other spheres: such as trade and agriculture, the education institutions, or the Arts, or medicine, etc. The keynote of the Cultural sphere concerns **freedom**; that is people being helped to find the most suitable and creative activity in life.

The keynote of the Legislative sphere concerns our **rights**; that is people having their natural rights recognized and protected. The keynote of the Legislative sphere is equality. The Economic sphere's natural keynote is **fraternity;** here this means ensuring that the goods of the world are available to all. Steiner wrote, The economic organization will develop on an associative basis, and this growth will arise from the links formed between various commercial associations. The work in this area of life will be purely economic in character, and will be carried out on the basis of the rights provided to it by the Rights sphere.[336]

---

[336] Rudolf Steiner, The Threefold Social Order, chapter Two, 'Meeting Social Needs', p.44.

Surplus funds are to provide the income for the non-commercial third sphere. Everyone would be working for everyone else, not for oneself; the goods or services one produces goes into the world, and one's own needs are provided from the work of others. What we now have is the worst possible inversion of this dynamic. Money should not accumulate in vast amounts in banks for individuals, whilst the contributions that others could make to society remain stifled because the funding is not available to them, or their career avenues are closed off, as they are not deemed to be profitable.

If in various countries somewhere on the planet, the social organism naturally develops a threefold structure, through activity undertaken widely across the social spectrum, then economics would cease to have its current role, a role which is so damaging to our lives. Steiner saw the way in which money is understood, or rather misunderstood, and consequently how it is misused by powerful financial institutions, in perpetrating immensely harmful influences upon the rest of society.

His lectures on economics have lead to the forming of wholesome banking institutions, such as the 'Gemeinschaft Bank' in Germany, 'Triodos' in Holland, and 'Prometheus Foundation' in New Zealand. In these institutions the effort is made to create a healthy role for money in society, where the interest rate is minimal and a fraternal concern for the initiatives of others is fostered.

With regard to Rudolf Steiner's teaching that selfless altruism is to be achieved in society via the economic life, this can be misunderstood. The selflessness is not going to occur solely through a spiritual force inherent in the economic life. Steiner explained that the sphere of rights should help to achieve this, by exerting a continual influence on the economic sphere, "The life of rights must always give directions to the commercial life, concerning the altruistic position that it naturally possesses."[337] On this theme he wrote,

> The first and indispensable thing to be worked for in public life today is the
> complete and thorough separation of economic life from the rights
> organization. As the separation becomes gradually established people will
> discover, that something else will happen. The two organisations will find that
> in the course of this process, each sphere will discover its own most
> appropriate method of selecting its legislators and administration.[338]

---

[337] GA 328, p. 90

[338] Rudolf Steiner, The Threefold Social Order, chapter Two, p. 45.

	VOWEL	SOUL or SPIRIT ASPECT	TREE	HIERARCHICAL BEINGS	METAL	GRAIN	LIFE ORGAN	Day of Week
☽	ei	Etheric body	Cherry	Angels	Silver	Rice	Brain	Monday
♀	a	Emotions: in both Sentient-soul & Spirit-self	Birch	Archangels	Copper	Oats	Kidneys	Friday
☿	i	Rational thinking	Elm	Principalities	Mercury	Millet	Lungs	Wednesday
☉	au	Ego-sense	Ash	Powers	Gold	Wheat	Heart	Sunday
♂	e	Vehemence of soul	Oak	Mights	Iron	Barley	Gall	Tuesday
♃	o	Spiritual-soul	Maple	Dominions	Tin	Rye	Liver	Thursday
♄	u	Subconscious Will, intuition	Fir	Thrones	Lead	Maize	Spleen	Saturday

28 Correspondences of the 7 classical planets from Rudolf Steiner

Looking again briefly at the Cultural sphere's focus in such a renewed society, its focus is to encourage the **freedom** of the individual. By 'freedom' here Steiner means that every person should be assisted to find opportunities in their working life through which they can manifest their inherent capacities and gifts. This would contrast wonderfully with what happens today in our all-in-one parliament. Today, politicians determine how easy or how difficult it shall be for school-leavers to enter various professions, by controlling the entry standards and funding for universities, etc.

But in a 'threefolded' society, the third sphere parliament would put in place systems to perceive what vocation is really of interest to school-leavers. Their task is then to facilitate these career aspirations. Thus if in a particular year, the national karma brings about a predominant interest amongst school-leavers in medical research, and or researching agricultural practises or musical creativity, then these impulses are facilitated.

A useful way to understand the basic dynamics is to compare the functions of the three spheres of society with those of the human mind. Rudolf Steiner taught that the three social spheres are directly similar in their dynamics to that of our thinking or feeling or will, respectively. The following two-page diagram makes this clear. This is only a brief introductory outline of the threefolding concept, and those interested in further knowledge about this topic need to read the core books by Rudolf Steiner on this, and also to check out the Internet sites mentioned that explore this idea. See the Appendix for more about the correlation of the human soul to the three spheres of society.

This concept of the threefolding of society presents many very striking ideas which require a fresh approach to how our society functions. For example, Steiner taught that the concept of an hourly rate of pay for work done is incorrect, and that rather the needs of the employee should be fully met by an employer, in return for the skills of the employee. This is an indication as to how the role of money would be totally changed in such a reformed society – to the huge benefit of everyone.

In this system of commerce and economics the global financial problems would be greatly alleviated. The banking system as we know it today, which treats money as commodity, would not exist. For in this new system, money would not be regarded as a commodity, but as a statement of the belief in the potential of a person's abilities to contribute to the needs of society.

Efforts were made in central Europe to bring about a development of this concept, but these efforts met severe obstacles. The reform to the education, agricultural and medical sectors for example, does encounter obstacles from established systems and yet much has been achieved in these areas by people working with anthroposophical ideas. But reform to the wealth structure and power politics of today's world naturally encounters far more entrenched resistance.

Further Reading
Rudolf Steiner :The Threefold Social Order,
         The Renewal of the Social Organism,
         World Economy (This is the main text that explains his views on the

role of money in society and economic policies.

Internet sites:
www.rudolfsteinerweb.com/Threefold_Social_Order
www.threefolding.org/essays

The following two-page diagram does not attempt to factor in the many complex issues discussed by Rudolf Steiner regarding governments and global financial issues. Nor does it reflect the re-structuring of society in terms of employer and employee, and how labour is to be remunerated, and how money as such is re-defined, taking on an entirely new position in life. Since the threefolding of society has to start as a natural grass-roots impetus, the outline in the diagram provides a way to re-think the current system, and from that, society could start to re-structure
the system of governance and finances.

Threefolding of Society: the dynamics inherent in each social

from Rudolf Steiner's 'Threefolding' teachings

HUMAN SOUL

	Wisdom, holistic insights	POSITIVE
THINKING	Deduction, logic, rationality	NEUTRAL
	Coldly clever, scheming	NEGATIVE

****

	Loving, caring, appreciation of art, beauty, purity of heart	POSITIVE
EMOTIONS	Enables emotions & wishes, and the capacity to feel the environs	NEUTRAL
	Sensual/selfish desires glamour, trivia, pettiness	NEGATIVE

****

	Humanitarian, socially-concerned, seeks spiritual renewal of society	POSITIVE
WILL	Impulse to action, pragmatic	NEUTRAL
	Unconscious acts, ego-centric Ambition, instincts (crime)	NEGATIVE

(**Third Sphere** = the Cultural Sphere: includes hospitals, universities,
- functions & infra-structure (roads, parks,

© Dr. Adrian Anderson

THE 3 SOCIAL SPHERES

Altruistic response to society & the environment
key ideal : **Fraternity** *(fraternal distribution of goods)*
finances the Third Sphere

maximum profit as the assumed goal   **COMMERCE**
isolated from Legislative sphere & Third sphere   **Parliament**

forcing the other two spheres to do its will.
use profits to enhance its power, environmental damage

****

empathetic to & guaranteeing people's rights,
facilitating morality in Comm. sphere & Third sphere …
key ideal: **Equality** *(framing the rights of each person)*

 balancing different needs & rights via   **LEGISLATIVE**
compromise laws, in our confused political system   **Parliament**

subservient to lobby groups in Comm. sphere or in
the 3rd sphere; making unwise/unfair laws

****

encouraging the creative potential of each person
key ideal: **Freedom** *(of will = facilitating initiative)*
supporting socially beneficial initiative

                                                   THIRD SPHERE
sustaining cultural/educat/ arts/medic   **Parliament**
relig-spir/vocat activities & civic needs

encouraging the lowest-common-denominator or even malignant
influences; rejecting leadership in initiatives

schools, centres for worship/spirituality, and all non-profit civic
the arts and social-welfare)

The Twelve senses, the Twelve-fold ego

We are accustomed to thinking that our interface with the world, in which we are placed by incarnating, is fivefold: hearing, seeing, hearing, smelling, touching. In recent decades this became sixfold when the sense of taste was added. In recent years science has expanded this list considerably adding such senses as pain, time, balance.

Rudolf Steiner taught that we have twelve senses, and that our consciousness when sensing something, also registers the inner life, as well as the outer sense world. The additional 7 are the sense of: warmth / balance / own limb's movement / life / mental-picturing (or ideas in a vague sense) / speech / ego. These 12 are linked to the zodiac. (The zodiac correspondences to the senses given here are in GA 169 & GA 115, in eurythmy lectures, in a 1913 Esoteric Lesson, and in Supplementary vol. no. 34. But a different correspondence of senses to the zodiac is given in GA volumes 183 & 199.)

The statements made in this section come from various books in the Complete Works.[339] As Rudolf Steiner explains, "A sense is that which enables the human being to so acknowledge an object or process that he or she is entitled to place this thing within the physical world".[340]

But our ego, in other words, our sense of being a specific person, is developed through our life in the physical world, not in the spiritual realms. Historically, it was in the Greco-Latin era and then on into Europe where the ego-sense first began to strongly develop. But in each life, we have a twelve-fold gateway of experience into the physical world, through having these 12 senses.

This twelve-fold interface is subtly giving us a twelve-fold, ego-based experiencing of life and of ourselves. So, our self or ego is gradually being formed into a twelve-fold reality in each lifetime: and thus into a kind of soul dodecahedron. The twelve senses are divided into four groups of three senses. And these twelve senses are themselves developed in us from spiritual forces raying in from the zodiac. Each sense has its origin in one zodiac force.

The First Group of three:
These 3 give: awareness of one's corporeality and hence one can sense oneself to be a being of the physical world.
The activity here is from the inner-nature of the human being's corporeality and manifests itself up to the boundary of the skin; in effect, what's going on inside the skin.
They are the senses of: life / own movement / balance

1 Life: Aquarius
This is the least defined, most general, most diffuse sensing capacity. It is our perception of the fact that we are alive. This is an experience which we become

---

[339] From GA 45, 115 and 107.
[340] GA 45, p. 31.

strongly aware of when we are unwell, or perhaps when a very intense moment of glowing health occurs. We would not know anything of how our living organism is going, without it; for example if the arm were numb, but we would not perceive this.

2 Own Limb's Movement: Capricorn

This enables us to know when a limb is in motion, which is very important ! Or even when the throat is moving, as in speech. All physical actions via hands, legs and jaws need this. With this we can detect how far we need to move our hand to catch a falling object, without looking.

3 Balance: Sagittarius

This sense involves an active awareness of the three dimensions of physical space, without which we could not make ourselves upright. All spatial orientation needs this. Once incarnate we are in 3-D space, we need such a sense. We are basically unconscious of these 3 faculties.

The Second Group of Three:
Reciprocal Interweaving with the External World

Our bodily nature is made manifest, to the extent that it responds to the stimulus from the external environment. Here the perceiving activity is mainly going **from outside our body, towards us.**

These are the senses of: odour / taste / sight

4 Odour: Scorpio

The sense of smell, the sense through which the human being comes closer to matter; but this close contact with substance, with the physical world is only allowed or possible through substances which are gaseous or **air**-borne particles.

It becomes active when the sense of smell is stimulated. As the odour particles enter the nose, astral substance presses outwards, like a feeler from the aura.

This faculty involves the spiritual-soul. So there is an intuitive insight possible with this sense, there is a deeper perception of which we remain unaware.

5 Taste: Libra

Rudolf Steiner comments that it is amazing that this is usually omitted. With this sensing capacity we are no longer just in touch with substance (matter), but now we also perceive its efficacy {upon the body}, it causes a more tangible response than normally a gaseous substance would. Here a watery-**fluidic** state of being is necessary, without this, there can be no taste, for example a sugar cube on the tongue – there is no taste until fluidic substances dissolve it.

This sense enables us to penetrate deeper into matter than the preceding sense, which only enters into the sense organ (the nose). For now with the sense of taste, it is the efficacy of the material upon the human soul which has the impact. And this impact (a taste) also draws forth a specific response for the human being to enable taste, namely digestion. So here we are making a second step into substance, a deeper step.

6 **Sight**: **Virgo**

Here we are drawn further <u>out</u> into experiencing the sense world, and we go deeper into our sensing of the external world. For the colour of an object tells us more about itself than a taste can, for whether an object shines in red or blue depends upon its own inner nature, the form, shape, texture-appearance, etc. Hence the eye is a more sophisticated sense organ, with its capacity to go deeper into an object. This sense corresponds to the sentient-soul; this is the active force of the soul which sends the visual experiences into the ether body.

The third group of three:
A Deeper Experience of the Ambient World

Here in this group, the human being perceives an <u>external</u> reality which is also **an inner-reality** which takes us out of ourselves.

These are the senses of: warmth / hearing / speech

7 **Warmth**: **Leo**

The warmth sense gives an indicator of the qualities which lie deep in an object, especially if due to the living-ness of a being. The astral body itself is active here; cold-blooded creatures have no manifest astrality, so they need the outer heat to warm up.

8 **Hearing**: **Cancer**

The sense of hearing brings us deeper into the nature of an object or being, the sounds these make reveal the inner nature of the substance or the being. Whether the cry of a raven, a sea-gull, a dog howling at the moon, the clanging of steel, the rustle of paper. This sense involves the etheric body.

9 **Speech**: **Gemini**

Here we can sense the presence of articulated, meaningful, structured sounds; this sense takes us deeper into the inner nature of a being, especially that of the human being. And by the sense of speech is **not** meant the **conceptual** meaning conveyed by the word, but the inner gesture of a vowel or consonant: as in a cry of pain or a moan of yearning. That is the articulated use of sound to convey soul meaning. It is a sense that gives us cognition without any associated activity of the intellect.

The fourth group of three:
We go **into the Inner Nature of another External Being**

That is, we are going further away from ourselves. These are the senses of mental picture (or idea) / ego / touch

10 **Mental-Picture** or **idea**   **Taurus**

We are aware of course of our mental images. This is an important sensing capacity. The sense for the presence of an idea, or of a mental picture, <u>prior to determining</u> just exactly what the concept is. But note that the idea is not only expressed in words, it could be in an object. For the usual human being, the awareness of a mental picture or general idea is the highest sense.

This faculty of sensing gives a <u>deeper sensing</u> than the mere sounds of speech sense; we get closer to someone when we grasp their concept. When someone is explaining some thing to us, we can say, "Oh, I like that idea !" Imagine if we did not have a sense for mental image / concept. There would be total isolation from others, and inability to use our own logic !

11 The Ego (another being's ego) Aries
This is described by Rudolf Steiner as the highest sense capacity of all. It has two sides to it. We perceive our own ego and we perceive, in an intuitive way, another ego. A still more intimate link to the external world is possible through the sensing of an ego, through which we feel at one with another, because we can perceive their "I". This faculty is about the ability to perceive the I of another human being, not our <u>own</u> sense of I. But the capacity to fully intuit the I of another person is actually very, very rare; it belongs to a high state of clairvoyance, for this is an **intuitive**-sensing capacity of the inner core of someone.

12 Touch: Pisces
This also has two sides to it; it is normally considered mundane. We become aware of texture, surfaces, of another object. This sense tells us from the impact on our own flesh, as to the nature of an object. But only via the skin, we don't go beyond, although our impressions/stimuli do come from beyond us

But the sense of touch also has a higher side to it. There is a high sensing capacity here as well; a subtle registering of the existence of a being upon our consciousness. This is a high, intuitive sensing, and this will be more developed in the far future. In effect, it is about the soul being touched by another bigger reality. And the sense of touch is present within the sense of odour, taste, sight and warmth; and it is also present in the sense of balance.

Finally, we note that there are five 'night' zodiac signs and seven 'day' zodiac signs. The 'night' signs refer to the fact that their influence is active in the subconscious, more than in the conscious mind. And the 'day' signs then refer to influences of which we are to some extent conscious, see Illustration 29.

For further reading in this theme check the Internet under "Rudolf Steiner twelve senses", many smaller useful articles will be found.

The 7-year Phases of Life
Rudolf Steiner taught that every seven years a new aspect to our human nature becomes active within us. These phases are derived from planetary influences. These new features give an added nuance to our mind, our soul-life. Following is a brief overview of this theme.[341]

From Year 1 to 7 the **Moon** has a predominant influence on the **physical body,** which develops its structure and organs at this time. The fresh moistness and roundedness of the little child reflects the lunar influence. This contrasts to the later dry, angular qualities of the aged person under influence of the Saturn forces.

---

[341] The underlying concept here is also to be found ancient Hellenistic Mystery wisdom; Claudius Ptolemy (2nd cent. AD) taught this in Book 4, Chapter 10 of his Tetrabiblos.

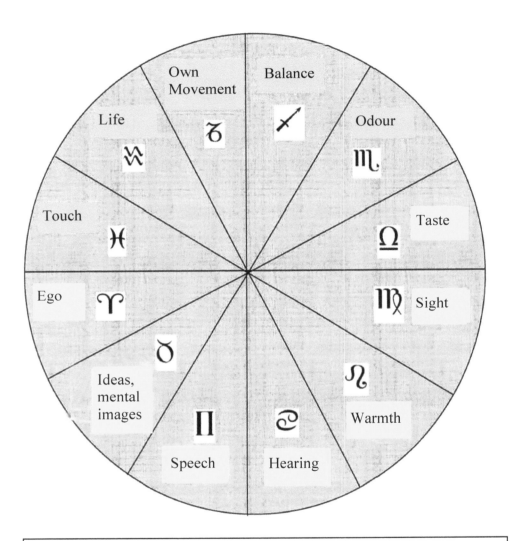

Blue = night signs, Scorpio to Pisces, still raying down, operative in the subconscious. Also called 'descending' influences as humanity has not yet consciously integrated these influences.

Yellow = day signs, Aries to Libra, operative in our consciousness. Also called 'ascending' influences, as humanity has integrated and ennoble these energies.

7 - 14 years **Mercury** influences predominate, and manifest in the **etheric body**.
This now emerges from the parental en-sheathing. At 14 years (more or less), the life-force organism (the etheric body) has fully developed, one of its functions is reproduction and hence puberty occurs.

14 to 21 years **Venus** influences predominate. The **astral body** emerges.
So now the teen-ager's personality becomes more obvious. In other words, the basic 'astrality' or personality is now free to manifest, but with only a faint ego being present. The teenager will then inwardly feel the need to go with their impulses. So they assert their own wishes, impulses, even if semi-consciously. They also may rebel against perfectly good advice, and practices and values of the parents.

21 – 28 years **Sun** influences arise (the beginning of the ego force).
The **sentient-soul** emerges: empathy, idealism, romance, and extreme or unbalanced impulses. The process of individualism intensifies; one is now much more consciously an individual. One feels empathy or solidarity with the world around one. The soul-life wafts over one's world, suffusing itself into the environs, linking the young person up to it. Because that is what feelings do, they are empathetic. One could say that, precisely assessed, that the young adult is no longer educated by what they experience in the interaction with the world. It is more the case that the young person is stimulated by their life experiences to educate themselves, to really learn from life.

28 to 35 years **Sun influences continue**
The **intellectual-soul** becomes awakened.
Young people become more analytical, more orderly. Previously they had flown down the river of life, at one with the swirls of the currents, the leaves and branches falling in. Now they are interested in looking ahead, seeing just where in time this current is taking them; and where the other currents could be taking them.

Also, bringing in here an astrological aspect which Rudolf Steiner mentioned, at 28/29 years of life, Saturn returns; i.e., it becomes **conjunct** to itself. That is, it returns to the place where it was in our horoscope when we were born. This creates an inner prompting about what kind of life one is leading, in terms of a purpose in life. The great beings called the Thrones in the Saturn sphere have a major influence in determining our karma; and Saturn forces endeavour to enhance our awareness of this.

35 - 42 years Sun **influences** continue
The **spiritual-soul** now emerges; this brings a spectator consciousness with it.
As Rudolf Steiner taught, "A self-sufficiency, an inner independence begins; one no longer just experiences something, one inwardly strengthens and consolidates what one experiences".[342] One's mind is now equipped with a potent new power, the power to intuitively discern the context of one's life.

42 – 49 years   **Mars** influences ray in.
The **Spiritual-Self** emerges. As Rudolf Steiner commented, "The soul becomes

---

[342] GA 96, p. 247.

freer within, hence from the influence of being in a body…The very first germinal beginnings of selfless love arises; a good-will towards the environment …nature and people…" [343]

49 – 56 years **Jupiter** influences ray in.
The **Life-Spirit** can emerge, in so far as a person has developed some of this. Menopause approaches, as the etheric body is closing down its reproductive power; but this still retains its full capacity, which now seeks an outlet in creative activity.

56 – 63 years **Saturn influences** predominate.
The **Spirit-human** emerges, to the small extent that it is developed. Just what it is and how it manifests is difficult for us to grasp. Perhaps the only indicator of inner change now is that any recall of earlier years brings a new and deeper atmosphere to the recalled scenes. See Illustration 30.

The remaining years
Since the human being consists of seven aspects, there are no further elements to us that can emerge after 63. Instead, we now have all seven aspects fully present, and we can have a much deeper soul-life; providing we are open to a deepening of the experience of life, and don't seek to stay on the surface of life. If we shy away from an inner deepening, then as Steiner taught, we hardly develop beyond the mind-set of the 21-28 year old person.

---

[343] From GA 96 p. 248.

30 The 7-year phases of life. Every seven years a new aspect to human nature begins to emerge and completes this process 7 years later. Each phase is influenced by a particular planet ('planet' used here in the sense of classical astrology)

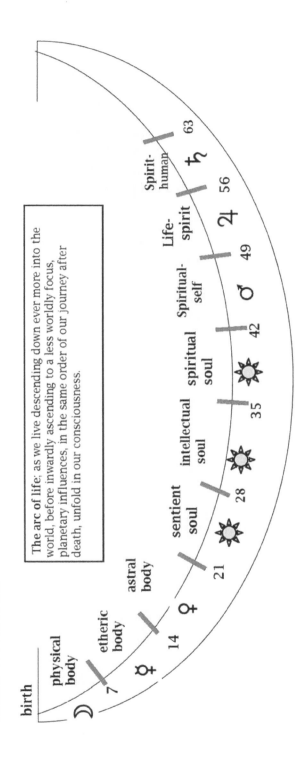

The arc of life; as we live descending down ever more into the world, before inwardly ascending to a less worldly focus, planetary influences, in the same order of our journey after death, unfold in our consciousness.

The order of the planets is: Moon, Venus, Mercury, Sun, Mars, Jupiter and Saturn. The numbers refer to the year of life, not the birthday year. So "14" here means, after the 13th birthday. The symbols for Venus & Mercury are reversed here ; see page 280 about the transposition of the two names.

277

14: Various themes: the Sciences
Age of Aquarius, astrology, astronomy,
extra-terrestrial intelligences, geology and palaeontology,
gems or crystals and the zodiac, technology.

The Age of Aquarius
According to Rudolf Steiner the Age of Aquarius is not happening now; it does not
commence until the 36th century AD. The timing of these Ages is caused by the sun's
motion gradually taking it into 12 divisions of the zodiac, reflected in the cosmic ether.
It is not caused by the sun's entry into the constellations. These cultural Ages
commence when the zodiacal energies are drawn down with the sun's rays into a
hemisphere as its motion causes it to enter one of these 12 divisions, on the day of the
spring equinox. In the northern hemisphere, this occurs on March 21st.

The reason for the choice of the spring equinox day is, that then the hemisphere is out-
breathing its subtle energies, it is very receptive to inflowing cosmic forces from the
strengthening solar rays. Until the equinox the hemisphere is still finalizing the closed-
off, introspective in-breathing process of the winter. Consequently, since the Earth has
two hemispheres, the situation is actually that the northern hemisphere is currently in
the Age of Pisces; but the southern hemisphere people are living in the Age of Virgo.
For the spring equinox in that hemisphere occurs on, or near to September 23rd.

At that time of the year the sun is in Virgo. So as the Age of Aquarius approaches for
the northern hemisphere in about 1,500 years, the Age of Leo will be approaching for
those living in the southern hemisphere. The impact of the zodiacal forces in each Age
appear to be quite subtle; they are active in the broader cultural nuances of these Ages.
So the difference in the cultural or inner spiritual mindset of people living in the two
hemispheres will not so obvious without the refined perceptions of a seer.

Astrology
Rudolf Steiner lectured very extensively on the influence of the planets and the zodiac
stars on humanity and in nature. With regard to the horoscope, he confirmed the value
and importance of the tropical horoscope, indicating that the sidereal zodiac is not
appropriate for a horoscope. The tropical zodiac (the basis of the zodiac signs) is the
one that has been used for millennia by astrologers for horoscopes. Steiner made the
following statement regarding the traditional horoscope, which is based on the tropical
zodiac,

> "The horoscope which has been cast for thousands of years for the individual,
> corresponded with infallible exactitude to the person….)"[344]

With regard to the zodiac constellations of stars (referred to as the 'sidereal zodiac'), he
lectured about the influences on the plant life and animals of the passage of the sun and
moon through the zodiac constellations. The visible starry zodiac is used for

---

[344] From an archive lecture not in the German Complete Works, Feb. 2nd 1911.

agricultural purposes. It is crucial in bio-dynamic farming, where the effect on plants and animals of the moon is carefully observed, when it is in the actual constellations (the sidereal zodiac), not the tropical zodiac signs.[345]

Steiner's extensive work with anthroposophical astrologers researching horoscopes (using the tropical zodiac) was done discreetly; it appears that he did not want to be associated with the superstitious astrology of the early 20th century. For ten years he supported and advised an anthroposophical astrologer about the interpretation of the horoscope. This person, Franz Seiler (1868 -1959), was one of his chosen assistants, and lived in the same building in Berlin as Rudolf Steiner. Seiler took official stenographic notes of some 800 lectures, and helped in administrative capacity in many ways, moving to Dornach when Rudolf Steiner moved there. There are however only a few books by anthroposophists concerning the interpretation of the horoscope.

But Steiner's attitude towards astrology was positive – if a horoscope is interpreted by people who strove towards wisdom and who had a living, competent knowledge of these influences. A comprehensive grasp of anthroposophical wisdom and psychological astrology enables one to see in the horoscope how the primary past life 'astrality' has been metamorphosed into the current personality.

From this author's work with clients over decades, merging an anthroposophical view of the soul with the insights of mainstream psychological astrology, it is evident that the analysis of the horoscope provides a way to achieve self-knowledge that is accurate and profound. The psychological profile that arises is detailed both as to conscious personality traits and impulses present in the subconscious. It is also a valuable way to perceive the interaction between the earthly ego and the higher ego. One can realize the true nature of the ego as twofold, by contemplating the horoscope anthroposophically.

It is not possible here to explore this anthroposophical astrology in further detail; but we can note that the planetary influences in the sevenfold human being are clearly discerned. The human being can be correlated to the seven planets. The so-called 'aspects' or angles between the planets become an invaluable guide to the nature of the astral forces in a person's soul. This enables the nature of the Double as well as the tendency towards the Spirit-self to be perceived. The manifestation of the Double or lower self through negative aspects in the horoscope involving Uranos and Neptune, in relation to the sun, is very revealing, when Steiner's comments about the beings in these planets are integrated into the analysis of the horoscope.

Three sequences of symbols were developed by Rudolf Steiner for each zodiac influence; these become a valuable guide to understanding the core personality traits of a person. Ancient evolutionary dynamics are discernible as an after-echo in the ego-sense of the personality in their respective zodiac sector or 'sun sign'.

---

[345] For more about his use of the tropical zodiac and the zodiac ages, see the author's e-booklet, www.rudolfsteinerstudies.com, *Rudolf Steiner and the tropical zodiac*, and also *The Origin and Nature of the Tropical Zodiac by Damien Pryor*.

Through what is called the south lunar node, the horoscope reveals a major zodiacal influence operative in the person's subconscious. When this is assessed in relation to the current horoscope, one sees a metamorphosis of the previous soul qualities into the current personality. And this shows clearly a progression of previous qualities and ways of being into the current soul qualities and external karmic events.

The transposing of the names Mercury and Venus
An unusual feature in Rudolf Steiner's approach to the solar system occurs when he is speaking about the journey of the soul after death. As we noted earlier, he reverses (transposes) the order of the names Mercury and Venus. Thus he explains that the soul enters the sphere of Mercury after leaving the moon sphere, and later enters the sphere of Venus, and finally approaches the sun sphere. But he does not transpose the names if he is talking about the planets as named in astronomy.

Steiner uses the names in this transposed sequence because, he says, in earlier times the names of these two planets were changed around. The problem this idea has created for anthroposophical researchers has been substantial, as it raises the question: to which planet do Venusian features belong, and to which planet do Mercurial features belong? The answer is, in brief, that these features belong to the planets as they are currently named, as if the entire matter of name-changing never occurred.

Further reading
A solution to the riddles raised by this view is given in the author's e-booklet; "Mercury and Venus, which is which?"

Astronomy
The science of astronomy has expanded enormously since Rudolf Steiner's death. With the advent of radio-astronomy, astronomers became able to detect invisible objects or energy-complexes that are emitting radiation in the electro-magnetic spectrum. And this opened up a truly vast, multi-layered universe, filled with unusual objects referred to as quasars, black holes, and so on. These are detected within the physical and electro-magnetic levels of existence. Since these were not known in Steiner's lifetime, he did not comment on such phenomena. Therefore a bibliography of articles by anthroposophists on astronomy, written from the 1930's up to 2007 rarely mentions the features of the galaxy and the intra-galactic universe as understood in today's astronomy.[346]

Rudolf Steiner's teachings about the cosmos mainly concerned its non-physical levels of being. But his research did at times allow him to know features of the physical or electro-magnetic aspects of the universe before scientific research discovered them. One such example concerns the phenomenon known now as solar CME's, or 'sun-spot derived Coronal-Mass plasma Ejections'. This means the ejection from a sunspot, out

---

[346] See „Astronomie: Aktualisiertes Kapitel aus dem Goetheanistiche Naturwissenschaft - eine Bibliographie" E. Hass, a 28 page document, undated. One article from 2004 refers to black holes, most articles comment on dynamics inherent in the solar system and the zodiac.

through the sun's corona, of huge quantities of electro-magnetic plasma (tiny particles of matter in an energy state). This plasma includes helium, oxygen, iron and other substances; but these substances are in the semi-ethereal 'plasma' state. Sophisticated late twentieth century technology discovered this solar sun spot process. But in November of 1923, Rudolf Steiner told his audience that,

> "If someone exactly observes the sunspot, they would find that from the inside of the sun the stimulus is continually being given for solar substance to be hurled out of the sun into the cosmos. And this substance appears in our solar system as shooting stars and comets..."[347]

This is a reference to CME's, and hence a very noteworthy achievement. Steiner simply mentioned it almost in passing, to explain other features of the en-souled cosmos. Another such discovery about the universe by Steiner concerns galaxies. It was only in 1922 that Edwin Hubble made the first theoretical discovery of these, but it was not until 1929 that his theory began to become somewhat known. Yet Steiner made a clear specific reference to galaxies in a lecture from 1909, when he told his audience that,

> "The Milky Way is not an oval shaped thing as the assumed, but it is in the shape of a lens, and this shape is found throughout the universe".[348]

Astronomy enthusiasts who are familiar with deep space imagery, especially M104, (the Sombrero Galaxy) will find this Steiner statement, from so early as 1909, very striking. All the more so, as the lens shape of galaxies was not known for some decades after Hubble's work, as galaxies were at first considered to be a kind of mainly two dimensional oval.[349] Steiner also taught that,

> "For every visible star there are uncountable other, invisible ones, but visible to those who are {looking} with another state of consciousness."[350]

But it is also apparent that he considered that there would be little value in making any more than a brief mention of such topics to his audiences. He rarely spoke in detail about the view of the universe that was being developed in astronomy circles. This science was in its infancy in his life-time, and it was being developed from mathematical hypotheses about sub-atomic particles and hypothetical energies. So Steiner usually reinforced the general feeling amongst his students for the spiritual qualities or the unearthly ambience, of the starry sky. An ambience that could still be commonly sensed a century ago in the dark night sky for both rural and city dwellers of those times. Steiner's approach of reinforcing the feeling for the spiritual ambience of the stars can be seen in a lecture from 1923,

---

[347] GA 231, lecture from 17th November 1913, p.111.
[348] GA 110, "Spiritual Hierarchies" lecture, 18th April 1909.
[349] Books on astronomy from the 1930's were still unsure about galaxies.
[350] From archive documents; notes from unpublished notes of a lecture in June 1904.

"...in regard to the world of the stars....in reality there are actually the beings of the higher hierarchies. In that people gaze up to the stars, basically they are gazing up to the spiritual beings of the higher hierarchies."

And in a lecture from 1924 he taught,

> "this expression of love for humanity resonating in the ether; that is what the stars are. This is what they really are; there {where they are} is nothing physical-material."[351]

For some anthroposophists these statements have lead to the conclusion that the universe, out beyond the moon, is entirely a spiritual thing, and thus non-physical. In particular, his very capable assistant, Dr. Elizabeth Vreede, sought to emphasize this spiritual approach. She was the primary anthroposophical authority on astronomy amongst the first generation of anthroposophists, back in the 1920's through to the 1940's. To the discerning student of Steiner's works today it is obvious the above statements are not denying the physical, material reality of the universe. They are rather poetic expressions, focussing on the spiritual dimension behind the physical universe.

But Vreede doubted the discoveries of astronomers that showed the universe to be physical-material and also as being so vast spatially. Her influence continues on for some students of Steiner today, for her collected writings were re-published in 2001, without a cautionary note, that some though not all of the ideas being expressed in them are now incorrect. Some of her caution is quite warranted, as we shall see below. But her works contain such cautionary remarks as,

> "People today still luxuriate in fantasies about cosmic worlds being born out of nebulae; the coming into being, arising and fading away of stars, or their destruction through gradually cooling down..."[352]

Here she is cautioning against the assumption of matter existing in the universe, because she has misunderstood Steiner's comments on this subject. And she continues,

> "According to this {modern scientific} view there are thus stars and nebulae that belong to "our" system and lie within the Milky Way and yet others that lie outside it and belong to "other" systems (galaxies). One sees that this is a strictly spatially conceived universe."

Here she is cautioning against firstly, the idea of the universe, beyond the solar system, as being a three-dimensional reality. Her point being that if the universe is 'spirit' then space cannot exist out there, at least not space as we experience it here on the Earth (and in our solar system). Secondly, she is also cautioning against accepting the idea of galaxies. But none of this should infer that Vreede was incompetent; she was a brilliant

---

[351] GA 239, lecture, 14th June, 1924, p. 245.
[352] E. Vreede, Anthroposophy and Astrology, reprinted Anthroposophic Press, Great Barrington, USA, 2001.

person, able to lecture on her subject in four languages. In September 1920, at the opening ceremony of the First Goetheanum, she gave a lecture on the viewpoint of anthroposophy regarding Einstein's Theory of Relativity (see below). It is more the case that in Vreede's lifetime, radio-astronomy was only its beginning and also Steiner's remarks on this topic are widely dispersed throughout his 25 years of lecturing, and were not available until at least the 1960's when the Complete Works of Steiner began to appear. In another article she writes,

> "Nebulae cannot be depicted, for they are something like visions, like dreams, in the world of the stars…"

Here she is taking up Steiner's wonderful poetic statement about a nebula being the "dreams of the gods", but she interprets it in such a way as to dismiss their physical existence. Yet Steiner meant that whilst the nebulae derive from the creative thoughts ('imagination') of the gods, they also do have a physical existence, too. For in some lectures he states that spectroscopic analysis does confirm the mineral-physical nature of nebulae. And in other lectures he states that such spectroscopic research brings confirmation of his own spiritual research in astronomical objects.[353] (Even though he did not support the accuracy of some spectroscopic analysis.)[354]

It is precisely the point that to Steiner they have an existence physically, but sensitive contemplation of their physical properties becomes a doorway into sensing their spiritual origin. (In the sense that all physical objects can be so contemplated, and their etheric or astral origins sensed.) So here with regard to nebulae, he takes the Goetheanistic approach to astronomy, wherein one tries to cognize a phenomenon in an artistic, intuitive way. Then the phantasmagorical shaping of their physical appearance and colours will speak subtly to the observer about energies that derive from the astral and etheric realms. And, as photos from the Hubble telescope reveal, these tenuous, metamorphosing cosmic fields of light and dust and gas do seem to manifest a world of cosmic dreams.

But normally, he restricts his comments on astronomy to a general approach of encouraging people to sense the presence of spiritual reality right across the heavens, or perhaps from specific zodiac constellations.[355] That Rudolf Steiner was aware of the now obvious fact that there is matter throughout the universe, is also seen for example in this statement,

> " the forces shaping the mineral kingdom extend far beyond our solar system… the mineral realm has a universal existence…"[356]

---

[353] GA 116, p. 114.

[354] GA 56, lecture, 17th Oct. 1907, p. 42. Doubt about spectrum lines analysis due to semi-etheric (plasma) atmospheric pollution were expressed in a lecture of 9th June 1923 (GA 350) but this would probably not apply to telescopes orbiting above the Earth or those placed further in space.

[355] He also gave instructions as to sensing the spiritual forces in the zodiac <u>signs</u> but since these exist in the ether, this is not a Goethean scientific process. (For more about the tropical signs, see the e-books at www.rudolfsteinerstudies.com.)

[356] GA 105, lecture 12th August 1908, p. 137.

And also this is seen in his summarizing of contemporary astronomical knowledge as at 1911,

> "..in the nebulae and in other formations which we encounter in the universe, there are present essentially the same substances, with the same material properties, as we find here on the Earth."[357]

A feature found in the view of astronomy by some anthroposophists is a reservation regarding the <u>size</u> of the universe; that is the vast distances between the stars in our galaxy and also between galaxies. This derives in part from Rudolf Steiner private comment (to Vreede) that, "No-one has actually seen parallax, they are all calculated."[358] His words here cast doubt upon the theoretical model used in astronomy to measure the distance of the stars from the Earth. This process involves trigonometrical calculations of a visual distortion phenomenon called 'parallax'. His statements were later studied and mathematically researched by another anthroposophical researcher, Wilhelm Kaiser (1895-1983), who concluded in 1964 that the parallax phenomenon was an invalid concept.[359]

In this book we cannot go into the specifics of this subject, except to note that the distances of stars are also calculated using a variety of other theoretical mathematical models, based on such factors as the luminosity of the so-called 'variable stars' and the Doppler red shift.[360] In regard to this theme, a number of scientists and amateur researchers have expressed similar doubt about the size of the cosmos.[361] And the recent instance of the discovery of star HD 140283 is a stimulus to these contrary views. When it was discovered, and the calculations about its features were completed, there was an impossible discrepancy between its (theoretically calculated) distance and its age. This prompted a re-working of the data to arrive at an outcome consistent with the current model of the universe.[362]

There are several other elements forming the basis of Rudolf Steiner's different view about astronomy. Firstly, he taught that the various laws of physics that apply to our planet, lose their validity the further we go from the Earth out into space. Another feature is that he did not seem to agree with the concept of light having a velocity. He never gave a detailed case for his alternative view, but the following statements are useful here,

---

[357] GA 60, lecture, 16th March 1911, p. 443. However some other elements of the then current astronomical view, though presented by Steiner in summary, were not necessarily being confirmed by him, in this lecture.

[358] Reported by Hans Reipert, *Über Stellar-Spekralanalyse* in *Mitteilungen aus der Anthroposopischen Arbeit in Deutschland*, 16. Jhrg. Heft 3, Nr. 61. 1962, p. 164.

[359] Mitteilungen aus der anthroposophischen Bewegung, Nr. 35, Ostern, 1965, p. 22.

[360] The Doppler effect occurs when a spectroscope reveals an object is moving away, by a kind of stretching out of its radiation, indicated by a red bar on the image.

[361] For example, on www.realityreviewed.com & www.oldshepherd 1935/thestellarparallaxdeception.

[362] This star near the stars of Libra, the Scales (γlib), is commonly referred to as the Methuselah Star; it was first seen in April 2013 via the Hubble telescope.

Light is not {a phenomenon composed of} tiny particles moving through space, but {rather} the luminous result, the trail or imprint, <u>of an effect</u> .. ....as light spreads itself, it is a continual imprint of an activity {occurring in the light-ether}. The physical surface of this imprint spreads out {as perceptible light}...[363] The phenomenon of light moving throughout space occurs because it moves within, or on the basis of, the ether.[364]

Or, as he once remarked, light does not travel, light is ![365] The above remarks from Steiner would appear to be incompatible with the concept of a light-year, the very basis of current astronomy's trigonometrical methods for arriving at the distances of stars.

As readers with knowledge of astronomy will have noted, Steiner's comments here reveal a disagreement with some implications of Albert Einstein's Theory of Relativity. Steiner did briefly lecture, in general, and also in mathematical terms, as to how his viewpoint was different to that of Einstein's.[366] His precise teachings on this topic are beyond the scope of this book, but we can briefly note Steiner agreed that Einstein's Theory of Relativity is correct – if one is an observer in the physical world, analysing the spatial world; the spatial world only.[367] For as soon as the interplay of the etheric realm into the physical is considered then, according to Steiner, Einstein's theory in some respects, ceases to be valid.[368]

The result of various statements of Steiner's about the spiritual aspect to the cosmos, has led many anthroposophists to conclude that some discoveries of modern astronomy would mean that it would be senseless to try to speak of a spiritual astronomy. This perspective is expressed very clearly by Wilhelm Kaiser. He writes, in his article, *Über das Weltall* (About the Universe, ca. 1940) that,

---

[363] GA 324A. Die Vierte Dimension, 7th March 1920, pp. 138-9.

[364] GA 88, lecture, 4th Nov. 1903, p. 40.

[365] The implications here are appears to include the highly 'heretical' one, that phenomena seen amongst the stars may be occurring as we see them, and not something that occurred millennia ago, but only seen now because light has to travel such vast distances. This is regarded as true in regard to astral and etheric processes, observed by a seer on the Earth.

[366] Albert Einstein's attitude to Rudolf Steiner revealed that he did not find the spiritual orientation of anthroposophical ideas of interest, nor did he sense Steiner's wide-ranging expertise. In March 1911 Einstein attended a public lecture by Rudolf Steiner held in Prague, and as they left the lecture hall he remarked to his friend, "The lecturer obviously has no awareness of the existence of non-Euclidean geometry." But in fact, Steiner had discussed this form of geometry extensively with several of his students, and discussed it in detail in various lectures, especially in GA 324A and 73A. (Incident witnessed by Professor Franz Halla, and reported in *Mitteilungen aus der Anthroposophischen Arbeit in Deutschland*, 9. Jhrg. June 1955, p. 74.

[367] This author attended an astro-physics seminar in the late 1980's in which NZ astronomers reported on the use of a military super-computer programmed to create a map of the universe; i.e., of the galaxy, as seen from the Earth, based on Einstein's cosmological theories. The resulting map, its areas of emptiness, of stars and of clusters, was 92% accurate to the actual structure and appearance of the galaxy.

[368] GA 324A, lecture 12th April 1922, p. 208-12.

"It cannot be true that the stars up there in the Milky Way are also suns like our sun, and thus could have planets, and thus perhaps be populated with humans, for this would be a senseless duplicating of the cosmic process which created us. Such a duplicating contradicts humanity's actual deeper experience of itself."

Precisely this sentence illustrates the difficulty for anthroposophists of Steiner's generation and their students to orient their mindset to the universe as presented in modern astronomy. It is a multi-galaxy universe, with other solar systems, and some of these have planets capable of supporting intelligent life. Yet Steiner taught discreetly that the universe is of this nature. He taught that there are populated planets existing in other solar systems, and hence Kaiser's conclusion about a 'senseless duplicating' is quite wrong; (see the entry in Chapter 14, Extra-terrestrial Intelligences). '

A spiritual view of the universe in the 21st century, which assimilates the sophisticated physical structure and energy-fields that astronomers report, to the multi-dimensional cosmos of anthroposophy is quite possible.[369] A primary feature of an anthroposophical approach to modern astronomical discoveries is to interpret the scientific data in the light of the activity of the ethers as they condense material objects into being. And also to attempt to discern the spiritual intentionality behind the various cosmic bodies or energy-fields that are discovered.

There are several major questions discussed amongst astronomers of interest to us here. One is whether the Big Bang ever occurred, and hence whether the Doppler-effect, which is supposed to verify this by revealing an expanding universe, is actually verifying this. From time to time free-thinking researchers, including accredited scientists question these two pivotal points.[370] As we noted in an earlier chapter, Rudolf Steiner's view of the Big Bang theory would be negative for in anthroposophy, the physical world condensed out of the ether.

Consequently his view of the Doppler-effect as something providing support for an expanding universe theory would probably be negative. He studied spectroscopy for two years at university, and did express reservations about some of the theories that derived from the Doppler effect.[371] But he does agree that the Doppler effect accurately reveals that stars are located at varying distances from the Earth, and that they are moving in specific trajectories. But this does not mean that thereby Steiner, in agreeing that there are varying distances of the stars, is agreeing with the actual vast distances currently theorised.

---

[369] The author has used a modest Maksutov-Cassegrain telescope and 100mm binoculars for some time and is familiar with astronomical theories.
[370] A scientist at the Max Planck Institute, Halton Arp, is well-known for his controversial theories, centred on the proposed 'redshift quantization' phenomenon. David Noel, Australia (aoi.com.au) and Jerrold Thacker, USA (www.deceptiveuniverse) and Assoc. Prof. Menahem Simhony, Israel, (epola.co. uk.) are a few more of the researchers who are presenting alternative theories on cosmology.
[371] GA 300A, 22nd Sept. 1920 p. 222.

Whether he agrees with the expanding universe model, and with the vast distances allocated to the stars, which is derived in part from the Doppler effect, remains unclear. It is worthwhile to note that over the past century various astronomical theories have been taught as scientific fact, only to be discarded some years later. Steiner did give a large lecture cycle on astronomy, but he stated that its content would not be derived from his seership, but rather from an intuitive approach to what was then current scientific thinking.[372]

However in general lectures on anthroposophical themes he also presents his research on other astronomical phenomena. This includes comets, and here he distinguishes between periodical and elliptically-orbiting comets. And he also gave a spiritually oriented view on the nature of the eclipses, the aurora, and (very briefly) the sun's structure. Here, we note that severe criticism has been made of some of his comments about Mars. This is mainly because in a lecture to the workmen who were building the Goetheanum, he appears to state that Mars is watery or gelatinous with some semi-dense parts, and it has people and animals living on it.[373] (!) The notes of the lecture in question are themselves very faulty, and these remarks can be ignored. For elsewhere he stated that, in regard to Mars, "people had never lived on this planet".[374] The editors of his books at times had to piece together faulty stenographic notes, to the best of their ability.

This is shown by an error in volume 99 in the Complete Works, which this author brought to the attention of the archive editors in September 1979.[375] It states there that the Lemurian epoch in which the Moon was cast out of the Earth occurred "thousands of years ago". But in fact Steiner taught that this event occurred some 18 million years ago, as other lectures also state. The stenographic notes of the lecture in question did state "millions of years" but the editors changed it to 'thousands of years' because of stenographic notes from some other lectures which referred to thousands, not millions, of years in other contexts. But unfortunately, it has become clear that these other notes were faulty, too.

With regard to the nature of Mars then, other lectures clearly state the opposite to the faulty Goetheanum workmen lecture notes. So what he really said in the lecture to the workmen is unknown. It records him saying that 'Mars' has parts that are jelly-like in their nature and other areas that have a more solid quality, with the consistency of antlers or horns. But this is actually a repeat of his statements about the density and structure of the Earth in the previous aeon (the moon aeon) as well as in the Mars half of this aeon, in effect in mid-Lemurian times. The faulty nature of the transcript is further revealed when the text says, that the more dense horn-like parts of 'Mars' form themselves from out of our Earth's ground, and then merge back again into the general ground (its soil and clay). This forming and re-forming of material objects is a feature of these two earlier epochs of evolution in our solar system, never of the current epoch.

---

[372] It is called GA volume 323, and is called "Third Scientific Lecture-Course: Astronomy".
[373] In lecture of 9th Sept. 1924.
[374] Archive document in author's library, "Die Namen der Wochentage und die Evolution des Menschen, unknown date.
[375] In the book "The Theosophy of the Rosicrucians" lecture of 3rd June 1907.

Steiner elsewhere stated, in more reliable lecture notes, that Mars is "a rigid, dry planet"[376] which does however give the impression of once having had water. And this last comment is quite striking, as this is precisely what the latest information gathered from Mars reveals. And consequently, astronomers are attempting to explore the nature of any water deposits or any past watery conditions on Mars. Consequently some of Rudolf Steiner's puzzling statements on astronomy, such as that space itself was created by the action of the sun, do merit further attention.

Criticism has also been made on the Internet of his remarks which affirm the existence of various faint, curved lines or 'channels' on the planet Mars. These were reported by several astronomers from 1877 to 1909 (popularly known back then as irrigation 'canals'). This led to a great deal of speculation as the whether Mars was inhabited. But the huge telescopes used today have failed to detect these channels. They are now regarded as a product of optical limitations of old telescopes, and the people who believed in these are dismissed as credulous.

Steiner taught that they are a faint, physical counterpart of etheric currents active above the surface of Mars. Private notes of a 1911 lecture clearly record that Steiner taught that Mars represents an earlier, older stage of evolution than our Earth, and that these channels derive from subtle energy currents that coursed across its surface.[377] It appears Rudolf Steiner was inferring that occasionally these can be visible from the Earth, when viewed at low magnification.

Extra-terrestrial Intelligences
Although Rudolf Steiner did not lecture on the theme of extra-terrestrial Intelligences directly, he did make indirect reference to it. Some brief remarks about this topic are therefore needed in this book; a fuller discussion of this very important theme will be left to a later book. This theme is a catalyst for several very significant questions about ourselves and our creator, about the universe in general. Questions that intensely interest astronomers, theologians, and spiritually minded people. But it is also a prominent theme in some New Age groups, in a manner that conflicts with the anthroposophical view. One needs to note that in recent decades various governments have officially confirmed that their defence personnel and associated intelligence agencies have concluded that physically real metallic craft have been in our atmosphere, many times. Some governments have even released videos taken by the air force pilots who were assigned the task of following these objects. These governments did this after decades of investigation which led them to conclude that the entities piloting these craft posed no danger to humanity.

Some people have accepted the idea of divine beings who inhabit a machine, a metallic craft. To these people, such high-tech entities have actually replaced the gods. They have accepted that the beings who are written about in sacred religious books – divine spiritual beings, operative from out of spiritual worlds – were really flesh and blood

---

[376] Archive document, an unpublished lecture, 30th Jan. 1905.

[377] Ludwig Kleeberg is one of three people who recorded the lecture, given in Kassel in 1911; L. Kleeberg, Wege und Worte, Mellinger Verlag, 1961, p.151.

humanoids, super technically advanced. This conclusion appears to those with an anthroposophical viewpoint as a potent expression of ahrimanic materialism.

However, the opposite has also happened; two anthroposophical writers have concluded that these sightings of 'space ships' are entirely non-material events. These anthroposophists view them as spectral visions, produced by ahrimanic powers.[378] That is, to them a UFO sighting is really the brief perceiving of a subtle etheric reality which becomes psychically distorted, through an inherent tendency to see everything in a materialistic way in today's world.

To this author, who like millions of people, has seen at night what is best described as a UFO sighting, this latter view is far too simplistic to be correct. There are other anthroposophists who do realize that there is also a physical reality to these craft. A personal student of Rudolf Steiner's, Fred Poeppig, in a 1952 article, cited statements from scientists including renowned astrophysicists that these craft are physical objects. He concluded that this phenomenon is therefore a significant challenge to anthroposophists.[379] Before we consider the theme further, it's essential to consider some comments from Rudolf Steiner relevant to this theme.

When given the opportunity to do so, Rudolf Steiner declined to dismiss the idea of other populated planets beyond our solar system. In 1921 a theological student asked him, "If there were beings beyond the Earth who are similar to humans, and whether they would need a similar event to the sacrifice of Christ." Rudolf Steiner replied,

> "Now, why would we want to concern ourselves with this question? We learn to know the world as a sensory reality and we attain to the spiritual in so far as our nature is placed within this spiritual reality….."[380]

In other words, in not denying this, Steiner was saying, "Yes, there are, but that is too huge a subject for humanity today, and quite inappropriate for theological students and priests trying to develop a deeper sense of the sacred in Christianity". For in fact, Rudolf Steiner had already spoken in terms of multiple inhabited solar systems many years earlier.

For example, in a lecture "What does astronomy have to say about the origin of the world?" he comments on the concept of the cooling down and dying away of the universe (called entropy),

> "Self-evidently it cannot be denied that *a* solar system – *perhaps like our solar system* – does approach the general destruction brought about by the cooling of the universe…"   (Emphasis added by this author).

---

[378] George Unger, "Flying Saucers, physical and spiritual aspects" and S. Prokofieff, in *The East in the light of the West*.

[379] Frd Poeoppig, *Ein undurchdringbares Geheimnis* (An impenetrable mystery), Blätter für Anthroposophie, 4. Jhrg. 1952, Nr.6, Juni, p. 224-227.

[380] GA 343, 9th Oct. 1921, p. 591.

But Steiner had also implied in earlier lectures that the universe is inhabited by other physical human-type beings. In a public lecture in 1908 about astronomy and the Kant-Laplace primal nebula theory, he discusses the relationship of the spiritual forces behind the plant and animal realms and how these are integrated into our planet. He then begins to become broader in his focus, speaking about planets in general, mentioning that the orbiting of a planet determines the existence of its animal life. And then amazingly, he comments,

> "The animal group-souls circle around *their* planet, and in this way they are independent of that planet {of its own orbital processes}. Every planet has its own plant life in common *with that solar system to which it belongs*. But each planet has its own orbiting capabilities, and thereby its own animal life; to the extent that *that planet* is capable of having any animal life." [381] (Emphasis added)

The statements here are directly indicating that there are numerous other solar systems which have plant and or animal life on them, and consequently human-like entities too. And in fact in almost all of the approximately 200 times that Steiner refers to "solar system" in his life's work, he refers to "**our** solar system", and not "**the** solar system". This unusual term is affirming the above position on this theme, namely that there are many inhabited planets.

In another lecture he refers to the existence of inhabited solar systems. He explained to his audience that the central 'ego' or foremost divine-spiritual creator of a particular solar system is outside of it: that is, above it (not in a spatial sense). Hence, he explained, we feel a solar system to be devoid of a central intelligence or 'ego'; unlike the case of human beings, whose ego is obvious to us, because it is inside everyone. He then comments that, with regard to the people in any solar system, the ego of these people is inside the general spiritual environment of that solar system,

> "Inside in the human ego, is the spirit – the spirit with which the ego has already filled itself. So the ego is the border between the general spirit outside everywhere around, and the spirit which lives inside the human being. This firm part or core of the human being {the ego} is the ego of **whatever solar system is under consideration**."[382]

So again in this lecture he is referring to the existence of other solar systems inhabited by human-like entities ! Truly an enormously mind-expanding concept, and we can conclude that Rudolf Steiner was aware that a prominent focus on this theme would undermine his work of helping people to become perceptive of the spiritual. It is important now to note again that, unknown to many people, various governments have officially confirmed UFOs as real. They concluded this from many sightings made by their defence personnel of physically real technologically advanced, metallic objects. And there are privately made videos of this kind. The Chilean government is just one

---

[381] GA 56, lecture, 26th March 1908, p. 259.
[382] GA 291 An early cosmology lecture, of 19th Jan. 1904, but with references to colour, was therefore put into this colour compendium book.

example here; it has made available a videotape taken by air force pilots of such an object.[383] The Brazilian government has released documents confirming that their experts confirm the existence of such physical, technological objects.[384] Many other examples exist, and they constitute a breach in the wall of secrecy thrown up by US authorities decades ago.

So on the one hand, there exists the tendency to a materialistic interpretation of sacred books, reducing the gods to alien astronauts. From this, various cults have been created which worship the entities that pilot these craft. This attitude destroys a sense for the spiritual worlds and also for the activity that divine beings have undertaken in creating and sustaining humanity over the aeons.

However it is also anthroposophically valid to conclude that the new faculty in people today of awareness of the ethers could become ahrimanically distorted through the effect of today's ahrimanically inclined thinking. But on the anthroposophical side, there has been a dismissal of the physical, technological reality of this phenomenon.

So for people interested in anthroposophy, no clear knowledge of this phenomenon has been established. Consequently there exists for anthroposophists and people in general a significant phenomenon that has not been integrated into their worldview. So what does all this mean for modern humanity? It opens up a vast, new perspective on the concept of God, and on our own position in the cosmos.

The exploration and encountering of the spiritual worlds and our own spiritual potential remains a vastly more significant reality than do technological craft from elsewhere on the physical plane; fascinating or ominous though that may be.[385] And the intrusion of this ultra-technological reality in our times in fact greatly intensifies the need for people to focus on the spiritual, rather than physical space. There is also an unpleasant psychic element to this very complex phenomenon; so in fact there are several phenomena involved.[386]

Summing up, it is hinted at by Rudolf Steiner that physical, flesh entities of a human-like state of mind, do exist elsewhere in the galaxy. So this means that reports of extraterrestrial physical objects are not incompatible with Rudolf Steiner's views. But this concept needs to be embedded into the spiritual view of creation and the creators that he gave to humanity. It will be the subject of a book from this author which will help readers to spiritually integrate such a potent intrusion of physical reality. Lacking this, various forms of spiritual confusion can arise.

---

[383] Filmed on April 2nd 1997 near Chacallula airport, Chile.

[384] The SIOANI of the Brazilian Air Force report on a 1986 sighting, signed by Brigadier J. P. C. de Albequerque.

[385] And this remains true, even when some craft can move in and out of visibility. The state of evolution of the entities involved can be related to comments made by Rudolf Steiner about the future of humanity, the non-spiritualizing branch, towards the end of the next large epoch.

[386] The author has carried out extensive research in this theme aware that it is not only a psychic phenomenon.

Geology and palaeontology

We have encountered many striking examples of how Rudolf Steiner came to radically different conclusions about human nature, history, psychology, nutrition, and many other subjects. In the area of geology, especially as regards the age of the Earth and its animals, we encounter another very different conclusion to that of modern science. This is the case also with palaeontology, or the pre-history of humanity (these two sciences are closely associated). Science regards the Earth as a very ancient body, having some billions of years of existence as a solid physical body, and accepts that there are skeletons of ancestors of humanity which are about two million years old. Palaeontologists are hoping to find a skeleton of an ancient primitive human which will be the missing link between the almost human skeleton and ourselves.

Rudolf Steiner has a very different perspective. In anthroposophy the human life-wave is an entirely separate one from that of the animals. Rudolf Steiner points to an error in Darwinism which has assumed that the inherently superior intellectual and spiritual qualities of the human being somehow emerges into reality within humans, out of animals. These higher qualities are simply not present in any animals, and hence cannot be magically conjured up out of their rudimentary consciousness by a gradual increase in the complexity of the genetic makeup of living creatures.

The more complex genetics of the human life-wave physically derive from the more sophisticated astral and etheric capacities inherent in the human soul, which is sustained by the intentions of spiritual beings that we can live on the Earth. His statements about geology and palaeontology are given in sparse and widely dispersed references throughout his life's work. So his indications here are not extensive, nor have they been prominent in the writings of anthroposophists. Since they also contradict the mainstream approach strongly, it is difficult to draw up a detailed presentation of his view on these subjects. Illustration 31 attempts to portray what he has stated and also the implications of his words.

In essence, he sees the history of the Earth as occupying a far shorter span of time, than modern geology does. In anthroposophy the Earth is less than 300 million years old.[387] One could also say that even this statement needs to be clarified, because the situation is complex. When Steiner dates the Earth to less than 300 million years, this is only within the context of geological ideas – that is, the length of time it has been a material, solid mineral planet ! (But he does not agree with Creationism, a religious viewpoint which says that the Earth is just 6,000 years old.) In terms of its actual age, which also includes the phases of its existence <u>prior to becoming a hardened mineral planet</u>, he would probably agree to an age of billions of years. But again this statement needs to be modified because the situation is indeed complex.

For in his worldview the rock would not have been existing as a solid and physical object for this vast length of time. It was existing in an etheric or astral form; but one cannot put a time-scale onto realms beyond the space-time continuum. In any event, simply put, in geological terms Steiner would not agree that a piece of rock has been solid for seven billion years or so.

---

[387] GA 319, p. 74. (Probably 30 or 40 million years old i.e., since it became solid.)

The whole Earth, and its life-waves, the mineral, plant, animal and human, existed long before it became a solid mineral object. To add further complex elements, he taught that in evolution there were phases when time ceased and the mineral world disappeared. So anthroposophical cosmology does not think in terms of a vast length of time that has simply proceeded on and on, continuously. Unfortunately the way to resolve the impasse between the geological assessment, which is based on the carbon-14 dating system, and Rudolf Steiner's views has not been found. But it is significant that Steiner refers several times to the actual measuring of time, the experience of time, as being inherently different in ages prior to the moon being cast out. So any attempt at reconciling these large numbers of years with his view of geology seems to be futile.

But, as the Illustration 31 shows, the ages of the geological stages of the Earth in anthroposophy are measured in much smaller time frames than in geology today. In geology, the earlier history of the Earth includes two upheavals that decimated much of life on Earth, as indicated by the fossil records in rocks. The first occurred at the end of the Permian era, when a wide-scale destruction of life occurred on the planet. Geologically, the Permian Era is dated to about 245 million years ago, and its cause is uncertain. In the anthroposophical view, this occurred about only 18 million years ago.

And this was caused by the ejection of the moon, bringing with it a catastrophic rupturing of the planet's eco-system. Later on, nearer to our times, geologists point to the second catastrophe, which lead to the extinction of the dinosaurs, and this is dated to about 65 million years ago. In the anthroposophical view, this event coincides with, and was probably caused by, the destruction of Lemuria about 26,000 BC. Lemuria was a large continent in the Indian Ocean, which extended from north of Madagascar down to the latitudes of the southern regions of Australia.[388] (See the illustration for a clear diagram of these two time-scales.)

As we noted above, it is an unusual feature of Rudolf Steiner's approach to this subject that the layers of rock did not become hard until Lemurian times, perhaps around 20,000 BC. And this statement opens up a line of thought regarding some really striking, enigmatic discoveries made by scientists and by many other people. Various accredited scientists, usually geologists, have discovered footprints of human beings alongside those of dinosaurs, in one case, actually walking over a dinosaur print. They remain a valid enigma, and are referred to as an anomaly. They reveal very substantial errors in either geology or paleontology.

Our illustration has a sample of two of these, in very small format, one has both human and dinosaur prints, and dates from the Jurassic era. This example was found by Professor Amanniyazov, in 1983, Director of Turkmenia's Institute of Geology. He expressed his shock at human footprints being imprinted into rocks that date from 150 million years ago. It remains classified as an 'anomaly'. The other example in our diagram, lower down, is actually a photograph of a human footprint imprinted in granite rocks, and found in the Cleveland National Park (USA).[389] But these rocks are dated to the Cambrian era, and therefore according to current geological theory, this

---

[388] GA 96, lecture 1st April, 1907, p. 276.
[389] Found in Feb. 2002 by James Snyder, 1,000 feet up on Gowers Mountain.

footprint was made about one billion years ago. A situation which is obviously impossible.[390] But please note that in our illustration, if it were to follow the anthroposophical model of geology, both of these footprint examples should be placed up in the Tertiary era, which anthroposophically considered, started about 26,000 BC. The reason for this is that both types of rock did not harden until then. These examples alone are sufficient to require the current geological models to be revised, and for Steiner's viewpoint to be taken as worthy of consideration; but there are many, many more of these. For example, the website *Ooparts* reports, in the following long passage,

> "In 1987 a palaeontologist, Jerry MacDonald, discovered a wide variety of fossilized tracks from several different species of animals and birds, located in a Permian strata. Among the various fossilized tracks were the clear prints of a human foot. However, the Permian strata has been dated from 290 to 248 million years ago. This millions of years before animals, birds, dinosaurs, and yes, man, was supposed to exist. How then can these prints be explained? In July 1992, the Smithsonian Magazine had an article on these tracks called "Petrified Footprints: A Puzzling Parade of Permian Beasts".[391] The magazine acknowledged the mystery, acknowledging "what palaeontologists like to call, 'problematic'.
>
> It described what appeared to be large mammal and bird tracks that, "evolved long after the Permian period, yet these tracks are clearly Permian." While it is commendable that MacDonald and the Smithsonian clearly acknowledge the existence of these tracks in a strata that contradicts the current evolutionary theory, it is noteworthy that they highlight only the mammal and bird prints, and don't mention the human footprint found with them. Interestingly enough, since these tracks have been discovered, evolutionists have not tried to argue their authenticity or debunk them. Nor have they tried to argue that the footprint isn't human. (Often they claim that it's a print that just "looks like" a human footprint.) Their silence is deafening."

Returning now to anthroposophical paleontology, the so-called first human skeletons, found in Africa mainly, are viewed by Rudolf Steiner as the remains of non-humans. That is, these are the skeletons of entities who in their evolutionary place, were somewhere between apes and humans who lived on after the end of Atlantis, as creatures referred to as the Yeti or by other names. Human beings did not form a fully hardened skeleton until early in the Atlantean era.

But in this era, there were also in existence large humanoid beings. These are referred to as giants in many ancient traditions of indigenous peoples, (and in the Bible. They were about 12 feet or 2 metres tall; skeletons of these people have been unearthed, but

---

[390] Granite outcrops are dated from ca. 900 million years at the earliest to 7 billion years for the older rocks.
[391] See "*Petrified Footprints: A Puzzling Parade of Permian Beasts*" by J. MacDonald, Smithsonian, July 1992, Vol. 23, Issue 4, p. 70-79.

again the mainstream science has by-passed them. The ancient folk memories of giants once existing on the Earth are verified as accurate by Steiner.[392]

Gems, Crystals and the Zodiac

Rudolf Steiner did indicate that there is a correlation of gemstones to the zodiac; but he also cautioned against any ungrounded, fanciful attitudes to crystals, which exaggerate their influences.[393] The following list derives from documents in the Rudolf Steiner archives,[394]

Aries   - Hyacinth: a fiery orange-red zircon
Taurus   - Aquamarine
Gemini   - Sapphire
Cancer   - Chalcedony
Leo   - Amethyst
Virgo   - Emerald
Libra   - Chrysoprase
Scorpio   - Jasper (heliotrope = green with red flecks)
Sagittarius   - Topaz
Capricorn   - Olivine (chrysolite-peridot)
Aquarius   - Carnelian
Pisces   - Sard-onyx (white/red-black stripes)

A key element in the anthroposophical view of crystals and gems is, that they came into being from zodiac energies in connection with the development of the human being. Rudolf Steiner taught that as a faculty in the human being was being formed, a particular gemstone arose. This was at a time when the earth was not yet solid, but partially etheric, partly fluidic-fiery.

The symbiotic link of gems and the human senses

Hearing   - Onyx
Sight   - Olivine (Chrysolite/peridot)
Touch   - Carnelian
Odour   - Jasper
Taste   - Topaz
Intellect - Aquamarine/beryl
Lungs   - Opal
Intuitive thinking - Ruby
Unconscious actions - Emerald
1st rudiments of entire body - Diamond
Warmth   - Carnelian
Mental picturing - Garnet[395]

---

[392] Rudolf Steiner confirmed the existence of these large entities, until late into Atlantean times in an archive document associated with a lecture # 2750A.

[393] Letter to Alice Kinkel from Marie Steiner, quoting Rudolf Steiner. 31st May 1917, in GA No. K. 51. p. 109.

[394] Published in GA K.51, „Kleinodienkunst as goetheanistisches Formensprache".

[395] The above information comes from lectures in 1906 and 1907, and supplemented from a question and answer session on this subject.

Name of era	geological dating millions of yrs.	anthrop. dating	Events and typical life-forms
QUATERNARY apes, anthropoids & later, humanity	1.8 mill.		
TERTIARY		Atlantean era ends in Ice Age	humans, giants and anthropoids
extinction of dinosaurs	65 mill.	24,000 BC	Destruction of Lemuria
CRETACEOUS	140 mill.	anthropoidal pre-humans: then humans, with at first a cartilaginous skeleton	
JURASSIC	200 mill.		
TRIASSIC			
mass extinction of life	245 mill.	18 mill. yrs ago	The moon cast out, mid-Lemuria
PERMIAN	290 mill.		
CARBONIFEROUS	350 mill.		
DEVONIAN	410 mill.		
SILURIAN	450 mill.		
ORDOVICIAN	500 mill.		
CAMBRIAN	550 mill. years ago	30 mill ??	

31 The different view of geological ages and of palaeontology

For a clearer description of the link between the human being in its evolution and the minerals, plant and animals, see the lectures from Rudolf Steiner, in the booklet "Two Gems".[396]

Technology

You may encounter what appear to be anti-technology statements in Rudolf Steiner's works and similar sentiments in anthroposophical circles (and in many other spiritually oriented circles). To understand why this is the case, we need to enter a little into his research regarding electro-magnetism. Rudolf Steiner lived when technology was at its infancy, but there are some important perspectives on this theme that can be derived from his work. There is a substantial reason in anthroposophical circles for some negativity with regard to technology and its associated EMR (electro-magnetic radiation) effects.

This reason is quite simply, that electro-magnetism as we discussed earlier in the book, derives from the ethers as they become worn out (in Steiner's words, decay). Obviously technology has enormously improved the quality of life in respect of so many areas of modern civilisation; in medical needs, transport, information dissemination, engineering, defence and communications, etc, etc. But the energy underlying all of this is based on the use of electro-magnetism, and therefore potent electro-magnetic radiation (EMR) smog problems now exist. This is enveloping our cities, our homes and the sky in dense but invisible smog. Decaying energies, like a decaying piece of food or animal carcass, are unhygienic; that is, unhygienic in regard to the ethers. So our modern technology is using the wrong energy. It would be so much better for the Earth's eco-system if etheric energy could be researched, and accessed for our technical needs, and not electricity.[397]

But unlike decaying physical substances EMR is almost un-noticeable. However, as is now well known, it can be cancer causing. But there is another side effect that Steiner mentioned back in 1924. When the possibility was discussed of using electricity in agriculture, to develop a way of preserving animal fodder, he replied that this was inadvisable. He explained that the more electrical devices permeate our lives, the less humanity will be able to use their minds, their consciousness, effectively. A 'dumbing down' of the mind is in effect what he was pointing to.[398]

In other words, there is an etheric pollution problem with electro-magnetically based technology. It has the effect of reducing the tendency towards an holistic consciousness, because the capacity for higher awareness is **dependent upon the health of the etheric body**. Electricity directly hinders the etheric energies. If all of our useful devices were powered from the ethers, there would not be this problem. But a further, more esoteric aspect of this problem is that our etheric body is interlinked to the soul or astral body, and Rudolf Steiner therefore cautioned that lack of ethics can

---

[396] From the website www.rudolfsteinerstudies.com.
[397] This had in fact already happened, in the 19th century by a brilliant inventor, John Worral Keely. But his secrets died with him, as authorities refused to take his work seriously.
[398] From the Agricultural Course, 16th June 1924.

become a feature in many souls directly through the prevalence of electrically based technology.[399]

In the light of Steiner's work the quest for 'artificial intelligence' is seen as dubious. A strongly ahrimanic tendency in thinking leads to interest in this. For Steiner points out that intelligence can never at any time arise from the dead mineral world, or from the electro-magnetic field. No computer will ever be able to manifest intelligence. For intelligence lives in the soul, it **is** the soul – whether of a human being, an angel or any other entities. However, ahrimanic elementals with a strong analytical intelligence exist. The question arises whether a computer system constructed with a refined and subtle electro-magnetic circuitry, might resonate with these beings.

Rudolf Steiner advised his students to empower themselves through an inner attitude, by understanding the basic principles of how technological devices function, so that one is inwardly informed as to their nature. And obviously an associated attitude is to keep them from subtly merging with oneself. Obviously the development of etheric technology would be a wonderful solution.

He did ask a student, Ehrenfried Pfeiffer, to carry out experiments to see if etheric energy could be utilised in his lifetime, but the results were negative. So Steiner concluded that humanity was not yet ready for it. But he also taught that to make use of the technology for good purposes is quite valid. However this does not remove the value of minimizing technological devices in today's world.

For etheric technology to develop there has to be some awareness of the true nature of what constitutes a living organism. People will need to acknowledge that all life is a manifestation of the ethers; it does not derive from chemicals and nerve processes. Without this awareness, the ethers won't be considered a factor of our existence, and hence won't be accessed by industry. So we considered the ethers in some detail in Chapter Eight. However Steiner did predict that at some time in the future it probably would occur.[400]

---

[399] In GA 273, Commentary on Faust, p. 109
[400] Or rather re-occur, since John Worrell Keely, had achieved this.

15: Various Themes: Health and Wellbeing
Alcohol: its esoteric significance,
Bio-dynamic agriculture,
Medicine, Nutrition

Alcohol: its spiritual significance
With regard to those people who seek to develop spiritually, Rudolf Steiner pointed out that alcohol has the power of stopping the development of the forehead chakra (the third eye). It is here that the first steps towards higher seeing occur.

It is interesting to note that recent medical research has discovered that alcohol actually travels upwards to the frontal lobe of the brain and dissolves some of its cells. Within seven seconds of being consumed it is in the forehead. This is the general area where, on the level of the etheric body, the third eye chakra develops. Alcohol blocks the processes in the etheric body that bring about the new higher spiritual seeing, upon which the spiritual renewal of civilisation greatly depends. So he advised his students in the esoteric schooling process that alcohol is forbidden.

They were of course free to leave this schooling in meditation whenever they wanted to, but so long as they remained in the esoteric schooling process, they were to avoid all alcohol. He also taught that alcohol creates a kind of opponent to the higher spiritual tendencies in the blood stream. This also refers to alcohol in such forms as liqueur chocolates and in food flavourings, such as vanilla essence, and in many medicines.

Bio-dynamic agriculture
This type of organic agriculture has several advantages over organic farming. In common with normal organic farming, it refrains from the input of toxic or artificial or genetically mutated substances. But in addition, it bans the use of human waste on crops, because this substance is permeated by malignant etheric energies, which are toxic to the human being's astral and etheric bodies.

Bio-dynamic farming is also pro-active in helping the Earth's own etheric energies, which is a very important task. Bio-dynamic farming uses homeopathic sprays of specially prepared compost material, such as herbs and minerals (called compounds '500' and '501') which Steiner taught have a unique power to enhance the actual etheric energies in the planet's etheric body. Bio-dynamics is the foremost method to achieve sustainability in agricultural practice.

The practise of bio-dynamic farming also re-connects agriculture to the cosmos, by showing how the phases and motions of the moon through the stars of the zodiac are crucial to successfully producing healthy and abundant crops. When this knowledge is used, there is no need for artificial and toxic chemicals. In his Agricultural Course to farmers, Steiner made it clear that the farm is an entity which is not limited to the land, the countryside; it extends upwards into the starry firmament, because the influences of the moon, the sun and the stars are an inherent part of the life cycle of plants. Here is where the so-called sidereal zodiac is to be used, that is the star constellations of the zodiac.

The bio-dynamic system of farming has spread to many parts of the Earth, with tremendous benefits to the eco-systems where it is practised. It is extensively practised in many countries; for example, as much as 50% of the Egyptian cotton crop is grown under the bio-dynamic method. This means that a large part of the Nile valley could be spared the high volumes of insecticides used in the cotton industry.

So this kind of farming restores vitality to the Earth's own etheric body and thus supports the microbial life of the soil. It produces vegetables and fruits which provide high-quality nutrition, which are also permeated by exceptionally healthy etheric energies.

Medicine, anthroposophical
Anthroposophical medicine is an approach to medicine offered by fully qualified General Practitioners who have also undertaken some form of additional training in the new modalities for health developed from the work of Rudolf Steiner. It combines aspects of conventional allopathic medicine with new types of therapies and medicaments derived from the research of Rudolf Steiner. These include hydrotherapy (incorporating plant oils dispersed in a complex manner), therapeutic eurythmy, music therapy, a new massage modality, colour therapy and also biography awareness.

Many of the medicaments used are created through an adaptation of the principles in homeopathy and naturopathy. Anthroposophical medicine is often referred to as complementary medicine, and socially this is its position. But if the principles underlying anthroposophical medicine were more clearly recognized in the community, then it could become an integral part of mainstream medicine. Currently there are nine hospitals in Europe based on this system of medicine.

An underlying requirement in anthroposophical medicine is for the practitioner to become alert to the way in which illness arises from the effect of the soul (the feelings, thoughts and volition) upon the etheric body and thereby upon the physical body. Sophisticated explanations were given by Rudolf Steiner in lectures to doctors concerning the interaction between these three elements of the human being, as a foundational element of health or disease. He wrote a book in association with a medical doctor, Ita Wegman, to explain to the wider medical community the underlying principles of anthroposophical medicine.[401] Several thousand doctors around the world use Steiner's approach to medicine and they work in conjunction with a wide range of therapists.[402]

---

[401] Rudolf Steiner and Ita Wegman, "Fundamentals of Therapy".

[402] A good place to get further information about anthroposophical medicine is the Internet site of, The Scientific and Medical Network: www.scimednet.org.

Rudolf Steiner founded the Weleda pharmaceutical company to produce the many medicaments needed for this new system of medicine. He also wanted such firms to produce medicaments that were free of alcohol for the household, and for practitioners. To make this possible Steiner instructed pharmacists as to how their organic, plant-based medicines could be preserved in water. This invaluable pharmaceutical process allows such products to have a shelf life of several years.

Today there are Weleda factories in various countries producing some 2,500 medical and general health products. And the Wala and Hauschka companies were formed as associate enterprises also producing such products (including skin care products).

Nutrition

Here we can only briefly note the main features of Rudolf Steiner's approach to nutrition. A primary element in his nutritional teachings is the rejection of the molecular or materialistic approach to the subject. The value of a foodstuff is not based on what useful nutrients it may contain, such as vitamins, or high protein levels or trace elements. Why not? Just consider, if it were to be discovered that the eyes of the tarantula spider have lots of vitamin A, or the liver of vampire bats are loaded with antioxidants, would you want to swallow a few capsules of this? The answer, for inwardly alert people is, no. The anthroposophical basis for selecting good foods is: **from what etheric and or astral source did the animal or plant condense into a material state**? Does the animal or plant have a sinister or repugnant quality? For we also swallow down with the food, whatever kind of life-force (and astral energies in the case of meats) exist in the foodstuff in question.

This brings us to another core element of anthroposophical nutrition, that the almost miraculous processes which occur in the digestive system are sustained to a great extent by the subconscious will of the person living in that body. Hence it is not seen as correct in anthroposophy to state that a diet must include all the proteins and vitamins that we need. This is because some people can create the nutrients they need from their food. Our food includes the etheric energies that lie behind the physical nutrient. This attitude finds support in medical data wherein vegetarians, who have no sources of Vitamin B12 in their diet (or extremely negligible amounts) will often have sufficient quantities of this vitamin, even in times of severe stress and illness.

So the question, as to who is a vegetarian, has to be answered as follows: it is that person whose will-force is sufficiently spiritualized and empowered to be able to create the needed proteins from a vegetable diet. But the fact has to be noted that some people who indeed have this inner power, may have to eat some meat, because of a variety of medical conditions or heredity factors. (If for example, you have had poliomyelitis, then some meat is virtually unavoidable.)

With regard to vegetarianism, Rudolf Steiner never urged a decision upon anyone that would impinge their free-will. He did however explain the impact of meat eating upon the soul and how it can leave an unpleasant after-effect in the aura. He mention that his vegetarian diet enabled him to carry out so much hard work. But he also cautioned that some people, though spiritually minded, would need to eat meat because of their personal situation.[403]

He described eggs as a manifestation of the general reservoir of astrality in the Earth's astral atmosphere. (So they carry only a little of animal astrality.) Fish are a milder form of animal life, but he mentions that they nevertheless do, like other animals, emanate a strong negative feeling towards people when being killed.

The next point to note here is that modern nutritional science, when viewed anthroposophically, has an over-emphasis upon protein. This fact, coupled with unawareness that the soul itself can, for those who are able, produce the full range of protein from vegetarian sources, often results in a recommendation of too much protein. It can also result in what amounts to irrelevant, standardized charts of how much of various nutrients a person needs.

But now arises an important question: on what does a person base their diet, who wishes to avoid meat? The grains are an excellent basis, providing a wide range of nutrients (which can be supplemented with seeds and nuts). Steiner did not recommend legumes (beans) as they are a plant in which some astral energies are present. Unlike nearly all other plants, they are not formed purely out of the ethers. Hence the flowers of the legumes take on the shape of insects (which are part of the animal realm). Summing up the various statements of Rudolf Steiner, one can say that legumes have a similar effect upon the etheric body as meat has upon the astral body.

A small amount of soya bean food is not harmful, as the ego can overcome its astral influence which tends to bring about an inner etheric hardening. The best sources of protein are the various grains. Instead of being used only to brew beer, and being fed to livestock, these wonderful foods, when properly prepared, give the vegetarian excellent nutrition. They provide sufficient protein, especially when combined with nuts and seeds. But they usually need to be pre-soaked, as this makes them more digestible. To best prepare the grains for a meal, see the diagram of the grains and how to pre-soak them. The pre-soaking makes it much more possible for the stomach to absorb the protein that they offer. See the following diagram that can be used as a guide to cooking grains for maximum protein assimilation. It presents the result of extensive work undertaken by researchers in Europe with an anthroposophical orientation.

One can also note that peanuts were not recommended by Rudolf Steiner. Nuts are a fine form of edible plant-life, but peanuts are in fact only a bean, which through an aberration in their biological evolution, became an underground bean plant. Its beans then developed an appearance similar to a nut, giving them an unfair advantage in the market place over true nuts.

The negative energies within a peanut is shown by the fact that aflatoxin, one of the world's deadliest micro-organisms, like to migrate through the soil and enter into any cracks that have formed in the peanut's shell as it is growing. Hence peanut paste

---

[403] The indications in these pages about fish, eggs, peanuts, legumes, vegetarianism, alcohol, mushrooms are in lectures from 25/4/06, 9/2/05, 13/8/08, 21/3/09, 13/2/03, 13/12/10.

manufacturers are under strict guidelines to kill off these toxins before the food is released to the public. To phase out peanuts and replace them with genuine nuts would be a good step forward.

Steiner also pointed out the nature of potatoes as inherently inferior to that of most vegetables, from the etheric point of view.[404] They are not an advisable staple food for those wanting to advance spiritually. No impediments arise for our consciousness by having some potato occasionally in the week. But from Steiner's statements, one can conclude that if they become a staple part of the diet, and thus are eaten almost everyday, then they would become a problem.

He taught that as they are being digested, they drain the etheric energies needed by the brain for active thinking. Whereas all other foods put demands on the stomach only, whether etherically or physically. Indeed strong potato soup is a remedy by some anthroposophical doctors used to help people with over-active, highly stressed minds, where the thinking process is over-active.

With regard to milk, Rudolf Steiner taught that the astral energies of the cow by-pass the udder.[405] Hence milk is of a reduced animal nature, and thus soured milk (cheese, yogurt, etc) is valuable for people, including vegetarians. But fresh milk, whilst good for children, is basically indigestible to adults.

Mushrooms

Mushrooms are <u>not</u> plants, they are a fungus colony. So they do not belong in a vegetarian diet. As a fungal growth, they are a throw-back to the ancient past of the Earth. They are a colony of bacteria with a marked ahrimanic disinterest in sunlight. They in fact do not <u>grow</u> at all, in the normal healthy sense of how animal and plants grow.

Plants, having a normal etheric body, can absorb the solar ether into their own etheric body. Then from out of the plant's etheric body, material plant cells condense. Through the sunlight the plant in effect brings about further growth, by producing new cells (a process called photo-synthesis).

By contrast, in the dark mushrooms are able to secrete enzymes that break down the decaying particle of rotting vegetation and then take those particles and incorporate these (together with water) into itself. Its body (mycelium) is actually made of 'chitin' which is the same substance as that produced by the spider or beetle, to form its legs or back. Rudolf Steiner told one audience,

> "Mushrooms are particularly harmful, they contain spiritually impeding or hampering lowly astral energies from the ancient primordial Moon aeon.

---

[404] lecture to Goetheanum workmen, 18th July 1923.
[405] GA 266a, p. 417.

Everything which arose on the Moon Aeon (and lives on un-metamorphosed today) is something which <u>hardens</u> the person's soul who eats it".

But since nature is in a continual cycle of birth, death and new growth, the role of such fungi as mushrooms is very important, down in the lowly area of life where rotting vegetation is in need of being recycled.

Rudolf Steiner could see the malignant elementals in unwholesome foods, as an incident connected to his lectures to doctors confirms. As he entered the lecture room and walked to the podium he paused to speak to two doctors and requested that they get up and be seated further back in the room, saying this is because, "You have been eating asparagus for lunch and the malignant elementals are now to be seen near your mouths." These two astonished medicos had indeed been eating this plant. Steiner pointed out in the lecture that asparagus could be grown between high furrows, forcing them grow higher. But this blocks the sunlight from their stems and malignant entities are attracted to these pale stems. Asparagus is described by Rudolf Steiner even when it is normally grown, as a lowly, unpleasant plant.[406]

---

[406] GA 275, p. 155.

HOW TO PREPARE "GRAINS" FOR THE MAIN MEAL.

		ADD WATER	SOAK		COOK	ADD 1 OR 2 HERBS	LEAVE TO SWELL	
WHEAT	Kibbled	1:2 1/2	2 hrs		1/4 hr	(Marjoram. Rosemary.	1 hour.	
	Whole	1:2 1/2	7 hrs		2 1/2 hrs	(Coriander.	1 hour.	
RICE	Brown	1:2	3 hrs		1 hr	(Curry. Thyme.		
	Kibbled	1:2	2 hrs	GENTLY OPTIONAL	1/4 hr	(Lovage. Parsley.		OPTIONAL
BARLEY	Whole	1:2	7 hrs		2 1/2 hrs	(Sage. Thyme.	1 hour.	
	Pearl	1:2	3 hrs		1/4 hr	(Pimento. Oregano.		
MILLET	Hulled	1:5			1/4 hr	(Ginger. Basil.	1/2 hour.	
	Unhulled: Use only when ground.					(Coriander. Marjoram.		
RYE	Whole	1:3	8 hrs		3 hrs	(Rosemary. Thyme.	1 hour	
	Kibbled	1:2	3 hrs	GENTLY OPTIONAL	1/4 hr	(Caraway.		OPTIONAL
MAIZE	Kibbled	1:4			1/4 hr	(Thyme. Oregano. Rosemary.	1/2 hour.	
BUCKWHEAT	Hulled	1:3			1/2 hr	(Marjoram. Hyssop.	1/2 hour.	
BULGHUR**	Whole	1:2	3 hrs		1/4 hr	(Parsley.	1/2 hour.	
	Parched	1:2	1/4 hr			(Basil.		
OATS	Whole	1:3	4 hrs		1 1/4 hrs	(Fennel. Hyssop.	1 hour.	
	Kibbled	1:2	3 hrs		1/4 hr	(Savory.		

HOW TO COOK THE GRAINS: A guide to preparing the grains for maximum protein absorption. A simplified diagram adapted from the work of Udo Renzenbrink and the "Arbeitskreis für Ernährungsforschung" in their books "Die Sieben Getreide" and "Ernährungskunde aus anthroposophischer Erkenntnis".

16: A GUIDE TO RUDOLF STEINER'S BOOKS

People can encounter problems when they begin to read Rudolf Steiner's works. Many of his books are the unedited transcripts of his lectures, as he travelled around Europe, giving talks, from 1900 to 1924. Of the 360 volumes of Steiner's works in German, only about three dozen of them were written down by Steiner as books. About 15 of these deal with his spiritual teachings, the rest of the books come from the time of his academic literary activity, prior to his teaching on spiritual themes. His written books are not designed to be easy to read; a certain amount of struggling necessitates the reader putting aside the normal focus of their earthly selves and putting effort into the quest for spiritual wisdom.

To present his spiritual teachings, he found it necessary to coin special phrases, such as 'the Life-Spirit', 'an Akashic image of divinity' or 'the thoughts of the Cosmos'. The reader has to make the effort to understand these unusual terms. Another difficulty can arise because the German language lends itself easily to a philosophical, transcendent style of expression, which is difficult to render into English. For example Steiner can refer to the 'Sinnlich-Anschauliche' which means that which is perceptible to our senses in a visual-pictorial manner, as distinct from the 'stimmungsgemäß Wahrnehmbare', which is something perceptible according to the mood of our feelings.

Another difficulty you will encounter in his more detailed teachings, and especially in his poetic verses, is a large number of 'neologisms'. A neologism is an especially created word, formed by joining of two or three well-known words together. Typical of his more subtle neologisms is his expression 'Kräftewesens', which, to be accurately rendered into English would be something like a 'forces-quiddity' which is a very specialised philosophical term. This term is wonderfully precise, but very difficult to render into everyday English. It can be rendered as, 'empowered Being-ness', and in my experience this expression serves well here. One can see that very puzzling phrases can be found in the English versions at times, where such terms have not been well translated.

With regard to the specialized terms developed by Rudolf Steiner for the sevenfold human being or the stages of aeonic evolution, etc, there are only two books written by Steiner in which he explains these special terms. He did explain them in his early lecture cycles, but then his audience consisted mainly of Theosophists, to whom spiritual ideas were acceptable and familiar. Consequently, since he was speaking regularly to members of the Theosophical Society (and later, the Anthroposophical Society) he had little need to explain these terms again. Knowledge of Steiner's technical terms is necessary to really grasp what he is communicating. So, it is important to read a volume in which these terms are explained. These are *"Theosophy; an introduction to spiritual knowledge of the world, and the destiny of humanity"* and also his book, *"An outline of Esoteric Science"*. This second book is easier to read than *Theosophy*. In this Handbook however, there is a glossary of such words.

One should also note that the lecture cycles were delivered to a specific audience, and people took notes without his permission, a situation of which he did not approve, but accepted. After some years (in 1917) a qualified stenographer was appointed to make the notes. But this situation means that the content of a lecture is often not intended for people outside the room in which it was given. Often when Steiner delivered lectures to a branch of the Society to which he returned again and again over many years, he would in fact subtly build on what he had taught on earlier occasions. But on other occasions he did deliver a talk that was intended as material for the general worldwide Theosophical or Anthroposophical Society. Secondly, it is necessary to realize that the lectures were not necessarily intended for someone living 100 years later in another part of the world. You may have already found passages in Steiner's material, which seem to lose their meaning, or even, appear somewhat bewildering.

It is especially in Steiner's verses that the reader may find texts which appear very interesting, but which at the same time, may also repel or at least confuse you, because the language seems odd and impossible to really enter into. Steiner did ask in 1920 that his books be updated to be more readable to the next generation but this has not really happened. So we may find old, apparently sexist or obsolete language in his books, and also Theosophical terms, derived from Sanskrit. We will deal with some of these terms later. You will find it helpful to know the special quality of those volumes, in deciding which one to read. The introductory books of Rudolf Steiner are:

Theosophy; an introduction to spiritual knowledge of the world, and the destiny of humanity. (1904)

An outline of Esoteric Science. (1910)

Knowledge of Higher Worlds, how is it achieved? (1904/05)

Christianity as Mystical Fact, and the Mysteries of Antiquity. (1902)

The Philosophy of Freedom (1894)

About These Books

Theosophy; an introduction to the spiritual knowledge of the world, and the destiny of humanity.

In 1904, Rudolf Steiner wrote *Theosophy*, which gives a detailed description of the soul and spiritual aspects of the human being, from Steiner's own spiritual research. The text owes much of its exceptional value to the fact that Steiner brings the precision and clarity of an epistemologist to the task of describing what his acutely conscious seer-ship revealed. Anyone who wishes to know precisely the constituents of human consciousness will find the book especially valuable, because of its clarity.

Rudolf Steiner starts by explaining the personality aspects of the human being, and the subtle energy-form which animates our bodily nature, and links it to the inner life of emotions, thoughts and will. Then the spiritual aspect of our nature is explained. He then gradually leads one out of one's inner life to discover what happens after death, in the realms of spirit. It goes from the microcosm of our human nature, as we experience it, up to the macrocosm. It provides a clear introduction to explore his insights about one's soul and spirit. But it is a demanding book to read.

The latest edition has been carefully updated in its translation, to try to form a bridge to modern times, and has a slightly different sub-title. Unfortunately the title, which also needs to be updated, has been retained, as traditions have a way of persisting in human society. A more correct title would be, "Anthroposophy: from the microcosm to the macrocosm", the human soul and the after-life". It derives from Steiner's own spiritual research and insights. The book does not derive from inspiration from what we today think of as 'Theosophy', with its strong links to Vedanta wisdom, and other ancient oriental traditions.

Steiner was the General Secretary of the German branch of the Theosophical Society at the time of writing this volume. However in 1912/13 when the new Anthroposophical Society was formed, he used the term, 'anthroposophy' to describe the wisdom which he was offering. But in fact he had already as from 1902, used this word 'anthroposophy' to describe what he was teaching. Although he had to use the term 'Theosophy', as a General Secretary of the Theosophical Society, he used it in the way it was understood in educated German and European society as a whole, where the term had a long history of usage, and was understood to mean divine wisdom.

A point to bear in mind with regard to the nature of the soul and spirit, and of the so-called 'ego', is that these aspects of our being are actually very complex, and they are transcendent, that is, their nature is radically different from the beings and objects which we meet here in the physical plane; they derive from other, non-physical realms. Their dynamics belong to higher realms, where space, time and causation are very different to what prevails in this world. Hence a purely straightforward elucidation of the soul and the spirit, even with the extraordinary clarity of Steiner's way of explaining spiritual realities, has its limits. This is because human speech is mainly intended for the physical world which is so different to the dynamics that prevail in the spiritual.

A careful study of the book *Theosophy* will answer many questions that you might have about the precise nature of the soul, but you will also find that quite a few questions are created by it, too. As you get to know it better, it becomes clear that Rudolf Steiner has composed it in such a way that the reader can certainly logically grasp many valuable facts about humanity's subtle nature (or 'subtle bodies' as they are also called), but in subsequent readings of it, one can also receive insights about deeper, transcendent truths of the soul and spirit. The text actually has a meditative depth to it, which means that if one goes back to it, even after years of studying his other writings, its sentences yield up profound insights.

But this book, which could be regarded as an 'introductory' book, is not designed to give an interested enquirer an easy to read, simple to grasp, description of higher truths. It is more difficult than reading Steiner's lecture cycles, because it is designed to take the reader on a probationary journey, where you are required to actually make an effort to grasp the ideas. The lecture cycles however, are readily understandable once you know the special terminology.

So the style of the book *Theosophy*, how it gradually unveils its treasures, reveals that it provides a parallel dynamic to the probationary requirements demanded in ancient cultures of those who wanted to achieve spiritual development. The Centres where people could strive to attain to higher consciousness offered a carefully structured, systematic experience of higher realties, which were referred to as 'the Mysteries'. Such Mystery Centres existed in ancient Egypt, ancient Greece and in Celtic lands, for example. People could apply to enter into an initiatory pathway in one of these centres, which offered a disciplined process of spiritual development. But in these initiatory centres such acolytes had to undergo a time of training, to purify and strengthen their inner being, so as to qualify for the special achievements which they were seeking to reach. *Theosophy* is intended to give the reader the equivalent soul training needed in the modern world: to learn how to **think spiritually**.

But since it is one of only two books actually written by Steiner, which provide the technical terminology, that is, the special terms that he created to describe what his research revealed, it is an essential book. In the latest edition there is an unfortunate choice of words to render Steiner's term for the divine spiritual realms, the realms beyond the Soul World, which we finally reach some decades after death. It is translated as "spirit country" in the English version, as distinct from the usual "Spiritland". But a better term is 'Spirit realm' or "Devachan" (a Sanskrit term from derived Theosophical literature). It could also be called the Realm of the archetypal Platonic Idea. It is also the 'Heaven' of Christianity.

An outline of Esoteric Science.
In this book Steiner gives a brief review of the nature of human consciousness and life after death, and then starts with the creation of the cosmos, the macrocosm, and how the solar system emerges from higher spiritual realms, and how humanity gradually came into being on the Earth. The book then follows the progress of history, from even before ancient Atlantean times and finally it speaks about the path of spiritual development. So it is a reversal in some ways, of *Theosophy*. If you have a feeling for the cosmos, for the question of how creation came about, and from that, our role in it all, this volume is of exceptional relevance.

It is larger than *Theosophy*, and is the second volume to offer a detailed explanation of the special terms used in anthroposophy. Its previous title was **An outline of Occult Science.** It contains a long chapter, the core of the book, describing in detail the process through which the divine-spiritual beings, as agents of the Godhead, bring forth the physical cosmos, out of higher realms, over aeons of time. If you resonate with ancient cosmological ideas from earlier cultures, this chapter will be a profoundly moving experience. But if these cosmic themes are not close to your interests, this chapter may be very foreign to you, and then it may be quite a struggle to read it. However apart from this chapter, the book is easier to read than *Theosophy*.

There is a profound spiritual intention in the fact the Steiner wrote these two primary texts about the esoteric truths of life. In the ancient Mysteries there were two main pathways to higher spiritual enlightenment: one was to 'the Gods below', and the other was to 'the Gods above'. The book *Theosophy* is in effect about 'the Gods below' which means the divine realities hidden within the human soul (and also the unethical tendencies).

By contrast, *An outline of Esoteric Science* is a way to 'the Gods above', which means an understanding of the spiritual energies in the cosmos, and their link to us. Its title is somewhat awkward, and needs to be updated. Think of it as, 'An Outline of a spiritual Cosmology, from scientifically rigorous spiritual research'. At the beginning of the twentieth century, science was seen as a saviour, and somewhat idolized; but it is also true that the rigour of scientifically precise work is indeed immensely important for the external progress of civilisation. If a new and more inclusive perspective in an established area of scientific knowledge was to be taken seriously, it had to meet these 'scientific' standards. In choosing the title, 'An outline of hidden/esoteric/occult Science' (all three words have been used at various times), Steiner sought to declare that the content of his cosmology did actually meet the same rigorous principles as scientific research. But in the 21st century, in view of the disasters and evident shortcomings resulting from a 'reductionist' scientific worldview, the emphasis on science is no longer so necessary, to establish social credence.

The book gives an overview of much that Steiner taught in hundreds of lectures, and it is not difficult to read. However, you may find the chapter on the creation of the cosmos difficult, because it is not an easy task to find earthly words with which to express clearly such vast realities. Steiner explains how we are currently in the fourth of seven vast evolutionary epochs. Our solar system has gone through three earlier such epochs. Unfortunately, following old Theosophical terminology these evolutionary periods are referred to in the book as 'planets'. This can lead to confusion. Thus these earlier vast epochs are called the "Old Saturn", the 'Old Sun' and thirdly, the 'Old Moon'; but these are also at times referred to as 'planets'. As we noted in the chapter on creation, it may be easier in the beginning, if you replace these three terms with, 'the First Aeon', 'Second Aeon' and 'Third Aeon', then much of the obscurity will disappear.

Knowledge of Higher Worlds, how is it achieved?
This small volume presents several of Steiner's essays written for Theosophists, on the actual way to develop higher consciousness, and the experiences which result from that. It is a text of immense value for those wanting to understand the potent inner development which a person undergoes who is actively seeking to enter into higher spiritual consciousness through meditation. The book is highly valued in anthroposophical circles for the esoteric revelations and clarity about the earnest and challenging experiences which befall one, when one crosses over of a kind of 'threshold' between this world and the higher realms. It is obviously written from direct personal experience.

However it does not address personal matters, such as hindrances to meditating, diet and life-style issues, timing and structure of the meditation session, etc. Nor does it provide practical advice on how to meditate, nor what to do with spiritual experiences when they occur, including the sometimes odd dynamics that may happen.[407]

---

[407] This author's book, The Way to the Sacred, provides this material drawn from Rudolf Steiner's life's work. It is a useful companion to Knowledge of Higher Worlds.

Christianity as Mystical Fact, and the Mysteries of Antiquity.
This book offers an orientation to the missing element in current understanding of Christianity; namely that it has a deeply esoteric and sacred aspect to it, which has a link to the esoteric "Mystery religions" of antiquity. It provides a fascinating and valuable background to understanding the esoteric environment from which Christianity arose. It fills in the gap which the non-spiritual, materialistic attitude prevailing in western society to religious and spiritual themes has brought about. Most committed Christians are unaware that Christianity has links to the Mystery Centres of antiquity, and that the Gospels are texts which contain, in a veiled manner, teachings about highly esoteric spiritual processes which occurred in Palestine 2,000 yrs ago. *Christianity as Mystical Fact, and The Mysteries of Antiquity* prepares the groundwork for Steiner's anthroposophical lectures, where he explains that the real core meaning of Christianity is about the entry into the soul of the Earth of a great cosmic being, the so-called cosmic Christ.

It is really worthwhile reading this book before taking up Steiner's lecture cycles on Christianity, especially as these were given after some 6 or 7 years into his lecture work, and hence contain his specific anthroposophical terms, which you need to know beforehand, and which are explained from the two books mentioned above. The Christological lecture cycles include those on the Gospels of St. John, St. Luke, St. Mark and St. Matthew. Steiner specifically advised that these be read before other more advanced lecture cycles on Christology, and indeed cautioned against reading the lectures about 'From Jesus to Christ' and also those about his research into the time of Christ, near to the time of crucifixion (which could be seen as forming a kind of additional 5th gospel about Christ), **until** the earlier cycles had been read.

Unfortunately, the publishers have not found it possible to designate Steiner's volumes with any sort of coding, to advise readers of the 'category' of a book, so the newcomer to his works can very easily select the wrong volume, and be "put off" because of the sheer 'newness' of the content, or by an inner shock which comes when one is quite innocently, but improperly exposed to esoteric knowledge, before being truly ready. The situation is much worse now, with the Internet, where any person can place whatever they wish into the public domain. You need to be aware that any deeper spiritual esoteric knowledge has to be gradually approached, and that sacred truths can appear to us as weird or impossible, until we have learned how to remove subtle materialistic attitudes from our mindset. This has nothing to do with allowing oneself to be indoctrinated with nonsense, it has to do with giving our mind a chance to learn of higher realities by degrees, and not plunge in all at once. This gradual process is very important. We need to orient ourselves to the higher realities; and there are many deep spiritual mysteries around the life of Christ.

The Philosophy of Freedom (1894)
This text also needs to be mentioned although it is not about anthroposophy; it was written in 1894, some 6 years before Steiner began to teach on spiritual subjects. It is not a text which makes any reference to spiritual realities. This book is also translated under the title "The Philosophy of Spiritual Activity". It has also been given the

English title, "*Intuitive Thinking as a Spiritual Path*", in an effort to present it in a more inviting light.

This is an 'epistemological' book, which means that it deals with an area of philosophy that examines the process of cognition, of how we actually become aware that we are perceiving a sensory object or a thought. It also explores the nature of human will, in order to examine the question of human inner freedom. In particular Steiner argues that we can achieve a highly ethical nature from developing an intuitive awareness of our mental processes, and it is this achievement that imbues our will with goodness, creating a source of morality inside our own soul. The person who achieves this condition has become, in Steiner's view, a 'free' human being. Freedom to Steiner refers to the condition of having spirituality flowing unimpeded through one's will.

This book does not provide an introduction to anthroposophy however, it is a very valuable preparatory book for all those interested in cognitional processes and in anthroposophy, for two reasons. [408] Firstly, it is a study in philosophical language, of how, in effect, the Spiritual-self can become present in the personality. So Steiner referred to it in his later anthroposophical work as being fully in the spirit of anthroposophy, and indeed providing a basis to understand to the spiritual reality behind cognition. Secondly, it trains the mind to more accurately and profoundly experience our own mental processes. As such it is an antidote to the subtle materialism which we imbibe from modern civilisation about the nature of our mind, and hence our essential humanity.

For many people materialistic ideas have become generally accepted, they are part of the fabric of modern attitudes to life; we are described scientifically as 'animals'. We are told that can never know whether what our senses tell us about the world is real or just a mental construct. And we are told that we can never have clarity about the motivating power behind our unethical deeds, that these are always hidden in the subconscious. This book indicates that it is a serious error in the mainstream view of philosophy that the truth about transcendent things can never be known because of inherent unchangeable limits to our ability to perceive with our mind. It is a book which argues the case for ethical individualism, and broadly refutes the Kantian 'limits to knowledge'.

Introductory lecture cycles,
There are a few lecture cycles suitable for enquirers. They include, "Founding a Science of the Spirit" (previously called, *At the Gates of Theosophy*) given in 1906, and also "The Theosophy of the Rosicrucians" from 1907. These provide straightforward overviews of anthroposophy, but you need to already have a firm acceptance of spiritual realities. Most of the lecture cycles require an acquaintance with the introductory books, *Theosophy* or *An outline of Esoteric Science.* So it is best to begin with these books, to become familiar with his special terms, and then on this basis proceed to read the lecture cycles.

---

[408] But philosophical books are more difficult to read than other books and so it is often better to study this with a person who has an academic background in philosophical ideas.

GLOSSARY of common anthroposophical terms

aeon: a long evolutionary time, there are seven of these,
      and we are now in the fourth such epoch.

Akashic Record: where in the cosmos the memory of all past events
      is stored; there are three different manifestations of this (see
      Chapter 12).

anthroposophy: a Greek word that literally means 'human
      soul wisdom'. In Rudolf Steiner's usage it means
      the wisdom that can dawn in a person's
      consciousness, in the spiritual-soul and which
      fully manifests when the Spirit-self is developed.

astral body: the soul, seen as the aura around the body.

astral plane: the Soul World or soul realms, above the
      ethers, but below the Devachanic realms.

astrality: soul energies, but often it is used to refer to the
      feelings.

Devachan: the realm of Spirit, above astral (soul) energies,
      the realm of Plato's archetypal Idea.

the Double: a term usually referring to the Lower Self

ego or self or I: the sense of self, but the eternal self is
      linked to this. Hence the ego is a dual or twofold
      thing.

egoism or egoistic: not quite the same as the well-known
      term egotism (which means conceit). Egoism is used
      by Rudolf Steiner to mean either the state of having
      a normal earth-centred ego, or that this earthly sense
      of self is behaving in a selfish way.

etheric body: is made of the four ethers and duplicates
      the physical body's appearance. From the etheric body, material
      substances, such as new cells, are condensed.

ethers: subtle energies which sustain all living things on the Earth.
      Electricity and magnetism are formed as they decompose.

Gemüt-soul: this German term is sometimes found untranslated in
      English-language books, because it is difficult to define. It

is, Rudolf Steiner explained, actually the intellectual-soul
or logical intelligence, but in the mode of experiencing
one's own inner life and mind, rather than assessing
external things. (GA 69a, p.170)

intellectual-soul: the rational, logical capacity.

intuitive-soul (see spiritual-soul)

imagination, inspiration, intuition: Latin words for the
three types of clairvoyance, but which mean
something different in everyday usage in English to
the meanings that Rudolf Steiner gives them.

imagination: the first stage of clairvoyance: this can be called
'psychic-image consciousness' as it results in astral
or etheric images being perceived. (In normal English
it usually means 'fantasy'.)

imaginations: astral thought-forms.

inspiration: this can be called 'cosmic-spiritual
consciousness'; it is a perceiving or 'breathing-in' wisdom,
from lower Devachan. (In normal English usually
means a strongly felt, creative urge or idea.)

intuition: this can be called 'high initiation consciousness', it
is a perceiving of, or inwardly becoming one with, another
being. This state allows the seer to perceive at an upper
Devachan level. (In normal English usually means an 'insight'
or semi-psychic awareness of something.)

intuition: can be used by Rudolf Steiner for the above
high seership, but can sometimes appear in English
anthroposophical texts in its usual English meaning
of 'insights', when translating such German words as
'ahnen'.

kama-loka: a Sanskrit term which refers to the four lowest stages
of the astral realm, but sometimes used for all the astral realms.

life-force: an alternative term for ether.

life-force organism: the ether body.

Life-spirit: the divinized etheric body, it is made of
Devachanic energies.
lower self: the soul qualities that are tainted with Luciferic

or Ahrimanic influences. It can be thought of as threefold; the lower thinking, feeling and will. But Rudolf Steiner also described it as sevenfold, being the lower qualities of the seven classical planets in astrology.

planets: the term 'Saturn' or 'Mars' for example, can mean the planet in our solar system. But it can also mean the aeon which is named after that current planet.

sentient-soul: the feelings, or emotional aspect of the soul.

soul: appears as an aura. It contains the sentient-soul, intellectual-soul and spiritual-soul.

Spirit-human (in older texts, Spirit-man): the divine forces underlying the physical body, present in our subconscious will.

Spirit-self or Spiritual-self: the result of the purified and enlightened threefold soul-body or astral body.

spiritual-soul: also 'consciousness soul', could be called the intuitive soul. This is the soul capacity which underlies intuitive decision-making or intuitive flashes of insight. But it is also the most individualized or 'ego-ic' soul capacity, and can tend towards a hardened self-centredness.

thinking: can be used to mean the exercise of our intelligence, but it is also used for any of the three clairvoyant states.

Appendix: More about the correlation of society to the soul.

The correlation of the 3 spheres of society with the 3-fold soul can be confusing; and there are only two places in the 20 volumes of Rudolf Steiner's works on this subject, in which the correlation is mentioned. And those familiar with anthroposophical ideas could ask, doesn't he describe the correlation differently in other lectures? That is, doesn't he correlate Thinking to the Third Sphere, and Will to the commercial sphere? No, he doesn't, it only seems that way. In *The Threefold Social Order* (Die Kernpunkte Der Sozialen Frage) it is described briefly, pp. 33-34, and in *Die Soziale Frage* (untranslated), lectures given in Feb/Mar 1919. In these 1919 lectures, R. Steiner is speaking about the fact of the 3-fold soul, and the general awareness of a possible three-folding of society. He goes on to say,

"What would result, what would be the most obvious outcome, if one were to play a game of analogy here? The most obvious outcome would be that one says, 'well, the social organism is also divisible into three sections… namely, the spiritual life…the economic life…and the political life.' And then, if one wished to play an analogy game, one might believe that the spiritual life of the social organism, which has its own specific dynamics, may have the kind of dynamics that can be compared with the dynamics of the human being's spiritual system, that is, the nerve-sense systems [*i.e. the head*]. Whereas, that which is the most coarse system in the human being, namely the metabolic [*-limbs*] system, would probably be compared in a mere game of analogy, with that which underlies the coarse, material economic life.
But the person who can observe for himself, who keeps a mere analogy game far from himself, knows that what is really the case is precisely the opposite of that which one arrives at through a mere analogy game.
For underlying the social organism, with regard to [1] **commerce**, to the production and consumption of goods, are those dynamics which in the human body underlie the [1] **nerve-sense** system [*head*].
And to be sure, the life of public **rights** [2], of the state, (which one often defines too broadly) is to be compared with that which is placed between the metabolic and the nerve-sense system, namely the…**rhythmical** system [2]….
The **spiritual cultural** [3] life, this life of the spirit in the social organism, this does not have dynamics which allow one to think of it as analogous to the dynamics of human talents [*head*]…but rather it has that which can only be compared with the dynamics of the most coarse system of the human being, the **metabolic** [3] system [*will*]. An objective observation of the social organism leads to this outcome…" (p.29-30)
(comments in [ ] by the author)

Now the lecture in which he appears to have an alternative correlation is one concerning the crossing of threshold by all humanity, from 11th April 1919.The following words appear there:

"This modern human being experiences in itself a division into a thinking life, a feeling life and a life of will…this present day humanity must find their thinking-life in an independent spiritual-cultural organism; find their feeling

316

life…in the independent life of rights; and the will-life in commercial sphere."(GA 190, p.162)

However, this does not contradict the correlation on the previous pages; but it is a passage which is very liable to cause confusion. The lecture in which this statement occurs is especially concerned with thinking, with the apparent incapacity of people to attain to spiritual thinking. For example, he comments,

> "But that which is thought – and this is illogical, what I'm now saying – is not something thought out at all, it is thoughtlessness. For what is {apparently} thought out, is in fact not thought out, rather {in this} thoughtlessness is being cultivated."   p.154

And a little later he comments,

> "One notices that when people in our times really think, that is, live in the thinking-process, they {only} have thought-shadows of something. One notices…that the soul moves as it were on the surface of the thoughts, and behind them is something which remains in the unconscious. But in this regard the soul must come <u>into</u> that within which it really has its life….."

Then soon after this comes the statement quoted above,

> "This modern human being experiences in itself a division into a thinking life, a feeling life and a life of will…this present day humanity must find their thinking-life in an independent cultural organism; their feeling life…in the independent life of Rights; and the will-life in commercial sphere."

He then proceeds to explain that the above correlation is about the need **for dynamics to occur** in human society, with respect to the 3folding of society. Steiner does not provide here in this passage a description of the dynamics **inherent** in the 3 soul forces and their **parallel** in the 3 spheres of society. The actual correlation of these two entities – as given on the preceding page – is about the fact that the same dynamic in a soul capacity occurs as in the corresponding social sphere; i.e., society is the macrocosm of the individual human (microcosm).

He proceeds to say in this second lecture that,

> "Once you look at things in this way, then you have the right basis on which to achieve three-folding. For then you will understand that everything which has to develop in the spiritual organism as thoughts <u>concerns the nurture of the individual capabilities of the human being</u>, and so in the spiritual organism (Third-sphere), **individualism** must predominate….Whereas in the life of Rights, **democracy** must prevail, and in the commercial sphere, the **associative** life must predominate."

As he explains in another lecture cycle from Nov 1919, " the social organism will only become healthy when one works one's way up from the usual way of thinking (which is described in this lecture as shadowy) up to the really living view of the healthy social organism." (GA 329 p.175)

CONCLUSION

Several facets of Rudolf Steiner's life and work inspired the author to set out on a path, some 45 years ago, to acquire a competence in the understanding and presentation of his worldview, so that other people may share in this.

The achievements of Steiner in the area of renewing various professions, such as medicine, education agriculture, by showing how a more spiritually aware approach can be developed, is unparalleled in the history of the western world. His contributions to deepening our understanding of what we are as human beings, and how we may imbue our life with a richer meaning and purpose are invaluable. His preparedness to work tirelessly to help humanity to achieve a higher spirituality, and to imbue the world with artistic beauty, is deeply appreciated.

This book has been written as an attempt to help you approach this heritage. May it be of real help to you !

Adrian Anderson, September 2013

INDEX

318

Select Bibliography

Reference works

Die Gesamtausgabe Rudolf Steiner, 354 vols.
Die Beiträge zur Rudolf Steiner Gesamtausgabe, 122 vols.
Altdeutsches Wörterbuch, Oscar Schade, ed. Vlg. der Waisenhauses, Halle,1866, 1 vol.
Meyer's neues Konversations-Lexikon, Zweite Auflage, Hilbburghausen, 1861, 15 vols.
Karl Simrocks Ausgewählte Werke in zwölf Bänden, M. Hesses Vlg, Leipzig, 1920, 4 vols.
Edda, Übertragen von F. Genzmer, E. Ciederichs Vlg, Köln, 1963, 2 vols.
Gering, H. redak., Vollständiges Wörterbuch zu den Liedern der Edda, Vlg. der Waisenhauses, Halle, 1903, 1 vol.
Goethes Werke, Hamburger Ausgabe, Trunz, Erich. ed. Hamburg: Christian Wegner Verlag, 1955, 14 vols.
Evangelisch-Katholischer Kommentar zum Neuen Testament, Benziger V1g, Düsseldorf, 34 vols.
Theologisches Wörterbuch zum Neuen Testament, ed. Kittel,
Kohlhammer Vlg, Stuttgart, 1932, 10 vols.
Deutsche Mythologie, J. Grimm, Ullstein, 1835 rev. 1981, 3 vols.
The Catholic Encyclopedia, ed. C. Herbermann, Encyclopedia Press, N.Y., 1907, 15 vols.
Grammar of New Testament Greek, J. Moulton, T & T Clark, Edinburgh, 1908, 4 vols.
The Golden Bough, J. Frazer, Macmillan, London, 1976, 13 vols.
Butler's Lives of the Saints, Christian Classics, Maryland, 1981, 4 vols.
Mackey's Revised Encyclopaedia of Freemasonry, Macoy Publishing, Richmond, USA, 1966, 3 vols.
Hastings Encyclopaedia of Religion and Ethics, T & T Clark, Edinburgh, 1908, 13 vols.
A Dictionary of the Bible, ed. J. Hastings, T & T Clark, Edinburgh, 1898, 4 vols.
ΩΡΙΓΕΝΟΥΣ ΤΩΝ ΕΙΣ ΤΟ ΚΑΤΑ ΙΩΑΝΝΗΝ ΕΥΑΓΓΕΛΙΟΝ ΕΞΗΓΗΤΙΚΩΝ, ed.
Cecile Blanc, Les Editions du Cerf, Paris, 1996, 5 vols.

Anthroposophical Movement, 1924-1928, London, 5 vols.

New Encyclopaedia of Freemasonry, ed. A. E. Waite, Rider Co. London, 1921, 2 vols.

Hermetica, ed. W. Scott, Shambala, Boston, 1985, 5 vols.

New documents illustrating early Christianity, ed. G. Horsley, Macquarie Univ. 1981 - 1994, 7 vols.

The Zohar, ed. Sperling/Simon, Soncino, N.Y. 1970, 5 vols.

Journals

Mitteilungen aus der Anthroposophischen Arbeit in Deutschland, Stuttgart, 1947 - 1981, 130 vols.

Blätter für Anthroposophie und Mitteilungen aus der anthroposophischen Bewegung 1948-1966, 72 vols.

Mitteilungen für die Mitglieder der Allgemeinen Anthroposophischen Gesellschaft, 1949 -1974, 50 vols.

Beiträge für ein freies Geistesleben, June 1946- April 1949, 17 vols

Mitteilungen der Deutschen Sektion der Theosophischen Gesellschaft, Cologne, 1905-1914.

Aquarian Theosophist, Sept. 17th, 2002.

Anthroposophy Today, London, 1986-1995, 25 vols.

Books & Articles

Aquinas, Thomas. Summa Theologica, Article 1; question 81.

Augustine of Hippo, Confessions, trans. R. Pine-Coffin, Penguin classics.

Beltle E. & Vierl K., Erinnerungen an Rudolf Steiner, Vlg. Freies Geistesleben (FGL), 1979.

Bock, E. The Three Years, C.C. Press, London, 1969.

Bockemühl, Schad, et al, Erscheinungsformen des Ätherischen, Vlg. FGL, Stuttgart, 1977.

Boos R. Die Hetze gegen das Goetheanum, Vlg. des Goetheanum, Dornach, 1920.

Buri, F. Der Pantocrator, Ontology und Eschatologie als Grundlage der Lehre von Gott, H-R Evangl. Vlg. Hamburg, 1969.

Campbell, J. The Mysteries, (Eranos Yearbook) Princeton, USA, 1978.

Carre, M. Realist and Nominalists, OUP, 1967.

Chapman / Lindzen, Atmospheric Tides, D. Reidel Publishing Company, Dordrecht, Holland, 1970.

Chadwick, H. The Early Church, Penguin Bks, 1993.

Clement of Alexandria, The Miscellanies, The Ante-Nicene Greek Library, translations of the Church Fathers, vol. 12, Clement of Alexandria Vol. 2, Edinburgh, 1882, p. 327.

Cloos, W. Lebensstufen der Erde, Vlg. FGL, 1970.

Coles, P. ed., The New Cosmology, Icon books, UK, 1998.

Crookall, Robert. The Supreme Adventure, J. Clarke London, 1961.

Crookall, Robert. What Happens When You Die, C. Smythe, London, 1978.

de Santillana & von Dechend, Hamlet's Mill, D. Godine Books, Boston, 1977.

Donnelly, I. Atlantis, the Antediluvian World, Rudolf Steiner Publications, N.Y., 1971.

Dornseif, F. Das Alphabet in Mystik und Magie, Vlg. Teubner, Leipzig, 1925.

Edwards, O. The Time of Christ, Floris Books, Edinburgh, 1986.

Fairweather, E. ed., A Scholastic Miscellany: Anselm to Ockham, Westminster Press, USA, 1956.

Frieling, Rudolf. *Erinnerungen an die Begründungsereignisse der Christengemeinschaft*, manuscript, Stuttgart, 1984.

Gause, Ute. *Friedrich Rittelmeyer (1872-1938)* in *Zeitschrift für Religions-und Geistesgeschichte,* 48. Jhrg.1996, E. J. Brill

Ghazi, A. & Watson, R. Intercomparison of Stratospheric / Mesospheric Data, COSPAR, Interdisciplinary Scientific Proceedings, Pergamon Press, Graz, 1985.

Gratus, J. The False Messiahs, V. Gollancz, London, 1975.

Goethe, Johann W. von. Faust, Vlg. TH. Knauer, Berlin, 1929.

Goethe, Johann W. von. Theory of Colours, trans. C. Eastlake, MIT, 1970.

Grosse, R. Die Weihnachtagung als Zeitenwende, Philos-Anthrop. Vlg, 1977.

ΚΛΗΜΕΝΤΟΣ ΣΤΡΩΜΑΤΕΩΣ, J.C. Hinrichs'sche Buchhandlung, Leipzig, 1905.

Hagemann, E. Weltenäther, Elementarwesen, Naturreiche, Vlg. die Kommenden, Freiburg, 1973.

Heidel, A. The Gilgamesh Epic and Old Testament Parallels, Univ. Chicago, 1949.

Heidenreich, A. Growing Point, C.C. Press, London, 1965.

Hildebrand, K. Die Lieder der Älteren Edda, Vlg. F. Schöningh, Detmold, 1912.

Hoffmeister, M. Die Übersinnliche Vorbereitung der Inkarnation, Vlg. die Pforte, Basel, 1979.

Holton, J. Dynamics of the Middle Atmosphere, D. Reidel Publishing Company, Dordrecht/Boston/Lancaster, 1983.

James, Van. Spirit and Art, Anthroposophic Press, USA, 2001.

Kleeberg, L. Wege und Worte, Mellinger Verlag, 1961.

Krück v. Poturzyn, M. ed., Wir Erlebten Rudolf Steiner, Vlg. FGL, 1957.

Kukal, Zdenek *Atlantis in the light of modern research,* Earth-Science Reviews, 1984.

Larrington, C. trans., The Poetic Edda, OUP, 1996.

Lievegoed, B. Phases, Pharos Bks, London, 1979.

Lindenberg, C. *Rudolf Steiner eine Biographie*, Vlg. FGL,1977.

The Nag Hammadi Library in English, Leiden, 1977, Brill.

Mahmoudian, A. & Scales, W. *Investigation of Dusty Space Plasmas in the Near-Earth Space Environment,* Oct. 2011.

Megner, Khaplanov, et.al. *Large mesospheric ice particles at exceptionally high altitudes*; Annales Geophysicae, 2009.

Meebold, Alfred. „Erinnerungen an einen Geistesriesen" unpublished.

Meyer, T. Rudolf Steiner's Core Mission, Temple Lodge, 2010.

Milner & Smart, The Loom of Creation, Spearman, London, 1975.

Myer, M. edit., The Ancient Mysteries, Univ. Penn. 1987.

O'Neil. G & G. The Human Life, Mercury Press, N.Y., 1990.

Philo: the works of, trans. C. Yonge, Hendrickson, USA, 1993.

Philonis Judaei. Opera Omnia, Lipsiae, Schwickerti, 1828.

Plato, The Republic, trans. B. Jowett, Barnes & Noble classics.

Plato, Timaeus and Critias, trans. D. Lee, Penguin Classic.

Plunkett, E. Calendars and Constellations of the ancient World. Senate Bks, London, 1997.

Ptolemy, Claudius. Tetrabiblios, S. Weiser, Chicago, 1936.

Πτολεμαῖος. Τετράβιβλος (www.astrologican.org/Ptolemy)

Poeppig, Fred. Abenteuer Meines Lebens, Novalis Verlag,

Schaffhausen,1975.

Poeppig, Fred. Rudolf Steiner, der Grosse Unbekannte, Vlg. B.- Woiczik, Vienna, 1960.

Poeppig, Fred. Rückblick, Vlg. die Pforte, Basel, 1964.

Prokofieff, S. The East in the light of the West, R. Steiner Press London, 2010.

Prasad, Rama. Nature's Finer Forces, T.S. publications 1894, Adyar.

Przywara, E. An Augustine Synthesis, Sheed & Ward. London, 1936.

Samweber, Anna. Aus meinem Leben, Vlg. Die Pforte,Basel, 1981.

Sandars, N. The epic of Gilgamesh, Penguin Classics.

Schneider, J. Michael, R-Geerig Vlg., Switzerland, 1981.

Schnelle, U. Antidocetic Christology in the gospel of John, Fortress press, USA, 1987.

Schöffler, H. Der Kampf um das Menschenbild, Vlg. am Goetheanum, 1986.

Schultz, J. Rhyhmen der Sterne, Philos-Anthrop. Vlg., 1977.

Sease, V & Brabant, M. Thinkers, Saints, Heretics, Temple Lodge, 2007.

Settegast, Mary. 'Plato Prehistorian', Lindisfarne Press, 1990.

Simrock, K. Die Edda, Deutsche Buch Gemeinschaft Gmb. H. Berlin, 1926.

Simrock, K. Handbuch der Deutschen Mythologie, A. Marchus Vlg, Bonn, 1874.

Singer, J. Boundaries of the Soul, Anchor Books, N.Y., 1973.

Sturluson, Snorri. The Prose Edda, Univ. Calif., 1966.

Soberman, Robert.K. Atmospheric Phenomena, Scientific American, 1963.

Speckner and Stamm, Das Gehemnis der Externsteine, Vlg.Urachhaus, Stuttgart, 2002.

Suwelack, G. The new dialogue with the spirit of the Earth, privately printed.

Sykes, Egerton. Atlantis Journal, May, Markham House Press, London, 1956.

Syncellus, George. XPONOΓPAΦIAZ Byzantinae 1832, Bonnae.

Tomas, A. Atlantis, Sphere Books, London, 1973.

Treichler, R. Die Entwickelung der Seele im Lebenslauf, Vlg. Freies Geistesleben, Stuttgart, 1982.

Tritemis, Iohan. Abbatis Spanheymen. De Septem Secundeis, Impressum Francoforti apud Cyriacum, Iacobum Anno Domini 1545.

Turgenieff, A. Erinnerungen an Rudolf Steiner, Vlg. FGL, 1972.

van Bemmelen, D. Zarathustra, Mellinger Vlg. Stuttgart, 1975.

Verniani, Franco. ed., Structure and Dynamics of the Upper Atmosphere, Proceedings of the Second Course of the International School of Physics, Erice, Italy: 13-27 June 1971.

von Eschenbach, Wolfram. Parzivâl, ed. H. Jantzen, Vlg. de Gruyter, Berlin, 1944.

Vreede, E. Anthroposophy and Astrology, trans. R. Koetsch, Anthrop. Press, USA, 2001.

Wachsmuth, G. Werdegang der Menschheit, Philos-Anthrop. Vlg., Dornach, 1973.

Wachsmuth, G., The Life and Work of Rudolf Steiner, Whittier Books N.Y., 1955.

Wallis-Budge, E.A. The Book of the Dead, RKP, London, 1969.

Wehr, G. Jung & Steiner, Anthrop. Press, USA, 1990.

West, A. Alcuin and the rise of the Christian Schools, Heinemann, 1893.

Wilkes, Fant, Klingborg. Die Holzplastik Rudolf Steiners, Philos-Anthrop. Vlg, 1969.

Witt, Georg. Height, structure and displacements of noctilucent clouds, Institute of Meteorology, Univ. of Stockholm, 1961.

Woodroffe, John. The Serpent Power, Ganesh & Co. Madras, 1958.

Yates, F. The Rosicrucian Enlightenment, RKP, London, 1972.

ILLUSTRATION CREDITS

Copyright the author
1, 8, 9, 11, 12, 14, 18, 19, 20, 22, 23, 26, 28, 29, 30, 31

Plus the diagrams:
Pond of life
3-fold Social Order & the human soul
Grains cooking (the complete, unabridged table is copyright to U. Renzenbrink.)
Elohim Creation Scene (adopting elements of Hilde Raske's version & Rudolf Steiner's original sketch)

Public domain
Note: the use of these images made available to the public domain does not in any way impute or imply that the holder of the License supports or agrees with any of the opinions herein regarding their image or images !

2 Mycenaean gemstone: this picture is in the public domain due to PD-US-no notice
3 tapestry from China: this picture is in the public domain due to PD-US-no notice
4 Egyptian painting: this picture is in the public domain due to PD-US-no notice
5 Renaissance paintings: this picture is in the public domain due to PD-US-no notice
6 Renaissance painting: this picture is in the public domain due to PD-US-no notice
7 Renaissance painting (Louvre museum), is in the public domain due to PD-US-no notice
10 Roman mosaic: this picture is in the public domain due to PD-US-no notice
13 Nacreous above: Creative commons Alan R. Light Attribution 2.0 Generic (CC BY 2.0)
    Nacreous below: Wikimedia Commons, by Mathiasm, 2008-01-20 GNU - FDL
15 Above: Storm sprite/elf, a Photo from **NASA** who holds the copyright to it
    Below: Storm sprite/elf, Wikimedia Commons by Abestrobi, 2008, C-C Attribution Share-Alike
16 Above: Noctilucent cloud, Wikimedia Commons by Martin Koitmäe, 26-7-2009 GNU - FDL
    Below: Noctilucent cloud, Wikimedia Commons by Mika Yrjölä, 13-7-2004, GNU-FDL
17 Above: Aurora, a **NASA** photo from the space shuttle who holds the copyright to it
    Below: Aurora, a **USAF** photo with ID 050118-F-3488S-003; this picture is in the public domain due to PD-US-no notice.
21 Mosaic from Monreale Cathedral, Sicily, this picture is in the public domain due to PD-US-no notice
24 Sculpture, Goetheanum, Wikimedia Commons, Attribution-ShareAlike 3.0 Unported (cc-BY-SA 3.0), colourised by author
25 Seals of the seven aeons, Copyright holder: Tree of Life, Kew Melbourne; artist: Russell Holland.
27 Left, photo from Bonn Landesmuseum
    Middle: Rhineland tourist map, public domain
    Right: the author
31 Images of primordial animal life: by Nobu Tamura GNU FDL, except Wikimedia Commons public domain images of Silurian fishes by Joseph Smit, of Acanthian Devonian fish a Cochise College image, of Dalmanites limulurus trilobite, by DanielCD, GNU FDL; and Woolly Mammoth by Mauricio Anton, GNU FDL; and the Permian

Milton Keynes UK
Ingram Content Group UK Ltd.
UKHW021846220823
427232UK00001B/20

9 780958 134156